The Lynching of Cleo Wright

The Lynching
of Cleo Wright

DOMINIC J. CAPECI JR.

THE UNIVERSITY PRESS OF KENTUCKY

Publication of this volume was made possible in part
by a grant from the National Endowment for the Humanities.

Scholarly publisher for the Commonwealth,
serving Bellarmine College, Berea College, Centre
College of Kentucky, Eastern Kentucky University,
The Filson Club Historical Society, Georgetown College,
Kentucky Historical Society, Kentucky State University,
Morehead State University, Murray State University,
Northern Kentucky University, Transylvania University,
University of Kentucky, University of Louisville,
and Western Kentucky University.

Editorial and Sales Offices: The University Press of Kentucky
663 South Limestone Street, Lexington, Kentucky 40508-4008

02 01 00 99 98   5 4 3 2 1

Library of Congress Cataloging-in-Publication Data
Capeci, Dominic J.
    The lynching of Cleo Wright / Dominic J. Capeci, Jr.
        p.   cm.
    Includes bibliographical references and index.
    ISBN 0-8131-2048-9 (acid-free paper)
    1. Wright, Cleo, d. 1942. 2. Afro-Americans—Civil rights—
Missouri—Sikeston—History—20th century. 3. Lynching—Missouri
—Sikeston—History—20th century. 4. Sikeston (Mo.)—Race
relations. 5. United States—Race relations. I. Title.
F474.S5C36   1998
305.896'077897—dc21   98-5635

This book is printed on acid-free recycled paper meeting
the requirements of the American National Standard
for Permanence of Paper for Printed Library Materials. ♾ ⊛
Manufactured in the United States of America

Per i miei maèstri

Reno Zuccaro
John J. Juliano
Albert Lopes
Van L. Perkins
Clarence E. Barnes
Donald C. Marsh
Edgar A. Albin

Contents

Maps and Illustrations

Preface

Beginning with James R. McGovern's case study of Claude Neal in *Anatomy of a Lynching* (1982) and running through Stewart E. Tolnay and E.M. Beck's comparative analysis of ten southern states in *A Festival of Violence* (1995), the recent interest in lynch law has provided valuable insights that reach far beyond the violence to tell much about black-white relations in changing historical eras.[1] The lynching of Cleo Wright extends this inquiry to Missouri, a state possessing neither completely northern or southern nor even distinctively border characteristics, but whose people and history have influenced important national issues.

First and foremost, this is the story of Cleo Wright, his victim Grace Sturgeon, and their respective communities in the city of Sikeston. Wright was not simply a socially pathological black youth and Sturgeon an isolated, helpless white woman; rather, his criminal act and her heroic response sprang from a past and a culture that explain much about all lynchings in the most basic of human terms. So do the actions of the lynchers who took Wright's life and the officials who failed to save it. Together, their acts reflect a contemporary society grown to expect senseless bloodshed of its own humanity and that of its forebears.

Moreover, Wright's killing influenced local, state, and national history as have very few lynchings. It revealed the disruption of transition from traditional to modern society in an urban setting marked by several regional and, more recently, southern influences. It happened in a state relatively unknown for racial violence yet one whose lynching record both paralleled and broke with patterns of the South, most notably in urban lynchings. It occurred at a time of national crisis that required unprecedented federal intervention, reinforced the reduction of extralegal public executions of blacks, and revised legal strategies the better to protect later generations.

Presented primarily as a case study, this interpretation also compares Wright's death with other lynchings in Missouri and throughout the South. In the process, it builds on the spate of recent studies, particularly those of Michael J. Pfeifer, W. Fitzhugh Brundage, and Tolnay and Beck.[2] It reinforces many of their findings, posits some variations, and advances a few theses. It analyzes the state's eighty-five lynchings from 1889 to 1942, aware of the difficulty in accurately identifying every such ritualized murder.[3] It provides an in-depth study of Wright's killing and suggests a direction for more comprehensive work on similar deaths throughout the state. Much more may be learned from these about race relations and racial violence at a time when society is becoming more pluralistic and, some would argue, violence-prone. An understanding of one death in one critical era can provide insights for citizens struggling to enter a new age of demographic change, scarce resources, and intergroup conflict. In that lesson lies the enduring significance of Wright's life—and that of every other lynch victim.

Acknowledgments

This study greatly expands my article "The Lynching of Cleo Wright: Federal Protection of Constitutional Rights during World War II," *Journal of American History* 72 (March 1986): 859-87, which comprises parts of chapters 3 and 8; the material is reused courtesy of the Organization of American Historians. Beyond that legal interpretation, which remains as originally written, recent secondary literature, additional archival material, and especially nearly one hundred interviews have enhanced and revised other aspects of the story. Whether they were speaking on or off the record, as noted in the bibliography, the courage of those who spoke is most appreciated. And because no one has been indicted, much less found guilty for having killed Wright, fictitious names have been given to those believed most responsible for his death.

Much of this information could not have been gathered without the assistance of a handful of individuals. In Sikeston, the late Walter Griffen of Sunset Addition; the Reverend Tom Geers, pastor of Trinity Baptist Church; and Michael L. Jensen, publisher of the *Standard-Democrat*, made many of the interviews possible. The Reverend Geers and Mr. Jensen also read the manuscript and provided thoughtful suggestions. Their encouragement and generosity during a decade of visits to Sikeston were invaluable, as were the microfilm editions of local newspapers, the photographs of the period, and the tours of the historic place provided by Mr. Jensen. In a very real sense, this book belongs to Walter, Tom, and perhaps most personally as a native son of Sikeston, Mike. I am most grateful for their unending help and most thankful for their heartfelt friendship.

The most important protagonists in this story could not have been understood without the unqualified support of Grace Sturgeon of Sikeston, the woman slashed by Wright, and Linetta Watson Koonce of Albuquerque, New Mexico, Wright's sister. They recounted what had happened from very different yet equally significant perspectives, while also opening the way for conversations with others and—in the case of Mrs. Koonce—permitting access to the records and supplying photographs of family members. Similarly, David E. Blanton of Sikeston provided several interviews revealing a third, legal perspective on the tragedy.

Likewise I thank former officials of Sikeston and Scott County: City Clerk Carroll Couch, County Sheriff Bill Ferrell, and County Court Clerk Lynn Ingram. And, at different stages of the research, Arthur Bruce, Don Culbertson, Angela Longstreet, and Tim Jaynes of Sikeston provided welcome assistance. Several other residents made available historical materials and are acknowledged in the notes.

I owe as much to officials and staffs of the Regional History and University Archives, Cape Girardeau, Missouri; Western Historical Manuscript Collection and State Historical Society of Missouri Manuscripts, Columbia; Missouri National Guard, Sikeston Armory; Missouri State Historical Society, St. Louis; Missouri State Highway Patrol, Missouri Board of Probation and Parole, and Missouri Department of Corrections and Human Resources, Jefferson City; Michigan Department of Corrections, Lansing, Michigan; Jefferson County Courthouse, Pine Bluff, Arkansas; Arkansas Department of Health, Little Rock, and Arkansas Department of Correction, Pine Bluff; University Archives, Tuskegee University, Tuskegee, Alabama; Federal Bureau of Investigation, Justice Department, Library of Congress, and National Archives and Records Service, all in Washington, D.C. A National Endowment for the Humanities Travel Grant (1988) and a Southwest Missouri State University Summer Fellowship (1990) financed the visits to some of these depositories.

My research was also advanced by others. Former State Representative Douglas Harpool and U.S. Congressman Gene Taylor assisted in the release of Cleo Wright's prison records and the search for his military records. Patrick J. Huber of Chapel Hill, North Carolina, and David Dickey of Scott City, Missouri, provided copies of their respective work on the James T. Scott lynching in Columbia, Missouri (1923), and on the Bootheel area in which Wright died. Attorney Lyman Russell Mitten II of Honolulu, Hawaii, shared his senior thesis on the Sikeston lynching. Professional counselor Carl M. Dawson of Springfield, Missouri, furnished information on drink and violence, while Emeritus Professor of Psychology Clifford I. Whipple of Southwest Missouri State University, contributed significantly to my understanding of Wright's personality.

In writing the manuscript, I profited from the suggestions of Lawrence O. Christensen of the University of Missouri–Rolla, David W. Gutzke of Southwest Missouri State University, Rick Boland of the Virginia Museum of Natural History, Jere L. Krakow of the National Park Service, and a reader for the *Journal of Southern History* who evaluated a preliminary essay. Similarly, James N. Giglio, Jack C. Knight, and Martha F. Wilkerson of Southwest Missouri State University, Frederick J. Blue of Youngstown State University, Stan Miesner of Springfield, Missouri, and Teresa Montseny of Tucson, Arizona, provided equally cogent remarks for the book-length draft. Comments by readers for the University Press of Kentucky, as well as the copy editing of Pat Sterling, improved the final version further.

Finally, I am beholden to several colleagues at Southwest Missouri State University. Matthew J. Mancini, head of the Department of History, provided research assistance through graduate students Jean Griffith and Brad Waddle. He also enabled departmental assistant Lyn Young to prepare the endnotes; indeed, Lyn single-handedly made it possible to deliver the revised manuscript on time. She and administrative secretary Margie von der Heide also aided me in countless other ways. I cannot thank enough Duane G. Meyer Library staff members: Lynn S. Cline and Frances K. Wolff, Carol Lynne Freeman, and Willa J. Garrett for numerous purchasing and interlibrary loan requests; Tammy Stewart and especially Byron Stewart for the collection of census data, which could not have been interpreted without the invaluable help of Professor of Sociology Wilkerson. Likewise John Wall of Photographic Services reproduced fifty-year-old newspaper photographs from microfilm editions.

And, as they have done so many times, Emeritus and Distinguished Professor of History Gerald D. Nash of the University of New Mexico, Professors Robert V. Haynes of Western Kentucky University, William D. Jenkins of Youngstown State University, and former colleague George J. Selement provided much needed encouragement. Given the controversial nature of racial violence, particularly when it has occurred in a small city where identities are well known and opinions strongly held, I alone am responsible for this version of one of the most tragic incidents in the history of Missouri. In 1942, it touched many lives yet benefited no one. Hopefully, its retelling can contribute to an understanding of Sikeston's racial past and assist present-day collaborative efforts of both races to improve race relations.

With deep appreciation for having taught me "real life" lessons, I dedicate this manuscript to Big Z, Little Caesar, The Professor, The Man, The Urban Leaguer, The Sociologist, and The Gray Fox. Above all, I have learned from them the need for individuals and communities to respect themselves and the humanity of others by remembering and learning from historical memory.

1 Sikeston

Within twelve hours on Sunday, January 25, 1942, racial violence erupted three times in Sikeston, Missouri.[1] It began in the dark, wintry morning on the southeast edge of town and ended in the daylight of early afternoon on the west side—in an area appropriately called Sunset Addition—where most black citizens lived. According to Grace Sturgeon, an unknown black man entered her home at 1:30 A.M., attacked her with a knife, and retreated into the night.

Thirty minutes later and within a short distance of the Addition, Cleo Wright stood before the headlights of a scout car. Covered in blood, he appeared to have stepped out of a slaughterhouse rather than the nighttime shadows. Arrested and placed in the vehicle, he soon rammed a hidden knife through the lower jaw of Night Marshal Hess Perrigan and, in turn, spewed forth his own blood as point-blank gunshots riddled his body, ending the second violent outburst.

Wright, Perrigan, and Sturgeon all received treatment at the tiny General Hospital, soon the site of a death watch as droves of residents responded to widely circulated stories of the assaults. Already anxious over the recent bombing of Pearl Harbor and U.S. entry into World War II, they grasped for resolution to the black brutalities that rubbed raw their white nerves. Some believed that it lay in still more bloodletting. How could public order be restored abroad, if not first at home?

Hence Wright's ordeal ended as it had begun, in cold blood. As he was shuttled from the hospital to his home and back to City Hall by policemen, instigators organized a lynch mob. As he lay semiconscious in a cell, having twice confessed to the crimes, knots of curiosity-seekers became crowds of spectators and, by noon, would-be lynchers. Dragged to the street and into Sunset Addition, he met death as a sacrilegious Sabbath blaze within view of black church services.

This final act of bloodletting ended Wright's rage. Occurring in the upper reaches of the Mississippi Delta, it bore the characteristics of a New South lynching. Yet coming early in World War II, it sparked international atten-

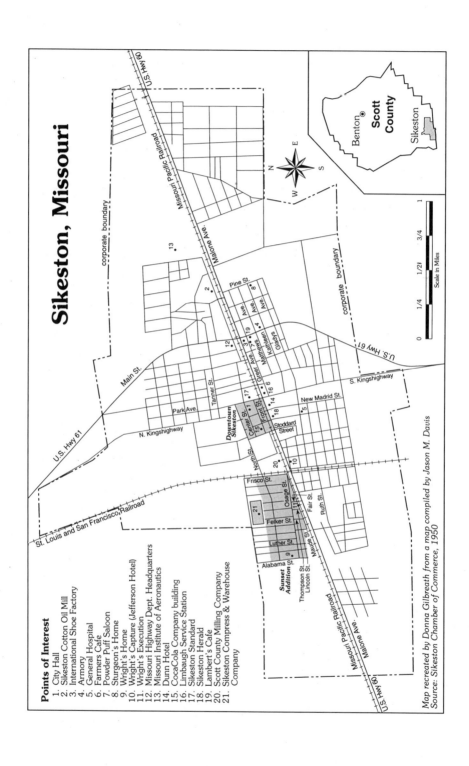

Sikeston, Missouri

Points of Interest

1. City Hall
2. Sikeston Cotton Oil Mill
3. International Shoe Factory
4. Armory
5. General Hospital
6. Farmers Cafe
7. Powder Puff Saloon
8. Sturgeon's Home
9. Wright's Home
10. Wright's Capture (Jefferson Hotel)
11. Wright's Execution
12. Missouri Highway Dept. Headquarters
13. Missouri Institute of Aeronautics
14. Dunn Hotel
15. CocaCola Company building
16. Limbaugh Service Station
17. Sikeston Standard
18. Sikeston Herald
19. Lambert's Cafe
20. Scott County Milling Company
21. Sikeston Compress & Warehouse Company

Scott County

Benton
Sikeston

Scale in Miles

0   1/4   1/21   3/4   1

Map recreated by Donna Gilbreath from a map compiled by Jason M. Davis
Source: Sikeston Chamber of Commerce, 1950

tion, federal investigation, and varying responses from citizens and officials, many of whom were feeling the impact of modernization—a centralized, depersonal, unpredictable world—which had begun during the New Deal and become accelerated by war exigencies. Similar to traditional lynchings yet unique in itself, Wright's execution revealed much about the evolution of black-white relations in changing southeast Missouri and even more about the roles of local, state, and federal authorities in stemming future racial violence. Thus it bears greater significance than most lynchings.

Until then, Sikeston had evolved as an ordinary community, though hardly one without historical meaning. Founded in 1860 by John Sikes, it sits in Scott County, one of seven counties that form the Bootheel of southeastern Missouri and, save for western Butler County, mark the northern edge of the Mississippi Delta: lowlands of rich soil, sweltering temperatures, and ample rainfall where, in time, cotton would become king. The city survived the guerrilla terrorism of area Confederates, who provoked hatreds that carried beyond the Civil War, and grew slowly as terminus of the Cairo and Fulton Railway (later the Missouri Pacific). Increasingly, it served as a major emporium for the upper Bootheel, which changed dramatically in the wake of turn-of-the century timber barons who cut over the entire area and stimulated the drainage of what had been known as "Swampeast." By 1910 Sikeston and its sister towns were catering to midwestern farmers entering their last "agricultural frontier" and southern laborers seeking work on the drainage projects.[3]

During and after World War I, townsfolk witnessed even greater economic change as the region evolved from a small-scale corn and wheat belt of predominantly white farmers profiting from wartime demand for foodstuffs to a larger-scale cotton kingdom of more racially diverse planters, ginners, moneylenders, and pickers chased north by advancing boll weevils.[4] "Our farms," exclaimed one former corn grower, "became plantations . . . peppered over with sharecropper shacks." Indeed, between the close of the war and the mid-1920s, established grain growers joined newly arrived planters to increase cotton plantings from 104,004 to 445,933 acres, producing 95 percent of the crop in Missouri.[5]

City dwellers in Sikeston and elsewhere profiting from this economic transformation must have noted its social impact as southern blacks entered the Bootheel in such numbers that by the end of the 1920s their race accounted for 24,877 persons or 12.7 percent of the population. Providing the largest increases in the three riverfront counties of Mississippi, New Madrid, and Pemiscot, blacks found themselves in a feudalistic sharecropping and wage-rate system akin to that of the New South, though tempered by absentee proprietors because high development costs benefited well-heeled landlords and speculators.[6] They entered a white-dominated caste system that included a "Tobacco Road," complete with poor whites, drafty shacks, slave diets, endemic diseases, and widespread illiteracy.[7]

Townspeople doubtless sensed that this hodgepodge of lowland people—the fastest-growing population anywhere in the state—accentuated traditional class and race conflict. In short, between 1890 and 1930, older families from the East, the upper South, and the border states combined with newly arrived hill people from Kentucky and Tennessee, farmers from Illinois and Indiana, and southerners from Arkansas and Mississippi to form a have–have not society that sparked competition. The transition from frontier to civilization merged Yankee and southern prejudice in the Bootheel, which became, in author Fannie Cook's phrase, "a sixth finger on the hand of the South."[8] Landlords imposed master-servant relationships, and white laborers, themselves exploited, sought to drive blacks from the region. Terror, rioting, and lynching burst forth during the first quarter of the twentieth century. This bloodshed stemmed from the interplay of a volatile population, frontier culture, pell-mell economic development, and occasional political party rivalries. But it also drew on racist beliefs and a historical context shaped long before 1890.[9]

Against this backdrop, Sikestonians and their lowland neighbors experienced further economic and social upheaval in the Great Depression. Throughout the 1930s both races—whether in city or country—encountered even greater poverty, though blacks suffered more, and some protested.[10] In 1934, Bootheel blacks, including some from Sikeston and its environs, heard St. Louis messengers from rival organizations promote imperial Japan and spread anti-white doctrines of "the most vicious type."[11] They abandoned the Japanese-sponsored activities within the year, however, as whites in the eastern- and southernmost counties retaliated with violence and arrests, effectively chasing organizers back to the big city they had come from. As significantly, large segments of the black population in southeast Missouri had found little of ideological or cultural value in the pro-Japan organizations.[12] Preachers and "reputable Negroes" spoke out against them, revealing class distinctions, religious beliefs, and leadership rivalries within the black community.[13]

One year later the Southern Tenant Farmers Union (STFU) began organizing in the Bootheel, and under the leadership of Rev. Owen H.

Whitfield, a black itinerant preacher from Mississippi County, launched a highly publicized roadside demonstration in 1939. More successful than the Japanese propagandists in connecting with a black heritage and an economic oppression shared by all farm workers, Whitfield mobilized nearly a thousand black and more than a hundred white sharecroppers in "a long, long showcase of human devastation" along U.S. 61 and U.S. 60 (which intersect at Sikeston). He protested the New Deal agricultural program that reduced cotton cultivation and permitted planters to release sharecroppers, thus simultaneously upturning the agricultural system and cheating laborers of their federal payment. Despite short-term gains, including Farm Security Administration (FSA) grants and construction of the Delmo Labor Homes for area croppers, Whitfield failed to convince politically minded officials that only a change in the law would force planters to treat farm workers more fairly.[14]

Nonetheless, Whitfield's protest accentuated the fifty-year march toward modernization that finally pressed in on southeast Missouri. Whereas the New Deal had recognized the area's hierarchy and outfitted planters in "new legal clothing," it stirred sharecroppers to action; whereas the New Deal had enlarged its role in the lives of landlords, it threatened federal intervention in their labor relations.[15] Beneficial government programs, in short, signified greater political centralization and challenges to the racial order.

On the eve of World War II, then, Bootheel residents confronted a whirlwind of change. Sikestonians experienced the clash of old and new most dramatically, for they serviced large segments of the region, interacted with the outside world regularly, and felt its pressures first. From a handful of settlers in 1860, they had grown to 7,944 in 1940—including 1,003 blacks—constituting one-fourth of Scott County's population.[16] They incorporated the town in 1874, established a mayor-aldermen government in 1891, and developed an infrastructure of telephone lines, waterworks, and some paved streets early in the twentieth century to emerge as the county's largest municipality thirty years later.[17] Following the influx of blacks in the 1920s and 1930s, townspeople lived, worked, and played along separate racial lines in a southern caste and class system.[18]

Most blacks—including many homeowners—resided in the Sunset Addition (see Sikeston map).[19] Their community of shacks and small houses lay approximately one-quarter mile west of downtown, across the Frisco Railroad tracks and immediately north of the Missouri Pacific tracks, which ran parallel to Highway 60 (also known as Malone Avenue).[20] Other blacks lived in cabins behind the northeast homes of wealthy whites, or in alleys back of some central and many southeast residences of working-class whites. Race aside, those in alley quarters experienced overpriced, unsanitary, and crowded conditions "unfit for human habitation."[21]

Members of both races worked in jobs that supported the surrounding farm community, though whites dominated the better-paying and supervisory positions. Most blacks hired out as field hands, performed common labor for large operations such as the Sikeston Cotton Oil Mill, and personal services for small white businesses and well-to-do families.[22] They received low wages in often dead-end jobs connoting master-servant relationships, while white men drew rank-and-file pay at Scott County Milling Company and, along with white women, the International Shoe Factory. Whites also dominated the professions and sales positions, as well as the businesses that provided all laborers with everything from groceries and clothes to restaurant meals and moving pictures.[23]

Neither race constituted a monolithic class. White discrimination still provided enterprising and educated blacks with economic openings and social standing. Carpenter John Dancler built many of the homes in Sunset, where George W. Scott operated a small grocery and Heavy Hunt ran a pool hall. And, given white aversion to pruning or burying supposedly inferior people, black barbers, beauticians, and morticians enjoyed virtual monopolies in the westside community.[24] So did the black pastors who led several denominations, Rev. Kater E. Crump of the First Baptist Church ministering to the hundred members of the largest congregation.[25] And since 1923 black teachers had instructed area students in kindergarten through eighth grade at Lincoln School. It boasted an active Parent-Teacher Association, an achieving student body, and a competitive athletic team.[26]

In addition to the impact of Jim Crow on socioeconomic status, blacks recognized their own diversity in terms of residency. Original founders, long-term proprietors, homeowners, and those who worked for wealthy whites made up Sunset's core, while less prosperous yet equally longstanding inhabitants and alley occupants who moved into the Addition were considered among its members. Class-conscious blacks, albeit in different terms, thought very much like those whites who distinguished homeowning "colored people" and hard-working "darkies" from shiftless "niggers."[27] Similarly, they looked down on "floaters"—seasonal workers who came in and out of the area to chop and pick cotton—and permanent cotton workers living on farmland beyond the city limits; thus they tended to ignore the Rev. Whitfield's roadside demonstration.[28]

To the majority of black townsfolk, Sunset was their turf and Sikeston their city. They had built the Addition from an informal immigrant community in the mid-1920s to an organized, ethnic community by the early 1940s, featuring religious and educational institutions and a wide range of recreational activities—from church fish fries to less wholesome nightclub drinking and gambling. They created a community within a city, embraced their families, maintained ties with relatives and friends living elsewhere in Sikeston and in the South, and preserved much of their folk culture and southern heritage.[29]

Whites, too—numbering 6,939 in 1940—comprised several classes and lived in well-established though mostly older neighborhoods throughout the city: wealthy and prominent in large northeast homes; business and working-class in smaller residences below Malone Avenue and some newly built houses west and east of South Kingshighway; common labor in rented houses and alley cabins of these southern quadrants or in downtown area roominghouses. Their accommodations varied more widely than did those of blacks; several neighborhoods still lacked streets and indoor plumbing.[30]

As much as class and residency, religion defined many, though hardly a majority, of white Sikestonians. Protestants predominated, establishing the earliest and largest churches, led by the First United Methodist (1867) and the First Baptist (1868), each with nearly a thousand members in the early 1940s. The First Presbyterian (1870) and several other denominations founded after World War I, in turn, claimed very few congregants.[31] The Catholics of St. Francis Xavier dated their presence in the city from 1885 and numbered one hundred families on the eve of World War II.[32] The Jews who inhabited the city at this time, perhaps fewer than fifty, journeyed to the B'nai Israel Temple in Cape Girardeau for worship.[33]

Congregants of each faith envisioned themselves a religious family and their place of worship a social community, but they related to one another in various other settings as well.[34] Thus Protestants, Catholics, and Jews all lived throughout the city rather than in religious neighborhoods; they patronized one another's stores, worked in similar jobs, and sent their children—save for St. Xavier's elementary-age students—to public schools. Some Protestants and Catholics also socialized together; some Methodists and Presbyterians even married members of St. Francis Xavier. That very few Baptists and even fewer Jews entered such unions indicated the opposition to interfaith marriages among more fundamentalist Christians and religious outsiders.[35] Clearly, like many nonchurchgoing whites, some Protestants expressed religious and cultural prejudice, referring to "Catlickers" and Jewish stereotypes; even more blatant bigotry existed beyond the city limits.[36]

For the most part, however, Catholic and Jewish residents were integrated in the public life of Sikeston. St. Xavier's parishioners viewed themselves as part of the larger white community and, accordingly, honored the color line; they employed blacks in menial jobs and held them at social bay.[37] So did Jewish residents, themselves much less assimilated into the gentile society. Their behavior toward blacks manifested an East European *shtetl* heritage, exemplified by Judaic dietary laws and celebrations, and the survival technique of a historically persecuted people aware of the region's potential for virulent anti-Semitism: tolerance in Sikeston could transmogrify into the kind of southern violence evidenced by the 1913 lynching of Leo Frank in Georgia.[38] Neither they nor white Catholics and Protestants played up their ethnicity, perhaps seeing it as an obstacle to living an "American life."[39]

Hence, most white townspeople, while understanding that the social and economic order favored sons and daughters "born here, raised here," considered themselves advocates of home, church, and school, of local autonomy, individual liberties, and hard work.[40] Protestants, Catholics, Jews, and non-churchgoers all embraced the "spiritual values" of democracy—for white people only—that had originated as a defense of slavery in the Old South.[41] This *Herrenvolk* egalitarianism ensured racial consensus regardless of religious or other divisions among white Sikestonians, who combined it with various aspects of southern tradition to create their own cultural heritage. Specifically, they practiced the "polite racism"—forged by diverse regional origins—found in border state cities.[42] They softened the oppressive nature of segregation and gave the appearance of racial harmony through "face-to-face relations" that advanced "a certain fulfillment of personality."[43] Indeed, "just about every" member of each race knew one another, whites seeming to love individual blacks while hating the race. Black city dwellers, like their forebears, understood and exploited this southern "personalism" as they did the paternalism that also carried over from the antebellum era.[44]

Whereas planters and entrepreneurs had protected and patronized slaves and urban blacks, twentieth-century white elites introduced a quasi-feudal system of "mutual obligations" to Sikeston. They imposed discipline and moral justification on their cotton-producing operations, providing black farm laborers and city dwellers with work, shelter, and protection in return for deference and loyalty.[45] In "a hangover from slavery," powerful whites "took care" of their black employees: first aid treatment for Sikeston Compress and Warehouse Company workers; easy credit; even gifts of property to favorite servants.[46]

So long as both races kept in their places of race and class, paternalists greatly influenced the social order. They succeeded by obligating themselves to individual blacks, thereby creating a dependency that discouraged racial solidarity and reduced collective resistance—when it did occur—to self-defense. As in the case of white personalism, however, blacks availed themselves of every benefit proffered, simultaneously accommodating and, however indirectly or individually, resisting the system.[47]

In fact, paternalism and personalism often interacted and shaped the lives of black city dwellers. Walter Griffen became well known as Dr. T.C. McClure's handyman. His reputation for honesty and his relationship to one of the community's most prominent elites brought him social status and economic leverage.[48] Called Walter "McClure" by clerks, he received respectful treatment in every downtown store. He benefited in other ways as a member of the doctor's family, perhaps one reason why landowner E.P. Coleman lent him the money to purchase a lot and build a home in Sunset. Griffen, in turn, hired John Dancler to construct the house, thus advancing the fortune of a fellow black man. Griffen represented those who assisted themselves and others to survive, while belying the notion that blacks were incapable of acquiring, constructing, or maintaining homes.[49]

Likewise personalism and, less directly, paternalism affected black political life. Perhaps several hundred Sunset residents cast ballots in the late 1930s and early 1940s, voting like other black workers in the region for New Deal Democrats. They lived in Ward 2 and followed the lead of party workers loyal to Grover C. Baker, a Democratic Party organizer, and undertook their assignments as much for money as for political belief. Their contact with Baker, a white operative, represented a form of clientage politics wherein a community member and a party notable collaborate for mutual benefit but voters receive little for their collective support.[50]

Certainly personal contact and paternal treatment blurred lines of acceptable behavior for blacks and whites, yet certain taboos were understood by all in the postslavery era of segregation and racial etiquette. Although blacks puzzled over being denied the use of restrooms in the Malone theater but permitted to share those across the street at the Frisco train depot with white travelers, they understood the "invisible line" that no one of either race dared cross no matter how inconsistent it seemed.[51] No transgression sparked a more violent reaction than real or imagined interracial sexual contact, savagely exemplified by the lynching of Roosevelt Grigsby in nearby Charleston during the mid-1920s for allegedly attempting to rape a sixteen-year-old white girl. Small wonder that black Sikestonians concealed their "more active feelings" from whites—until they were brought forth by a crisis.[52]

Meanwhile, individuals of both races stirred the social order in annoying if not cataclysmic ways. Blacks and whites were arrested for drunkenness, fighting, disturbing the peace, shooting craps, and, usually in the case of whites, prostitution.[53] In these activities, however, save for a handful of whites who gambled with Sunset and alley residents, they rarely crossed the color line. Given this fact and the supposed "petty" nature of the crimes, Police Judge Brown Jewell meted out evenhanded justice for like violations regardless of race.[54]

More disquieting was the violence that occurred in Sikeston and its vicinity. Some dice games ended in arguments, fights, and even killings, reminders of southern and hill culture influences that had taught individuals to resolve disputes through the use of force.[55] Aggressors and their victims tended to be of the same race, as were those who assaulted lawmen in surrounding towns and farms, including Illinois youths who killed a Bootheel state trooper in 1941. Both blacks and whites were also lost in highway deaths, among the highest in the state—graphic reminders of the impact of modernization.[56]

Labor strife too pushed at traditional society. In 1941 Sikestonians chose sides as the International Brotherhood of Teamsters, Chauffeurs, Warehousemen, and Helpers of America (AFL) shut down Scott County Milling Company in their city, Dexter, and Oran. The impasse was settled in favor of unionists by federal officials who considered wheat "a necessity for national defense."[57] Simultaneously, workers of the International Shoe Company were approached by organizers of the United Shoeworkers of America (CIO), but the sizable female work force generally identified with the local factory, which townsfolk had contributed to building eighteen years earlier. Neither incident sparked violence in the nearly all-white shops; mill managers refrained from employing black strikebreakers, and shoeworker leaders understood the area's anti-union heritage. Yet no one in town could have missed the intrusion of government and outsiders on the local economy and power structure.[58] "We will continue to oppose 'changes' we do not believe desirable," wrote the *Sikeston Standard* editor, criticizing the shoe factory campaign directly and, one suspects, similar assaults on traditional society.[59]

Ironically some changes were brought about by bumper crops and world war. Prosperity returned with bountiful cotton harvests that provided work, raised wages, and reduced relief rolls throughout the area.[60] Blacks shared in the good fortune, paying off mortgages, laying away staples, and joining in the spending sprees that characterized Saturdays in Sikeston and Charleston.[61] Some instances appeared haughty and sparked white resentment. When a store clerk referred one shopper to the store basement for a dress, she insisted, "No, sah, I want a regular teaser." Scenes such as this recurred from September through the Christmas shopping season and, though likely overlooked by many in the holiday spirit, ruffled some whites.[62]

During this same period Sikestonians witnessed the physical transformation of their community, which had begun the previous year. They built numerous homes and businesses: a Sikeston Compress and Warehouse Company storage facility expanded the locale's cotton economy; a Kroger supermarket, one of the largest "self-service" stores in the region, boosted its consumerism.[63] City councilmen considered widening Front Street to facilitate the growing business of downtown retailers. And before the new year, local investors took the first step toward establishing a commercial radio station.[64]

Townsfolk also sensed the abrupt shift to military preparedness. They expanded severalfold the Missouri Institute of Aeronautics, which trained cadets from every state for the U.S. Army Air Corps and required establishment of the Sikeston General Hospital—"a district infirmary"—the previous year.[65] In late August and in early October 1941 they observed 6,000 members of the U.S. Army's Fifth Division of Fort Custer, Michigan, pass through Sikeston to and from maneuvers in southern camps. They realized that the city served as a permanent link in the state defense council's communication plan, and experienced the scarcity of materials that soon led to systematic rationing.[66]

Essentially, then, Sikeston denizens found themselves in transition between traditional and modern ways. They possessed much of the politically provincial, economically uniform, and socially hierarchial order established by early settlers and later migrants, particularly those from southern, mountain, and delta regions. In fact, despite modernizing modes of communication and transportation, and commercial links beyond the locale, their racial world turned on rigid communal mores. The "traditional personality" of white residents, including those from northern areas, required—however personal or paternal—segregation and social control. Townspeople of both races felt the impact of the Depression and, more immediately, the war: in-

trusions that fostered increasing political centralization, economic diversification, and social egalitarianism. Simultaneously, they operated in "different spheres" and moved in "contrary directions," a dichotomy shattered by
the bombing of Pearl Harbor and, following swiftly on its heels, bloodshed
of a more local kind.[67]

2 Bloodshed

Despite the economic boom and the festive preparations for Christmas that characterized early December 1941, Sikeston residents experienced anxious moments amid glad tidings. They knew of draft calls over the past year and of area youths already stationed in "danger zones": the Hawaiian and Philippine Islands.[1] Little did they realize, however, how soon blood would be shed there—and elsewhere.

Indeed, townspeople reeled with the reports of Japan's "unprovoked and dastardly" attack of Pearl Harbor on December 7. "Congress Declares War on Japan" screamed local headlines, which soon included Germany and Italy as enemies; "severe damage to American naval and military forces" and "many American lives . . . lost" confirmed President Franklin D. Roosevelt, who outlined the Japanese surprise offensive throughout the Pacific and along the East Asian coast.[2]

Against the slogan "Remember Pearl Harbor!" Sikestonians declared their patriotism and shared the anger of their newspaper editors. "At last the brown bellied Japs have struck," snarled the *Standard*'s C.L. Blanton, while his counterpart at the *Herald*, Clint H. Denman, prophesied defeat for those "who would destroy the freedom . . . [God] has willed His people."[3] Townspeople prepared for war and experienced tension as young men "assumed that they were going to have to go," and everyone realized that the war might be closer to home than first thought.[4]

For white residents, Company K best exemplified past glories and present anxieties. Formed as a National Guard unit in Sikeston on August 25, 1917, it had become part of the 140th Infantry, Seventieth Brigade, Thirty-fifth Division; it had fought valiantly in the Meuse-Argonne offensive and served as part of the occupation force in Europe. Disbanded during the spring of 1919, only to be reorganized within a year, Company K secured rail centers during the railroad workers' strike of 1922, Poplar Bluff streets after the tornado of 1927, and Mississippi River levees in the floods of 1927 and 1937. Its numbers surged during 1940 as conflagration spread worldwide and Roosevelt pledged all aid short of war to the Allies. By presi-

dential decree, guardsmen mobilized on December 23 for a year of training, a mobilization that in fact lasted for the duration of World War II.[5]
    Shortly into the new year of 1941, the 140th Infantry arrived at Camp
Joseph T. Robinson, near Little Rock, Arkansas, where Company K and other
guardsmen drilled for eight months, returning to Sikeston periodically for
a parade or furloughs.[6] Then, in August and September, they participated
in the massive Louisiana Maneuvers of the Sabine Valley, which transformed
them into soldiers. Back at Camp Robinson, they marched in the Armistice
Day celebration at Springfield, Missouri, and came home on leave as often
as possible.[7]
    With the bombing of Pearl Harbor, however, the men of Company K
called mothers, wives, and sweethearts, clogging telephone wires with word
of their departure to an unknown destination—many thought the Philip-
pines. "Like a fighter on a fine edge," in the words of Sgt. James D. Sturgeon,
Company K wanted "a chance at those Japs." Guardsmen departed "smil-
ing," perhaps in anticipation of dealing out "plenty" to the enemy or in an
effort to mask their own or their loved ones' anxiety.[8]
    As city residents bundled up in the face of cold temperatures and snow
flurries early in 1942 they knew that Company K had been assigned to the
Western Defense Command in California and that "winning the war" meant
home-front sacrifices such as tire rationing, "less frivolity, fewer luxuries,"
"uncertain business conditions," and longer work hours.[9] Some of them also
knew that in southernmost Pemiscot County, planters had broken up a meeting sponsored by the Southern Tenant Farmers Union on January 16 and,
after cursing and striking its organizer, had run him out of Caruthersville.[10]
    Surrounded by modern warfare and traditional race conflict, Sikes-
tonians entered the last weekend of January enjoying uncharacteristically
warm weather and anticipating a Saturday night of entertainment—and
escape—possibly at the Malone theater, where *West of the Cimmaron*, star-
ring Tim Tyler and Bob Steele, played for less than two bits.[11] Expecting attacks overseas or even on the West Coast, where Company K was securing
beaches, fuel dumps, and transportation systems, they hardly imagined the
acts of violence about to erupt among themselves.
    The bloodshed began early Sunday morning, January 25, at 847 East
Kathleen Avenue in the so-called shoe factory district of southeast Sikeston.
There, Grace Sturgeon resided with her eight-year-old son Jimmy and her
sister-in-law Laverne Sturgeon, sharing the house while their husbands—
brothers James and John—served in the armed forces. Grace Sturgeon awoke
twice, first hearing noise in the kitchen around 1:00 A.M., where someone

attempted to open the back door by cutting its glass and reaching in to undo its lock. Thirty minutes later she heard the bedroom window being raised and warned the intruder to come no farther.[12] She sat up as a man entered the room, cursing her and waking Laverne, who thought that Grace had had a nightmare until she saw the stranger and heard him say, "Shut your mouth or I'll kill you."[13]

Both women jumped from bed and bolted for safety. Laverne, screaming as she passed through the living room and the dining room (where Jimmy slept), tried to exit through the kitchen door. Unable to open it because—as the prowler had discovered earlier—the key was missing from its lock, she backtracked to the living room, phoned for assistance, and then ran out the front entrance. Meanwhile, Grace also entered the living room but did not get far; the man caught her from behind.[14]

Grace Sturgeon turned to face her attacker, who reacted to her defiance like a "mad bee." Spat upon and threatened, she blocked his six-inch folding knife from cutting her throat, nearly losing three fingers on the hand that saved her life and surprising him with her strength. Staggering under a barehanded blow to the head, she fought on, a "stout S.O.B.," he uttered in amazement before slicing her lower abdomen as easily as one could make "a deep pin scratch." She "burned like fire" as her intestines "just unfolded" and fell from her body, and she wondered if her heart would follow.[15] As she grasped her dangling insides with one hand and the front door with the other, an approaching auto frightened the assailant away. She was standing on the porch in her own blood when H.D. Davenport, her step-grandfather, arrived moments later, still in nightclothes and armed with a corn knife.[16]

Suddenly, help appeared from every direction. Nearby neighbor Jesse Whittley came running and Sikeston lawmen drove up, one responding to Laverne's screams and the others to her frantic phone call (which the operator had relayed by police signal).[17] Whittley joined Night Marshal Hess Perrigan and searched the grounds, while Officer Roy Beck entered the house, called an ambulance, and alerted other local and state officers.[18]

A terrified Grace Sturgeon reentered the premises only after Beck's probe. Inside, her son lay petrified on a cot in a corner of the dining room.[19] Awakened by Laverne's screams, Grace's directions to her, and the intruder's "low, muffled voice," Jimmy moved only after his mother returned, flicked on the lights, and called to him. He advanced to behold her blood-splattered body: a towel-filled left hand cupping intestines, a truncated right hand displaying laid-back fingers! Obeying her instructions, he crossed the street to stay with his maternal grandmother.[20]

Grace Sturgeon, accompanied by Beck, was soon taken by ambulance to the General Hospital, where she underwent emergency surgery. Dr. M.G. Anderson sewed her three fingers and closed a six-inch abdominal slash that had punctured her large bowel. More critical than these wounds or the loss of one and a half quarts of blood, however, was the life-threatening infection that followed.[21] Conscious throughout most of her ordeal, Sturgeon survived the first act of violence.

Meanwhile, the hunt began for her assailant, who retreated the way he had come, through the east bedroom window, leaving bloodstains on the sill and dragging a curtain several feet. Perrigan and Whittley followed his tracks around the house and west behind Kathleen Avenue before they petered out.[22] Believing that the culprit had fled through the rear alley or along the adjacent street, they jumped into the police car and first cruised the neighborhood, then extended their dragnet to skirt the city limits and Sunset Addition's eastern edge. Crossing Malone Avenue into southwest Sikeston, they came upon a black figure walking calmly with hands in the pockets of blood-splattered pants. They stopped Cleo Wright in front of the Jefferson Hotel on the corner of Prosperity Street, due east of the Frisco railroad depot and within seventy-five feet of the tracks themselves. Thirty minutes into the search and approximately a mile and a quarter from the Sturgeon home, Perrigan and Whittley believed that the twenty-six-year-old oil mill worker was their man.[23]

Perrigan searched Wright and found a "long keen bladed knife" banded in red and white, which he claimed had become bloodstained in a fight with other blacks. Within moments, as Whittley slid into the driver's seat, he heard a blow and turned to see Perrigan strike Wright a second time with his pistol, apparently for resisting arrest. He entered the fray, as policeman and suspect struggled for the Smith and Wesson, hitting Wright over the head two more times with a flashlight and clinching him around the neck. Whittley incurred an arm bite before he and Perrigan forced Wright into the back seat of the car, then Perrigan piled in behind him with drawn firearm.[24]

Whittley was chauffeuring them onto Malone Avenue, back toward City Hall, when their prisoner lashed out again. Perrigan fought for his life as Wright plunged a previously hidden scout knife through his upper lip and jaw, smashing some teeth, puncturing the tongue and cutting an artery beneath it. Additional blows slashed his face and left ear. In desperation, Perrigan fired four times, his bullets slamming through Wright with .45 caliber force. He collapsed under Wright who continued to battle until Whittley

Hess Perrigan and Jesse Whittley in 1942. Courtesy of Michael L. Jensen.

hit the brakes, opened the door, grabbed the prisoner, and beat him about the skull with the revolver until he fell out of the car. Perrigan owed his life to Whittley, who alone escaped serious injury.

Amazingly, both combatants remained conscious as Whittley drove a few more blocks along Malone Avenue to the Dunn Hotel. "I got the son-of-a-bitch and he almost got me," Perrigan boasted to Beck, who arrived from the hospital and took charge of the prisoner.[25] As Beck, Whittley, and Wright proceeded to City Hall, the night marshal sought medical attention. He walked into the General Hospital and stoically comforted Grace Sturgeon as they both awaited the arrival of Dr. Anderson, he assuring her of Wright's capture and she calming herself by "talking ninety-miles-a-minute." Perrigan's grave condition required immediate treatment, and on the operating table the blood gushing up from under his tongue "like a fountain" proved difficult to stop. He lived through the ordeal, though he was unable to talk for several days and lacked teeth for the rest of his life.[26]

Wright endured even more pain, and greater misfortune. Taken to the jail in City Hall by Beck and Whittley, he got very sick, and Beck, who discovered his gunshot wounds for the first time, called Dr. E.J. Nienstedt and an ambulance. Accompanied by his captors to the hospital, where Whittley had his arm treated before leaving for home, Wright waited a short time in the emergency room for the physician.[27] In the basement facility, his wounds—eight bullet holes—were dressed and his broken arm set. Wright, though still conscious, received no narcotics, for Dr. Nienstedt feared that an anesthetic might prove fatal. He had withstood six blows to the head, four bullets passing completely through the midsection, right chest, and right arm, and enormous loss of blood.[28] When visited after surgery by his in-laws, Richard and Minnie Gay, he was unconscious. Nor did he recognize his wife, Ardella, shortly before daylight, when full hospital rooms and emergency-only treatment for blacks required his removal by ambulance to his home in Sunset Addition, escorted by Policeman Grover H. Lewis.[29]

Visited by Beck and Lewis, just before they went off duty, and Assistant Police Chief Harold Wallace, Wright appeared to be dying at 6:30 A.M.[30] His pregnant wife and worried in-laws soon feared for his safety and considered themselves incapable of either caring for him or incurring his burial expenses.[31] At their pleading Wright was moved back to Sikeston by ambulance, this time under the direction of Wallace, and placed on a cot in the women's detention room of the jail shortly before 9:30 A.M.—left to die alone as the second act of violence played itself out.[32]

By now, much of Sikeston knew of the dying prisoner's attacks on Sturgeon and Perrigan. From 1:30 until 6:00 A.M., when she went off duty, the operator who received Laverne Sturgeon's "Mayday" and directed police to the crime scene handled 666 calls, five and a half times more than the normal number. That a cab driver informed Maxine Croder of the assault almost immediately suggested the content of most phone conversations. Word that "a white woman had been slashed . . . by a negro"—first reported by lawmen requesting an ambulance for Grace Sturgeon—spread so rapidly that townsfolk converged on the hospital and could not be "pushed out" of its small confines.[33] Patrons of Lambert's Cafe, for example, received phone calls from friends and passed the story along in private conversation, so that youths heard of it while driving about town. Some residents arrived even before Sturgeon; others came already aware that Perrigan had had "his tongue about hacked in two." Few individuals laid eyes on Sturgeon or Perrigan at the hospital, but several witnessed Wright's entry and surgery in the much more accessible emergency room.[34]

Significantly, the rapid transmission of information by phone and the easy mobilization of residents on a Saturday night combined modern technology and traditional mores to transpose a criminal act into a communal affair. Unnamed whites were in Sunset inquiring about Wright's condition shortly after officers took him there. By daybreak at least two black residents sensed the possibility of mob violence and wanted Wright moved out of the Addition, their fears later reiterated by his mother-in-law who "knew trouble was coming."[35] At about 7:30 A.M. groups of two and three white males circulated among downtown garages and cafes, enlisting recruits to mob "the negro."[36] Hence, when Richard Gay walked into town to call Wright's mother at 9:00 A.M., "he saw what was going to happen"; recognizing that "righteous look" of whites that time and again announced "the faggot, the whip, the fist," he retreated back to the black community.[37]

Comprising both would-be lynchers and mere curiosity seekers, the crowd gathering outside City Hall "kept growing." Excited individuals called friends and fellow workers, urging them downtown to take part in the anticipated action. Churchgoers returning from services and Sunday visitors from outlying communities filled Center Street.[38] Several flight school cadets stood across from the historic building, erected in 1908; handfuls of spectators looked down from second-story decks on the opposite side of the thoroughfare; and a few women sat in parked cars beyond the mob.[39] All knew about the vicious knifings and the grave condition of Sturgeon and Perrigan.

Doubtless, word of Wright's confession also enlarged the mob. Some heard that he had admitted twice to attacking the woman, slashing her with "the long keen knife"—he told Beck in the hospital—and blamed his actions on "bad whiskey."[40] Several hours later in City Hall he acknowledged to Wallace, Coca Cola Bottling Company manager Milburn Arbaugh, and former service station employer Milem Limbaugh that having been drinking, he wandered "down there," broke into the home, and cut Sturgeon.[41] The mob might have learned of Wright's guilty pleas through police officers (though no evidence suggests this), or one of its own ringleaders may have overheard his conversation to the businessmen (themselves innocent of spreading its contents).[42] In any case, even before Wallace, Arbaugh, and

City Hall, Sikeston, Missouri, erected in 1908. Courtesy of Michael L. Jensen.

Limbaugh left Wright at 10:00 A.M., his executioners said that "something ought to be done."[43]

State Trooper Melvin Dace, approaching City Hall one-half hour later, found it bereft of police protection and overrun by "an unusually large crowd": seventy-five people were inside trying to break into Wright's chamber with an iron bar. Dace ordered them out without much opposition—though some threatened to get their guns and "burn nigger town"—and called for help: fellow troopers in Sikeston, reinforcements from Troop E headquarters in Poplar Bluff, lawmen from the sheriff's office in Benton; he also notified Mayor George W. Presnell and County Prosecutor David L. Blanton. Almost immediately, Sergeant Dace was joined by Troopers Vincent P. Boisaubin and John Tandy and Police Chief Walter Kendall, who appeared from the street where the horde numbered 700 persons. For nearly an hour they "discouraged" several attempts by the mob to enter the building.[44]

At 11:35 A.M. the crowd began to buzz like "a hornet's nest slowly stirred."[45] At this moment County Prosecutor Blanton arrived from the country, where Dace's message had caught up with him. He conferred with the trooper and, in an effort to defuse the situation, addressed mob members from the building's entrance. He ordered them to vacate the premises, only to hear—from all directions—boos and shouts: "What are we waiting for?" "Let's go get the black S.O.B." Turning to one of the mob's leaders, Blanton threatened prosecution "if you have murder on your mind and do anything." Suddenly someone slipped under one of the trooper's arms, enabling others to surge through three sets of glass-paneled double doors and push by the prosecutor, who sustained a broken rib.[46]

With the lawmen, Blanton rushed down the corridor, unsuccessfully trying to beat the mob to the women's detention room. He climbed on a stool to address the throng once more but found himself forced off and the troopers roughed up. As the crowd smashed the upper panel of the wooden door shielding Wright, Blanton watched helplessly. One of the mob tossed the battered prisoner into the hallway, then climbed atop the broken door, jumped down on his chest, and kicked him several times. Blanton saw no more, but four others dragged their prey back down the corridor and through the entrance, enveloped by the multitude and spurred on by shouts: "Let's take him to Sunset and burn him."[47]

Under the portico of City Hall, with its graceful white columns framing their brutality, ringleaders paused while others kicked Wright.[48] They quickly pulled him feet first, arms overhead and skull bouncing down seven concrete steps amid the kind of cheering that follows "a ninety-nine yard touchdown" run.[49] Once beyond the sidewalk, members of the mob first jammed him into the trunk of a Ford idling in Center Street, then changed their minds and pulled him out, hooked his legs behind the car bumper, and drove off to the blasts of honking horns.[50]

Packed into the maroon sedan-turned-deathmobile and standing on its runningboards, lynchers headed for Sunset Addition. They moved west on Center, turned south on Stoddard, stopping for traffic signals—obeying the law, said one wag; avoiding a traffic ticket, recalled another[51]—west again on U.S. 60 and, leading a cavalcade of fifty vehicles, raced toward the black community.[52] Shortly beyond the Frisco railroad tracks, they entered the Addition at Fair Street, circled via Maude, Thompson, Osage, and Lincoln, and returned to Maude, Sunset's southernmost street, separated from U.S. 60 by Missouri Pacific tracks.[53]

Meanwhile, Blanton, Dace, and Tandy, among the last to emerge from the recesses of City Hall, rushed to Sunset, while Boisaubin, at the prosecutor's request, retrieved his camera to photograph the culprits. Blanton and four other citizens—including *Standard* newsman Paul Bumbarger and photographer Roy Wilcox—rode in Dace's patrol car; Tandy accompanied

Trooper John N. Greim, who arrived at that very moment from Dexter (one of the officers mobilized by Troop E headquarters in response to Dace's call).[54] Since their vehicles faced east on Center Street, they headed in that direction one block, turned north on Kingshighway, and then west on North Street, which fed into the Addition. Entering the community by "an entirely different route" from that taken by the car dragging Wright, they divided at the first intersection and, fearing "a massacre" should the mob encounter any blacks, chased them off the streets before converging on the lynching site.[55]

Horror-stricken blacks believed themselves under siege as state troopers and white residents poured into Sunset, some in vehicles, others afoot, everyone turbulent and—it appeared to many blacks—crazed.[56] Some whites even got to the execution site ahead of Wright's mangled body. As the "lynch parade" swung onto Osage, blacks attending the Church of God in Christ at the far end of the street received word that "a terrible thing" was happening and crowded at the door to see.[57] Meanwhile, on nearby Luther Street a neighbor's child informed Minnie Gay of her son-in-law's fate. She rushed to her daughter's home, where Ardella collapsed upon hearing the news amid car horns squalling and people yelling.[58]

Within moments, George W. Scott, standing on the front porch of his Osage Street grocery store, watched the cavalcade speed by him, while eight-year-old Arthur Renfro froze in his steps as it passed Felker Street. Witnessing a near-naked body being hauled behind the lead car and armed men riding the running boards of several vehicles that followed it, he ran up Felker and into his home; with eyes as big as saucers he kept repeating: "I seen 'em! I seen 'em! I seen 'em!"[59] Alberta Gardner of Lincoln Street came to the front door of her home thinking that the noisy entourage turning off Osage must be a parade. Instead, she reeled at the sight of Wright in tow, "bobbing up and down," and police, men, and women—some even in housecoats and slippers—all "rejoicing" as if on a picnic.[60]

The mob halted on Maude, near the schoolhouse and within view of both Smith Chapel and the First Baptist Church.[61] As lynchers placed Wright on the Missouri Pacific Railroad easement, just north of the tracks and U.S. 60, authorities closed in from each end of the street. Blanton worked his way through the crowd of three to four hundred, while Dace and Tandy stayed with their vehicles, trapped in traffic and buffered by humanity two hundred yards deep. Blanton alone entered "the inner rim" of the men, women, and children who formed a circle around Wright, just in time to see a middle-aged man in coveralls douse the victim with five gallons of gasoline brought

Lynching spectators view the charred body of Cleo Wright, January 25, 1942.
Courtesy of Michael L. Jensen.

from a nearby service station and a younger, inebriated man unsuccessfully
try to set him ablaze. From behind the county prosecutor someone flipped
a lighted match onto the saturated ground, which sent flames racing up
Wright's naked body and caused him to cry out once. Blanton became nau-
seated as fire and smoke engulfed the victim, whose arms contracted in the
heat and reached skyward as if pleading for a mercy that did not come. Cleo
Wright perished in the third and final act of violence.[62]

Across the way, Rev. J.B. Ross considered the commotion outside Smith
Chapel a typical distraction from his sermon. He looked through a window,
mistook Wright's funeral pyre for a burning car, calmed his congregation,
and continued to preach.[63] As the "terrible sounds" persisted, someone entered the church and informed him of the killing just a few hundred feet
away. Children soon followed with similar messages, and churchgoers filled
the windows, frightened by the sight of "black smoke" and screaming
whites.[64]

Others in that noonday crowd seemed gleeful, irritated, or unmoved,
and throughout the Sabbath many more whites came from church services

and family dinners to view what became a charred sphinx: human face, distorted torso.[65] Witnesses to the burning—which for several minutes threw off so much fire that few could recognize what was ablaze—described a piece of flesh "blistered up" and distinguished by lattice-like designs.[66] Later viewers came upon what more nearly resembled "a roast pig": body naked, charred, and drawn up; human features mocked by a cigarette inserted between the lips and a match placed in the nose.[67] Like Blanton, who left the barbaric scene quickly, some became ill, and few ever forgot the sight and smell of Wright's burnt carcass.

Still, until late in the afternoon whites entered Sunset Addition to look at Wright's body and, inadvertently, to see blacks fleeing their community. Several dashed across fields; many more trekked along U.S. 60 and adjacent railroad tracks laden with bundles and suitcases, reminding one witness of Exodus; still others, carrying whatever they could in cotton sacks, boarded buses and trains, hopped railroad cars, piled into farm trucks, or offered car owners like Fred Smith "any kind of price" to drive them out of town.[68] Their numbers mushroomed, ultimately exceeding one hundred persons.[69]

Numerous seasonal workers headed east to Charleston, north to St. Louis, and south to Dixie. Some white employers sent their servants to temporary refuge or offered haven in their homes—mirroring acts of southern paternalism during periods of racial violence.[70] Other blacks survived the crisis, as their forebears had done, by drawing on religious associations, family bonds, and personal courage. Milton Brown, his family, and members of their congregation also "got the hell out of Dodge" and, through their affiliation with the Church of God in Christ, stayed in New Madrid with Rev. B.B. Gillispie.[71] Some led their wives and children to the homes of relatives in nearby communities such as Morley and left the women to watch over the family while they returned to Sunset Addition, revealing anew the historic role of females as protectors during periods of male absence and the significance of return journeys to home fronts, however close by, during periods of crisis.[72]

Women left alone in Sunset Addition, by choice or circumstance, protected themselves and their children in other ways. Single parent Julia Renfro walked her two sons downtown, passing whites "on every side," and headed north to her mother's alley cabin on Kingshighway, where they spent the night. Her promenade, which could never have been contemplated by most black males, especially those without contacts among powerful white families, indicated the gender distinctions—in this case established by white males—within the color line. Her bravery, daughter-mother relationship, and guardianship of her children bespoke a self-reliant life and a female slave heritage.[73]

More directly in line with traditional "mamas"—those outspoken, elder women who enjoyed respect within the community and whose successors would play a major role in the next generation's civil rights struggle[74]—Mattie D. Smith reacted more demonstratively. She witnessed Wright's burning from Smith Chapel and returned home immediately. When the mob stayed at the site, she called city officials and, receiving an unsatisfactory response, went downtown. In the company of her thirty-eight-year-old son, she demanded that Mayor Presnell and Police Chief Kendall take measures to protect all of Sunset's residents from further violence. "For her own protection," Mattie D. Smith stayed that night at the home of a member of the prominent Matthews family.[75] One of the founders of the chapel and the funeral business that bore her name, and one of the black community's largest property owners, she benefited from white southern personalism and class concepts.

Black men, particularly those with roots and property in Sunset Addition, also drew from their heritage and readied for combat. Immediately after Wright's burning, some assembled on the streets and others gathered in George Scott's grocery. They seemed "badly scared" yet incensed that lynchers hauled Wright through their streets—an affront they would have challenged with Winchester rifles had they known of it in advance, and women would have stayed and fought alongside their men in a "double war."[76]

Several homeowners—including Fred Smith, the son of Mattie—armed themselves and, as individual sentries, guarded family homesteads.[77] Those who met at Scott's store organized to collect weapons from house to house and place loved ones beyond harm's way. They regrouped that evening—perhaps seventy-five strong—in the First Baptist Church, aware of subsequent white threats: "We will be back tonight." Called together by Scott, Ross, and Walter Griffen, they inventoried munitions, divided into squads, and guarded the Addition's five entrances: no white person would pass save lawmen. "If whites came," recalled Griffen, who bore a weapon loaded with cartridges taken from his white employer's gun case, "a lot of folks would have died."[78] For reasons of duty, survival, and cultural beliefs that deemed their homes "a state of mind," the source of their sense of community, and a link between generations, Sunset's men mobilized and risked race war, prepared to defend themselves as individuals and as a people: "No one," said Alberta Gardner, "had the right to run them out."[79]

The threatened attack did not occur, mainly because authorities stepped between the races. Almost immediately after the lynching, Governor Forrest C. Donnell learned of the incident from a state trooper in the Cape Girardeau area and phoned Mayor Presnell, whom he told to await further instructions. Throughout the afternoon he spoke with several officials, specifying that Colonel M. Stanley Ginn, superintendent of the Missouri State Highway Patrol, and Sheriff John Hobbs assign additional men to the lynch scene. Meanwhile. Presnell called city councilmen into special session and appointed extra policemen to prevent further "acts of violence." Then he visited Sunset Addition and tried unsuccessfully to reason with frightened residents intent on fleeing the community.[80]

Presnell's deputies joined several troopers that night and sealed off the Addition. Six everyday citizens—including Jesse Whittley, who had assisted in Wright's capture and saved Perrigan's life—and a handful of American Legion members received instructions "to keep the peace" by keeping the races apart.[81] Their numbers were augmented significantly by nineteen troopers under the supervision of Sergeant Dace. In truth, Dace, Tandy, Boisaubin, and Greim remained in the community after Wright's killing, as did John Morris and Morley G. Swingle from Troop B (Cape Girardeau), who arrived shortly thereafter. Fully sixteen of southeast Missouri's twenty-two-man unit, including its commanding officer, secured Sunset. Local deputies and state troopers ordered residents inside and turned back whites seeking to enter the black community, while other troopers cruised its streets in a safety truck and official cars. They also patrolled downtown, and one trooper manned the Sikeston office, ready to call in reinforcements.[82]

Learning that blacks had armed themselves and fearing that whites might consider it a challenge to be answered, Dace spoke to Sunset homeowners about disarming. His efforts failed, largely because blacks questioned whether "they could depend on the officers for protection."[83] They believed that Dace had led the very procession responsible for Wright's death. Moreover, having failed to protect one person, how could he possibly shield many more from a mob?[84]

Consequently, while the "showing of strength" by lawmen imposed order through the night, Sunset residents carried their worst fear—of a racial pogrom—into Monday. The Reverend Ross called Governor Donnell early that morning, concerned about the role that state troopers had supposedly played in Wright's killing and the immediate rumor that Sgt. J.D. Sturgeon had arrived in town saying "a new crew" would attack the Addition that day.[85] Throughout the afternoon, Ross and three others insisted that blacks lacked "adequate protection" and, according to state troopers who questioned his motives, kept that entire population in "an uproar." Contacted by the mayor, Ross reminded Presnell of his own Sunday remark that there would not be "enough laws or guns to keep a mob from coming to the colored section" if Grace Sturgeon or Hess Perrigan died.[86] He also knew that several blacks received anonymous phone calls throughout Monday, indicating that they would be harmed and their property destroyed should the woman pass away.[87]

No doubt it was because of Ross's concerns that most lawmen stayed on duty until Tuesday afternoon. Only two troopers left the area the previous day and returned to their home station in Cape Girardeau, which required their services in court and on patrol.[88] In fact, from Sunday evening on, Dace believed that the crisis had passed and Presnell reported Monday morning that things were "more apprehensive" than dangerous; but the mayor's belief that quiet could quickly change to tumult should the woman die "in the next day or two" gave weight to black fears and the governor's decision to guard Sunset another day.[89]

Although little was said to Donnell, many whites also expressed unabashed fear at the prospects of black revenge for the lynching and, ironically, dreaded the thought of a race war.[90] And well they should have, for weapons were abundant among Sunset blacks raised in a southern tradition of hunting and self-protection. Unknown to white residents, younger blacks between the ages of seventeen and twenty had to be talked out of retaliatory violence by Scott, Ross, and Griffen, who supervised them in the community patrols that lasted through Wednesday night.[91] For good reason, then, troopers who knew better played down the rumor that blacks were heavily armed.[92]

In reality, the brutal slaying of Wright had ended the violence. At 4:00 P.M. on Sunday, as Sturgeon and Perrigan lay hospitalized with wounds that would take weeks to heal and thoughts that would never pass, Wright's scorched remains were gathered up unceremoniously and hauled away in a city dump truck to sit overnight in the City Hall, where street department workers built Wright's coffin out of twelve-inch pine boards. Claimed by neither his family nor frightened black or affronted white morticians—though all were contacted by municipal officials—what remained of Wright was loaded back on the truck, driven north to McMullin, and interred in the "potters field" of Carpenter Cemetery at the City of Sikeston's expense.[93] Presnell made all these arrangements, Coroner Clyde Poe deeming an inquest into Wright's death unnecessary.[94]

The carnage was finally over, but its impact on black and white Sikeston had just begun. Blacks who happened upon Wright's dragging and burning never forgot, and youthful witnesses experienced nightmares for some time afterward.[95] Others too endured indelible anguish. Griffen, for one, stood vigil in Sunset for three nights, while his wife, Mattie Lee, a half mile away in their cabin on Dr. T.C. McClure's property, clutched a .38 Colt pistol. They talked periodically by phone, but Alberta Gardner knew much less about the fate of her husband, who also patrolled the Addition. From Morley, she listened to the radio and looked for daily messengers. She prayed often—alone, with her family, and sometimes with several families—seeking consolation and deliverance as had slaves in a perilous South.[96]

 Little is known about the nearly one hundred residents who fled but never returned to the community. Many were seasonal workers or individuals without property, who like many earlier and later black migrants controlled their lives and protested their treatment by leaving areas of bloodshed.[97] Swept up in the "mass hysteria," they abandoned the locality rather than remain even more servile to whites. The "colored boy" who washed dishes at Gilbert's Cafe, for instance, and was whisked to the safety of his country kin by a concerned employer as the lynchers organized, never set foot back in town.[98]

In contrast, those refugees with greater stakes in Sunset Addition returned within a matter of days or weeks. They had waited out the period of uncertainty in nearby Charleston, Cairo, and elsewhere, reappearing in Sikeston once the threat of further violence had passed.[99] Even those who remained in the community throughout the ordeal talked about finding new homes elsewhere, but "financial conditions" prevented them from doing so.[100]

Perhaps most significantly, blacks who patrolled under Ross, Scott, and Griffen quickly organized a local chapter of the National Association for the Advancement of Colored People (NAACP). They met on Monday, electing Rev. S.V. Wolfe president and carpenter John Dancler secretary. More than redress for Wright's murder, they sought protection from further mob violence.[101] Gradually, they transformed themselves from a paramilitary unit to a paralegal organization, trading weapons for monthly dues and the chance of race war for the prospects of racial peace, organizing in modern society for self-preservation and social order.[102]

During the last week of January, after the most immediate threat of white invasion had passed, most black Sikestonians sought to move beyond the killing and reestablish peaceful, if strained, coexistence with whites. By Tuesday, influential blacks informed local newsmen that "the best thing" would be for everyone to think of the bloodshed as "a bad nightmare"—presumably to be forgotten. No doubt several black customers of white merchants, who later denied ever knowing Cleo Wright, fixated on the frightful vision of themselves bouncing behind a car driven by cold-blooded racists. Others, however, wanted to forget the lynching because of the self-destructive anger that it engendered; they hoped to avoid the further tension that would surely come should their emotions be channeled into protest. Black residents privately discussed the brutal slaying and its traumatic impact on their community, but ultimately they manifested, if not believed in, Minnie Gay's fatalism: her son-in-law was dead, and everyone ought to "forget about the whole thing."[103]

White Sikestonians responded to the shocking events along more segmented lines of ideology, class, and gender. Those who caused or observed Wright's death considered it righteous. Immediately after the killing, several said in effect, "He got just what he had coming." Their numbers were augmented by law-abiding citizens of both southern and northern backgrounds who, discussing the execution throughout Monday, expressed neither remorse nor disfavor. Customers of a seed company, for instance, reached a "general consensus" endorsing lynch law.[104] Predictably, C.L. Blanton—unreconstructed southerner, influential editor, and father of the county's prosecuting attorney—captured the essence of community opinion: the vigilantism served as "solemn warning for the night prowlers to leave the community."[105] Like their forebears, townspeople sought to reestablish "their sense of order" by sanctioning the "display of brute force."[106]

Some individuals used the violence as an opportunity to express attitudes usually kept beneath the surface.[107] Men and women agreed on the justification for Wright's death, though from diverse perspectives. Only "cowards and dogs" would "sit idly by" while their women and peace officers were attacked, reasoned a northern-born paralytic who—had he been mobile—would have joined in the mob. Only a woman alone, reinterpreted a wife and mother of one child whose husband worked a night shift, could "describe the fear that Mrs. Sturgeon must have experienced."[108] For many, male pride and female fear turned on issues of power and sexuality.

Other whites demonstrated fear of another kind. Apprehensive of "what the colored people might do," they prepared for the worst and exhibited relief when the threat of retaliation—which blacks never seriously considered—faded. They also expressed shame for the lynching, an act the town could not be proud of.[109] Perhaps for this reason, some residents considered Wright's death unfortunate or, more quietly, condemned it. Troubled by rope-and-faggot justice, they wished that Wright's fate had been determined by the legal process. Occasionally someone even admitted sorrow for "the man who got lynched." Churchgoers expressed greater reservation than others, believing that "by the laws of God it was wrong," yet neither they nor their ministers publicly reproved the lynchers.[110]

Although residents such as *Herald* editor Clint H. Denman contended that no other community in the state applied the Golden Rule more than Sikestonians, only Rev. Joseph P. Read of the Christian Church directly addressed the subject of Wright's burning. On February 1, in "As I See Mob Violence," he preached on the bloodshed that caused "a tragedy" and gave the city "much unfavorable publicity."[111] Other pastors appeared to shy away from such controversy. "Church News and Announcements" carried no lynching-related titles of sermons nor do congregants of the major churches recall hearing their ministers speak out from the pulpit. Following southern tradition, Protestant leaders—during and after the killing—failed to step between mob and victim.[112]

Clearly, ministers were as shocked as any churchgoer by Wright's assaults and his own death. Such bloodshed, remembered one, "never happened before."[113] Given the heinous crimes of Wright, the anger of townsfolk, and the southern tradition of Sikeston, some clergymen may have believed in lynch law; more likely, they feared to aggravate an already volatile situation. In either case, they considered the lynching "a hot potato" which, if condemned (or endorsed), would drive "a wedge" into their congregations.[114] While most preachers thought their hands tied, at least one reacted out of personal fear: within three weeks of the incident the recently arrived fifty-year-old Church of God of Prophecy minister resigned his pulpit and returned to North Carolina "scared to death." Ironically, he was Grace Sturgeon's pastor.[115]

More representative was Rev. Elbridge W. Bartley of the First United Methodist Church. The son of southern, formally trained Methodist parents, he shared the segregationist views of his congregation and, in the larger community, practiced its personalism toward blacks.[116] Occasionally, as in his most famous sermon, "If I Had Wings," he injected self-mocking racist humor: "I am like the good old colored brother, who stoutly refused to fly, saying: 'Ah stays right here on dis terrah furmah, de more furmah de less terrah.'"[117] A thoughtful, seasoned pastor, who had graduated from Vanderbilt University's School of Religion and administered church affairs with authority, he considered violence un-Christian and could never endorse it. Yet he refrained from publicizing his opposition to the lynching. Having settled in the city only four months earlier, perhaps he felt in need of better rapport with his congregation before confronting such a loaded issue. Moreover, his

*since it would
be an improbable
setting—*

sizable church membership was divided into three distinct classes, which made speaking for everyone impossible.[118] Though he realized that his silence gave comfort to those who wanted nothing said, he knew that an effective pastor could ill afford to antagonize congregants or lose their trust by addressing controversy, particularly if he expected to serve as a conciliator among them. Hence he kept quiet rather than split his church—or lose his pastorate. The latter was improbable, since his appointive position came from the Methodist Conference; fellow ministers who answered the direct call of a congregation were much more vulnerable. Thus, his friend Rev. E.D. Owen, whose First Baptist Church resembled his own congregation in numbers and class structure, also remained silent.[119]

Much like Bartley and Owen, who pastored the largest Protestant congregations, and those ministering to smaller ones, Father John J. O'Neil confessed only to himself. Privately, he considered the lynching an immoral intrusion upon God's jurisdiction but refrained from saying so during mass. He had arrived in Sikeston six years earlier, an Irish-born and -trained priest, who had studied at a St. Louis seminary and served a parish there before being assigned to Saint Xavier's. He also took a "lively interest" in civic affairs, which exposed him to controversial issues—none more volatile than race. He surely understood that some parishioners accepted the lynching while others condemned it, indicating anew how race and culture transcended religious beliefs. And he must have sensed that because of the unity among local Protestants and Catholics, who supported segregation and each other's fund-raising activities, his congregants never imagined themselves—a religious minority—as potential lynch victims.[120]

Smaller in number, more culturally distinct, more historically persecuted, and without religious leadership in Sikeston, Jews felt less secure than Catholics. Some Catholic youths witnessed the lynching, for example, whereas Jewish residents apparently shied away from it. They experienced shock and resignation when learning of the execution but publicly remained silent. In part, their silence reflected personal beliefs that pogroms were "acts of God" and that *sheyneh layt* (fine Jews) like themselves were peaceful people.[121] Though they were hardly cowards, their passivity also reflected a primordial understanding that Jews could replace blacks as "shock absorber[s]" for white southerners facing change. Certainly, Leo Frank had served as "a surrogate" for both the black rapist and the industrial revolution that threatened the New South thirty years earlier.[122] For this reason, one Jewish proprietor spoke for many when he condemned the lynching years later. He denied the possibility that Jews could have become victims like Wright, yet contradictorily admitted that they avoided trouble in 1942; speaking out against the bloodshed would have accomplished little and exposed them to ridicule or worse.[123] However subconsciously, Jewish residents invoked a survival technique that many blacks also employed: personal umbrage, even denial, and public quietude.

In this atmosphere, blacks stayed clear of whites for the week or so following Sturgeon's attack and Wright's killing. They remained close to home and even closed their school on Monday. That day very few domestics appeared at white homes, and only twelve of sixty employees reported to the Sikeston Cotton Oil Mill, forcing it to shut down for several days.[124] And when laborers did return to the company that had employed Wright and that was located across town, they worked their shifts and "got the hell back home quick." Most Sunset women waited even longer before they ventured downtown, warned by their men to get the shopping done with haste.[125] Many whites reacted in kind. Immediately after the lynching, cabdrivers refused to enter Sunset, and residents throughout the city locked their windows and doors. Also for the first time in memory, women were escorted, especially after dark, and their movement restricted; they "just didn't go anywhere by themselves."[126]

Predictably normal race relations did return over the coming weeks and months, its pace largely determined by individual impressions of the violence and personal white-black connections. As in the antebellum era, white paternalism and personalism hastened the reconstruction of racial civility. Prominent citizens sought to protect their domestics and handymen against "aggression and abuse."[127] One evening shortly after the mob violence, for instance, Walter Griffen waited in his car for a friend shopping in a downtown drugstore, only to be harassed by a local constable. He exchanged words with the officer, attributed the altercation to a C.L. Blanton suggestion for a black curfew, and complained to his employer, Dr. T.C. McClure. He played his part well, hinting that he would have to quit working for the physician lest he be arrested while running errands. He enjoyed knowing that McClure gave the mayor "hell and hallelujah" and that Presnell, in turn, reprimanded the offending lawman.[128]

Reestablishing race relations was hardly smooth, but most whites understood that someone like Griffen was an entirely different person from Wright. In the wake of bloodshed they needed to insist—as would later white southerners facing the tumult of an emerging civil rights movement—that the races "lived in utopian harmony." So did some established blacks such as Alvin Dotson, who remembered no recrimination among people who "got along like two peas in a shell."[129]

Boosters and officials, too, moved to protect Sikeston's image. Following a week of "unfortunate publicity," attorney Ralph E. Bailey Sr. appeared before city council on Tuesday, February 2. He presented for its consideration a resolution expressing "horror" over Wright's crime and the lynching that it sparked; "deep regret" for the mob violence, particularly in the City Hall; and "united willingness to assist in any possible way" the apprehension of those responsible for the crime and "for bringing humiliation upon the city." Bailey's petition, which also declared appreciation for local policemen, state troopers, and the county prosecutor—who did "everything in their power" to prevent the murder—received the unanimous support of Presnell and councilmen.[130]

Bailey, a former congressman, called on Governor Donnell three days later in Jefferson City. Representing the bankers, businessmen, and other "substantial citizens" who had initially asked him to prepare the council resolution, he reiterated that "strong sentiment" existed in Sikeston for "a complete investigation" into the tragedy and the "punishment" of its ringleaders. He delivered the facts to Donnell, a fellow Republican, without presenting new evidence or requesting state intervention. In fact, acknowledging that divided opinion existed in Sikeston and doubtless having traditionalists such as C.L. Blanton in mind, he met with Missouri's chief executive primarily to tell the world that local modernists opposed mob violence.[131]

That same day, February 5, Denman, one of three prominent Sikestonians who originally sought Bailey as their spokesman, penned "We Stand to Defend." He too condemned both Wright's "terrible crime" and "the disgraceful mob violence," yet focused on the law-abiding people of Sikeston who regretted that "passions ran riot." Presenting a long history of their assistance to black residents, he criticized the undeserved scorn heaped on the community by outsiders. In "Don't Be Misled," the *Herald* editor, again like Bailey, deemed that citizens throughout the nation expected Donnell to keep "the name of Missouri above reproach by insisting that local officers bring the guilty to justice," openly challenging those like C.L. Blanton who charged the governor with political motives.[132]

Planter E.P. Coleman Jr., another of the organizers responsible for Bailey's councilmanic resolution and gubernatorial visit, responded to a *New York Times* editorial written immediately after the lynching, commending the editor's sensitivity to the shame of most townsfolk. His letter, which appeared in that newspaper's pages on February 7, reiterated the modernist position: neither "one wild Negro" nor "300 white hoodlums" represented black or white Sikestonians.[133]

Others shared the outlook of Bailey, Denman, and Coleman. Between Bailey's appearance before city council and his visit with the governor, members of the American Legion adopted a resolution designed to parry external criticism. They unequivocally condemned the lynching, while commending the efforts of state police officers. In rapid succession "other civic and service clubs," such as the Lions, endorsed the legionnaires' resolution. Civic and business leaders thus revealed the reluctance of many white residents to assume responsibility for the violence, seeking instead to marginalize and reduce its significance for the entire community.[134]

Whites also moved to ease the anguish of Grace Sturgeon. Council members donated $50 from municipal funds toward flying Sergeant Sturgeon home from California, and local Red Cross members quickly collected an additional $150 that brought him to his wife's side.[135] In a similar gesture of good will, employees of the International Shoe Company, where Grace worked, contributed to a purse for her hospital expenses. And, perhaps most personally uplifting, churchgoers from various congregations filled "sunshine baskets" with an assortment of gifts.[136] By assisting the victim, townsfolk set themselves on the long process of recovery.

In contrast, white—and black—Sikestonians thought less immediately of Ardella Wright. Councilmen never considered her plight. A Red Cross representative, sensitive to St. Louis inquiries and feeling compelled to assure the public that there existed "no color line when serving humanity," specified that shortly after the lynching his organization had offered to help Ardella Wright but received word from her family that no assistance was needed for the moment.[137] Sunset blacks, perhaps believing with Red Cross officials that Ardella Wright preferred to be left alone, or fearful of being associated too closely with Cleo Wright, seemingly provided little if any aid to his wife. Within two weeks of the bloodshed, however, St. Louis area donors organized by Nanetta Mitchell, wife of the *Argus* business manager, began contributing to a fund for Wright's widow that ultimately exceeded $200.[138] Ardella Wright needed and welcomed the kind of support that she could not accept from those who killed her husband or could not get from those who lived as her neighbors.

To a significant degree the bloodshed focused whites' attention on themselves, some never forgetting the horrific, indelible events. Several adults who witnessed the dragging and burning of Wright no doubt experienced the same nausea that had forced David E. Blanton to leave the killing site. Certainly, more than a few youths were devastated: one teenager woke up from nightmares for some time afterward, and a twelve-year-old was so "overwhelmed" that fifty years later he remembered his sick feeling.[139] Perhaps it was most psychologically debilitating to the children of five years and younger who were paraded by Wright's grotesque, seared corpse as an object lesson in the proper treatment of an inferior race.[140] At least one child from a family of one daughter and two sons whose father escorted them past the carcass required a doctor's care before the sun set. Small wonder that earlier antilynching crusades stressed the emotional damage of mob violence on children.[141]

Nonetheless, teaching racism through "direct observation," wherein blacks—symbolized by Wright—were cast negatively and treated brutally, achieved its purpose among other white youth. One eighteen-year-old, surely typical of many whose families hailed from eastern mountain areas, grew up on a farm where violence occurred as a way of life. Having butchered livestock, killed rabid dogs, experienced corporal punishment, and seen blacks physically abused, he felt neither emotional nor queasy upon witnessing Wright's fiery death, and he knew of no one traumatized or made ill by it. If anything, the bloodshed reinforced what he and many others had been taught about blacks and justice in a frontier society.[142]

Such a lesson also "took" with numerous school-age children who viewed Wright's immolation, his corpse afterward, or photographs of both without ever flinching. Within days of the savagery a "bunch" of students brought photographs of his body into their classrooms and later displayed them about their neighborhoods. Their parents had snapped most of the pictures, though some may have come from vendors, who hawked them for twenty-five cents apiece.[143] With or without visual props, pupils joked about the lynching's impact on blacks who exited town like "rats leaving a sinking ship." One youth entertained his classmates with the image of a fleeing black pushing "a wheel barrel" down the highway.[144] Given the racial judgments learned from adults, siblings, and peers as well as from observation and socialization, some students shifted easily from mocking to terrorizing black residents: several weeks later they taunted and stoned "Negro girls on their way to and from Sunset Addition."[145]

Blacks also understood the lynching message: the races were not to mingle; if they did, what happened to Wright would happen to all transgressors. In fact, Sunset men venturing past the execution site were baited by lynchers to "come and look. You may be next"; and Sunday School children leaving nearby churches trembled at intimidating remarks: "Here's what we do to your kind."[146] Elderly blacks experienced similar terror. Caroline Brown, a seventy-year-old widow who fled Sikeston within days of the lynching, died several weeks later in St. Louis, her health having declined in part because of worry over "memory of the terrible mob."[147]

Long before the lynching, of course, mothers admonished children to be careful around whites because of their past brutalities. They preached a golden rule yet warned that some people were just bad. Like female slaves before them, they taught their progeny survival techniques: namely, obeying white society in order to avoid "pain, suffering, and death," yet not to the point of "unconditional submission" or at the risk of jeopardizing kin.[148] Following Wright's slaying, mothers comforted their children, particularly those who suffered terrifying dreams after having seen Wright dragged. Julia Renfro, for one, held her younger child every night for a month and said little to her elder son, believing the lesson of white violence self-evident.[149] Thus, some youths dealt with the incident by thinking for themselves, while men like Griffen found comfort in the belief that whites were fully capable of distinguishing between Wright and other blacks.[150]

Like those whites who found humor in the bloodshed—including one Sikeston youth enrolled in a southern military school who playfully warned a black waiter to serve well lest he experience the fate of Cleo Wright—black youths exploited the horror.[151] In Sunset Addition, pranksters singled out Julia Renfro and her young sons. Soon after Wright's destruction they knocked on and shook her door "a good number of times," until a friend reversed the scare tactics one evening. Upon hearing a man's voice for the first time, they "hit the street flying." This group demonstrated an insensitivity to lynching crises and an ignorance of nightrider folklore, both powerfully embedded in southern black culture.[152]

Either through personal experience or by word of mouth, then, graphic details of Wright's violence and of his demise very quickly became common knowledge in the close-knit community. Phone conversations and church contacts on Sunday and press coverage and store or workplace meetings on Monday spread the story, sometimes inaccurately: many blacks believed that state troopers led the mob in Sunset; some whites heard that Wright's body was "packed in a sack, covered with acid and then dumped into a hole outside of town."[153] Most persons, however, transmitted the basic facts correctly and remembered them years later.

Black residents in nearby communities east and west, such as Charleston and Poplar Bluff, heard the story firsthand from refugees fleeing Sikeston. They well understood the historical pattern of racial violence in the South and feared its eruption in their own locales. "When those things start," recalled one prominent leader, "you don't know where in the hell they're going to end."[154] And blacks below Sikeston, aware that planters had broken up the tenant farmers' meeting in Caruthersville, envisaged Wright's lynching as one more example of "mob rule" in the Bootheel.[155]

Unlike all previous racial violence in southeast Missouri, however, the lynching of Cleo Wright became a cause célèbre. Its impact extended beyond local residents—themselves divided both along and within racial lines—and evoked national censure that generated state and federal investigations. Coming as Sikeston moved toward modernization and as the nation entered World War II, Wright's public execution raised questions about personal responsibility and civic duty in a democratic society founded upon law and order.

3   Law and Order

News of the lynching quickly spread beyond the immediate area via radio broadcasts and newspaper copy. State and national reporters, including representatives of the Associated Press, Associated Negro Press, and Southern News Service, soon followed the story into Sikeston to pepper local officials, newsmen, and residents for information. Several gravitated toward Paul Bumbarger, staff writer for the *Standard* and author of its major lynching story, which became the basis for accounts published near and far. But since journalists of both races found him "very polite" yet cautious about becoming "mixed up in a racial situation," they also sought their own material.[1]

As black Missourians heard broadcasts and read news reports, they called on officials to investigate the bloodshed. Within twenty-four hours and in advance of what the *Pittsburgh Courier* would soon label the "Double V Campaign," residents and organizations statewide pressed Governor Forrest C. Donnell for a democratic victory at home as well as abroad.[2] Arthur Euing of St. Joseph, a combat veteran of World War I, opined that all citizens needed protection under the law; Lorenzo J. Greene, a professor from Jefferson City, contended that in order to "erase the stigma" of lawlessness the lynchers must be apprehended.[3] Groups as ideologically disparate as the Communist Party of Missouri and the St. Louis Urban League added that Wright's death—"an act of vicious Hitlerism"—endangered national unity, sabotaged war preparations, raised suspicion among nonwhite allies, and gave "hope to Hitler and his Axis partners." Such an occurence, asserted the St. Louis YWCA Public Affairs Committee, should make white Missourians "feel ashamed and degraded, and fearful of the future."[4]

Black leaders, especially from St. Louis and Kansas City, quickly transformed private outrage into organized protest, inspired by the National Association for the Advancement for Colored People (NAACP) and the hope of democratic victory worldwide. Shortly before the lynching, for example, the president of one NAACP chapter had received word from national executive secretary Walter White that the "destiny of Negro America" would be determined by the war; for this reason, the association's work "must be expanded, rendered more effective and made a vital part of the life of every community." His message reflected the thinking of many local officers who understood immediately that Wright's slaying in broad daylight and within weeks of Japan's bombing of Pearl Harbor was "made to order for the N.A.A.C.P."[5]

St. Louisan Sidney R. Redmond led the way, probably having provided the national office with some of its earliest information on the lynching.[6] As a result of phone conversations with Walter White he called members of his chapter together within forty-eight hours of Wright's cremation, organized a meeting with Donnell on Thursday, and planned a mass rally on Sunday. He broadened the base of protest by drawing on eight chapters and several business and civic groups for the gubernatorial conference.[7]

On January 29 Redmond arrived in Jefferson City with eighty-seven persons. Their names, reading like a Who's Who of Missouri's black elite, included St. Joseph's Dr. William A. Simms, Charleston restaurateur Marshall Currin, *Kansas City Call* editor C.A. Franklin, St. Louis attorney R.L. Witherspoon, Columbia's Rev. Ernest S. Redd, and Jefferson City's Professor Lorenzo J. Greene. That they thought alike reflected longstanding personal, class, and racial solidarity; Kansas City NAACP president Carl R. Johnson and National Negro Business League regional vice-president U.S. Falls of St. Louis, among others, had protested to the governor well in advance of Redmond's call for action.[8] That they acted as a group evinced equally well-established networks and cooperation among more than NAACP affiliates: rival editors Franklin, J.E. Mitchell of the *Argus* and N.A. Sweets of the *American*, for instance, protested in person and in print.[9] At least fifteen women, many elite and most from Jefferson City, and less well-known Missourians such as Lee Johnson from Sikeston, marched as delegates.

Redmond's delegation came from all parts of the state. Anchored in Jefferson City with twenty-eight participants, it drew heavily from St. Louis in the east and Kansas City in the west, which respectively provided twenty-two and twelve delegates, added four and nine from nearby Columbia and Mexico, one from south central Lebanon, five from northwest St. Joseph, and three from northeast Hannibal. Southwest Missouri was not represented, but three members hailed from southeast Charleston and one from Sikeston. Only the last and the delegate from Lebanon lived in cities without NAACP affiliates.

Clearly, the association's officers, themselves elite, interacted with the black vanguard to forge an impressive statewide activism. Redmond ensured that achievement by gaining an audience with the governor, creating a bonafide coalition, and sharing authority with its members. The group gathered in the state capitol at 11:30 A.M., chose spokespersons, and adopted a resolution. Editor Sweets chaired the delegation. The St. Joseph and Kansas City NAACP presidents, a St. Louis minister, and a Kansas City resident representing all women of the state addressed Donnell at 1:00 P.M. Attorney Witherspoon then read the resolution aloud, charging what blacks everywhere believed: that Wright had been left unguarded, without medical care, and in an insecure place; that police and prosecutor neither threatened the lynchers with arrest or firearms nor identified and apprehended them afterward; that Sgt. Melvin Dace led the mob to Sunset Addition and with other officers watched idly as the victim burned. Given this "breakdown or impotency or complicity" of law enforcement, the petition asked that Donnell investigate the activities of Dace, Sheriff John Hobbs, and their subordinates; relieve David E. Blanton of his duties in this case and replace him with a special prosecutor; and call the state legislature into special session to enact an antilynching law.[10]

Delegates heard Donnell respond in "a sincere and satisfactory manner," promising a thorough probe and regretting that state law did not give the chief executive power to remove sheriffs and prosecutors from office for failure to perform their duty. They also listened as Blanton informed the governor that "some progress was being made toward" identifying those in the mob. Thus they departed fully expecting Donnell to bring those responsible before "the bar of justice." "We Negroes," Franklin reminded Donnell afterward, were learning "how to handle the tools of democracy."[11]

Franklin, of course, understated the savvy and contribution of neoabolitionist editors like himself, Mitchell, and Sweets. Upon first hearing reports of Wright's death, Franklin and Mitchell had wired Donnell for his comments. They sent reporters into Sikeston, while Sweets himself journeyed to the killing field.[12] Simultaneously, as they conferred with the governor on January 29, they printed graphic coverage of the execution. "Southeast Missouri Lynch Mob Escorted by Policemen," charged *Call* headlines, while the *Argus* screamed, "Sikeston Lynch Orgy Stirs U.S." In accompanying editorials, "Missouri Shame!" and "That Sikeston Mob," Franklin and Mitchell stressed the lynching's savagery, the doubt that justice would prevail, the challenge to war aims, and—in Mitchell's "Anti-Lynching Bill"—the call for a federal measure to protect black life and deliver on the promise of democracy.[13]

This activity, combined with that of the conference and the white dailies, whose stories began the day after the lynching, quickened the pace of black protest. Perhaps because of the proximity to Sikeston—which lay 135 miles due south and easily reached by U.S. 61—and because of the enormous coverage given the incident by the local NAACP and journalists, St. Louis area residents, more than any others in the state, demanded justice. Virgus C. Cole, for one, inquired about the supposed freedom in "this great Democratic form of government." Members of her race could not attend white schools or work in numerous industries and, worse yet, lived unprotected lives: men were "shot down and burned like dogs" and women raped without retribution. Yet in this crucible, her twenty-one-year-old son prepared to risk his life for the defense of "a White Man's country" that reduced black hope to belief in a vengeful God who "sees all things."[14]

Divine intervention aside, 3,500 individuals like Cole attended the NAACP mass rally in St. Louis on Sunday, February 1. They filled to overflowing the Pine Street YMCA's gymnasium and two lobbies, forcing organizers to turn away another 2,000 people, start the program a half-hour early, and hold meetings both upstairs and down. For three hours they heard some twenty speakers of both races and several affiliations. Audience and press attention, however, focused on three voices: Rev. J.B. Ross repeated his charge that Sergeant Dace had led the lynchers, former congressman Leonidas C. Dyer renewed calls for a federal antilynching law, and Mayor William Dee Becker pressed for a state grand jury inquiry. Those listening agreed—particularly with Becker's contention that the lynching stemmed from "the same kind of class hatred this nation is fighting a war against"—and passed resolutions expressing dissatisfaction with the state police report, which defended trooper action, and support for the NAACP's efforts.[15]

Significantly, then, between Thursday and Sunday Redmond raised the level of protest. He expanded the crusade from eighty-seven elites to include hundreds of everyday citizens, liberal white leaders, and another political power in the mayor of St. Louis. Also renewing the drive for an federal antilynching law, which the national office had sought since 1918, he pushed the governor for state legislation, billed the mass meeting as an antilynching rally, and raised $150 among its participants to carry the association's drive further.[16]

Redmond's well-publicized activities encouraged additional programs and assisted some already planned. On February 6, delegates from the Negro Baptist Ministers' Alliance of St. Louis trekked to Jefferson City, met with the governor, and urged a "complete inquiry" into the lynching. That Sunday St. Louis businessmen and housewives held a mass meeting, as did

NAACP affiliates throughout the state. The St. Louis County branch, for instance, drew 500 persons to Douglas High School in Webster Groves, where they heard some of those—including Robert L. Witherspoon—who had conferred with Donnell ten days earlier, adopted a resolution condemning Wright's murder, and donated $43.23 to the antilynch law fund.[17]

In fact, the series of NAACP gatherings on February 8 were planned by the Kansas City chapter's president shortly after Wright's burning. Carl R. Johnson responded to the crisis as quickly as Redmond, cooperated in his preparations for the gubernatorial conference, and may have provided him—indirectly via Walter White—with the idea of mobilizing branch members to assure its numerical success.[18] Johnson's handiwork demonstrated the far-reaching extent of black protest.

Personal and group agitation continued throughout the state during the first two weeks of February. Some came from previous sources such as Rev. C.B. Johnson of Jefferson City, a member of the NAACP delegation to Donnell, who prophesied that his God, mindful of "all the evil" done by white men, would have "a hand" in meting out justice.[19] Other protesters voiced their anger for the first time. Members of the Negro Community Council of Sedalia took up the familiar cry to punish the lynchers lest government officials appear to condone the very "atrocities that make civilization blush." And the Butler County Negro Citizens Committee questioned Sergeant Dace's conduct and requested gubernatorial action. Regrouping in the face of a killing only forty-eight miles east of their headquarters in Poplar Bluff, committeemen and -women claimed to speak for all "law-abiding Negro citizens" in the vicinity.[20]

Similar protest mounted nationwide. From late January through early February, black citizens and leaders responded almost in lockstep with their counterparts in Missouri. Sparked by radio, white daily, and black weekly press coverage of the lynching in every major urban center, they spoke to editors, officials, and leaders in "Double V" language.[21] Representative of numerous correspondents, a thirty-three-year-old husband, father of three and U.S. Customs Guard from Brooklyn, New York, asked Franklin D. Roosevelt what 13,000,000 black Americans and the "Dark races" worldwide were to think of Wright's murder: was "Democracy just for the white American?" Franklyn R. Johnson also requested that the president abolish Jim Crow throughout the nation, push for a congressional statement on the "un-American slaying of Cleo Wright," and thus give blacks the "heart to fight and die for America." Hopeful that others would back up his call, he gave Walter White permission to publish the letter.[22]

Of course, the NAACP executive secretary had already acted publicly on several fronts. He telegraphed Roosevelt on January 26, immediately upon hearing of Wright's death, that nothing short of "positive," affirmative action"—specifically, enactment of an antilynch law—would assure "citizens of all races" that democracy "applies within as well as outside of the United States."[23] White also released his telegram to the press and contacted Redmond for the latest information, reaching the St. Louis president the following day. In a series of phone conversations they laid plans for the conference with Governor Donnell on Thursday and the mass meeting on Sunday.[24]

Before those efforts came to fruition, White inquired whether Redmond could send a "competent investigator" into Sikeston. The suggestion stemmed from both longstanding NAACP policy and personal experience as the association's lynching authority, one who had investigated mob violence and published *Rope and Faggot, A Biography of Judge Lynch* in the 1920s. White recommended Mary Taussig Tompkins, a white St. Louisan who knew southeast Missouri.[25] She and her husband, L. Benoist Tompkins, visited the lynching site on January 29 and 30. They interviewed several black and white residents—including "leading citizens"—to ascertain "the trend of community feelings," but "made no attempt to obtain evidence for the prosecution" of lynchers.[26]

White collected information from other sources as well and pressed the protest nationally. In addition to the Tompkins report he received personal statements about Wright's killing and ensuing events from Ross and from Redmond, and an advance copy of the *Kansas City Call* lynching stories based on the visit to Sikeston of reporter Lucille Bluford.[27] From these references he forged a strategy of propaganda to promote greater protection of black life.

White understood well the need, in the words of St. Louis County NAACP members, to strike "while the iron is white hot." Hence, in a series of press releases between the date of the lynching and early February, he linked the bloodshed in Sikeston to the brutal attacks on black soldiers in Alexandria, Louisiana, and both to the question of democratic war aims. Within two weeks of Wright's death, White's battle cry became "Remember Pearl Harbor . . . and Sikeston, Missouri!"[28] Perhaps he or association staff members originated the powerful slogan, but others arrived at it independently. "What Pearl Harbor was to international law, Sikeston was to our national law," opined Rev. Russell S. Brown as early as January 28; "Truth Truly" informed Governor Donnell of the exact saying four days before it appeared in an NAACP press release; shortly thereafter a Chicagoan urged *Defender* subscribers to adopt—in the face of the Pearl Harbor battle slogan—"our own cry for the things we hold dear": "Remember Sikeston, Mo."[29] Regardless of its origin, White's association popularized the "new national slogan," and black editors soon pushed it in print.[30]

White also continued to work with chapter presidents, especially Redmond. He cooperated with the latter's plans to gather petitions endorsing an antilynch bill, send a delegation to Washington, D.C., and organize a silent parade to protest racial pogroms: NAACP tactics developed in the wake of the East St. Louis race riot of 1917 and designed to bring redress through exposure and pressure.[31] To advance that purpose further, White and his staff planned for a pamphlet on Wright's murder to be distributed "to congressmen, senators, and other influential Americans."[32] Meanwhile, he released excerpts of the Tompkins study, particularly its emphasis on "the feudal nature of southeast Missouri," where blacks were viewed as brutes to be kept subservient and where tension was promoted between poor white and black laborers; alleged black assertiveness and white solidarity across class lines wrought bloodshed. Quoting the Tompkinses, the NAACP press release made much of "breakdowns in our legal system" when local judges and jurors "believe in lynching." Widely published by the black press, the Tompkins probe reinforced the association's drive for federal prosecution of lynch mobs.[33]

White also received advice from E.T. Summytt, president of the St. Louis County chapter, who passed along the legal ideas of prominent whites and advocated involving federal authorities in the case.[34] In fact, White's legal representatives, led by Thurgood Marshall, had already begun negotiations with the U.S. Justice Department and, by mid-February, had received its Criminal Division's "investigative attention."[35] Significantly, NAACP and Justice Department lawyers initiated a legal strategy requiring neither a federal law nor, therefore, dealings with the conservative, southern congress members who had filibustered all previous antilynching measures.

Success on any front, White realized, required relentless public pressure on local, state, and federal officials. He knew, too, that NAACP members not only provided the core of such protest activity (as Redmond and Johnson had demonstrated to Donnell and Becker) but, in doing so, raised the association's stock. Thus, both to advance the challenge to Wright's lynching and to build the association into the most powerful civil rights organization, White's office worked to enlarge Missouri's chapters.[36] On the heels of the Pine Street YMCA meeting of February 1, for example, Redmond requested field representative Daisy E. Lampkin's presence to start his chapter's membership drive; St. Louis was "in fever heat" and "hundreds of people" were volunteering for work. Within two weeks he and Lampkin launched the drive and soon added 3,331 members.[37] Small wonder that White's national staff considered printing the pamphlet on Wright's burning complete with a "membership blank" and "sales stuff."[38]

NAACP efforts also fostered white protest, though much of that came spontaneously from several parts of the state. Within days of the atrocity, St. Louis area residents expressed their disgust to editors and officials. Attorney Dyer, perhaps the best-known champion of an antilynch law in the 1920s and 1930s, wrote that "burning a human being at the stake" proved the presence of lawlessness in the state and the need for federal legislation to restore equal justice. "Misguided persons," added an everyday St. Louisan, should never be permitted to destroy "the fruitage of civilization," and a Columbia professional reiterated that lynchers' setting themselves above Missouri law could not be tolerated.[39]

Similarly, citizens from southeastern communities, including those of the Bootheel, mourned—in the poetry of H.H. Lewis—Wright's "cringing tones," "muffled moans," and "spirit downed."[40] Like the Cape Girardeau bard who wrote these lines during the Great Depression, contemporary protesters associated the lynching with "lags in our Southeast Missouri civilization," which they condemned—according to one Lilbourn modernist—as "too prevalent for a presumed intelligent democracy." They also linked it to the war against "heel-clicking Nazi militarists" and their anti-Semitism, which showed one traditional resident of "pure southern stock" and slaveholding ancestry "how disgustingly terrible race hatred can be."[41]

Organizations in the largest municipalities gave added weight to individual complaints. Religious groups led the way, with the Ministerial Alliance and the Council of Churches of Kansas City censuring mob violence as "a menace to all free institutions" and the Inter-racial Commission of the Metropolitan Church Federation of St. Louis redoubling efforts to "build a true democracy."[42] St. Louis area affiliations of the Council of Catholic Women, Fellowship of Reconciliation, and Young Men's and Young Women's Hebrew Association reinforced the point, as did several secular associations.[43]

White journalists, too, landed hard on the lynchers and more than any other segment of society articulated the modernist view so prevalent in urban centers. Editors from St. Louis, Kansas City, Independence, and Joplin berated mob violence as a shameful reversion to "a state of mass barbarism" which permitted Hitler to "sneer at our hypocrisy."[44] "Not In Poland, Not In

Conquered China—but Right In Missouri" read the caption of a *St. Louis Star-Times* cartoon that depicted gleeful, club-wielding, Neanderthal-like mobsters standing over the burning body of Cleo Wright, whose face grimaced in pain and arms stretched skyward as an oversized forearm and fist inserted above the bloodthirsty horde grasped a rope attached to his neck.[45] Only papers in "Columbia, St. Joseph, Springfield, and other communities" that had experienced lynchings, noted one prominent editor, failed to condemn "the Sikeston mob" and cover its activities fully.[46]

Once again, the *St. Louis Post-Dispatch* proved most outspoken. Its editors publicly pressed for the prosecution of those guilty of Cleo Wright's murder. They privately advised local black leaders about possible federal violations by the lynchers, and perhaps played a role in the St. Louis Newspaper Guild's resolution for prosecution of the perpetrators "in accordance with the best interests of Democracy."[47] Sikeston residents, even some who opposed the lynching, wondered why press coverage "had to go on and on"— that of the *Post-Dispatch* in particular; "dragging it to the coals." What did it take "to quell the nation's outrage?"[48]

The answer seemed to be justice for all. Exactly because the lynching challenged democratic tenets during a war against totalitarianism, it drew national attention and demands for state and federal action. Newspapers, magazines, and radio announcers "played up" the tragedy "for all it was worth-and-more," or so it seemed to Clint H. Denman of the *Sikeston Herald*.[49]

Former residents living in Illinois, Michigan, and New York expressed shame for their "old state," as did an Ohioan, who deplored the presence of racial hatred when survival called "for unity against Hitlerism."[50] Others also living beyond the Show Me state felt disgrace that members of their own race had carried out this lynching. One citizen knew of nothing four-legged "so wantonly cruel"; another envisioned the lynchers as "traitors to their country."[51]

Numerous organizations across the nation protested in the same idiom. Kentucky members of the Association of Southern Women for the Prevention of Lynching deemed mob violence indefensible, and Arkansas representatives of the Women's Society of Christian Service likened it to the conduct of America's enemies.[52] Northern associations—for instance the Federal Council of Churches of Christ—believed the bloodshed disgraced everyone, violated democracy, and undermined Christian ideals. And nearly five hundred Ohio University students called for the "immediate passage" of the antilynching bill.[53] Other groups endeavored to provide direct redress. "What happened in Sikeston too closely parallels events in Nazi Germany," admonished officers of the National Federation for Constitutional Liberties in Washington, D.C., who suggested a $5,000 reward—themselves pledging a tenth of that sum—for information leading to the lynchers' capture and punishment.[54]

Opposition to the lynching appeared in the national press, ranging from eastern liberal dailies to more moderate publications elsewhere. "It was," noted the *Washington Post*, "an act on a par with the diabolical murders perpetrated by Nazi and Japanese gangsters"; it raised questions, contended the *Tampa Daily Times* of Florida, about "what kind of democracy we claim to be fighting for." Many other dailies agreed and, like the *Chicago Sun*, expressed concern for black patriots or demanded federal legislation to end a barbarism that would cause even Heinrich Himmler to blush.[55]

Though never embarrassed for himself, Governor Donnell broke with traditional gubernatorial indifference to local violence long before the protest emerged and well ahead of its peak in mid February. Hearing of Wright's death within an hour of its occurrence, he immediately arranged for Sikeston and state officials to protect Sunset residents. He also wanted the law "fully enforced" and those responsible for the bloodshed apprehended, telling David E. Blanton to make "an example" of them.[56] He concurred with the Scott County prosecutor's suggestion for a state grand jury and, by early evening, had issued a public statement calling for "a searching and thorough investigation" of the lynching. His decisive action and view of the incident as "a disgraceful blot" on the state drew the praise of many, including those who soon organized the statewide protest.[57]

For many reasons Donnell set precedent, though the need to restore order and demonstrate justice during a war against lawless, racist, totalitarian powers loomed large. He desired, as had earlier modernists, a regulated society free of "violent encounters."[58] A devout Methodist, he promptly declared Wright's death wrongful; a pragmatic thinker, he moved to prevent Wright's lynching from becoming a pogrom; a governor believing in "stewardship" and "strict construction," he criticized the denial of due process to Wright and determined that his murderers would face its full force. Donnell also reaffirmed the superiority of democratic values, as had most American intellectuals, jurists, and politicians who feared the authoritarianism of Italy, Japan, and especially Germany.[59] A Phi Beta Kappa recipient, University of Missouri Law School graduate, thirty-third degree Mason, and Republican

Party leader, he knew—as Dyer later reminded him—that blacks were fighting and dying for democracy abroad while "in our own state" the law was "thrown to the winds."[60]

The public outrage over Wright's killing simply accentuated Donnell's predilection for state intervention. In the weeks following his unhesitant resolve, he received more than a hundred letters, postcards, and telegrams, as well as some petitions.[61] He met with delegations and learned of the demonstrations held in several Missouri cities. Some black Missourians contended that democracy meant "less than a promise from Hitler." Liberal whites bolstered their ranks, as did members of both races outside the state who considered the lynchers "more barbaric" than the Nazi leader and more threatening than saboteurs. Almost everyone felt shame that "this dirty deed" had smeared state and nation.[62] Their protest raised a basic question: if government could not protect its citizens, who could it protect?

Donnell's reply depended on the Scott County prosecutor. Protective of state rights, he had little choice but to rely on Blanton and the state grand jury process rather than call in federal authorities. The governor's duty, advanced the *Herald* editor, required that he respond to national protest and keep "the name of Missouri above reproach by insisting that local officers bring the guilty to justice." If Donnell did otherwise, concluded his Sikeston supporter, he would be an unfit chief executive.[63]

Given the almost immediate criticism directed at Blanton and Sergeant Dace—he heard from several sources that the county prosecutor claimed himself unable to identify individual lynchers and that the trooper had led the mob—Donnell anticipated the necessity of a state grand jury investigation in order to protect their reputations, his genuine effort, and the state's integrity.[64] The governor certainly understood that criticism of the Scott County prosecutor heightened because of his residency in a southern town, his initial belief that an inquiry might be unsuccessful, and his father's editorial remark that the lynching "was deserved."[65]

Of course, personal and party concerns also motivated the governor. He had emerged as the only Republican in Missouri elected to state office in 1940, winning his first campaign ever despite Roosevelt's third-term triumph; he had benefited from the collapse of the Pendergast machine in Kansas City and its statewide effect.[66] It was noteworthy, however, that his victory by only 3,613 votes required an overwhelming majority in St. Louis County and strong support in traditionally Democratic St. Louis and Kansas City. He knew that some blacks had deserted the Democratic Party because of former Governor Lloyd C. Stark's handling of the tenant farmers' roadside demonstration. He knew further that many whites of both parties had supported him in the aftermath of the election when disgruntled Democrats, in an unsuccessful effort to "steal" his office, charged voting irregularities.[67] Sensitive to these political realities and aware that most of the protest over Wright's killing came from black and white supporters in St. Louis and Kansas City, Donnell acted quickly in their behalf. "For God's sake and ours, don't let us down at a time like this," pleaded a black St. Louisan.[68]

To be sure, the lynching was "a hot potato."[69] Donnell knew of the backlash as some whites criticized him for interfering in a local issue: the law that governed whites "will not control a beast," contended one St. Louisan; another sent Donnell a newspaper clipping of his order for the lynching investigation with the message "NIGGER LOVING GOVERNOR."[70] Many letter writers, however, supported Donnell's efforts, as did the delegations led by Redmond and Sikeston attorney Ralph E. Bailey. Donnell, of course, understood the political stakes, but his decision came unequivocally, before any indication of public support and for reasons that transcended politics.

President Roosevelt, through the United States attorney general, set precedent for similar reasons. Francis Biddle reacted to what became over three weeks a nationwide outcry. Politics, public opinion, black protest, and war diplomacy made him "vitally interested in this case."[71] He knew that "flocks of telegrams" and messages were pouring into the Justice Department, White House, and Capitol Hill, where black Congressmen Arthur W. Mitchell of Illinois demanded—two weeks after the lynching—that the president "speak out in condemnation of the Missouri terrorists."[72] He knew, too, that NAACP and Justice Department representatives had conferred several times during the same period.[73] Quickly, then, Biddle agreed with Victor W. Rotnem, head of the department's Civil Rights Section (CRS), and Assistant Attorney General Wendell Berge, director of its Criminal Division—which included the CRS—that the lynching was more than "a local problem." Distressed by Japanese propaganda depicting Wright's death as an indication of what East Indians might expect if the democracies won the war, on February 10 Biddle ordered an FBI probe into the incident.[74]

Biddle was also disturbed by the lynching's impact on black morale, national unity, and probably his own liberal sensibilities. Certainly he knew that Wright's murder had delivered—in Walter White's words—"the most crushing blow to Negroes."[75] Even more than discrimination in defense industries or segregation in the armed services, it struck at the heart of citizenship: the right to live in peace. Perhaps he also feared A. Philip Randolph's prediction that "wild outbursts" like the Alexandria military riot and the

Sikeston killing would soon get "out of hand"; the international president of the Brotherhood of Sleeping Car Porters raised anew the specter of more racial disunity.[76] In sum, Biddle, a Harvard-trained Philadelphia lawyer of distinguished ancestry, patrician bearing, and New Deal sentiment, considered the denial of basic constitutional rights a "tragic mockery" and a threat to victory.[77]

Consequently, the attorney general concluded that some action on his part—within very carefully drawn parameters—was imperative. He must have realized that the president would not support renewed calls for an antilynch bill, which he had evaded throughout the 1930s for fear of alienating southern Democrats whose votes he needed to pass New Deal programs. Nor would Roosevelt embrace Randolph's suggestion for a Negro Citizens' Committee to advise him on racial matters; another upstart body might—like the recently appointed Fair Employment Practices Committee that the black leader had forced on the president—incite even greater southern reaction. Given the established politics and priorities of Roosevelt, who concentrated on the Depression and the war rather than on race relations in either era, Biddle focused on legal approaches within his department.[78]

As solicitor general, 1940-41, Biddle had participated in the Justice Department's early efforts "to breathe new life" into the civil rights statutes of the Reconstruction era; now, as attorney general for less than six months, he brought to that office "the eager flame of reform." Upon being confirmed by the Senate in 1941, Biddle had reflected on his philosophy and record, which advocated "respect for all human beings." Despite Biddle's role in the internment of Japanese Americans, the war accentuated his liberal tenets, placing them in a global context and imbuing them with a life-and-death urgency.[79]

Biddle's actions in the Wright case reflected the political reform and judicial activism of the 1930s. Indeed, early in that decade Roosevelt and his New Dealers envisioned citizens in "the conglomerate, as 'one third of a nation' rather than individually," and stressed positive government.[80] While they never emphasized racial equality, they included blacks in separate administrative programs. Even Attorney General Homer S. Cummings, who stood aside "as the battles over lynching raged" from 1933 to 1939, invoked federal statutes in nonracial cases that set precedent for later civil rights suits.[81]

More revolutionary judicial activists acknowledged the theory of "discrete and insular minorities" and the need to protect them.[82] By 1938 both political and judicial forces were poised to expand civil rights for blacks and respond to NAACP pressures for change. In that year Roosevelt publicly pro-

This is an effort
(A-9) to fix the
efforts)

posed the federal investigation of all lynchings, and the high court handed down *Missouri ex rel. Gaines v. Canada*, incomplete but highly significant steps toward shielding blacks and smashing segregation.[83] In line with those developments and pressure from organized labor, in 1939 Attorney General Frank Murphy, a New Dealer, judicial activist, and former NAACP board member, marked "a turning point in official thinking" by creating the Civil Liberties Unit (CLU) in the Criminal Division of the Justice Department. Over the next two years, CLU attorneys developed strategies and changed the unit's name to the Civil Rights Section (CRS). When Biddle (succeeding Robert H. Jackson) became attorney general in 1941, the stage was set for federal activity in civil rights. Biddle signified his intentions very early, filing an amicus curiae brief in support of Congressman Mitchell's suit against segregated transportation.[84] He also seemed ready to go beyond Supreme Court cases and, through the CRS and the FBI, protect black citizens.

In short, Donnell and Biddle realized, as did most liberals, that the presence of Nazi-style racism during a war for democracy brought into question "the moral integrity of white America." Wright was the first lynching after the bombing of Pearl Harbor and therefore required their immediate attention. Neither had much choice under the circumstances, though both officials expressed genuine concern for the constitutional rights of black citizens. Biddle, whose commitment to civil rights predated the tragedy, may have thought that the "remote likelihood" for the conviction of lynchers in the border states could serve to deter mob violence in the Deep South.[85]

Initially slowed by questions of political concern and federal jurisdiction, Biddle soon followed Donnell's lead. On February 10 he informed the governor of the FBI investigation, giving assurances that it would "in no sense conflict" with the state inquiry. Three weeks later, on the eve of the state grand jury hearing, he responded positively to the governor's request for a copy of the FBI report and permitted the federal investigators to testify in the state proceeding.[86] Indeed, Biddle broke precedent all along the line, from ordering the first federal lynching investigation to conducting an FBI probe "for the benefit of state authorities."[87]

Meanwhile, responding to Biddle's order for an investigation into Wright's death, two FBI agents from St. Louis—both named Jones—journeyed to Sikeston. They interviewed forty-three witnesses during the week of February 15, either at the State Highway Department building on Main Street or in a parked car near an individual's place of employment. Although they "worked quietly and with no publicity," according to the *Herald*, their presence was known about town and mocked by some white residents.[88]

Occasionally, they came upon an unsuspecting subject who considered their introduction as "the Jones boys" a practical joke being played by a friend. Once they flashed their credentials, however, "the real Joneses" conducted anything but humorous interviews.[89] They also collected editorial comment, newspaper clippings, photographs, and a floor plan of City Hall. By February 23 the agents had submitted their fifty-page report to their superiors, who passed it along to CRS lawyers.[90]

The FBI effort overlapped that of county and state personnel. In fact, federal agents interviewed the prosecuting attorney and area lawmen, attempting to identify lynchers and prospective witnesses.[91] But "under no circumstances" were they "to investigate the case jointly" with the state attorney general's office or identify confidential sources.[92] Bureau investigators cooperated with the county prosecutor but protected their agency's jurisdiction and informants.[93]

David E. Blanton began his own inquiry immediately after the lynching and, from personal memory and unnamed informants, compiled a list of mob members. Quickly he engaged Sergeant Dace and Trooper John Tandy who recalled more names, ran down clues, and located onlookers and participants in Wright's murder. He remarked later that the troopers never presented a written document of their interviews, and federal agents uncovered "what we already had." Soon enough, however, the county prosecutor benefited from the FBI probe.[94]

State and federal investigations described the lynching, named those responsible for it, and provided extensive clippings; in addition, Blanton gathered photographs. No doubt he heard about the many snapshots taken by ghoulish, event-minded, or entrepreneurial spectators, who shared them with friends, sold them locally, proffered them to out-of-town newspapers, or hid them. And, of course, he knew of several pictures taken by local newsmen.[95] He seemed to believe that these photographs belonged to private citizens fearful of the investigation or that they depicted close-ups of the victim and distant shots of large crowds rather than identifiable portraits of mob members. Thus only the five prints he received from the camera of State Trooper Vincent P. Boisaubin—which showed Wright's charred body, the vehicle that dragged him, and the mobs before City Hall and at the lynching site—bore the credibility necessary for legal prosecution.[96]

Blanton also heard that motion pictures had been taken of Wright's killing. Although mob members were said to have seized one film and the photographer to have destroyed a second, he was alleged to have received a third;

shot with a telephoto lens, which identified the lynchers beyond a doubt.[97] He later denied having received or viewed any movies of the incident, however, a recollection borne out by FBI files.[98]

Early on, Blanton requested that a member of the state attorney's office assist him in the grand jury proceeding, since he himself might be "a witness for and on behalf of the State."[99] Consequently, Governor Donnell arranged for Assistant Attorney General Harry Kay to work with him—placing the State of Missouri even more directly in the case—and armed him with a copy of the FBI report, which he had requested for the grand jury presentment. Four days before that body convened, Kay arrived in Sikeston to prepare for the prosecution.[100]

Meanwhile, Blanton arranged the entire proceeding. He considered bringing the case before local justices of the peace, yet feared "forcing their hands" only to have them bring an abrupt end to the legal process by releasing all suspects. Believing it difficult to sway judges directly affected by public opinion, Blanton sought another strategy.[101] He placed "every confidence" in Circuit Court Judge James C. McDowell, who—upon viewing the evidence—agreed to place the crime before county jurors in the first grand jury called in five years.[102]

State law authorized the judge to assign the selection of jurors to either the county court or the sheriff. McDowell slated the proceeding for March, when his docket would be clear, and asked John Hobbs for, in the sheriff's words, "a panel of 'good men.'" Among those chosen McDowell designated R.H. Mackley, a Blodgett merchant-farmer, foreman of the twelve-man jury; the others were insurer F.M. Craig and merchant Theodore Horn from Illmo; druggist L.D. Lankford and building and loan officials P.N. Keller and M.H. Stubblefield from Chaffee; merchant Frank Frobase from Benton; barber Edwin Burger and retired farmer Tony Gosche from Oran; banker Joe Matthews, mule dealer–realtor R.D. Clayton, and garage operator Charles Eakers from Sikeston.[103] For reasons of ill health, Matthews and Stubblefield were replaced by Benton land overseer William English and merchant Wade Miller.[104] Essentially, jury members reflected judicial tradition: all male, all white, and all proprietors of varying wealth, representing various—if largely central—sections of the county.

On Monday, March 9, McDowell empaneled the jurors at the Benton Courthouse, a two-story stone edifice dating back to 1883 and located in the heart of Scott County.[105] For fifteen minutes he instructed the jurors to exercise their duty without influence from outside interference, local intimidation, or racial prejudice; to indict any one who violated the law; to keep the proceeding secret. "We want," he concluded, "law and order in this county."[106]

So did Blanton and Kay, who summoned thirty-eight witnesses that day and the following morning. Blanton questioned the lawmen, alleged lynchers, and knowledgeable spectators; Kay interrogated the county prosecutor himself, helped with several others who testified, and kept notes of the statements.[107] They elicited charges and denials, even some unintended humor as when Kay referred to the trunk of the car behind which Wright bounced as a "trundle." Concentrating on the identity of those responsible for his lynching, they nevertheless touched on the accusation that state police had led the mob; serious about uncovering lynchers and pinning down gossip, they included four black witnesses. They concluded late Tuesday morning, March 10, believing their evidence sufficient for indictments.[108]

The jurors, however, failed to return a single indictment. They deliberated for three hours and, upon Judge McDowell's return, issued their verdict at 4:30 P.M. to a courtroom of fewer than fifty white persons. They found "insufficient evidence to return a true bill" and, indirectly dismissing the allegation that troopers had collaborated with lynchers, complimented the highway patrol and county officials for their efforts in the face of the mob. They adjourned quickly, as McDowell accepted the fifty-two-word report without comment.[109]

Nor did Blanton or Kay immediately respond to the verdict, though they must have sensed the reasons for it. In fact, the jurors identified closely with the area. Living in small towns linked to a rural setting, they either shared multiple social relationships with some of the defendants or well understood the significance of such ties. Consequently, they no doubt gave consideration to future encounters with friends and townsfolk who based their close-knit society on an amiable, broad network of socioeconomic interests.[110] These jurors, rather than having been members of the mob (as suggested by some) or protecting themselves for roles in future violence, as did nineteenth- century jury members, simply respected community mores.[111] They knew that most people, even among those who condemned the lynching, expected them to go through the motions and then "let dead dogs lie."[112]

Moreover, many jurors considered themselves southerners and their locale part of the South, where racial justice operated in a for-whites-only framework.[113] Their identities, combined with a state structure that granted judicial districts enormous leeway and permitted one dissenting juror to scuttle the proceedings, prompted many observers to predict the verdict—

"an easy guess"—well in advance. Grand jurors understood, as did one black editor: "You can't indict a community."[114]

That "no mob formed against the mob that formed" also revealed the disdain of area residents for outsiders.[115] Significantly, McDowell had instructed jurors not to be "intimidated" by journalists and protesters from beyond the area, contending that "the best citizens in the world" lived in Scott County and that they did not need "anybody else to enforce the law." He warned against holding local blacks accountable for Wright's misdeed, yet mused that protest elsewhere "might stir up more trouble" and prove "more injurious to the colored race" than had the Sikeston mob. In other words, he called for "law and order" within well-established community and racial parameters.[116]

Given this frame of reference, jurors claimed that no evidence justified a true bill. They readily accepted the denials of would-be lynchers and disregarded the testimony of officials, in essence taking the word of the accused (and thus defending the community). They easily set aside the presentations of prosecutor and lawmen, in part because of their own loyalties and in part because of McDowell's instructions, which were "a model of caution, reserve and legal punctilio."[117] They heard the judge refer to Wright as the person "who was supposed to have been mobbed" and issue instructions to return verdicts "if" rather than "because" the law had been violated, thereby pointing up the absence of an antilynching law.[118]

Some jurors must have read McDowell's earlier public contention that the "most important question" of the case turned on Wright's condition: if medical testimony established that Wright was dead at the time of his abduction from jail, it was "very unlikely" that indictments for murder would be forthcoming. Of equal importance, Dr. E.J. Nienstedt, who had treated Wright hours before the lynching, testified before the grand jury that Wright "was certain" to have expired, though he could not say how soon.[119] In reality, the paramount question for jurors involved Wright's guilt or innocence, not whether alleged lynchers had apprehended, dragged, and burned a living human being or a cadaver. And jurymen, like the white constituents from which they were drawn, believed that Wright was the "son-of-a-bitch" who assailed Grace Sturgeon and "got what he had coming." They deemed him "the right man," thereby making insignificant the conundrum of when he died—and at whose hands.[120]

On the heels of the grand jury verdict, Judge McDowell openly confirmed his true feelings. Denounced by Mayor Becker of St. Louis for originally having said that he was "too busy" to call a grand jury, he lambasted

the mayor in turn for having played to black voters by accusing county officials of the failure to protect Wright, and he chided FBI agents for entering
the case and stirring local racial divisions. Furthermore, he called protest
meetings, such as the NAACP rally where Becker held forth, "just another
form of mob rule." The son of southern parents and a longstanding Charleston attorney with "extensive farm interests," McDowell spoke in part for the
besieged community; in part, he spoke for himself as a former prosecutor
and state senator and a recently elected member of the court who resented
the assertion that he needed only "order his clerk to summon the jury—the
Prosecuting Attorney can do the rest."[121]

In retrospect, McDowell appeared "cold toward the investigation," influential with the jury, and representative of most area residents.[122] He made
no mention that "the dignity of the State had been outraged," seemingly more
concerned about the reputation of southeast Missouri. Hence the jurors received coded instructions and the witnesses lost their memories in a proceeding opposed by most local opinion and, consequently, destined to fail.
Judge and jurors responded collectively, like earlier southern elites who opposed mob rule yet were taught to fear centralized government and defend
local autonomy.[123] They evinced their own and their white neighbors' deep-
seated parochialism and historical memory, resenting—in the phrase of the
Charleston Enterprise-Courier editor—interference from "upstate sociological
busybodies."[124]

Despite the hope of judge and jurors that the grand jury report would
end the matter, Kansas City and especially St. Louis "busybodies" protested
loudly. The *Post-Dispatch* editor referred to the proceedings as a "fiasco," as
did white communists and black sorority sisters.[125] "Another Blot on Missouri" vented the *Argus* editor, having predicted earlier that "powerful forces"
possessed "brushes all ready for a general whitewashing of the case" and officials prepared, like Pontius Pilate, to permit it.[126]

The editor went on to ponder the governor's sincerity, and the vice-president of United Electrical, Radio, & Machine Workers of America (CIO) accused him of having requested long before that the federal government
withdraw from the case.[127] Donnell refused comment on the grand jury verdict until he had consulted with Kay and State Attorney General Roy
McKittrick, then publicly announced—almost as the charges were leveled
against him—that he had met with the state attorneys. On March 13 he assured the United States attorney general of his interest in "the possibility of
proceedings based on the violation of Federal Statutes" and of his full cooperation in prosecutions stemming from the lynching.[128] He also privately

informed the union official that his charge regarding gubernatorial efforts to keep Biddle from investigating the crime "was mistaken."[129]

Donnell's clarifications notwithstanding, critics were more concerned about pressing the case. "The state authorities made a miserable failure in bringing the lynchers to justice," declared the St. Louis NAACP branch president.[130] Most blacks had questioned the wisdom of giving responsibility for the state investigation and presentment to Blanton and Dace, who were themselves suspect, lived in the area, probably had friends among the lynchers, and in the county prosecutor's case depended on public support for reelection.[131] Blacks also wondered how a grand jury composed of jurors from the lynching area—and themselves the lynchers or "friends, relatives, and sympathizers" of the lynchers—could mete out justice.[132] Perhaps they knew that mob members rarely faced legal action and that of those in Missouri who had, only 3 percent had drawn convictions.[133] Thus blacks, supported by white allies, renewed demands for federal action.[134]

Both races were aware that U.S. Attorney General Biddle had launched a federal investigation shortly after the lynching. In cooperation with the governor's effort, however, he had delayed the decision to empanel an independent federal grand jury until the state jurors had returned their verdict. Now he acted unhesitatingly, undoubtedly more sensitive to black feelings and international opinion because of a recent racial clash over federally built houses in Detroit.[135] On March 11, one day after the jury's decision and two days before Donnell's pledge of cooperation, he announced that the Justice Department would continue its lynching investigation.[136]

Biddle quickly set another precedent by assigning the case to the Civil Rights Section (CRS), whose lawyers pursued legal strategy set forth two years earlier. Formulated by Albert E. Arent and Irwin L. Langbein under the direction of the section's first head, Henry A. Schweinhaut, the scheme rested upon Reconstruction statutes (Sections 51 and 52, Title 18, United States Code) but advised using those laws only "in cases of flagrant and persistent breakdown of local law enforcement," since their application might arouse antagonism over states' rights.[137] Clearly, CRS attorneys considered Wright's death more shameless and embarrassing than constitutionally or politically explosive.

Led by section head Victor C. Rotnem, CRS personnel endeavored to bring Wright's murderers within "the purview of existing federal criminal statutes." This required challenging Supreme Court interpretations that limited the Fourteenth Amendment and jurisdiction over lynching to state action.[138] Since the amendment protected the right to due process of law, the

attorneys contended that it also permitted federal assistance to protect that
right when state governments failed to do so. They maintained further that
Sections 51 and 52, respectively derived from the Enforcement Act of 1870
and the Civil Rights Act of 1866, pertained to lynching cases. Section 51 pro-
hibited private citizens from conspiring to deny another citizen his or her
constitutional rights, making such conspiracy punishable by $5,000 fines,
ten-year prison sentences, and ineligibility for federal office. Section 52 pro-
hibited lawmen under the color of law from willfully depriving citizens of
"any rights, privileges, or immunities secured or protected" by the Constitution and federal laws, and punished violators with one year's imprison-
ment, a $1,000 fine, or both.[139] It appeared to departmental lawyers that
 Wright had been willfully denied equal protection of the law and deprived
of his life, without due process, by private conspirators and local authorities who failed to shield him from the mob.[140]

Rotnem and his staff knew that convincing grand jurors and, ultimately,
Supreme Court justices of their legal position would not be easy. Preliminary studies under Schweinhaut's direction found that Section 51 had been
used solely against the crime of conspiracy—leaving "some of the most fundamental constitutional rights" unprotected—and that Section 52 had been
little used, perhaps because of the vague wording "color of law" and "willfully."[141]

Lacking other alternatives, however, Justice Department attorneys
moved to forge Sections 51 and 52 into an antilynching law. They seemed
buoyed by district and Supreme Court rulings in 1940 and 1941. In *United
States v. Sutherland* (1940), a suit involving southern police brutality (which
was subsequently dropped), the district judge ruled that a lawman exceeding his authority acts "under color of law" to deprive his prisoner of equal
protection rights, thus violating Section 52. Supreme Court Chief Justice
Stone endorsed that ruling on the misuse of power in *United States v. Classic* (1941), when the Justice Department prosecuted Louisiana election com-
missioners for primary election fraud. Stone also found that the officials
violated Section 51 by conspiring to deny citizens their voting rights. CRS
attorneys believed these cases, especially *Classic*, expanded legal interpretation of the Fourteenth Amendment and of Sections 51 and 52 to enable prosecution of lynchings.[142]

As federal lawyers concentrated on overturning past Supreme Court
rulings, Berge sought Thurgood Marshall's advice on the department's prosecution theory. And Rotnem considered the NAACP counselor's request—
originally suggested by a St. Louis area chapter officer—for a federal case

led by representatives from Washington, D.C., rather than the United States attorney for eastern Missouri: Harry C. Blanton, brother of the Scott County prosecutor and supposed friend of the Sikeston police.[143] Berge and Rotnem went further; they decided to name a "Special Assistant to the Attorney General" (probably for reasons of departmental politics regarding Blanton). They asked prominent St. Louis attorney and former president of the American Bar Association Jacob M. Lashly to serve and discussed the case with him for two weeks before he agreed, on April 11, "to come in."[144] Their desire to please the NAACP, combined with Lashly's procrastination, delayed official announcement that a federal grand jury would investigate the lynching. When it came, however, the special appointee's high profile and the recent "vigorous action" for black Detroiters in the housing controversy brought Biddle's office double kudos from liberal organizations.[145]

The Justice Department benefited further from Donnell's unwillingness to release Kay's account of the Benton Courthouse testimony and from its own publicity efforts. When State Attorney General McKittrick decided that grand jury notes could be delivered only to the county prosecutor, for example, he and the governor looked disingenuous after having vowed to cooperate with the federal probe.[146] And, while Lashly pondered the special prosecutor offer, Justice Department officials informed the news services of their "moving on a wide front to protect the civil rights of Negroes" in Arkansas, Florida, Georgia, Kentucky, Texas, and, of course, Missouri.[147]

Meanwhile, CRS lawyers quietly acquired the state grand jury notes from Harry C. Blanton via David E. Blanton, the sole person deemed legally qualified by the state attorney to possess the telltale evidence.[148] In line with Lashly's request, they assigned Irwin Langbein—special assistant to the U.S. attorney general and an originator of the antilynching legal strategy—to assist with the federal grand jury presentment in St. Louis.[149] And they ordered FBI agents back into Sikeston for additional interviews focusing on specific details and the actions of local lawmen.[150]

Much work still lay ahead as the CRS lawyers and Lashly debated theories and culled Kay's notes, Blanton's photographs, FBI reports, and Justice Department summaries for evidence. Before the end of March, Berge and Rotnem approached Lashly about Section 52. Sikeston lawmen, they contended, could be accused of having taken either "positive steps to avoid their duties" or "willful 'inaction'" in the face of the lynchers; though the inaction thesis lacked "substantial precedent," the *Sutherland* and *Classic* decisions bolstered the first theory.[151] Berge and Rotnem also raised "the possibility of indicting members of the mob as aiders and abettors" of the policemen under Section 550, Title 18, United States Code, or as violators of Wright's guarantee of due process under Section 51. The first approach, they admitted, necessitated proving that the lynchers knew of the officers' intent to violate the victim's civil rights, and the second required reversing judicial interpretation.[152]

As Lashly questioned all theories without offering alternatives, CRS attorneys settled on Sections 51 and 52.[153] Believing that omitting mob leaders would weaken the case "appreciably" for jury and propaganda purposes, they selected Section 51 over Section 550; it seemed precise enough to indict lynchers for interfering with the state's obligation to provide Wright a fair trial, yet narrow enough not to offend "ordinary ideas of federalism."[154] Realizing that their theory contained "several fundamental weaknesses" and necessitated going at least "one step beyond which the Supreme Court" had thus far "seen fit to go," they argued that the Fourteenth Amendment guaranteed Wright due process "at the hands of the state" and freedom "from any lawless intervention by third parties"; and that *ex parte Riggins* (1904) provided precedent for interpreting Section 51 as an exercise of necessary and proper congressional power to protect due process, thereby permitting the prosecution of lynchers who interfered with state officers discharging their constitutional duty. But CRS counselors believed that the case against the officers was legally stronger. Relying on Section 52, they cited positive steps taken by lawmen—state action—that cost Wright his life. Indeed, FBI reports revealed names and detailed activities.[155]

Nevertheless, Lashly and Langbein were in no hurry to appear before the grand jury. Reputable witnesses had identified Wright's murderers, but indicting them on the basis of Section 51 appeared—in Lashly's words— "pretty tenuous."[156] Shortly before the federal grand jury convened, his superiors admitted that such a theory would move quickly "to the Supreme Court on a direct constitutional question." The wisdom of "this or other theories" could still be debated internally: since U.S. Attorney Blanton determined jury dates, Lashly and Langbein put testimony before the grand jury in May but withheld their indictment until June.[157] They would benefit from the split session "to put a good shine on the indictment" before presenting it.[158] Essentially the case against the lynchers was important for indicting Sikeston policemen.

On May 18, then, in the courtroom of U.S. District Judge Charles B. Davis, Lashly and Langbein began "United States v. Walter Kendall, et al." Unlike prosecutors in the state case, who focused solely on the lynchers, they sought primarily to determine whether Wright had received adequate protection by lawmen. They called fifteen witnesses over three days, drawing heavily on David E. Blanton, Sergeant Dace, Trooper Tandy, Police Chief Kendall, and Assistant Police Chief Wallace, as well as Ardella Wright, Richard and Minnie Gay, and suspected lynchers.[159] Identifying lynchers through the testimony of Blanton, Dace, and Tandy, Lashly and Langbein prepared the ground for an indictment based on conspiracy as defined in Section 51. In fact, they knew that hours before the lynching several whites had inquired about Wright's wounded condition and that at least three whites had solicited townsmen interested in "mobbing the negro."[160]

The Justice Department lawyers also attempted to demonstrate the various roles that officials played in Wright's apprehension by lynchers. Despite black allegations that Blanton had given prior approval to the lynching, other black witnesses admitted that the county prosecutor had been sincere, if "completely ineffectual," in his effort to disband the crowd at City Hall. And against the accusation that he had led the mob to Sunset Addition, federal attorneys confirmed that Dace and fellow troopers had done "everything within reason" to protect Wright and warn black residents; the prosecutors accepted Dace's decision not to fire into the crowd for fear of harming innocent people and, no doubt, his Paul Revere–like ride through Sunset streets as displays of "reasonable judgement."[161]

Thus, Lashly and Langbein focused their attention elsewhere. They considered the conduct of the police chief and his assistant "most reprehensible" and in violation of Section 52.[162] Although Chief Kendall stood against the mob from 10:00 A.M. until it abducted Wright, he never saw "the Negro" and made no effort to follow the lynchers. Instead, he stayed in his office while they murdered his prisoner, then went home for lunch. Wallace appeared even more cowardly to federal prosecutors. After taking Wright's confession at 10:00 A.M., he went about his "regular police duty." Returning to City Hall at 11:15 A.M., he noticed three or four hundred "very quiet and orderly" people out front, and within twenty minutes departed to answer a police call. Shortly after lunch he drove to Sunset Addition, saw the large crowd, and "turned around"—only to go back that afternoon and recover Wright's corpse. "I happened to be out there," he told FBI agents.[163]

Hard evidence notwithstanding, Lashly and Langbein lost their bid for indictments against lynchers and lawmen. Following their initial presentment, the grand jury recessed from May 21 to June 3 and again from the afternoon of June 4 to July 1, and did not issue its verdict until late that month. To be sure, Lashly and Langbein sought additional information to bolster their case, examined thirty-five witnesses in all, and elicited 1,091 pages of testimony.[164] Long before the jurors publicly issued their special report on July 30, however, federal prosecutors knew that no indictments would be forthcoming and discontinued ongoing FBI investigations.[165]

The jurors' report officially condemned the incident as "a deplorable blot upon the reputation of this State." Since Wright was dead or near death, however, they considered the violence "useless." More puzzling, even though admitting that lynchers had denied Wright due process, they concluded that "the facts" did not constitute "any federal offense." State troopers did "a fine job," and municipal police apprehended Wright quickly but thereafter "failed completely to cope with the situation." To prevent the recurrence of such "a tragic breakdown of the protections of government," the jurors urged Missouri authorities to study the law enforcement agencies that dealt with the lynchers.[166]

Not everyone agreed with the verdict. Liberal editors labeled the jury's report a whitewash and called for a federal antilynching law. National and state reputations would suffer in the face of Nazi propaganda, editorialized the *Post-Dispatch*.[167] More bitterly, black Missourians charged the jurors with purposely overlooking facts and condoning Wright's murder in a country where even saboteurs received fair trials.[168] And CRS personnel must have wondered, as did Rotnem, how jurors could admit that Wright had been denied due process yet conclude that the lynchers had committed no federal offense.[169]

The expertise and commitment of Justice Department officials had failed to overcome legal precedent, internal differences, racial prejudice, and probably resistance to federal interference. Throughout the grand jury proceedings, federal lawyers developed their legal theory, only to find the jurors unconvinced of its logic or unwilling to overturn precedent. Laypersons serving on the jury must have found the complicated thesis, law terms, and Supreme Court references exceedingly difficult to comprehend. What constituted "conspiracy" by citizens or willful denial of rights by lawmen? Which of the half-dozen federal cases cited challenged or upheld existing litigation? Such sophisticated legalities were all the more baffling for having been presented over several weeks interrupted by recesses. Jurors heard the strongest witnesses on the first days of the proceeding and those who denied culpability or claimed forgetfulness afterward: Blanton, Dace, and Tandy corroborated the federal case in May, but alleged lynchers and frightened onlookers undermined it repeatedly until the time that the verdict was reached weeks later.[170] Small wonder that the jury seemed unprepared to make history by adopting legal theory that countered "a long unbroken line" of Supreme

Court cases and itself would require verification by the highest tribunal. Some of the jurors abhorred Wright's lynching but found federal arguments for indictment wanting.[171]

Their skepticism may have mirrored Lashly's, for he never fully embraced the CRS's theory. From the beginning, he doubted that lynchers and police could be linked satisfactorily "to supply the conspiracy requirements" (Section 51) or that lawmen could be shown conclusively to have deprived Wright of his rights (Section 52).[172] Apparently he based this contention on the initial FBI investigation, which "did not give very much encouragement to the case"; nor, supposedly, did follow-up inquiries. The facts, he later told both Biddle and newsmen, failed to place "the offenders . . . within the coverage of any federal criminal law."[173] The special prosecutor's reasoning puzzled federal attorneys; even the conduct of Wallace and Kendall did not, according to Lashly, "rise beyond negligence, lack of foresight and inefficiency." Admitting that the indictment against the Sikeston police commanders "might be sustained," he objected on "psychological grounds" to bringing charges against one or two individuals when so many more were culpable; he considered it "unlikely to bring constructive practical results."[174] He seemed unconcerned for the trauma experienced by Wright or the need, in Walter White's phraseology, for examples of "vigorous affirmative action" to "stem lawlessness against Negroes and other minorities."[175]

Lashly's position, pervading all aspects of the government's case, apparently influenced some jurors. Justice Department officials had selected a special prosecutor with impressive credentials. An Illinois-born, Missouri resident, avid Democrat, former partner of Governor Donnell (1927-32), a man well thought of in legal circles state- and nationwide, he possessed all the necessary political and public characteristics for the sensitive, historic assignment. Yet he lacked the prerequisite most required for legal victory and judicial revolution: grand jury and criminal law experience. His reputation rested on "liquidation and bankruptcy matters."[176] Consequently, Lashly relegated the preliminary work to junior members of his law firm, supervising them in "frequent short conferences." Within a week of the grand jury date, however, he had not given the case "very much solid time," and his assistants seemed to be "thrashing over old straw" already covered by Arent and Langbein in their "civil liberties bible" and by Jim Doyle in the *Classic* case.[177]

Despite Langbein's efforts, Lashly resisted the embroidery of Sections 51 and 52; even a high-level conference with Biddle and Berge midway through the grand jury proceedings failed to change his mind. They had followed NAACP advice and appointed a special prosecutor, only to err drastically by selecting a strict constructionist to present a brief grounded in an elastic interpretation of federal law.[178] (Ironically, Lashly had been recommended by Roger N. Baldwin, director of the American Civil Liberties Union.)[179] "Under existing laws nothing else could have been done by the grand jury," he told the press.[180] Morover, he aided its efforts to save face. After adjournment on July 1, he was approached by some jurors who desired help "in getting up a report" that would prevent the public from considering their action "a condonation of the lynching." He raised their request with Berge and Rotnem, also noting that the grand jury wished "to hold the result in secret until some later time."[181]

Berge took his time responding, and Biddle misled the public by denying reports that "the grand jury had completed its investigation," thus giving the Justice Department time to consider its options.[182] Clearly, CRS attorneys influenced the jurors' carefully crafted statement and at the same time prepared a news release that stressed the crime against Wright, the state grand jury's failure, and the call for more effective "machinery" if local, county, and state authorities were to retain "exclusive jurisdiction in lynching situations." Above all, both documents released on July 30 reiterated CRS theory; the press release concluded that "the blind passion of a mob can not be substituted for due process of law if orderly government is to survive."[183] Instead of an indictment, overstated one insider, the Justice Department "got an excellent report from the Grand Jury."[184]

Still, Biddle, Berge, and Rotnem must have wondered why Lashly ever agreed to head the federal inquiry. Perhaps he acted—in Biddle's words—for reasons of "unselfish patriotism," realizing the case's "national importance" for the war effort. Win or lose, Biddle had assured him, his participation would strengthen "the forces of law and order throughout the country." As "an outstanding Missourian" and former American Bar Association president, one suspects, Lashly relished the recognition and opportunities for public service provided by the assignment.[185] Nor could he, as a lawyer, pass up such "a provocative challenge," one dealing with the "flagrant breakdown of order and failure of government."[186] Until the end, he insisted that he welcomed the chance to improve that "deplorable situation."[187]

In addition to the differences between Lashly and CRS attorneys, racial bigotry worked against their efforts. Everyone, including the attorney general, realized that the case was "fraught with prejudice."[188] Though it is difficult to document the racism of individual members, the jury shared the popular belief that stereotyped Wright as a dying black rapist undeserving of civil rights. Ignoring the law—which clearly stated that if the victim was alive when taken by the mob, his rights had been violated— jurors considered that the lynching mattered little because Wright was dead or "would have been dead within a short time." Further ignoring the law—which clearly assumed one's innocence until proven otherwise in court—the jurors declared Wright "a brutal criminal" guilty of assault. He was denied due process, but their great concern lay with future, "entirely innocent" lynching victims."[189]

Moreover, the jurors, like those on the state grand jury, disapproved of outside interference. If the citizens of southeastern Missouri resented upstate busybodies challenging local authority, they certainly disliked federal attorneys threatening states' rights. Wittingly or otherwise, the jurors projected the conservative reaction to New Deal encroachment that had already occurred in Congress and in some state houses, especially on racial issues. Doubtless, "state rights and strict constructionism remained remarkably healthy" in their minds, despite the previous decade's centralization.[190] Perhaps some recalled the Missouri roadside demonstration, perceiving—as had Governor Lloyd C. Stark—federal farm administrators as "troublesome." Others may have seen in Nazi totalitarianism further justification for disapproving big government.[191] Harboring those beliefs, they reconciled within themselves the injustice done Cleo Wright.

Although seated in St. Louis, drawn from the entire eastern district, and supposedly "less influenced by local climatic conditions," the federal jurors resembled the Scott County jurors in important ways. Most were bankers, businessmen, insurers, and realtors; some were ranking officers in sizable companies; and all were "more or less responsible persons" with a stake in society; most had their residences in a concentrated area, that of St. Louis and its suburbs.[192] Predictably, then, as white male entrepreneurs, they displayed their own concept of the status quo and federalism, if not racism and provincialism. Like area church members and university professors approached by petitioners seeking signatures for a federal antilynching statute, they indicated that rapists "had it coming" and that communities—whether in urban centers or Bootheel hamlets—needed the shield of white supremacy.[193] And, unlike Benton jurymen who found only an adversary in the county prosecutor, federal jurors who may have genuinely opposed lynching associated closely with Lashly's own doubts about the case; he was one of their own, geographically, socioeconomically, and philosophically. Why else would four or five or more jury members have approached him throughout the month of July about "our grand jury problem"? Clearly, they sought—both directly and "casually"—his assistance with their final report.[194]

For the moment, that report closed the case. State and federal prosecutors had raised many issues, even if neither jury addressed them, and local residents heard numerous rumors about Wright, his victim, his captors, his protectors, and his killers. Yet although they may have thought that law and order had been restored, perhaps even that justice had been done, important facts remained elusive. Like Wright himself, whose killing was granted no inquest and whose body received no postmortem, the acts of bloodshed and the community's response needed an autopsy.[195]

4 Autopsy

Among numerous questions posed by the lynching, the most significant involved those touched by violence. Beyond names that suddenly blazed across wire services and headlines, who exactly were Cleo Wright and Grace Sturgeon? Was he a black beast and she a white innocent, or were they lovers whose passion turned to bloodshed? And, their personal relationship aside, what drove him to such a savage act and her to such an indomitable desire for life? Indeed, the responses to these queries pushed beyond sexual innuendo to reveal much about a racial and cultural heritage that fostered Wright's aggression and demanded Sturgeon's defense.

Since few in Sikeston admitted knowing Wright, both black and white reporters described him simply as a young cotton oil mill worker with a prison record; sometimes they misreported his age. NAACP representatives identified him as a transient cotton picker or simply ignored him in their lynching investigation.[1]

Wright remained a mystery in part because of his recent arrival and erratic behavior. Born in Jefferson County, Arkansas, nearly twenty-six years before these events, he had come to Sikeston in the spring of 1937. That fall he was caught tampering with an automobile belonging to a state police commander and served sixty days in the county jail.[2] He then settled in the black community for nearly two and a half years before committing a second crime. On May 16, 1940, Wright burglarized the Sikeston Sales Company, taking $15.95. He again admitted his guilt, was sentenced to two years in the state penitentiary, and served seven months at Jefferson City before being released on parole. From February 18, 1941, to January 3, 1942, he reported regularly to Police Chief Walter Kendall, held a job, avoided trouble, and became a free man—three weeks before the assault on Grace Sturgeon.[3]

Before that tragedy, Wright appeared to be no more than a petty thief. In 1937 he found employment as a laborer for Milem Limbaugh and, once released from county jail, for J.C. Oden in 1938 and part of 1939. He worked as a cake stripper at the Sikeston Cotton Oil Mill later that year, and during his parole from the state penitentiary in 1941 and into 1942. Both at

Limbaugh's service station on the corner of Kingshighway and Malone Avenue and at the mill farther east, where Malone Avenue turned into U.S. 60, Wright impressed his white employers as "a good worker," industrious and dependable, never causing trouble.[4]

Wright's personal life also seemed respectable. He courted Ardella Gay, married her on February 10, 1940, in nearby Benton, and established their home in Sikeston at 207 Luther Street. There, in the west end of Sunset Addition, he and Ardella enjoyed a sense of family with his in-laws, Mississippians Minnie and Richard Gay, who lived close by. During the period of his parole, Ardella became pregnant with their first child.[5]

Those who knew Wright at that time liked him. Although he rarely attended church—in part because he worked on Sundays— ministers of the community considered him "a pretty nice sort of fellow." Rev. S.D. Woods of the Second Baptist Church, for example, had supported his request for parole.[6] Sunset residents such as Walter Griffen, who managed the baseball team for which Wright played outfield, verified that he got along well with teammates; and when on occasion Griffen obtained his temporary release from the Scott County Jail to play in games, he never proved troublesome.[7] Similarly, white citizens such as Lynn Ingram remembered Wright as "neat looking" and "friendly," never resentful.[8]

Likewise, Ardella and her parents gave the impression that all was well. The Gays belonged to the Church of God in Christ and considered Wright, himself raised a Baptist, a quiet, "decent man." Cleo, said his wife, "had been good to her."[9] Although concerned over Wright's prison record, Richard Gay supported him. So did Minnie Gay, who considered him "a nice boy." Not surprisingly, then, friends and relatives of the Wrights and the Gays recalled "just a big happy family."[10]

After Wright's lynching, those who had known him said little. Clearly, blacks were frightened: the Gays had distanced themselves from their son-in-law when police officers sought to leave him in their care during the last hours of his life. Whites, too, feared repercussions from the lynchers, and in some cases embarrassment for having sponsored Wright for parole; in fact, petitioners had included Mayor George W. Presnell, City Attorney Robert A. Dempster, and Justice of the Peace W.R. Griffin. Their endorsements revealed personalism, paternalism, and even tenderheartedness. "This boy," contended City Collector J.W. Mathis, "will make a good citizen if given the opportunity." Perhaps they, like southerners elsewhere knowing of black economic hardship, expected his thievery, even gave it tacit approval as proof of black inferiority and, therefore, justification for the color line.[11] That

Cleo Wright, about 1937.
Courtesy of Linetta Watson Koonce.

Wright returned to the oil mill at a time when white employers refused to
hire "real mean" black males indicated further the positive view that many
whites had of him, or the influence of trustworthy black petitioners such as
Richard Gay and the Reverend Woods with white power brokers.[12]

Thus Wright's attack on Sturgeon shocked everyone and hinted at a
more troubled personality than one simply wearing the mask of survival and
deceit demanded by white society. Yet no one questioned whether he had
indeed slashed Sturgeon and Night Marshal Perrigan. Partly this reflected
the impact of his confessions, though it is doubtful that they were legally
acceptable admissions of guilt. In shock and pain from batterings, gunshot
wounds, and loss of blood, Wright must have been spent and certainly less
than alert—conditions never given "a thought" by those who arrested him
or by the county prosecutor; they simply accepted Wright's self-incrimina-
tion and the circumstantial evidence surrounding it. Accordingly, they dismissed without investigation his initial explanation of having been bloodied
in "a fight with two Negroes" just before encountering Perrigan.[13]

Many other whites believed Wright because he gave his confession while
dying and because it fit the facts of carnage: the attacks on Sturgeon and
Perrigan. Still others, one suspects, embraced his guilt rather than face the
horrifying thought that a crazed black rapist remained at large. Wright's

confession, as well as any evidence, hearsay, or fabrication that identified him as the culprit provided relief to Sturgeon's neighbors, for instance.[14] In a final analysis, journalist Paul Bumbarger speculated on "the essence of all mob violence: the guy is guilty, so let's go hang him."[15]

Black townsfolk too deemed Wright guilty. Many followed the thinking of whites in believing that his attack on Perrigan offered proof of his attack on Sturgeon.[16] Some had heard that he was "bad with a knife," and others had known him to be belligerent when drinking, quite capable of having cut both victims. And, given the pattern of residential segregation in Sikeston, they realized that he had no cause to be in Sturgeon's neighborhood other than for theft or "whore chasing."[17] Several blacks acknowledged Wright's wrongdoing for reasons of personal survival. Aware that whites needed an immediate captive to ease anxieties about a black brute, they feared widespread terror should Sturgeon's assailant prove elusive. In other words, Sunset residents accepted Wright's guilt as dictated by his capture and, most important, by the message of his death for all blacks who dared "step out of line." Significantly, they emphasized that he acted alone. Sikeston blacks, like their nineteenth-century southern counterparts, understood both the possibility of Wright's guilt and, should they condone or ignore it, the certainty of their own annihilation.[18]

Less certain than Wright's attack on Perrigan was his assault on Grace Sturgeon. Neither she nor her sister-in-law, Laverne Sturgeon, could positively identify the assailant because it was dark inside their house. Laverne told reporters that she looked up from her bed to see "a Negro man" by the window, and that he had been watching the premises "for some time."[19] A month later, when interviewed by FBI agents, she and Grace again identified the intruder as "a Negro because of his voice" and his body odor. Grace also remembered that while being treated at the hospital, she heard Wright—himself receiving medical care in the basement—exclaim "Oh, God!" in "the same voice that she had heard in her bedroom."[20]

If these flimsy descriptions hardly proved Wright's culpability, his encounter with Perrigan and Jesse Whittley lent credibility to his guilt. He appeared one and a quarter miles west of the Sturgeon home within thirty minutes of the assault, wearing blood-soaked trousers and carrying a "very bloody" knife in his pocket. That he attempted to run as soon as he saw the vehicle left no doubt in Whittley's mind that "he was the one who did it."[21] His resistance to arrest followed by his assault on Perrigan seemed the reaction of someone who had done much more than fight with other blacks (an act that would have brought no great punishment from white society). Given his usual demeanor before white authority, attacking Perrigan made no sense unless Wright had been provoked, a possibility denied by Whittley, or unless he had committed an even greater crime than that of attempting to kill a white lawman—itself an act inviting violent reprisal. Cutting the night marshall with the same ferocity demonstrated by Sturgeon's assailant also suggested more than the coincidental patterns of different slashers. Like other black men trapped in a system that assumed their guilt and obliterated their humanity whenever they crossed lines of sex and authority, Wright, when cornered—in the Sturgeon home and in the police car—acted as if he believed it necessary to kill in order to live. Surely this was why Sturgeon's would-be slayer commenced his attack upon her with the pronouncement, "You'll never live to tell this."[22]

For all these reasons, Wright's confession at City Hall was believed to evince his guilt. What he is purported to have told Milburn Arbaugh, Milem Limbaugh, and Assistant Police Chief Harold Wallace contained information that, if actually given and correctly repeated, clearly indicted him. Beyond admitting that he had cut "that white woman," Wright retraced his steps that evening. He told of patronizing the Farmers Cafe until 9:00 P.M., reporting for work at the oil mill a half-hour later only to discover that his shift would not work that evening, and then heading south to Sturgeon's home. His movements until he left the mill had been confirmed by eye-witnesses and were restated separately and without significant deviation by Arbaugh, Limbaugh, and Wallace.[23] Nor did Wright repeat his first claim that he had been fighting with unidentified blacks just before his capture, or offer any other alibi.

Years later the Sturgeon women reiterated that the assailant spoke and smelled like a stereotypic black man, but for the first time Grace claimed to have caught a glance of him passing her hospital room before descending the basement stairs to the emergency room for treatment. Whether or not this sighting occurred, she repeated that Wright's voice identified him as her assailant, though she acknowledged again her inability to recognize him visually.[24]

While fighting for her life in a darkened room and at close quarters, however, Grace Sturgeon knew well her intruder's size and clothing. Standing 5'6" and weighing 135 pounds, she had traded blows with a "broad-shouldered," "muscular" man two or three inches taller than herself and wearing a leather "waist coat"; she desperately clung to the slick jacket in an attempt to deny him the space needed to wield his knife. Still, her intestines spilled out as he cut from her left to right, revealing himself to be right-handed.[25]

In addition, Sturgeon insisted that her slasher fought and spoke like a sober person. Very sensitive to the smell of alcohol, she sensed no trace of it on him.[26] Neither did a black policeman when he conversed with Wright four hours before the attack; nor did Perrigan and Whittley upon apprehending him half an hour after it.[27] To be sure, Richard Gay testified that Wright reeked of whiskey shortly before daybreak and long after his capture, apparently having been plied with it by an unknown samaritan intent on easing his pain. And Wright's own midmorning confession of having attacked the woman while drunk represented the impact of shock, trauma, and alcohol as much as conscience.[28] Significantly, however, whatever he did during the late hours of Saturday and early hours of Sunday, he did with a clear head.

Sturgeon's descriptions fit Wright in several categories. He stood 5'10", weighed 175 pounds, and possessed a "husky," athletic build. When caught, he was wearing a "jacket" or "waist coat," though his captors never described its composition. And, as a baseball player, he batted and threw right-handed.[29] In other words, Wright resembled the intruder in voice, height, weight, size, dress, use of hand; he had not been drinking on the night of Sturgeon's attack; and he shared with her slasher the choice of weapon, ferocious aggression, and blood "all over his clothing."[30]

The individual pieces of evidence regarding Wright's whereabouts and actions during the early hours of January 25 appear moot, but taken together they provided a cumulative weight that persuaded most townspeople, black and white, of his guilt. And, regardless of their own divergent and often self-serving reasons, they seem to have been correct in condemning Cleo Wright. In all probability, it was he who slashed Grace Sturgeon—but for what reason? Did he intend to take her money, her honor, or her life? Or was his activity, as rumored among Sunset residents, more scandalous than whites dared assume?

Given his previous thieving, Wright might have intended to steal from Sturgeon and then overreacted when discovered. Conceivably, he had been responsible for the citywide rash of burglaries that had occurred the previous November. That thief slid in and out of white homes through windows, lifting wallets from trousers and handbags from bureaus until suppressed by police patrols. Some of his robberies occurred while victims slept, and at least one took place on Kathleen Avenue. When caught in the act, however, the notorious "Negro purse snatcher" had fled, not fought. His slight build did not fit the description of Wright, nor did the items he stole—for example, a .32 caliber pistol—appear ever to have been in Wright's possession.[31] Moreover, when Wright entered Sturgeon's home, he never mentioned theft and gave no indication of seeking loot.[32] And five weeks after his death, another black man, perhaps the renowned burglar himself, attempted to break into 811 Gladys Avenue, almost directly behind the Sturgeon premises—which closed the subject of Wright's motivation having been thievery.[33]

Most white townsfolk, of course, believed that Wright had intended to rape Sturgeon. Their racial and sexual beliefs dictated such thinking long before the police chief publicly confirmed it. Some Sikestonians in fact assumed that Wright *had* raped her. Even Sturgeon's step-grandfather, H.D. Davenport, who came running to her rescue and knew her situation firsthand, inexplicably spread the rumor. In truth, Sturgeon had not been raped; only Wright's declaration that he intended to kill her triggered her fierce resistance: "I said to myself, 'Oh, no you're not!'"[34]

Whereas whites envisioned Sturgeon the random victim of "a lust mad negro buck," blacks in Sikeston believed her to have been Wright's lover. Supposedly, she had followed him from Arkansas, and on this particular night he was discovered—by visitors or a neighbor—entering her home. Others claimed that his detection occurred because of a lovers' quarrel, which led to her knifing. In any case, alleged blacks, Sturgeon cried rape in order "to keep her clothes clean."[35]

Given the history of the South, blacks found this story plausible. They believed that some white women were attracted to black men and, if discovered having sexual relations with them, were absolved of all wrongdoing (which was untrue); they believed, too, that other white women possessed "racially heightened imaginations" and claimed rape where none occurred (which was true).[36] Sunset residents realized that "racial orthodoxy" and white male jealousy required the denial of any mutual desire between Sturgeon and Wright, which meant that accusations regarding their encounter would point in only one direction—his.[37]

Lacking firsthand evidence, black Sikestonians launched the rumors about the Sturgeon-Wright affair as angry payback for his death and their powerlessness. Walter Griffen, for one, believed that these stories were a way for blacks to "get by," to inflict revenge without incurring white reprisal: such gossip served as "a universal form of aggression," however passive, and perhaps an effort to manage the frightful situation.[38] If Wright had acted out of sexual motives based on an established relationship with Grace Sturgeon, there was no reason for whites to destroy or condemn other members of the black community.

Significantly, the rumor of sexual liaison surfaced only after the assault on Sturgeon and in contradiction to the testimony of Wright's wife. Black police officer Henry Bartlett told federal agents that Wright "had been going with Mrs. Dillard Sturgeon regularly" but provided no evidence for his claim (which appeared to have come from a black newspaper); he based his speculation on a remark of Ardella Wright that her husband's death "was no more than I expected." However, on two separate occasions Ardella denied any knowledge of Cleo's having "relations with a white woman"; she clarified her so-called death premonition by saying "she had a peculiar feeling that something was going to happen to her parents."[39]

Long afterward, Ardella changed her story to claim that Cleo had been Grace's lover: she told Wright's sister of having confronted Sturgeon about the affair before the lynching.[40] Yet though she might have lied to federal investigators about Cleo's relationship with Sturgeon for fear of physical harm by whites, she had little reason to give friends the impression that such charges against her husband were trumped up.[41] Furthermore, given southern etiquette, her altercation with Sturgeon would have been unacceptable and much talked about in both black and white circles. Ardella would have had to visit Grace in her home, at her place of work, or in downtown Sikeston—all locations where neighbors, workers, or shoppers could hardly ignore an interracial argument by married women over one of their husbands. Very young and sheltered by the Gays, Ardella did not seem self-assured enough to press the issue. Nor did any source, black or white, then or more recently, substantiate her contention. Her showdown with Sturgeon appears to have been concocted after Wright's death as a means to save face. Ironically, whatever humiliation Ardella felt over Cleo's love for a white woman resulted from rumors that blacks originated and that she could not stop by denial or affirmation.[42]

Sturgeon steadfastly denied ever having met Wright's wife.[43] Though a handful of whites described Grace as "a loose woman" who ran around while her husband served in the military, they did so only after the lynching without knowing her personally and without naming Wright—or any other man of either race—as her lover. They based their portrayal solely on hearsay, probably endeavoring—as did white counterparts who lynched alleged black rapists elsewhere—to distance themselves from the supposed rape victim's humiliation. Consequently, they impugned Sturgeon behind her back in order to protect their own reputations as white people, their illusions of racial purity, and their need for an impenetrable color line; because of their minuscule numbers, however, they made no attempt to ostracize her from the community. Instead, Sturgeon became a counterimage for their white supremacist psyche, "a shady character" who crossed the black-white barrier one time too many.[44]

In sharp contrast, most white residents protected the racial order by unequivocally supporting Sturgeon, whom some knew personally. Next-door neighbor Glenda Whittley, wife of Jesse, judged the Sturgeon-Wright rumor impossible. Eight months pregnant with her first child during the time of the supposed affair, she had been staying at home all day and noticed nothing of the sort; Grace, she insisted, was "not like that." Similarly, prosecuting attorney David E. Blanton described Sturgeon as "a fine person" and dismissed the gossip as baseless. So did such townsfolk as cafe owner Gilbert Clinton, who knew Sturgeon and her family less well but considered them upstanding.[45] Numerous individuals interviewed by federal agents echoed these sentiments, leaving them to conclude that the sexual encounter never occurred and that Sturgeon's reputation and "moral character" were "above reproach."[46] They seemed correct: if she and Wright were lovers, why did he not know about Jimmy or Laverne? Why did he prowl around before entering Grace's home? And why did he come in it through a window? A paramour would surely not have been so ignorant or acted so oddly.

Still, the rumors persisted, and for over a year "threatening letters" came to the Sturgeon home. One bore a mock marriage proposal from a Potosi mate-seeker who said that he had fallen in love with Grace's newspaper photo. Another from a St. Louis resident accused her of being "crazy about" black youths, including one in 1931 whom she had tried to have lynched for attempting "to quit her."[47] These letter writers drew the attention of lawmen, who investigated the 1931 incident, denounced it as false, and reported Sturgeon "perfectly innocent of all charges."[48] Sturgeon, for her part, believed that the correspondents were black, delivering retribution for Wright's death. She anguished over their emotional impact, crying "many a tear" for a very long time.[49]

Those accusing Sturgeon of having gone dancing with Wright or sending him love letters, however, unwittingly touched on the possibility of more widespread race mixing in Sikeston. Given the rumors about herself, Grace soon heard about white women who frequented the "dives" in Sunset or sat with black customers in the rear of downtown establishments such as Farmers Cafe, which Wright patronized. Proprietors and waitresses denied such conduct, and respectable residents both black and white played down interracial affairs as rare.[50] They loomed as intolerable, far worse than one-night stands with streetwalkers who peddled themselves to willing customers, particularly white cadets from the Missouri Institute of Aeronautics.[51]

Hearsay about Sturgeon and Wright, then, brought to the surface the question of forbidden racial behavior—and Cleo's reputation. Officials produced evidence that he had chased white women before. Sgt. Melvin Dace said he thought of Wright "as soon as he heard" about Sturgeon's assault, because three years earlier Wright had written to a reputable young woman in Sikeston—not Grace—"requesting a photograph of her and telling her that he was in love with her." Dace had pursued the issue, only to determine that Wright had violated no law.[52] Similarly, U.S. Attorney Harry C. Blanton, brother of David, reported that a nineteen-year-old from St. Louis claimed to have been raped by Wright in 1941 while she was in Sikeston selling merchandise. She had entered a car driven by Wright and contended that he compelled her to "have intercourse with him"; she had said nothing afterward because of her "humiliation" and his warnings that she "would be ruined."[53] Though few, if any, citizens knew of these accusations, state police and federal authorities believed them further proof of his guilt.

In truth, though the evidence is sketchy, Wright did become attracted to white women and engage in a pattern of escalating sexual transgressions that ended with the assault on Sturgeon. His letter of 1939 to the married woman in Sikeston implied that she had a child, though not necessarily his, and that he feared contacting her but missed her and wanted to return to her: "Just a few lines to let you hear from me. This leaves me O.K. and hope it will find each of you enjoying life like birds in the springtime. I been going to write you ever since I been back [in Arkansas] but was afraid to but this morning I had to if it cause the world to turn up. . . . I can't rest at night for dreaming and thinking." He asked her to send a picture, for it would provide "a lot of consolation" should he never see her again, but he preferred to see her if she would "say so." Poetic and yearning, he closed by extending his "love and greatest wishes."[54] While Sergeant Dace gave the impression, supposedly suggested by the woman handing over the letter "immediately upon receipt," that Wright's feelings were unwanted and unrequited, his troop commander, Sgt. O.L. Wallis, considered them "rather sentimental."[55] In any case, Wright's letter indicated an affair with someone who had ended it (most likely because it threatened her way of life in Sikeston's white community).

Perhaps Wright raped the St. Louis teenager two years later, though that is very questionable. He had been a chauffeur just before he burglarized the Sikeston Sales Company in 1940.[56] On parole the following year, he could have been moonlighting as a driver at the time of the alleged assault, but he showed no signs of aberrant behavior until shortly before the attack on Sturgeon. Wright's accuser, furthermore, seemed somewhat unsure of his identity. She had never encountered him before—or apparently after—her visit to Sikeston; she might have seen a photograph of him in the St. Louis press immediately after his death, but it was another two months before she came forward with her accusation. In fact, between the lynching and the rape charge, the same girl made news by claiming to have been swindled by a man who had impersonated the brother of cowboy actor Gene Autry and who absconded with her money and property after promising to marry her. For this reason, and perchance because she was "rather buxom, attractive, well-built," Harry Blanton considered it "barely possible" that she was seeking publicity.[57]

Whatever the truth of her story, Cleo Wright had been sexually active in Sikeston. He believed himself stricken with gonorrhea, though he probably misdiagnosed his condition; he told prison officials in July of 1941 that he thought himself cured without having "taken shots"—an impossibility. Nor did Ardella or their child, born after his death, show signs of that or any other sexually transmitted disease.[58] Nevertheless, that Wright thought himself infected revealed extramarital affairs and verified the later suspicions of his wife, who shortly before his death accused him of "running around with other colored women."[59] In truth, he had been sexually intimate with at least one white woman before his marriage and possibly more than one black women after it, deceiving members of both communities and, for a long time, Ardella. Few, if any, knew him as a lady's man, perhaps because Wright's survival among whites and, one also suspects, his standing among blacks—who deemed circumspection in affairs "a virtue"—required utmost discretion.[60]

Certainly his liaison with a white woman, much less his assault on Sturgeon, would have been unthinkable to those who had grown up with Wright twenty miles northeast of Pine Bluff in rural Arkansas. Delivered by a midwife in 1916, he lived behind Gilliand Road, across from the Gilliand plantation and slightly northeast of Gethsemane. There, on Highway 31, he frequented the convenience store of Henry Walker Jr., which provided groceries, gasoline, and credit. He also attended the local Baptist Church and grade school, just beyond the tiny emporium, and played baseball in the field behind it. On weekends he ventured nearly seven miles due south to Altheimer, on Highway 79, where one could buy a "fresher" or see a movie. Or he journeyed northeast on that route to Wabbaseka for a ball game.[61]

The young Wright's everyday world, however, was fixed within a plantation economy. Those about him raised cotton for profit, vegetables and livestock for personal use. Whether sharecropper, tenant farmer, or property owner, all worked long hours and understood their subservient position. The hundred families of croppers and renters who worked the Gilliand place benefited from the cabins, school, and even burial payments funded by a paternalistic owner, who also dispensed self-serving justice and exploited their labor. Lillie Clorah, who had worked in the fields as a youngster and young adult, remembered that life in the area was "as close to slavery as you can get." Though a smaller number of blacks, like Wright's family, lived beyond the estate, they too realized that "the big man got the big end of it." And while those who owned or rented land fared better than seasonal laborers working on plantations, they rarely expressed class bias. Among blacks, recalled John Henry Rasberry, who rented directly across from Gilliand, "there was no big Is and little yous." Individuals doing well shared their bounty with less fortunate neighbors; hog killing in hard times became a social event, filling bellies—and warming hearts.[62]

At times, blacks and whites cooperated. The Walkers lived across the road from the Oliver Mason family, for example, and got along well enough to share water pumps and stay in touch later in life. Like other blacks in the area, most of whom traced their origins to the slave South, Henry Walker Jr. and his wife, Leona Banks Walker, instructed their twelve children to work hard and mind their own business. Whites had the advantages, they admonished behind closed doors; and blacks must know their place in a society of Jim Crow schools and theater seating. That would bring success, as it had for the Walkers, who owned the store and seventy-two acres of land that their sons parlayed—through loans from white bankers and business dealings with other blacks—into three hundred acres.

Wright, of course, had learned similar lessons. His mother's parents, James Woolfolk and Lucy Moorehead, had migrated from Alabama. Each had been previously married; he was the father of Prince and she the mother of Willie. They met in Arkansas, accumulated 160 acres of farmland, and raised three more children together: Caleb, John, and Alonzo. In 1907 at the age of twenty-one, Alonzo married Temp Humphrey, a farmer fifteen years her senior and father of teenage daughter Bettie. She settled on his sixty acres off Gilliand Road and soon became pregnant, but their union ended in tragedy when lightning struck Temp. Within a few months of Temp's death she gave birth to their son, Wiley Arnett, and faced a lawsuit over her inheritance. She yielded fifteen acres to Bettie, then married and raising a family.[63]

Nearly a year after that litigation, on January 26, 1910, Alonzo married Albert Leak Watson. He worked as a logger and lived on Gilliand Plantation, where his parents James and Parthenia had settled upon leaving Pine Bluff. Little is known of them or his sisters Cornelia and Alice, but they were all residing in the Gethsemane area when he married Bessie Lusby of Wabbaseka in 1904. That union ended in divorce, despite the birth of a daughter; Bessie took baby Willie to Pine Bluff and ultimately remarried, while Albert met and wed Alonzo, and moved to the Humphrey homestead. Over the next fifteen years he kept in touch with daughter Willie and helped raise stepson Wiley, while she gave birth to their own family: Cleodas (1916), Alice (1920), James (1921), and Linetta (1925).[64]

When they married, Alonzo (twenty-four) and Albert (twenty-six) seemed opposites. She was a Baptist, he a member of the African Methodist Episcopal Church (AME); she college educated (having studied at Branch Normal School in Pine Bluff for two years), he grade-school literate; she outgoing, dominant, sometimes high tempered and hard edged, he reserved, easygoing, a "very nice man." Yet they complemented each other, and their faith ran deep: Alonzo came from a family of preachers, and Albert taught Sunday school.[65] They attended services regularly in Gethsemane, their churches and their Christianity divided only by the pavement of Highway 31. They also balanced each other in the secular world. She taught school throughout the area, and he read the newspaper every evening. She as a teacher and he as a farmer, they both contributed to the family upkeep—as did their children, who helped Albert raise cotton for cash, corn and hay for livestock, and vegetables for food. And they both had a say in major financial dealings, though Alonzo did the negotiating.[66]

Most significant, they cooperated as parents. They permitted their children to choose between the Baptist and Methodist faiths, revealing neither personal disappointment nor marital difficulties as each child joined Alonzo's church. They established house rules together and closed ranks on discipline, though Alonzo served as the lone enforcer until the boys became so big that whipping them required Albert's assistance. As in business dealings, they played different roles according to their personalities.[67]

In Gethsemane the Watsons enjoyed a reputation as "one of the most respected families." Alonzo and Albert labored hard, feared God, and meshed well with their neighbors. Though neither wealthy nor prominent, they drew status from her land ownership—Alonzo, many knew, would add to her holdings with the inheritance of thirty-seven acres of Woolfolk property—and profession: she came into contact with numerous families, teaching sev-

Alonzo and Albert Watson, with two of their children, James and
Linetta, in 1942. Courtesy of Linetta Watson Koonce.

eral grades in one-room schools, for many years on the Gilliand Plantation.[68]

Alonzo's own children also mixed well. Like their peers, they worked in
the fields, attended church and school, and enjoyed their free time. The boys
hunted, fished, and played baseball; the girls watched the games or played
jacks. Both went swimming in warm weather, when the boys also stole wa-
termelons or engaged in other high jinks. In the colder months school programs provided some entertainment, as did church socials, concerts, and
Christmas observances. Occasionally everyone, including adults, watched a
movie in Altheimer, separated from white patrons by only an aisle.[69] Older
teenagers and young adults enjoyed more leeway. Perhaps they "barrel-

housed," gathering spontaneously for some home brew, music, and dancing. In contrast, married couples attended more formal affairs such as birth
parties and fish fries. Given the absence of speakeasies in the area, blacks
created their own social outlets beyond home, church, and school.[70]

Still, strict rules applied to dating. Mothers, like slave women before
them, belied the myth of black promiscuity and endeavored to slow down
boy-girl relationships. Even when walking to church, they admonished their
daughters to stay within sight: "Sister, I can't see you."[71] Girls did not date
until sixteen years of age, when boys could visit them in their homes under
"the watchful ear" of parents. At seventeen they enjoyed much more freedom, stepping out with boyfriends to a school play or accompanying them
to basketball games in Altheimer, Humphrey, and Pine Bluff. Those with
access to an automobile took rides or, against parental dictate, attended house
parties.[72]

Serious courting occurred in the upper teens, culminating in marriage
as early as age eighteen for girls and twenty-one for boys. Couples wanting
to marry earlier were limited by parental influence and economic reality:
hence the usual three-year age discrepancy between brides and grooms. Girls
who married before their eighteenth birthdays usually did so because of
pregnancy and because their lovers consented freely to matrimony or were
pressured into it. Where boys refused to enter wedlock, however, pregnant
girls were shunned by nonfamily members of the community. Separated
from their age group and sheltered by their parents, they wore loose-fitting
clothing to conceal their condition. But once they gave birth, all was for-
given; the family expressed joy; the neighbors, acceptance. Young mothers
of illegitimate children now associated with wives and mothers usually older
than themselves. They also dated again, many marrying without stigma individuals other than the fathers of their children. Illegitimacy thus revealed
double standards, family love, and community tolerance.

In contrast, interracial dating and miscegenation was unacceptable for
either teenagers or adults. Both races considered this intimacy the major
taboo. Some parents lectured their children on the subject; others never approached it directly, but all children understood its gravity. Boys, in particular, were taught "how far to step" and sometimes frightened by the possibility
of overstepping into a lynching. "I didn't even want to get close to a white
woman," recalled one Gethsemane youth.[73]

In the home of Alonzo and Albert, Cleo and his siblings also learned
how to lead productive lives. Alonzo constantly encouraged them to "hold
your head up, you can be anything that you want." They lived under a rigid

set of rules that stressed obedience, accountability, and religiosity. Everyone ate together and returned home by sundown unless on a date (for which the boys enjoyed later curfews); everyone attended Sunday church services and participated in a revival once or twice a year. Family members stayed in prayer meetings until adjournment; no one left early. As they grew older, if they decided to forgo a worship service, they were confined to the house. Alonzo and Albert also discouraged gossip, shared few secrets with their children, and imposed rigid discipline.[74]

For the first eighteen years of his life, Cleo thrived in this atmosphere. He related well to his brothers and sisters, despite age differences and occasional rivalries. He attended church regularly, completed the eighth grade, and learned to tap dance and play the piano.[75] He excelled as a pitcher whose fast ball, according to catcher James Walker, could "knock a mitt off your hand!" Cleo's Gethsemane team defeated the likes of Wabbaseka and Dudley Lake. They played hard, inciting curses and fist fights that kept their games off limits to younger teens.[76]

Beyond his athletic talent, Cleo seemed ordinary for Gethsemane during the period between the Great War and the Great Depression. His family and friends considered him friendly, pleasant, and trusting. He accepted people easily and made friends quickly, which sometimes led to disappointment and confrontations. He was never a bully, but if provoked or ridiculed he made his tormentors "pay the price." He backed down from no one, exhibiting a fierce temper and muscular physique that few dared to challenge. Yet he held no grudges.[77]

More than to anyone else, Cleo looked up to Wiley. Eight years older, his half-brother had completed ninth grade, had an easygoing personality and a temper. He could be "pretty mean"; though he did not look for fights, he never permitted himself to be pushed around. Still, he would do almost anything for friends. He enjoyed barrelhousing and gained the reputation of a fancy dresser and playboy. In time, he became disenchanted with family rules and his stepfather. Believing that Albert Watson treated him differently from the other children, he left home at age seventeen to live in St. Louis with his uncle Caleb Woolfolk.[78]

That occurred in 1925, when Cleo was nine years old. Seven years after this he quit school, saying later that he had to work with Albert because of the Depression. Cleo also began dating, however; he developed a fondness for older women and thus needed additional income at a time when few males in his world valued schooling and when he sought more distance from his well-educated mother. Given his new-found independence, he chafed under her admonitions. Like Wiley, albeit for reasons of personal freedom more than of personal rejection, and probably because of Alonzo more than Albert, he left home; in 1934 he went to a Civilian Conservation Corps (CCC) Camp.[79]

Cleo came back, though, and for several weeks in the summer of 1935 found himself reunited with Wiley. His half-brother had returned a convicted felon. After living for a number of years in St. Louis, he had struck out for Detroit, where—in the depressed economy of September 1930—he broke into a store and served five years of a fifteen-year sentence before making parole.[80] Back in Gethsemane, Wiley related better than ever to Cleo, their respective ages of twenty-seven and nineteen enabling them to share experiences that had been impossible when Cleo was younger.

Having few choices, Wiley moved back into the Watson home. He came to an understanding with his compassionate stepfather and mother which, of course, required Wiley—an adult and a carouser—to live by the rules. The toughest was that anyone out after curfew stayed out until the next morning; hence, though he kept his clothes in the house, he came and went every two or three days in order to avoid a middle-of-the-night confrontation with his parents. "More or less freeloading," he still found time for Cleo. He also carried a gun and on one occasion drew it during an argument with his half-brother. Under these circumstances, Alonzo worried about her elder son's influence on the younger.[81]

It was likely through Wiley's experience that Cleo understood what home life held for him and decided to break away permanently. On September 3, 1935, he enlisted for four years in the U.S. Navy, specifying a desire to travel and begin a military career. Designated Mess Attendant 3d Class, he reported to the Naval Training Station at Norfolk, Virginia, and then the Naval Hospital at Portsmouth, Virginia. In mid-October he became ill and returned to Norfolk. There he slept on duty, refused to obey orders, and received "five days of solitary confinement on bread and water." Nevertheless, he completed his training in mid-December and reported to the USS *Wyoming*. Cleo's ordeal was not over, however: from February 7 to 9 he lost three days "on account of sickness due to [his] own misconduct"; on March 1 he disregarded orders and again dined on bread and water for three days; and immediately following that punishment he received an undesirable discharge for "reason of unfitness."[82] Ironically, he had discovered military rules to be as stifling as those of Alonzo and Albert. Rather than finding more liberation in the service, he found naval commanders who deemed him immature and dashed his dream.[83]

Cleo hardly noticed that his undesirable discharge was less serious than a dishonorable one, which would have required a general court-martial.[84] He wrongly believed himself to have been released without honor and in March 1936 cared only about returning to Arkansas. There he continued his quest for independence, choosing to live in Pine Bluff, where he found work as a truck driver. He visited his family on holidays but rarely stayed overnight—though he and Wiley, who still resided in the family home, spent time together despite their twenty-mile separation.[85]

Just as it appeared that Cleo might turn his life around, he found himself unemployed.[86] Increasingly, he visited with Wiley, and the two brothers, along with William Moorehead and Bob Johnson, robbed a store in Wabbaseka. Moorehead remained in the car while Cleo, Bob, and Wiley entered Beye's grocery in the late evening of May 9, 1937, and, without using force, took $80. Needing money but bearing no animus toward the Chinese proprietor, they held him up during store hours and without wearing masks. They proved themselves doubly foolish if they also believed that Beye's race would dissuade white authorities from hunting for them.[87]

Wiley was identified within days—possibly with planter assistance—and arrested the following Sunday at the Gethsemane Baptist Church. He told Altheimer and Pine Bluff lawmen where to find the loot, shocking Alonzo and Albert when a search revealed that hiding place to be their smokehouse! He astounded them even more by fingering Cleo as an accomplice. Why he named his half-brother but neither cousin Moorehead nor friend Johnson puzzled everyone in the family, particularly Alonzo, who experienced "a double force of grief."[88]

Indeed, Alonzo had suffered much in recent months. On January 29 she had lost sixteen-year-old Alice, named in honor of Albert's sister, to pneumonia (following an appendectomy). That bereavement, combined with the belief that Wiley dragged Cleo into the crime and then identified him for authorities, resulted in Alonzo's refusal to aid her eldest son. She had mortgaged the family homestead seven years earlier in a vain effort to prevent him from going to prison in Michigan. This time, with Albert's assistance, she concentrated on saving Cleo.[89]

On the evening of Wiley's apprehension, Albert and Alonzo's brother John Woolfolk visited Pine Bluff to warn Cleo—only to find themselves behind bars alongside Wiley, accused of assisting the younger thief to escape. Soon released, they returned to Gethsemane. Wiley pleaded guilty to highway robbery and, given his record and parole violation, drew a seven-year term at the Cumins State Farm in Gould.[90] He paid for the crime alone, never mentioning Moorehead or Johnson. Only Cleo felt "so hot" that he quick-stepped to Missouri.[91]

In Sikeston he began a new life as Cleo Wright (an alias to fool officials). His clumsy attempt to steal a pistol from the state police commander's car that September revealed the anxiety of a novice on the run. Twenty-one years old, unemployed, alone, and influenced by Wylie's gun-toting example, Cleo sought a weapon for protection and perhaps self-confidence. His awkward theft of the cash box came three months after his marriage to Ardella in February 1940, when he was jobless again and feeling greater responsibilities. Freed after six months, he lived an exemplary life for several months before suddenly becoming a monster.

Only Cleo's wife sensed radical change in his behavior, but without realizing its portent. Near the end of his parole, in December 1941 he began coming home in the wee small hours. He claimed to be frequenting pool halls, but she suspected him of running with women.[92] Equally revealing, in responding to the request "State any difficulties you face" in his final probation report that same month, Cleo pleaded: "Please at once, let me know what I'm suppose to do now. My time is up Jan. 3rd."[93] Plainly, he received no instructions, for his behavior became more unpredictable in the following weeks and included casing the white neighborhoods south of the oil mill. Finally, on Saturday, January 24, he left home in the afternoon, though his shift did not begin until 10:00 P.M. He appeared at Farmers Cafe that evening, reported for work on time, learned of his shift's cancellation, and disappeared for nearly three hours before striking the Sturgeon home. Cleo's aggression seemed impromptu and sober, yet it erupted from deep-seated frustration and escalating resentment that fostered a predilection, if not a precise date, for destruction.

Indeed, his savagery marked both transmogrification[94] and the abrupt end of a short-lived life in search of itself. His journey had taken him from rural Arkansas to small-town Missouri, through four distinct stages of development: country boy, struggling teenager, troubled youth, and desperate young adult. Shaped by the interaction—and inherent contradictions—of an achieving family and a limiting racial milieu, his situation ultimately proved unbearable. Unlike thousands of other young black males born into a southern society that denied their very manhood, he snapped under its weight.

From birth to age eighteen, Cleo experienced both idyllic and stressful circumstances. He enjoyed a close-knit, successful family—educated mother, religious father, loving siblings—and an equally cohesive black community.

Encouraged to succeed by parental example and conversation, he also faced house rules that every brother and sister deemed too rigid. Unlike James, the youngest male, whose quiet personality resembled that of his father, Cleo—like Wiley—challenged the strictures.[95] He rebelled against lessons that taught survival in a racist society and, in the process of building character and shaping citizenry, also stifled his humanity and—increasingly—his masculinity. Thus his defiance of rules, especially as a teenager, became an assertion of individualism and manhood. So did his reputation both as a fast ball pitcher and as someone never to cross, "an idealization of personal violence" that drew admiration in rural southern communities.[96] Perhaps his attraction to older women revealed further a desire for recognition as a mature male.

Joining the conservation corps and, more decisively, the navy, Cleo disclosed an even greater longing for freedom. He knew that remaining in Gethsemane meant stifling home rules, arduous work for room and board, and little opportunity for self-fulfillment.[97] Possibly inspired by Wiley's example, he left home, only to discover in military life—as Wiley had in Michigan—more intolerable and depersonalized conditions; his misconduct brought familiar punishment from offended superiors.

Cleo returned to Arkansas in 1936, still determined to succeed on his terms. He ran with Wiley but pursued his own dream, only to have it dashed by unemployment. In the face of this final setback, brought on by a depressed economy that dogged the crucial decade of his coming of age, he crossed—for the first time—the legal line and joined Wiley in highway robbery. He succumbed to his devotion to Wiley, whom Alonzo judged the "rotten apple."[98] Cleo certainly looked up to his half-brother: the older, self-assured, gun-carrying, sharp-dressing lady's man who openly defied parents and authorities and, even though jobless, steadfastly refused to work the family farm. As his own world collapsed, Cleo embraced Wiley's deviance. More than younger brother having been led astray by older brother, however, they shared very similar responses to their very similar upbringing: namely, rebellion against the peasant life expected of them and the struggle for manhood in a restrictive home and society. As their experiences intersected in the spring of 1937, Cleo saw himself in Wiley—in part because his urban environment accelerated changes in his self-perception and his expectation for race relations. Unable to reconcile with either the world of his parents or the wider one of Pine Bluff, he reverted once again to disobedience. In this context, he joined Wiley to steal from the Chinese merchant.[99]

Cleo's experiences, like Wiley's, signaled more than insolence and, in

Sikeston's urbanlike if not urbanized setting, became full-blown defiance.
Beyond the problems at home, he battled racism. While his naval record fails
to specify what orders he disobeyed or whether his actions were a response
to race-baiting officers, as was likely then, Cleo's thefts in the Bootheel did
bear racial connotations. He endeavored to pilfer the highway patrol
commander's pistol and money from the employer who laid him off, risky
expressions of resentment and revenge toward white authority. More point-
edly, shortly before his assault on Sturgeon, he had indicated preferring arrest "by a colored officer" rather than a white lawman. That he never had
been known to challenge the caste system while in Arkansas accentuated the
significance of his evolving racial animus.[100]

Even more provocative, between criminal acts he struck at the caste
system's core in 1939 by establishing a sexual relationship—the greatest of
taboos—with a white woman. Again, he acted "out of character" and broke
with his past.[101] In Arkansas, he had dated black females and "never went to
the other side of the fence"; he knew well that a black man caught with a
white paramour "wouldn't have the chance of a rabbit."[102] That he gambled
with his life in such a liaison signified, like his escalating theft of white property, movement through a range of emotions—rage, anger, and hatred—toward hostile and violent behavior.[103]

On the eve of his attack on Grace Sturgeon, Cleo stood teetering between southern traditions that pitted—especially for men—servility against
antisocial behavior.[104] Thus far, like all black males, he had experienced in-
consistencies in parental teachings: love that fostered obedience and crushed
"aggressive styles" in a white world; ambition that limited success according to white proscription; caution that engendered fear of but dependency
on white people.[105] Hence, for most of his life Cleo had worn a mask of deception, which slipped—for example, in the navy—when its slavishness became too heavy. Always in the past he had reassumed the masquerade, most
successfully in Sikeston where neither blacks nor whites sensed his bitterness; always in the past he had begun anew the struggle to step out of his
assigned "place" and find himself. Suddenly, in December of 1941, he realized that whites, whether in Gethsemane or Sikeston, would never permit
him to be human "except in rejection, rebellion, and aggression."[106]

Cleo's mask became oppressive as the self-hatred inherent in a life of
subservience finally overwhelmed his drive for manhood. His forced migration and repeated jail terms subverted his efforts to succeed: instant flight
delivered him from the clutches of Arkansas lawmen but consigned him to
racial restrictions, marginal economics, and personal limitations in Sikeston;

county and state prison terms forced him to focus on his immediate misfortunes and bleak future in Missouri.[107] Married to young Ardella, about to become a father, and working long hours at the oil mill, he was an ex-convict living close to in-laws and in a segregated society. He wanted much more at the very moment that his obligations became most weighty and his status most devalued. If shame involves a sense of failure and loneliness, he expressed both, simultaneously seeking directions from the parole board and distance from Ardella.[108] By entering Sturgeon's home, Cleo as much as admitted failure.

Cleo's sister Linetta suspected that he smarted at failing to live up to the standards set for him by Alonzo and, less assuredly, Albert.[109] He identified more with his mother, who with her "desperate love" of rules and corporal punishment—like devoted black mothers before and after her—sought to prepare him for survival.[110] He knew, too, that Alonzo's life "set the emotional tone" for his own life, again much as the lives of her counterparts had done for other sons throughout the South.[111] Perhaps for these reasons, he joined Alonzo's church and seriously considered marrying someone like her: a woman older than himself who taught school at Gilliand.[112] In time, Alonzo's domineering personality and Albert's powerless presence, both as a father and as a black man, combined to chase Wiley out of the home and drive Cleo to Wiley as his model. Concurrently, he tried to deliver on his mother's teachings and his own freedom, only to be frustrated by personal immaturity in the navy and economic depression in Pine Bluff.

On the run in Sikeston, he kept in touch with Alonzo and continued to find strength in their mutual "truly worthwhile acts." He attended the funeral of her mother, Grandma Lucy Woolfolk, during the winter of 1938 and returned the following summer with Ardella. In turn, Alonzo visited him in 1941, and between these reunions they exchanged letters; she also corresponded with his bride and mother-in-law.[113] Even after landing in the penitentiary, Cleo articulated his mother's lifelong influence, desiring further education and impressing officials; he wanted to complete high school and projected a cooperative attitude, some initiative, and "fair" morals.[114] A year and a half before turning from thief to assailant, he still dreamed of personal deliverance from a demanding family and a bigoted society.

Cleo's aspirations clashed not only with his upbringing but with unending race barriers. Given his earlier failures and the botched robbery that resulted in Wiley's incarceration, he had arrived in Sikeston with "some realistic paranoia." His bitterness grew in the face of hard times, further law-breaking, and prison sentences; though he never manifested psychopathic symptoms, living in an urban environment accentuated his anomie, loneliness, and racial conflict. Of normal intelligence, he struggled with self-image and societal strictures yet remained fairly stable until the very end.[115] Then he exploded in an act of violence, stemming from his personal failure in a racist system, which for a moment probably seemed "psychologically liberating" and physically empowering.[116] At that instant his life changed drastically.

So did that of Grace Sturgeon. Born twenty-nine years earlier on September 25, 1912, in Marston, Missouri, the daughter of Golda Jane Haynes and Charles Franklin Skalsky, she had grown up in New Madrid County with brothers Harold and Orville and sister Millie. Her mother came from Rector, Arkansas, and her father from Daviess County, Kentucky, respectively from Irish-Indian Kentuckians and German Jewish immigrants. Her father farmed 280 rented acres of land; he employed two hired hands in the summer and several pickers in the fall. Family members pitched in to raise "a yard full of chickens, hogs, geese, ducks, and turkeys"; they killed their own meat, grew their own vegetables, and enjoyed "plenty to eat" but made little money.[117]

Raised by poorly educated but "loving parents," Grace received both secular and religious teaching. She attended schools at Conran, Kewanee, and Matthews, completing the eleventh grade, as did her sister; her brothers advanced through ninth grade. She had embraced her mother's and father's Baptist faith yet worshiped at the Methodist Church, the only available meeting house in the neighborhood. There she participated in church socials but also enjoyed hearing the music and watching couples dance at "play parties."

Grace too learned about race. Living in the upper Bootheel, which experienced fierce economic competition along racial lines in Marston and a lynching in New Madrid at the beginning of the twentieth century, she came of age in a rural society characterized by white paternalism and black subservience.[118] She noticed little outward tension, recalling that a nearly blind black man sometimes worked for her father, at the same dollar-a-day wage paid white laborers, and played the piano at white dances; he was one of the few blacks residing in the area. Whether permanent or transient, the children of black parents attended a segregated school. Grace knew, moreover, that those who came in for the harvest were known as "cotton picking niggers," reputed to be lazy, guileful, and in need of a firm hand.

Perhaps in part because of these racial attitudes, Grace considered herself less than handsome. Though no one ever cast aspersions on her appearance, which was, in fact, appealing, she was conscious of her coal black hair, brown eyes, and especially dark complexion. As a very young child she mourned the equally dark-headed youngest sister who had died in infancy; she had named Carletta Marie and admired her light skin. Similarly, she thought Millie better looking than herself despite the freckles that accompanied her red hair and, most favorably, fair coloring.[119]

In addition to an aversion to black people, Grace learned about sex. Her mother warned that men, especially those with "slick tongues," were capable of getting young girls in trouble. Given the racial order and its open condemnation of miscegenation, these maternal cautions, surprisingly, transmitted no special fears about black males, though Grace, of course, comprehended the supremacist credo that white teenagers like herself should never "get connected" with black men. Nor did she receive explicit lessons about intercourse and pregnancy. Shooed from overhearing female gossip and from observing barnyard births, she nevertheless understood the concern about rape. She took her mother's frequent admonition "Watch your corners!" to mean that "there could be harm."

In 1929 Grace carried these beliefs into Sikeston when, forced to leave the farm because her father became ill, the family moved to Ruth Street. She matured quickly as the oldest sibling at sixteen and, along with her sister, found employment at the International Shoe Company doing piecework for Depression wages. While they contributed much-needed income to the family, their mother cared for her school-age sons and declining husband. After Grace's father died at the age of fifty-three in 1932, the Skalsky family remained a close-knit one.

In the early 1930s Grace accompanied her recently converted mother to the Church of God of Prophecy, where she met J. Dillard Sturgeon. She married him in 1932, moved to 847 Kathleen Avenue, and in 1933 converted to Prophecy and gave birth to James Dillard. She named Jimmy after his twenty-three-year-old father, the son of Roberta Waters and Simeon Sturgeon, who had grown up in Sikeston with siblings John, Charles, Ralph, Donald, Nina, and Fannie May. Grace must have seen in Dillard qualities that she possessed, those of a quiet, gentle person. She admired most his deep religiosity and scriptural knowledge, which he expressed easily as a result of having completed the eighth grade in Sikeston and attended Bible school in St. Louis; perhaps, too, she related to his being the grandson of a Baptist minister. Grace in turn touched the core of Dillard, who described their relationship as "a lifelong romance." When she met him, however, he was recuperating from a traffic accident that ended his bible studies, boxing career,

Jimmy, J. Dillard, and Grace Sturgeon in 1942. Courtesy of Michael L. Jensen.

and truck-driving job. Thereafter, he found work with the Scott County Milling Company, Works Progress Administration, and finally the local armory.[120]

Sturgeon's affiliation with Company K aided him in becoming caretaker of the drill center, located on U.S. 61 between Matthews and Kathleen, within three blocks of his home. There, during the last days of the Depression, he taught Jimmy to clean rifles or gave him the run of the building. He also trained older boys for Golden Gloves competition, empathizing with those who shared his religious beliefs or impoverished upbringing. And despite the segregation of Sikeston, he permitted Jimmy to converse with black sharecropper children living in the fields below Kathleen Avenue.

Having risen to the rank of supply sergeant, which resulted in everyone calling him "Sarge," Dillard also personified Company K. Assigned to Camp Robinson, Arkansas, in early 1941, he served as personal adviser to several guardsmen and informal spokesperson for their unit. He assisted younger enlistees—sometimes as outright ghostwriter—with family letters or newspaper stories, and became popular as secretary of the regimental chapel and one of five of its choir members from Company K.[121] Predictably, when Japan bombed Pearl Harbor, family members and friends called Grace for information about the future of their loved ones; they trusted Sarge's interpretation of events more than that of their own men. Before the "day of infamy," however, Grace and Jimmy stayed in contact with Dillard. They journeyed to Little Rock six or seven times throughout the year—as often as possible given the family's limited income— riding the bus or traveling with the sisters of other guardsmen. Dillard wrote letters, called periodically, and visited when he could; at home he assisted Grace and "rolled all over the yard" with Jimmy. On the afternoon of December 7 he called, finally getting through telephone lines abuzz with anxious conversations and verifying Company K's orders to depart almost immediately for the West Coast: Bakersfield, California.

Grace adjusted to wartime sacrifices in Sikeston, believing that she and Jimmy could survive. Their situation eased in early 1942 when Laverne Sturgeon, wife of Sarge's brother John, moved into the Kathleen Avenue home. During the previous year she had met John at the Second Baptist Church in Little Rock while he too served with Company K at Camp Robinson and married him after he transferred to the U.S. Army Air Corps at St. Louis. Laverne accompanied John to Scott Field in Bellville, Illinois, but they soon found themselves separated by the events at Pearl Harbor; he reported to Savannah, Georgia, and she stayed for a time with his parents at their farm near Blodgett, Missouri.[122] Not liking it there, Laverne found a job in Sikeston and arranged to live with her sister-in-law.[123]

Although younger than Grace by six and a half years, Laverne also came from a rural background. She had lived on a farm near Prescott, in southwest Arkansas, with two sisters and their father and mother, James Blant Willson and Minnie Baker. She never knew her mother well; Minnie was a victim of stomach cancer very early in Laverne's life. Soon she found herself being raised by James's second wife in Hope. She came to love Alice Ward and adapted easily to life in the small town, where her father operated a furniture business and farmed in the area. Raised a Baptist in "a very strict home, a very good home," she graduated from high school and beauty school in Little Rock.[124]

Having left the Prescott farm at age seven, Laverne nevertheless absorbed the racial beliefs of her father and mother, as well as her stepmother, whose parents had owned slaves. She recalled a segregated, personable society of landowning whites like her father—an Arkansas native—and sharecropping blacks; she spoke with black "old ladies" and experienced neither fear nor tension. Even as a small child, however, she was "not close" to black children and recalled no interracial activities other than sitting together at revivals. In time, she learned the paramount taboo against dating across the color

Laverne Sturgeon in 1942.
Courtesy of Michael L. Jensen.

line. Though not given to derogatory language like "nigger," she wanted noth-ing to do with blacks.

Laverne's sister-in-law's house in Sikeston was located on the far east side. A small frame dwelling—kitchen and dining room in the back, bed-room and living room facing the street—with one rear door and two front entrances that opened onto a porch, 847 Kathleen anchored the southwest corner of that unlit road and Pine Street, which ran north for a quarter-mile to intersect with U.S. 60 directly across from the Sikeston Cotton Oil Mill. It was within walking distance of the armory, due west, and a quarter-mile from Grace's and Laverne's jobs on Greer Avenue, two blocks north. Though in a sparsely settled area, the Sturgeon house occupied the same side of the street as the Whittleys', separated only by a vacant lot. It faced the home of Grace's grandmother, cater-corner across the street, and lay one block south of her own mother's place on Matthews Avenue. Out back, beyond a hand-ful of homes on Gladys Avenue, stretched farmland occupied by black share-croppers, while east, across Pine, there was pasture.[125]

Isolation characterized wartime life for everyone in Sikeston, including the Sturgeons, who worked long hours and rarely socialized. They rose early, Grace getting Jimmy ready for school and herself off to work by 7:00 A.M.,

leaving him at her grandmother's until classes began, and returning to collect him sometime after 5:30 P.M.; Laverne opened the Powder Puff Beauty
Shop an hour later in the morning but stayed until eight o'clock for evening
customers. Both women worked more than five days a week and generally
walked to and from their jobs, though Laverne took a cab during inclement
weather. While Grace awaited Laverne's arrival in the evening, she washed
and hung out clothes, or ironed them. Grace attended church services on
Wednesday night and sometimes worked half-days on Saturday, but only
Sunday provided a day of rest and family get-together: morning worship,
midday dinner, afternoon leisure, evening rest.[126]

January 24 began as a routine Saturday. After breakfast, Grace left Jimmy
with her grandmother and went to the shoe factory until 11:00 A.M. Back at
home, she ate a light lunch and cleaned house, scrubbing the front porch as
the last chore on a pretty, sunny, unusually warm day. She visited with her
mother and an aunt from Michigan, remembering the day as the eve of the
tenth anniversary of her father's death. After they left, Grace prepared sup-
per and waited for Laverne, who was working a full shift that day. Later she
helped Jimmy with a lesson, took a bath, and wrote to Dillard, while Laverne
turned in early. By 10:30 P.M., everyone was under the covers and soon "sound
asleep."

Grace awoke to the noise of someone tampering with the back door and,
thirty minutes later, to the sound of the intruder raising her bedroom window. Everything imploded: he entered, cursed, slashed, and retreated; Grace
bled all over her house and her porch, cleaned so immaculately a few hours
hours earlier; Laverne ran through the rooms, screamed into the phone, and
scurried across the street; Jimmy awoke, was riveted to his cot by fright, and
then brought to life by the sight of his wounded mother. Mercifully, the violence ended almost as quickly as it had begun, and later that morning Grace's
blood and Jimmy's footprints through it also disappeared under the scrub
brushes of several neighbors.[127] But their trauma and Laverne's remained
forever, periodically brought forth by images and sounds of what many believed had begun as an attempted rape.

In fact, Cleo Wright fit many characteristics of most modern sexual assailants: attractive, young, married, of average intelligence, respected by
neighbors (and prominent whites); he also possessed a criminal record,
seemed insecure during the weeks before the assault, acted on a weekend,
and, significantly, planned his moves in advance.[128]

Several incidents shortly before the assault led the Sturgeons, their neighbors, and lawmen to conclude that Cleo had been watching the house "for

some time."[129] One woman had seen a black man run across her yard; another reported having been grabbed by a black man near her outhouse; others purportedly observed him in several different places; and Assistant Police Chief Wallace announced that Cleo's footprints indicated he had prowled the vicinity. Despite the absence of positive identification, few now doubted that "the Negro" in every instance was Cleo.[130]

Certainly Grace and Laverne later believed that Cleo had tried more than once to enter their home. The Thursday evening before his breakin, the rear screen door had slammed shut, and the next day Laverne found "big footprints out back." Though Grace initially thought that a dog had run against the door, Laverne considered loading a shotgun for protection, but she dismissed the idea for fear Jimmy and his friends would hurt themselves. And of course, on the night of the assault, Grace heard noises at the back door thirty minutes before Cleo appeared in the bedroom window.[131]

In all probability, Cleo somehow came into contact with Grace or Laverne and followed her home. Each woman denied ever having met him, but Grace recalled three black males, middle-aged and younger, who walked down her street in the early mornings and late afternoons, presumably to and from the oil mill—though this seemed far afield for Cleo's normal route to work. Grace suggested, too, that perhaps he had seen Laverne in the beauty shop, one block south of Malone Avenue, which he did travel to work.[132]

Laverne believed that Cleo found Grace "all by herself" in the late afternoons and spied on her from the back lot.[133] But Grace remembered that about a week before the attack Laverne thought she had been followed two or three times through the armory park. One wintry night she heard somebody behind her and "tried to run." She never saw anyone, male or female, black or white, but neighbor Glenda Whittley agreed that "that's who the man was after": Laverne's late working hours and solitary walks home had caught Cleo's eye.[134]

In this way, like later rapists, Cleo apparently mustered courage for his plan to attack. More than simply having watched the Sturgeon home, he seems to have stalked Laverne and approached her home more than once; doing so with impunity bolstered his confidence, and—assuming he was the neighborhood prowler—he emboldened himself further by sneaking about houses, running across back yards, and laying a hand on the woman next door. That he acted alone, again like most later rapists, required several preparatory acts of bravado.[135]

If Cleo was seeking Laverne, his plan went awry in the face of Grace's unexpected presence. Unlike most adult rapists, he confronted her without having imbibed much, if any, alcohol and with a weapon common to younger assailants.[136] He unleashed a barrage of threats and obscenities designed to control and demean Grace: the "verbal strategies" of all rapists. Entering, he said that he intended to kill and, upon seeing Laverne and Grace, expressed utter surprise: "There are two of you son-of-a-bitches!"[137] He continued to curse as Grace absorbed his physical charge and turned his psychological abuse to her advantage, repeating to herself, mantralike, that he would not kill her. Cleo probably felt betrayed, having so completely misread his prey, and certainly felt trapped in the grasp of Grace, who held onto her life; he fought savagely until a car backfire sent him scurrying. Though lacking the history of violence that characterizes most rapists, his street brawls, his reputation as a punishing opponent, and his search for manhood prepared him for this very moment when the drawing of blood came easily.

What began as an attempted rape escalated to assault but fell just short of murder. Cleo did not evince the characteristics of a sex killer: one who chokes his victim, engages in sadism, and suffers from sexual dysfunction. He chose a stranger rather than an acquaintance to attack, as rapists and sex killers often do, but nothing indicated an original desire on his part to slay; indeed, he flashed his knife only after entering the house. Even then, Cleo's repeated death threats came forth as predictable terrorist chatter rather than final sentence—at least until Grace repulsed his initial assault. Within hours of his having slashed her and Perrigan, he revealed an intention short of taking life; entering the hospital for first aid, he exclaimed (or so Grace contended years later): "Oh God, I did not mean to kill them!"[138] That Cleo blamed his actions on alcohol disclosed further the alibi of a rapist rather than a rape murderer.[139]

Like that of most historical figures, Cleo's motivation can be analyzed only through his behavior. His response to racist barriers and personal difficulties revealed contradictions that were both independent of and linked to one another; they reached back to slavery and, like more acceptable forms of accommodation and resistance, "arose within a complex psychological framework."[140] Struggling in a one-sided relationship that accentuated white power, fostered black resentment, and ultimately confirmed his own failure, Cleo evolved from aspiring black youth to "bad nigger" and turned his nihilistic rage on Grace.[141]

Initially, Cleo's resentment manifested itself in the seduction of white women. His love affair with a Sikeston woman in 1939 corresponded with his nonviolent, masked personality. His alleged rape of the St. Louis teenager a couple of years later, true or not, would have been consistent with the shift toward the greater fury and consequent risk-taking that drove him to steal from a former employer. After his stay in prison, his repressed impulses broke through. He became more angry and intrepid; his attack on Grace completed the emotional journey of endeavoring to be a black man in a white society by violating one of its women. Cleo advanced from taking property to figuratively stealing the one human object that every southern male had been taught to place on a pedestal.[142]

Surely Cleo's genuine relationship with a Sikeston housewife and assault on Grace indicated the intensity of that idealization. He, like most black males, confronted the greatest contradiction in black-white relations: the double standard that idealized white women and placed them beyond reach of black men while permitting white men the pick of all females.[143] He, like some black males, ascribed to white women a mystique and found them—without doubt because of the taboo—"intensely exciting" sexually.[144] He, like very few black males, crossed from a loving relationship—in which he sought verification of his self-worth (perhaps even prideful conquest)—to a vicious attack upon the white goddess.[145] Thus, on leaving Farmers Cafe, Cleo was said to have boasted that "he was going to get himself a white woman that night."[146]

Cleo struck where he could hurt white men the most. Like that of black males historically, his aggression, however deviant, stemmed in part from social injustice and evidenced racial protest. And had he not been captured, his payback could very possibly have escalated from rape to sex killing.[147] His nuclear family, rural upbringing, and small-town living, however, hardly resembled the urban ghetto experience of oppressed males in more recent times, with its increasing socialization toward violence.[148] Neither normal nor heroic, Cleo's aberrant behavior should not be stereotyped as representative of all black men or dismissed as the fanatical exception of a few. Shaped by variants of racism, it demonstrated anew that viewing women as objects "fueled racial hostility."[149]

Cleo's violence occurred in a gender context, yet one never completely free of racist intrusion. His assault on Grace targeted women generally, combining the characteristics of a power rapist who engages in sexual conquest as compensation for "feelings of inadequacy" and (much less) of a sadistic rapist (without the ritualistic cruelty) who seeks revenge by punishing a random female. Thus he planned his attack in advance, selected his victim according to her vulnerability, even stalked her, and used force readily. He also displayed some traits of an anger rapist, who retaliates for imagined wrongs, especially those by women, and expresses his fury physically and verbally.[150] Although it is difficult to type a rapist who failed, Cleo reacted brutally to Grace's resistance—as anger and sadistic rapists would do—when he may in fact have intended a sexual conquest. His declaration in the cafe that night implied as much, and his actions to the point of encountering his victim fit those of a power rapist—the largest proportion of modern offenders—in search of his manhood. Whatever his type, Cleo's actions, like those of all rapists, were triggered by "unresolved conflict." Coming off parole, he seemed purposeless and emotionally spent—"except for anger."

In fact, the source of Cleo's anger most likely included his parents and, quite possibly, his wife and in-laws. He chafed under the dominant, over-protective, sometimes punitive Alonzo and the aloof, largely uninvolved Albert—though the former never appeared seductive, and neither seemed cruel.[151] He was estranged from Ardella, who accused him of infidelity, probably argued with him, and definitely "did not want him" in his wounded condition. Her pregnancy and fear accounted for this behavior, but so must have the influence of Minnie Gay, who believed "he would die any minute," and Richard Gay, who did not want to "stand the expense of burying him."[152] Whether or not Ardella hurled racial epithets at Cleo during arguments, thereby reinforcing his self-hatred, her (and her parents') rejection of him in life and in death indicated limitations in their relationship. At critical times in his life, then, he perceived the love of his parents, wife, and in-laws as conditional. Just as racism molded the manner in which he was raised, it also affected the nature of his marriage. Nevertheless, he attacked a white, not a black woman, revealing the depths of both his own racial animosity and his tie to Alonzo; he could not strike his mother or a symbol of her, even in rage.[153]

Most provocative, Cleo's origins posed another possible explanation for his rampage. Born Ricelor Cleodas Watson on June 16, 1916, he changed his name in 1937 in order to evade the law after robbing the Chinese grocer. He abbreviated his middle name and combined it with a supposedly ficti-tious surname, which may have been that of his natural father: "Henry Wright of Pine Bluff."[154] Learning this name from Ardella, federal prosecu-tors hoped to present the elder Wright's testimony before the St. Louis grand jury and sent FBI agents in Arkansas to search for him. They followed nu-merous clues, including the names of Henry Wright, Henry Watson, Cleo Wright, R.C. Watson, and A.L. Watson. They combed Pine Bluff, Varner, and

Gould, where they found a postal clerk who recalled handling mail for Henry Wright and Cleo Wright, but that lead petered out. Finally, through the Jefferson County jail records of Wiley's conviction for the Beye robbery, they located Albert Leak Watson.[155]

In Gethsemane, Albert told FBI investigators that his wife, the mother of Cleo Wright, had been married to Henry Wright. His testimony was verified by Alonzo, who elaborated that she had been separated from Cleo's father twenty-two years earlier when he lived in Mississippi. She never heard of his having visited Sikeston; neither Ardella nor Minnie Gay had mentioned him in their letters. And, with that, bureau officials ended their search, unaware of the possibility of Cleo's illegitimacy or the implications that it bore for the attack on Grace.

Why Albert would deny being the father of Ricelor Cleodas, and why Alonzo would verify that denial is baffling. Perhaps he preferred to avoid the agony and embarrassment of traveling numerous miles to bear witness in an investigation of his son's horrific death. An intensely private, quiet man, he farmed, attended church, and went into town "if he had to" but rarely anywhere else; he had never visited or written Cleo. Possibly because of pride and religious belief, Albert felt disgraced by his son's reputation as a rapist; ironically, he and Alonzo believed Ricelor guilty as either the spurned lover or sexual assailant of a white woman. Said Alonzo: "When you do wrong, wrong will come to you." Together, they kept Ricelor's death from most of their relatives and neighbors, and forbade their other children to discuss it.[156]

Nevertheless, if Ricelor was their first-born, Albert's rejection seems incomprehensible. He had warned Ricelor when police sought him in the Beye robbery. Hiding Ricelor's identity made sense then, and ignoring him in Sikeston—except through Alonzo—seems in keeping with Albert's self-possession, but cold-hearted in the face of a son's lynching. For a father who treated Ricelor as his own and exhibited little strain in their relationship, he reacted to him in death more as he had responded to stepson Wiley in life: when Wiley landed in jail, Albert expressed most concern for Alonzo; when Ricelor died, he again concentrated on her. Neither Albert nor Alonzo ever inquired as to Ricelor's cemetery plot, believing that nothing remained of his burned corpse or, like his own wife and in-laws, that burying his memory proved more necessary.

Albert's unfatherly response to Ricelor's killing could be explained by the youth's having been someone else's son. If so, it meant that Alonzo had an affair and gave birth to Ricelor while married to Albert. Worse yet, if accurate, her statement to the FBI indicated that she had separated from her lover, Henry Wright, in 1920, four years after Ricelor's birth and ten years into her marriage to Albert—in other words, that she and Henry Wright had shared their attraction for a very long time. Whatever the nature of their relationship, at least one neighbor claimed years later to have heard a rumor among blacks in the area that Ricelor was the child of Alonzo and an unnamed fieldhand who lived behind the Watsons and worked land owned by "ole man McDonald of Altheimer." And Ricelor's very dark complexion was said to resemble that of his natural father; Albert was much lighter and possessed straight hair.[157]

In direct contradiction, Ricelor's surviving sister and their mutual friends remembered no such scandal. Linetta recalled that Albert treated Ricelor "like he was his father," no differently from any other child in the family. She knew of relatives in the area named Wright, most notably Willie Wright, husband of Alonzo's cousin Lucandia, and his brother Milton Wright, but no Henry.[158] Nor had John Henry Rasberry, backyard neighbor and grandson of Alonzo's first husband, ever heard gossip that Ricelor belonged to anyone other than Albert; he considered impossible the idea that Alonzo had run around, for the Watsons seemed a loving, reputable couple. Others from Gethsemane and Wabbaseka, themselves unrelated to either Alonzo or Albert, echoed these opinions.[159]

Ricelor himself confounded the issue. When he enlisted in the Navy on September 3, 1935, he named Albert Watson as his father and next of kin, yet five years later in prison he identified his father as one "George Wright," who had died in 1919 at the age of forty-seven; he referred to Albert Watson as his stepfather.[160] Between these revelations, Ricelor married Ardella and told her and her parents that his father was "Henry Wright": hence the FBI inquiry.

George or Henry notwithstanding, Ricelor's father seems to have been Albert Watson. Though Alonzo filed no birth certificate for Ricelor Cleodas Watson, Cleo Wright, or any combination of those names in either Arkansas or Mississippi, that oversight was hardly unusual for the period or for rural births attended by midwives; in fact, she officially recorded the birth only of her youngest child, Linetta, which occurred nine years later.[161] And, significantly, no marriage or divorce records for Alonzo Watson and either Henry or George Wright were recorded in the Jefferson County Courthouse from 1906 to 1920, years during which George Wright supposedly died or Henry Wright presumably separated from Alonzo; only her marriage to Albert Watson was registered officially. Clearly, the story of George or Henry

Wright having been the husband of Alonzo was a hoax; if either had fathered Ricelor, he was illegitimate.[162]

That legal issue aside, the paternity of Henry or George Wright still appeared suspect. No concrete description exists for the very black-complexioned, younger, transient fieldhand who worked back of the Watson property but did not stay very long (as Alonzo suggested of Cleo's father), and who appears incongruous with his rival. And the only George Wright in the area was dark brown, much smaller, and much older at the time of Ricelor's birth. He had entered the Gethsemane area at age four with his parents in 1871 and remained a member of its community for the rest of his life, but he was known neither as having toiled behind Alonzo's homestead nor as someone whom Ricelor resembled facially and physically—height, weight, build—save for skin color. Moreover, he came from Georgia, not Mississippi (as Alonzo implied of Cleo's father). Remembered as a hard-working, law-abiding man, though one who stayed clear of church, George enjoyed whiskey, tobacco, and female companionship; still, this diminutive 5'3", forty-nine-year-old commoner, taught by his father always to be "obedient," hardly seemed a likely paramour for the younger, dignified, class-conscious Alonzo.[163]

Moreover, the Watson neighbor who reinforced the allegation of Ricelor's illegitimacy said that the rumor about the fieldhand had been launched *after* the lynching, and he described it in racist terms: "Niggers told me he looked like his daddy . . . just as black as tar."[164] Less self-serving and more believable, Ricelor's sister and some of the family's friends doubted the charge but did not dismiss it out of hand. Linetta confided, "All I can say is I don't know and I never heard of it."[165]

Most telling, the chronology and content of Ricelor's and Alonzo's testimony smacked of a poorly rehearsed alibi. Ricelor never claimed anyone other than Albert as his father until after he fled from Pine Bluff and changed his name. From then on, he and Wiley protected one another, Wiley not listing him on his own prison survey that year and Ricelor returning the favor three years later: he acknowledged an unnamed half-brother but lied about his record.[166] Ricelor's telling those same officials that his father was George Wright—not the Henry Wright that he had earlier identified to Ardella and that Alonzo later confirmed to FBI agents—disclosed either an error made by the prison interviewer or evidence of his bogus story. The latter seems very obvious: he claimed that his father, George Wright, died in 1919 when he, Ricelor, "was an infant and his mother remarried," whereas Alonzo contended that his father, Henry Wright, separated from her in 1920 and implied that he was still alive in 1942. Moreover, Ricelor fused parts of Wiley's experience with his own, telling the interrogator that his early home life had been "somewhat broken" because of his natural father's death but that his growing up with a stepfather had been as pleasant as the "lack of financial means would allow."[167] Essentially, Ricelor and Alonzo told variations of the same tale, a cover for his transgression in Arkansas, which one or both of them confused for lack of use.

As revealing, Ricelor misspelled his alias in the 1939 letter to his white lover, identifying himself as "CLEO WRITE [while] there in Sikeston." Spelling the surname phonetically exhibited his limited education; he appears to have corrected his error only after having been incarcerated in Missouri, possibly as a result of observing its spelling by prison officials. And, consistent with a person of legitimate birth, he signed the love letter "R.C. Watson," thereby disclosing—at considerable risk—his true identity: wanting the woman he adored to know him for who he really was, as do many people who believe themselves in love.[168]

It was probably Alonzo rather than Ricelor, just shy of twenty-one and still very much influenced by her when he fled Pine Bluff, who concocted the fable of his father. That she repeated the lie after her son's death exposed the depths of her grief and embarrassment rather than callousness. And Albert, given his own shame and sorrow, played along with the fiction, though he must have found this issue very unsettling, coming nearly six months after Ricelor's death. And as one who lived rigidly within the dictates of white society, Albert also had reason to fear for himself outside of Gethsemane: facing white prosecutors, lynchers, policemen, and journalists miles away would have been a terrifying prospect.

In part, Albert consented to Alonzo's deception because he *was* Ricelor's father. He treated Ricelor like James, his other son, but very differently from Wiley, even though both older boys shared their mother's personality and looks rather than his own. He recruited Alonzo's brother John, in a classic example of extended family support, to warn Ricelor that Wiley had identified him in the Chinese merchant theft; he never assisted Wiley in a comparable way during his troubled youth. His perennial conflict with Wiley, a stepson, suggests that neither his love for Alonzo nor his religious faith would have been enough for him to accept an illegitimate son for twenty years. Perhaps most telling, Albert consented to plans for Ricelor to receive a portion of the family's property on an equal basis with his siblings.[169]

Ricelor himself acted like a natural son long after having appropriated a bogus surname. That he took the alias from Alonzo's side of the family hardly seemed in keeping with some sudden realization of having been illegitimate and his mother promiscuous; rather, that he selected a sobriquet protective of Albert and the family's identity suggests the act of a loyal son and a calculating mother. Thereafter, he visited his parents twice, played host to Alonzo once in Sikeston, and corresponded with her. Ricelor's family relationships appeared much as they had before 1937: he was somewhat distant with Albert, very close to Alonzo, and seemingly free of the pain or resentment of a bastard child.

Alonzo suffered pangs of conscience over Ricelor's death and sought vindication. She met her brother Caleb in St. Louis, contacted the NAACP, and considered filing a lawsuit against the police and City of Sikeston. She never pressed the issue, however, wanting neither a "blood money" settlement nor, most disgraceful, further publicity about the rape charge against him and the manner in which he died. Having always taken care of the family business, Alonzo managed the death of her son with little demur from Albert.[170]

Tragically and unintentionally, she contributed to Ricelor's undoing. Inspiring and loving yet hard-nosed and rigid, Alonzo argued with her children, tore them up when they did something wrong, and monitored their futures, for example, permitting Ricelor to enlist in the CCC. She stressed propriety and respectability, urging her offspring to make something of themselves, yet she could not parry—much less fully understand— the pressures of racism that so truncated the manhood of Wiley and Ricelor. In the family matrix of Albert's weakness and Wiley's defiance, Alonzo proved most influential in the life of Ricelor; consequently, when he failed to reach the status that she imagined for him and that he strove for, he held her responsible. Yet though she failed with Wiley and Ricelor, she succeeded with James and Linetta, whose honest, industrious lives disclosed that more than his upbringing led to Ricelor's fatal rage.[171]

Had Ricelor actually been illegitimate, he might have fled home for that reason and, for psychological comfort, invented a natural father who departed honorably. But in fact he left Arkansas because of the Wabbaseka incident and created an imaginary past in order to dodge the law. He came to emulate Wiley, ignore Albert, and resent Alonzo, who centered his life and— along with white society—came to seem the cause of his emasculation which, in turn, fostered resentment of all women. As a young man he neither talked back to his mother nor treated women roughly, acting the "pussy cat" around them while being "high-tempered" with men. In the most revealing and demonstrable of acts, he overturned that chivalry and refocused his deep-seated outrage on the morning of January 25.[172]

Like all rapists, Ricelor directed his hostility toward one female, Grace Sturgeon, though both she and Laverne Sturgeon became his victims. Grace fit many of the characteristics of modern rape victims: she was the approximate age and from the approximate class of her assailant, and smaller in size than he. Like them also, Grace never considered the aggression a sexual act; rather, she feared for her life from the moment the intruder came forward.[173] Unlike them, Grace fought off her attacker, who failed to rape her—an important fact in her ability to cope with the traumatic happening and placate a racist and a sexist society that demanded "evidence of 'utmost resistance' . . . [and] corroboration by other witnesses." Indeed, she resisted in heroic proportions, insisted that she had not been raped, and in time spoke frequently, perhaps therapeutically, about the incident. Having been told almost immediately by Perrigan, an officer of the law, that she had done nothing wrong and unhesitatingly supported by family, friends, and townsfolk, Grace escaped the worst of the guilt feelings and humiliation that haunt many rape victims. Her mother especially helped, repeatedly assuring Grace of her innocence from the night of the attack until her own death several months later.[174]

Dillard, too, helped Grace over the hard times. He left California by military transport without knowing whether or not she was alive and, because inclement weather grounded his flight, arrived nearly a week after the attack. His St. Louis destination remained a military secret, further slowing his return, as no one knew where to meet him. Finally in Sikeston, he remained twenty days. He felt "torn up" and vengeful but acted calmly, wanting the issue to die down so that Grace could get well. Dillard never blamed her for what had happened, and there were no "problems" between them over it, yet they both worried that people would portray her wrongly, as a promiscuous woman. When an Oklahoma lawyer suggested that he sue the *St. Louis Post-Dispatch* for its supposed racy coverage, Dillard opposed the idea rather than prolong Grace's ordeal. He even spoke of moving the family away after the war.

Dillard also expressed concern for his son. Jimmy lived with Grace's mother and younger brothers, Orville and Harold, while she recuperated. He visited her in the hospital, where they told each other stories; he well understood Dillard's encouragement to be brave and soon returned to school. But despite the attention of his father and his uncles, he manifested signs of stress: he ran a temperature, found sleeping very difficult, and was under a doctor's care for three weeks. Eight years old, Jimmy struggled with the new routine of living with his grandmother and, worse, the fear of losing his own mother. He also found the lynching talk of adults, more than rumors by classmates, very upsetting; like his father he believed that people should be left alone to work through such a tragedy. Jimmy recovered faster than Grace, yet both agreed that things got much better when Dillard returned home permanently following his discharge for respiratory problems in August 1943.[175]

Grace herself endured numerous difficulties. She lay in a hospital bed for nearly three months, then moved in with her mother and rented out the Kathleen Avenue house for nine years before finally selling it. Despite this escape from the trauma scene, she slept only twenty minutes at a time for three years after the attack and, with the slightest nighttime noise, was "wide awake and up."[176] She found ridding herself of "his smell" difficult and struggled constantly with flashbacks, pushing them away with good thoughts. Grace recalled: "You don't forget," but if you dwelt on the assault "you'd lose your mind."[177] She also suffered physically, having to learn to walk again and struggling with regulatory problems. She lost her slim figure and much of her strength.[178] Unlike many contemporary victims who experienced similar psychological and somatic complaints, however, Grace continued to enjoy an intimate and tender relationship with Dillard.[179]

Predictably, Grace found some days very hard. Before she could walk again, Assistant Police Chief Wallace asked her to testify before the federal grand jury, a request that brought her to tears and required her doctor's intercession to prevent. She also received numerous letters threatening to string her up or harm her child, and once out of the hospital she drew attention wherever she went. Some individuals pointed her out as having been sexually assaulted; one party from Effingham, Illinois, even showed up at her front door a year after the incident to see "the lady who had been cut up by the colored man." For two or three years she cried frequently and displayed other signs of anguish sparked by public insensitivity, especially the allegation that she and Wright had been lovers. In spite of familial and community support, Grace thought about what she could have done to prevent the assault.[180]

Laverne, too, suffered from the harrowing experience. A very nervous person, she unraveled under the attack, racing through rooms, screaming into the phone, and rushing across the street. Though surely in shock, she received no treatment at the hospital but soon called her husband, who came

Prison photos of Cleo Wright in 1940. Courtesy of Michael L. Jensen.

on emergency military leave. She left with him for Savannah, Georgia, within ten days of the assault. She and her six-month-old son returned in early 1943, when John Sturgeon was serving overseas, but lived only a short while with Grace before departing permanently. Laverne never recovered fully from that fateful evening; she sustained great damage to her nervous system and physical health. For the next seven years she lived like a rape victim, failing to sleep well and jumping at every sound, which had to be investigated; fearing for her physical safety, though without singling out black men.[181]

Laverne's emotionalism, one suspects, stemmed in part from guilt feelings. Even before the assault, she had told Grace of having been followed; afterward, she speculated that since only she had regularly come in late and had been followed several times, she had been Wright's target. That Laverne later forgot—possibly repressed—her own interpretation suggested pangs of conscience because Grace had absorbed the violence, as did her visiting Grace in the hospital for several days and doing everything to comfort her before suddenly leaving town, unable to talk about the bloodshed without becoming upset. Ultimately, she overcame the trauma by seeking "the Lord's help" and relying on her husband—a Baptist minister—for comfort.[182]

In varying degrees, then, Grace, Laverne, and Jimmy suffered the post-traumatic stress disorder common to victims who survive or witness others in life-threatening episodes. They experienced depression, anxiety, difficulty sleeping, and physical symptoms such as Jimmy's fever but were unable to express anger even years later. Grace endured "recurrent and intrusive recollections of the event," and Laverne soon fled the area.[183] Each woman struggled with her psychological recovery. Grace's physical injuries provided "concrete evidence" of the attack: her fight for life sparked more widespread sympathy than accusation, and her very survival reduced self-recrimination. Laverne identified with the attack; she had saved Grace by running for help and, in her mind, nursing her for a long time afterward, but her recovery was hampered by her high-strung personality and probably a feeling of being blameworthy.[184] In many ways, Grace dealt with the tragedy better, but no one involved, including Jimmy, recovered easily or fully.

However unwarranted, the victims and their families, like their assailant's family, felt shame. They reacted similarly: both the Sturgeons and the Watsons wanted the entire maddening episode to go away quickly; they neither discussed it among themselves and their loved ones nor sought vindication through attention-getting litigation; they kept their children as uninformed as possible, Dillard never elaborating on the acts of violence to Jimmy, and Alonzo telling the story of her son's death only in small parts to James and Linetta. In truth, members of both families coped with their wounds, but none of them forgot Cleo.[185]

In the final analysis, Ricelor Cleodas Watson metamorphosed into Cleo Wright and embarked on a path of self-destruction. His life had been one of submissiveness to parents, employers, naval officers, prison authorities, and perhaps even in-laws—a life extracted "rather than freely given," requiring him to conceal his true feelings and pay a high cost in shame and self-hatred.[186] He had searched for himself at home as an adolescent and in several refuges as an adult, only to encounter one crisis after another. When in early January 1942 he entered the Sturgeon home to strike at his enemies, he slashed and ran but soon reappeared, bloodied and calm, an easy suspect for Perrigan's one-car dragnet; he failed to conceal himself well enough to avoid capture, as if the violence on Kathleen Avenue had stripped away a "self-blinding" to reveal the truth about himself as a disappointing son, poor husband, and—powerless man.[187]

What specific incident set Cleo off may never be known, but his annihilation, like his earlier manifestations of alienation, involved white women and racial taboo. He lent credence to James Weldon Johnson's "clear and certain truth" that race relations centered on sex, and he reinforced stereotypes of black rapists. White fears aside, he acted as an individual—not for all black men—in a crucible of racism that shaped and exaggerated his sexual transgression.[188]

Cleo Wright represented both black beast and black victim, one who stumbled and fell harder than most black males facing relentless oppression. And with his death, lynchers and lawmen alike sought his quick burial.

5 Burial

Cleo Wright's lynching prompted questions that focused on the citizens and officials of Sikeston. Which townsfolk took his life and why did they do so, knowing that he already lay on his deathbed? And what resistance did would-be lynchers encounter from lawmen who held Wright in their custody? Those who sought answers, most notably the county prosecutor and federal attorneys, faced major obstacles as members of the mob and local policemen scrambled to escape prosecution. They, and most town residents, wanted the entire tragedy buried as quickly as possible.

Certainly, Sikestonians knew who executed Wright, having witnessed the lynching directly or heard of it within hours. And since members of the mob circulated outside City Hall among hundreds of spectators and struck in broad daylight without the cover of masks, their names tumbled easily from the tongues of townsfolk living in a close-knit community. Whites who disapproved of vigilante law deemed the lynchers "hoodlums," while blacks who remembered past violence judged them "outlaws."[1] Yet no one came forth to finger the killers.

Fearing conflicts with friends and neighbors, and sharing their racial beliefs, white bystanders near enough to see Wright's eyes roll as he bounced down the steps of City Hall said they recognized none of the lynchers.[2] Journalist Paul Bumbarger, who came "to get news," initially claimed that he had lived in town only fifteen months but later admitted that for his own "protection" he had deliberately looked away when close to the action.[3] Cafe owner Gilbert Clinton, heeding the advice of those around him, destroyed the movie that he took rather than be "run out of Sikeston." Other entrepreneurs kept quiet to avoid having their businesses closed by boycotts.[4] Even those who seemed unafraid for themselves and who opposed lynch law believed that little would be gained by prosecuting the participants.[5] For various reasons, then, white residents understood their own reticence as only to be expected in an autonomous, provincial community that functioned through face-to-face relations, mutual dependence, and local pride. They lived in a traditional society and responded to a set of socioeconomic mores that outsiders viewed too simply as a "conspiracy of silence."[6]

Blacks also said nothing. According to NAACP investigators, one south-ern-born resident who witnessed Wright's dragging and burning "could iden-tify the chief lynchers" but was terrified: "I ain't talkin' to no white folks."[7] Black journalists visiting from Pittsburgh and Kansas City charged that there were Sunset inhabitants willing to name members of the mob before the grand jury in return for protection and, in one instance, relocation funds. But none stepped forward, realizing the suicidal nature of bearing witness against whites and, given Wright's fate, the inability of police to protect them. Nor did they draw the interest of official investigators. Believing Wright guilty and prosecuting attorney David E. Blanton's probe just "another case like Mississippi," they chose safety over justice.[8]

Not surprisingly, like white counterparts Bumbarger and Clinton, the handful of prominent black witnesses who did come to the attention of au-thorities also feigned ignorance. George Scott, who observed the procession that pulled Wright past his grocery, told federal agents and state grand ju-rors that he recognized none of the white people. Similarly, Rev. J.B. Ross, who held services within view of Wright's execution, heard others name four of the lynchers and revealed their identity to Governor Forrest C. Donnell and St. Louis NAACP officers but later testified that he possessed "no first-hand information of the affair."[9]

Essentially, city and county lawmen responded no differently. Neither Police Chief Walter Kendall at City Hall nor Sheriff John Hobbs at the ex-ecution site, for instance, recognized a single person in the mob of three hundred. Their inability to identify people whom they had policed for nearly twenty-five years bespoke the community mores that regulated all wit-nesses.[10] If officials—including Henry Bartlett, the lone black patrolman—would not identify those responsible for Wright's killing, why should Sunset Addition residents?[11]

Prosecutor Blanton stated within a week of the lynching that the "bet-ter elements" of the community did name mob leaders.[12] If they did, their identities never appear in the records. Perhaps well-known citizens such as cleaner Tip Keller and landowner Leo Fisher, who told federal agents noth-ing, confided in Blanton privately, or others such as Dr. T.C. McClure sur-reptitiously passed him names provided by black servants.[13] Possibly Governor Donnell relayed Ross's list of culprits to Blanton; more certainly, "Informant TA" did furnish FBI agents with the identities of "agitators" in the mob.[14]

While private citizens assisted in the identification of twenty mob mem-bers, county and state officials knew firsthand those most responsible for

Wright's apprehension, dragging, and immolation. Blanton, of course, prepared the state grand jury case and, along with Sgt. Melvin Dace and Troopers John Tandy and Vincent P. Boisaubin of the State Highway Patrol, testified before it, describing the role of each mob member.[15]

Ted C., Preston H., and Nigel J. led the pack, the latter declaring its desire to "get the negro" and dismissing Blanton's threat of prosecution. Stan E., Carl S., Rob K., Sam M., Steve N., Ned B., and Lance W. followed close behind, the first wave of shock troops that pushed into City Hall and drove Wright's protectors back. Someone struck Blanton, fracturing his third rib, and Preston H. repeatedly punched Dace in the stomach. None of those fighting the mob recognized the person who then broke into the women's detention room and hauled Wright out, but Edward Z., Ivan D., Art U., and Wade L. were seen in the hallway or spilling into the street; their presence as second, third, and even fourth rearguard units assured front-line assailants of their mission.[16] Once outside, lynchers attached Wright to the Ford driven by Martin X. and sped toward the Addition in a procession of vehicles, those closest to the front operated by activists such as Yancey T. and those bringing up the rear by spectators such as Richard D.[17] Once the lynchers had laid Wright on the railroad easement, Kirk V. poured gasoline on him. After Matt R. failed to set the helpless captive afire, another man—blacks said Lou O.—stepped from the crowd to flip the match that instantly ignited him.[18]

A handful of the mob members were victims of circumstance. Martin X., accompanied by fellow mechanic Ollie I., was driving his father-in-law's car home from the garage when, in front of City Hall, he was blocked by lynchers who fixed Wright to his auto and then piled into and on it. Directed to Sunset, Martin X. became "half scared to death" and alighted from the automobile—as Ollie I. had done moments sooner—before entering the black enclave. He stood at the roadside as a lyncher slid behind the steering wheel and drove on toward the execution site. Only after Wright's killing did he retrieve the Ford.[19]

Unlike the two auto mechanics, however, most of those identified were guilty. Predictably, lynchers told federal agents and—in sworn testimony—grand jurors otherwise. Ringleaders Nigel J. and Preston H., respectively, denied having spoken with Blanton or seen, much less struck Dace; they were at City Hall for a short time, they said, but left before "the negro was taken out." Ted C., the third leader, became hard to locate. Shock troopers also pled innocent: Lance W. observed events from his parked car and then departed; Carl S. entered City Hall but left when ordered out by lawmen; Steve N. was pushed in by the crowd that apprehended Wright but did not go to Sunset;

Stan E., Rob K., and Mike A. were nowhere near the siege, though Mike A. overheard Wright's midmorning confession. Likewise, executioners Kirk V., Matt R., and Lou O. said they arrived too late to have set Wright afire.[20]

Support troops in Wright's apprehension and pilots in his funeral possession followed suit. Edward Z., Ivan D., and Art U. contended that they were outside during the charge on City Hall. More insistent, Richard D. and Wade L. swore that they were never in sight of the building when the mob attacked, a position that Yancey T.—a close friend of Wade L.—would also have taken had he been summoned by the grand jury.[21] All lynchers, regardless of their individual roles, testified as blameless spectators and, in effect, called the county prosecutor and state troopers liars.

Pictures of the lynchers would have undermined their testimony (though without necessarily bringing indictments from empathetic jurors), but members of the mob had confiscated the movie camera of one freelance photographer; another destroyed his own equipment; a third supposedly preserved his efforts but never shared them with law enforcers. Those responsible for the violence did not prevent Trooper Boisaubin from snapping the only prints that Blanton deemed worthy of presentation, but those photos proved inconclusive: individuals were difficult to recognize or stood among others.[22] Since there were no shots of lynchers assaulting officers or manhandling Wright, the subjects stated alibis with impunity.

Courtroom proof aside, mob members were "just folks."[23] Despite black and white recollections of the presence of "lower- class people" and "outsiders," Blanton more accurately described them as longtime residents of Sikeston. They were mostly males, mature, educated, hard-working, and in some cases churchgoing: normally law-abiding citizens, if "not the prominent people that would make a community function."[24] Certainly the twenty individuals whom Blanton investigated fit this profile.

The lynchers themselves were men. Although white women appeared at every stage of the violence, even in the circle of death, they were only spectators and their numbers were small.[25] Their limited activity revealed the passive nature and separate spheres demanded of females by the "cult of the true womanhood" that carried over into the twentieth century, assigning to males violent license and power to define public events.[26] Female presence also indicated a fear of sexual aggression by black men, an endorsement of their punishment, and—though less assertively than in the 1930s—"a means of self-expression" in a patriarchal society.[27]

No one described the women's characteristics, but the men varied from young adult to middle age—from twenty to fifty years old, the median age nearly thirty-five. In part, this reflected the impact of war; for several months before the lynching, Scott County youths had been reporting for military duty.[28] Hence the mob leaders and the "six youngsters" who hauled Wright's body to Sunset were in their mid-twenties and early thirties, while the executioners were nearing the half-century mark. Fully half of the lynchers were married; at least six had children.[29]

It is impossible to determine the schooling of all the mob members, but their occupations indicated a typical, if not advanced, Sikeston education and middle-class or upper-middle-class status. Three of the lynchers had earned high school degrees and two received pilot training; information for the remaining fifteen is unavailable.[30] Seven small businessmen and one manager (most of whom provided food or entertainment to townspeople) dominated the ranks of the seventeen lynchers with known occupations. Three craftsmen, mechanics and the like followed, and, surprisingly, professionals equaled the number of operatives (i.e., somewhat skilled labor): two of each in jobs ranging from flight instructor to truck driver. One service worker and one sales worker rounded out the group's occupational profile, which clearly boasted substantially greater percentages in the more affluent categories—especially proprietors and craftsmen—than did county residents collectively.[31] None were laborers; contrary to popular late-nineteenth-century perceptions of southern lynchers, Wright's most demonstrative murderers sprang from the ranks of budding entrepreneurs and skilled and semi-skilled workmen. Indeed, one already had run (unsuccessfully) for public office, another would succeed as a lawman, and two would become prominent in Sikeston's postwar economic development.

Though their religious commitment is difficult to assess, few of the mob's vanguard seemed true believers. None of the known lynchers practiced Judaism, and only one Catholicism: Richard D., who attended mass the morning of the lynching.[32] If asked their religion, most would have identified with Protestantism, though only Steve N. appeared on church rolls (First Baptist), having been baptized several years earlier; Lance W. was not a recorded member but admitted to frequenting services at the First United Methodist Church.[33] Others surely considered themselves God-fearing, worshiped on occasion, and later in life joined a church. Those who played the most active roles in killing Wright may have participated in prayer services occasionally or even regularly, but they appear to have been nominal Christians rather than "devout church members" who had been baptized or con-

firmed and served as deacons or committee members.[34] And a handful—
led by gambler Lou O., who seemed "a person of immoral character" to later
authorities—possessed little, if any faith.[35]

Repulsed by these realities, Rev. E.W. Bartley of the First United Methodist Church quipped that if Sikeston's citizens were to be believed as to their
whereabouts during the lynching, every church experienced an attendance
that Sunday "double the size of its largest-ever Easter crowd!" His humor,
biting yet safe, chided members of the mob and their apologists for hypocrisy.[36] The "spirit of bigotry" that an earlier critic had blamed on an emotional Protestantism, and held responsible for rural mob activity in the
South, seemed much less influential in Sikeston.[37]

However the twenty lynchers envisioned themselves religiously, most
were longstanding town residents. Sixteen lived in Sikeston, several had done
so for ten years or more. Of the twelve for whom origins are known, eight
came from Sikeston or within fifty-five miles of it, two from Kentucky, and
one each from Tennessee and Texas. Most of the active mob members, in
other words, were scarcely "outsiders" or southern newcomers, though
Blanton admitted that some in the crowd hailed from "nearby communities," and another witness speculated on the presence of "rednecks."[38]

In fact, Preston H. had been born in Texas and had arrived recently from
Georgia to instruct cadets at the Missouri Institute of Aeronautics, supposedly one of numerous southerners on a staff that some blamed for the lynching. He served as a ringleader—inciting others and striking Dace—whose
southern upbringing might well have permitted him to violate community
norms of law and order more easily than could those born and raised in the
area.[39] But only one other flight school employee—Kentucky-born mechanic
Carl S.—took an active role in apprehending Wright, and, perhaps fearful
of disciplinary action from the school commander, none of the students at
the air field entered the fray. Instead, twenty-five trainees watched the action from across the street.[40] And given the area's demography of southerners
from Arkansas-Mississippi and mountaineers from western Kentucky-Ten-
nessee, longstanding residents manifested the racial and violent heritages of
their forebears once Preston H. and two other leaders, one a lifelong area
resident, provided direction.

Two of the three executioners, themselves longtime townsfolk, also bore
one trait very different from leaders or shock troopers. Both over forty and
tradesmen, Kirk V. was intoxicated when he doused Wright with flammable
liquid and Matt R. so drunk that he was unable to light the original match.
When later questioned by federal agents, Kirk V. again "appeared to have been

drinking." Only one other lyncher, shock trooper Sam M., showed signs of drinking (perhaps of being an alcoholic). In short, only three of twenty mob members required libations to fortify themselves before killing in cold blood; the other seventeen, as well as the crowd that abetted and bore witness to their murder, needed no such bromide. They acted "sober" and with malice aforethought.[41]

Unrepresentative too were the few rank-and-file lynchers with arrest records or personal vendettas. Rob K. had served a sentence in the state penitentiary for armed robbery; Lou O. appeared before local justices for gambling activities; shortly after the lynching, Stan E. faced a charge of driving while intoxicated; and Ted C. sought personal revenge for the alleged killing of his father some time earlier by another black man.[42] Rob K.s' social deviance and Ted C.'s blood vengeance certainly explained their participation in the mob, particularly the latter's leadership role, but not that of Lou O., Stan E., or Wright's sixteen other murderers.

Lance W. represented the core of the twenty lynchers: the shock troops that overwhelmed Wright's protectors and drove him to his death. Born in a nearby town twenty-eight years earlier, he was one of three children whose parents owned property, attended church, and advocated hard work, self-sufficiency, and respectability. He graduated from high school, worked for a grocer, and soon set out on his own to sell merchandise beyond city and county lines. Meanwhile, he married and began a family. Already successful in 1942, Lance W. had built a home in Sikeston's southwest quadrant and hired blacks for domestic and yard work, never considering them qualified for his business; he also believed in segregation. A respected entrepreneur, responsible family man, and regular churchgoer whose local roots reached back into the previous century, Lance W. epitomized those upper-middle-class townsfolk caught up in the violence.[43]

Lance W. was unaware of the early morning bloodshed that Sunday until he drove downtown to check his mail at the post office before going on to church. He parked on Center Street, across from City Hall, and learned what had happened from individuals in the crowd whose numbers soon swelled to several hundred. Within an hour he found himself pushing at the municipal building doors.[44] He heard Blanton address the crowd and most likely participated in the charge that brought Wright to the street; his agitation clearly set the stage for and helped precipitate the siege. Thereafter, he is said to have left the scene, collected his family, and joined his parents for Sunday dinner. When he returned home late that afternoon, he heard "about the lynching."[45]

When questioned by federal agents, Lance W. claimed that he had nothing to do with the mob. He admitted going to City Hall at 10:30 A.M., when the street contained "very few people" and was open to traffic, but claimed that he left shortly for the Sabbath meal. He later embellished his story before the grand jury, saying that he drove someone from the scene to give Grace Sturgeon a blood transfusion at the hospital, after which he and his wife (mentioned for the first time) returned to City Hall but never got out of the car and never saw the troopers or prosecuting attorney. Again, Lance W. ended his testimony by stating that he departed for the family dinner before the ruckus that claimed Wright's life began.[46]

Similar denials came from Wade L., representative of the rear guard whose numbers proved indispensable to Wright's captors. He had come to Sikeston at a very young age. Born on a farm southwest of Benton thirty-five years earlier, he was the oldest of several children, completed high school, and learned a trade from his father. Although exposed to religion, he appears not to have been a regular parishioner. Except for a period during World War I he lived in town; he practiced his trade and earned a modest income. By 1942 he was operating his own shop and sharing an apartment with another bachelor. He was a well-thought-of member of the working class.[47]

Very early on Sunday morning, Wade L. sat at a local cafe and learned, in a phone call from his roommate, of the attack on Grace Sturgeon and Hess Perrigan. He went to the hospital to see how badly Perrigan, a friend, was wounded and inadvertently walked in on Cleo Wright being doctored. He left without visiting the lawman, but by early afternoon he had reappeared in Sunset Addition. He told FBI investigators that he "knew nothing" of the crowd and "took no part whatsoever in the lynching," admitting only to have visited the death site "later in the afternoon."[48] He too changed his story before grand jurors, elaborating that he rose at 10:45 A.M., learned of the mob action from a visitor, and arrived in time to see the burning. In fact, he got there early enough to talk to Kirk V. before that self-appointed executioner sloshed gasoline on the victim, and to stand within twenty feet of the cremation. That Wade L. seemed among the first to reach the black community, in short, indicated his presence at City Hall when the procession left with Wright in tow. And his camaraderie with one lyncher and favored vantage point evinced much more than the role of a late-arriving curiosity-seeker, who should have been several rows back. Small wonder federal agents considered him among "actual participants" or those present at City Hall.[49]

If shock troopers and rear guardsmen such as Lance W. and Wade L.

represented a socioeconomic cross section of the townspeople involved (as opposed to lower-class "nitrogen" in turn-of-the-century southern violence), spectators reflected similar distinctions. Like those who attacked City Hall, some were "roughly dressed, and others in their Sabbath best."[50] Ranging from prominent to "middle-run citizens," most came from town—many arriving directly from church services—though their ranks also contained individuals from outlying areas, such as Morehouse, who heard of Wright's assault by word of mouth.[51] Men dominated, but women, children, and cadets also filled Center Street, rushed to Sunset, and witnessed the execution. Their behavior varied: many acted like small-town sightseers viewing a big time "happening"; some whooped it up; a few served as cowardly "mischief makers" and milled through the gathering, goading others to do their killing.[52]

More wittingly than not, spectators, like earlier witnesses to lynch law activity, "figured prominently in the proceedings." For one thing, their numbers rendered impossible any defense of Wright: state troopers never drew their weapons, in part for fear of shooting bystanders. And it was because of the congestion inside City Hall and the traffic jam on Center Street that they failed to reach Sunset ahead of the lynchers and prevent Wright's immolation.[53] Spectators also encouraged and empowered the lynchers, legitimizing their actions. Sensing their anonymity, they believed themselves immune from legal reprisal; realizing their oneness of thought, they deemed themselves righteous—even moral. "If acting individually," recalled Blanton, "they would have been most reliable." Spectators knew that they could overwhelm authorities and resolve their rage. However momentarily, they considered their actions personally beneficial, scarcely irrational.[54]

In a substantial way, lynchers and spectators succeeded because others cowered. Clerics and residents who opposed the mob stood clear of its wrath, presuming themselves outnumbered and fearful of "what their friends would think."[55] Only two individuals stepped forward to assist officials at City Hall. Jack Johnson, an eighteen-year-old airport employee, accompanied Trooper Vincent P. Boisaubin and helped "hold out the crowd." More surprising—given that the ritual of lynching usually included kinsmen of the female victim—an unidentified man who claimed to be related to the Sturgeons pleaded with those outside "not to seize Wright."[56] More in keeping with tradition, a mob of seventy-five, backed up by several hundred additional persons, easily overran the prosecutor, police chief, three troopers, a teenager, and a relative.

Throughout the siege at City Hall, the parade to Sunset, and the burning of Wright, however, a handful of town elites stood close by. When Blanton arrived on the scene, attorney Roger A. Bailey, landowner Leo Fisher, and cleaner Tip Keller positioned themselves off to the side. Once violence erupted, Bailey retreated home, though he would surface later to condemn the lynchers. Fisher and Keller joined Blanton and Sergeant Dace in an effort to "beat the mob to Sunset" and warn black residents off the street.[57] Similarly, millionaire Joseph L. Matthews appeared to chase sightseers from Wright's remains and, afterward, housed a frightened black.[58] While these civic and commercial leaders neither doubted Wright's guilt nor objected to his death, like elites elsewhere they understood the danger of rampant violence should the mob turn from one "inner enemy" to the entire black community.[59] They countenanced reestablishing a broken color line but opposed a pogrom that would destroy innocent people (including their own employees), bring outside interference, and prove them incapable of ruling their own creation. No pogram ever occurred, thanks to action by state troopers and black residents and, as importantly, the fear of race war on the part of many whites—both in and beyond the crowd—who considered Wright's death lesson enough.

No one but the authorities, however, questioned the taking of Wright's life in such an open display of white savagery. That two or three ringleaders could organize large-scale support within hours, including that of many churchgoers and normally law-abiding citizens, revealed a conspiracy that grew to public proportions and, as quickly, ceased to be secret. Large numbers became caught up in the mob hysteria, which unified them further in the belief that Wright threatened the racial order and their personal safety.[60] Enraged both as individuals and as a community, they channeled their anger and calmed their fears by killing Wright for very specific, interrelated, and racist reasons.

From the moment Perrigan told the night operator that a white woman had been slashed by a black man, word spread like wildfire. Whites heard that Wright had attempted to rape or had raped Sturgeon, reports that turned their world "upside down."[61] Like their forebears, they feared this transgression more than any other, for it challenged the foundation of white supremacy: racial purity. Hence they proved susceptible to the rumors that shaped their violent impulses. Many remembered hearing "nigger raped a white woman" again and again; it was the single most important reason given to justify lynching Wright.[62] By 9:00 A.M. Sunday, even blacks in Sunset had heard talk of lynching Wright because of "the nature of the offense," gossip verified by the lynchers. Lance W. spoke for many who confronted troopers at City Hall, asking what they would do "if it had been their wife who had been mistreated."[63] Likewise, numerous individuals who witnessed and endorsed Wright's death repeatedly declared, "That will teach him not [to] fool with white women."[64]

That Wright had assaulted Sturgeon in her husband's absence in the military incited lynchers further and, given the war atmosphere, served as a "call to colors."[65] That ringleader Preston H. trained would-be combat pilots seemed more than coincidental. Again and again Wright's killers declared their need to protect a neighbor's wife: "If I was away in the army," Steve N. told Trooper Boisaubin as he struggled to enter City Hall, "I would not want a black [bastard] to rape my wife, and I am going to do what I can to get him out."[66] His "patriotic fervor" ran even among individuals to whom the Sturgeons were strangers.[67] Some lynchers soon bragged to Jimmy Sturgeon that they "got revenge" for his mother and that his father "would be proud of what they had done."[68]

The lynchers thus revealed a heightened sense of honor, duty, and manhood. Raised in a culture shaped by nineteenth-century southern and mountain traditions, despite the passing of years or influence of town living, they violated Wright as their ancestors would have in order to avenge Sturgeon's and Sikeston's honor; conscious of their obligation, they showed themselves, again like their forebears, "men enough to assume the big [community] responsibilities."[69] Several booed Blanton's effort to disperse them, for it was their "duty to take care of" Wright. Mindful of Sgt. J. Dillard Sturgeon's military sacrifice and their own prospects of fighting abroad soon, they lynched Wright in a tension-filled atmosphere that drew together memories of "black beasts," real or imagined, and uncertainties of their own and their loved ones' safety in a world war.[70]

Mob members found another reason to take Wright's life in his attack on a lawman, a transgression that historically drew the death penalty for blacks—and whites—in southern and mountain regions because it weakened respect for authority.[71] They deemed Wright's cutting of Perrigan, "a duly appointed officer of the law," serious in itself but intolerable in combination with his brutalizing "the wife of a solider." Thus they let down "all the bars" to secure their manly reputations and, more significantly, their white world.[72]

That many lynchers knew both victims intensified their wrath, provided wide-range "social support," and prevented public opposition to Wright's death. Everyone in town knew everyone else; even members of the mob who lived beyond city limits were "not far outsiders."[73] Despite clear lines of socioeconomic hierarchy requiring "your great, great, great grandfather" to have been born in Sikeston, most townsfolk enjoyed close-knit relationships.[74] "Who ever wasn't kin" was probably a longtime resident, and more recent arrivals, especially northerners, felt some distance but not hostility.[75] The Sturgeons, of course, had been well established: J. Dillard was from the area; Grace had lived in town since 1929.

Significantly, Sergeant Sturgeon was no ordinary citizen. Lou. O., Richard D., Yancey T., and Wade L. were old friends of his—Wade L. recalling that he had been raised "in our end of town"—and Mike A. grazed horses in the pasture opposite the Sturgeon home. No doubt others in the mob had gone to school with Sarge.[76] Still other lynchers and townspeople knew that he "had been one of the first to volunteer in the Home Guard" and had cared for the armory, and that he was serving younger members of Company K as confidant, exemplar, and guardian at the very moment his unprotected wife fell before an intended rapist's knife. They knew further that two of Sarge's brothers had begun their service in Company K and that the wife of one of them, air corps cadet John Sturgeon, had barely escaped her sister-in-law's fate.[77]

Members of the mob also empathized with Perrigan, who, as a police officer, was well known and had befriended some of them even before becoming night marshal the previous year. They knew him as a native of Union City, Tennessee, thirty-seven years old, married, and father of a young daughter. A former oil mill worker and barber, he lived next door to Sarge and Grace.[78]

Given these relationships, and particularly because Sarge symbolized much more than friend or citizen, lynchers drew ready support as their actions became a communal event. Some approached Grace's brother Orville at the hospital, inviting him to join their ranks, but he and younger brother Harold stayed at their sister's side. Presumably, they also contacted Sarge's father and the youngest brother, Charles, then living in Blodgett, though apparently with no more success. Other members of the family, most notably brothers-in-law of Grace, appeared outside City Hall but did not join Wright's abductors. Sometime later lynchers proudly offered Grace a souvenir of her courageous stand: the red-and-white-striped, celluloid-handled folding knife that Wright had used to cut her (she demurred). They also helped financially to bring Sarge to Grace's side.[79]

Precisely because Sturgeon and Perrigan were known and respected, lynchers deemed Wright a perfect enemy, "evil that had to be eradicated."[80] They viewed his double act of violence—which threatened racial order and devastated personal relationships—as a communal and intimate reason for killing him immediately. Doing so required that they portray Wright as a stranger rather than the familiar member of the community that he had been for five years.

It also required that they treat all black Sikestonians as possible threats, undeserving of the racial etiquette that operated during peaceful moments. Therefore members of the mob dragged Wright through Sunset and burned him in full view of black residents, signaling much more than personal rage or revenge. Calculatingly, they sought to prevent future attacks on other white women. Steve N., for one, expressed the need to "teach these niggers a lesson," a phrase assuming that all Sunset males were desirous of raping Sikeston women.[81] Lynchers also reminded white women of their vulnerability before black beasts and their need for white male protection, reinforcing well-understood patriarchal beliefs of race and gender in a traditional society. Those who abducted Wright referred time and again to Sturgeon's having been "unprotected." In contrast, they said nothing about black women, who were vulnerable to the white male advances that had historically pushed aside black male protests.[82]

Given this racial and sexual tension, lynchers killed a hated enemy who would have died shortly anyway. So said Dr. E.J. Nienstedt, who stated what had been obvious to those involved in dragging Wright from deathbed to funeral possession. They preferred him alive when captured, which he was, according to several witnesses.[83] That he gave at least the appearance of breathing was necessary for their psyches and an object lesson for black rogues and white maidens. They frightened many males and females into believing that rape and lynching—involving them—"might happen again." Nor were the teachings of lynchers lost on black women shocked by the bloodshed and worried about their men. Even black wives who had been sheltered from white male aggression realized the unmistakable message of indiscriminate "racial hate."[84]

In part, it was that hatred—and its accompanying fear—that prevented members of the mob from being identified publicly, much less indicted. Although blacks beyond Sikeston hoped for convictions, those in the area knew that lynchers such as the Caruthersville vigilantes who had broken up a Southern Tenant Farmers Union meeting the week before Wright's death would "never get justice"; like a greased eel, W.M. Tucker of Holland predicted accurately, "they will slip out." And yet both black outsiders and locals thought that state and federal authorities might impose punishment, if only on lawmen who allegedly assisted the lynchers.[85]

Initially, Governor Donnell received numerous complaints that state troopers had led the death motorcade and had made no effort to identify lynchers or execution witnesses. He heard similar versions of the same story from delegates of the National Association for the Advancement of Colored People, officers of the United States Negro Democrats of Missouri, and members of the Butler County Negro Citizens Committee.[86] Clearly, the charge emanated from Rev. J.B. Ross, who gathered information from Sunset residents and within twenty-four hours phoned it to the chief executive: Sergeant Dace drove patrol car 84, "led the parade," and told Rev. Kater E. Crump to get off the streets because "they were going to burn the nigger."[87]

That Ross passed the same information on to Sidney R. Redmond, who in turn spread it to black activists and white liberals throughout the state, explained Donnell's inundation with near-identical charges from such a wide variety of organizations and citizens. The pastor, of course, reported the experiences of those who had been in the street and contended that "a state police car was in front [of the procession]."[88] Since Ross and his informants had not seen Dace, Boisaubin, and Tandy struggling to protect Wright at City Hall or entering Sunset by an alternative route, they assumed that the officers were escorting the mob. Hearing that Dace was looking for him almost immediately after his call to the governor, Ross "got out of town." He surfaced in St. Louis and repeated his charges before the NAACP mass rally a week later, logically believing, as did most blacks in Sikeston, that highway patrolmen had played the traditional role of coconspirators in southern violence.[89]

In direct contrast, within hours of having observed the defense of City Hall and the race to warn Sunset residents, white elites praised Dace and his fellow officers for doing "everything in their power to prevent the mob violence." The city council's resolution prompted similar action by the American Legion, Lions Club, and Kiwanis Club. Ralph E. Bailey, well-known attorney, Republican Party member, and former U.S. congressman, presented the declaration to councilmen and visited the governor in Jefferson City. He represented "a large number of businessmen and civic leaders" who "wanted the world to know" of their opposition to lynching and reaffirmed widespread local support for the highway patrolmen.[90]

Caught between the biracial protest from St. Louis and Kansas City reformers and the counteroffensive of civic and commercial elites in Sikeston, Donnell weighed the statements of Dace and his superiors. One week after Wright's death he heard "a brief oral report" from Dace, who also presented his official written account to Highway Patrol Superintendent M. Stanley

Ginn. So did Sgt. O.L. Wallis of Troop E, Dace's supportive commanding officer. Within hours, Donnell knew that Ginn had exonerated Dace, Tandy, and Boisaubin; they had done "all they could do to prevent the lynching." But he knew, too, that Reverend Ross held to his story and that NAACP rally participants were criticizing Ginn's report.[91] As late as March, and unquestionably because of the state grand jury's failure to indict a single lyncher, Donnell received a request from the St. Louis association to remove Dace from his post. He replied that according to the evidence the trooper had done "everything within his power" to shield Wright, and asked for evidence that would justify suspending him.[92] None was forthcoming.

In fact, Dace emerged as one of the area's most reputable lawmen. Born May 27, 1907, in Sullivan, 125 miles northwest of Sikeston, one of six children, he had served as an original member of the Highway Patrol in 1931. He spent his entire enlistment with Troop E, headquartered at Poplar Bluff, and patrolled the Sikeston area. He married Ann Childress of nearby Bertand, settled in the vicinity, joined the First Baptist Church of Sikeston, and became a highly respected member of the community.[93]

Very early on January 25, when someone beckoned Dace to "investigate a serious crime" at Kathleen Avenue, he arrived shortly after 1:00 A.M., learned of Grace Sturgeon's cutting, searched unsuccessfully for her assailant, and proceeded to the hospital. He was there when Perrigan and Wright underwent surgery, and he spoke at length with Jesse Whittley, Roy Beck, and Laverne Sturgeon. He did not disturb Grace Sturgeon but later was the first lawman to visit her and offer his assistance. He departed for home at 4:30 A.M., reported the incident to Troop E headquarters, and excused himself from regular duty.[94]

Dace did not sleep in, however, for Sergeant Wallis phoned him five hours later to ask if he had shot Cleo Wright. After correcting this rumor, Dace decided to pursue a statement made at the hospital by Wright's in-laws that their daughter had "expected something like this would happen." En route to Sunset Addition at 10:30 A.M., he saw the crowd outside City Hall and thought that Wright must have died. Finding it necessary to chase would-be lynchers out of the building, he called for reinforcements and contacted city officials. He, Tandy, Boisaubin, and Kendall kept the mob at bay for the next hour until, along with Blanton they were overrun. Following the lynchers out, mindful of their excited "state of mind" and repeated intentions to burn Wright in Sunset, Dace instructed fellow troopers to warn blacks off the streets.

Since the patrol cars faced east, troopers entered the black community

Sgt. Melvin Dace examines the knife
used in the assault on Grace Sturgeon.
Courtesy of Michael L. Jensen.

from a different direction than the lynchers and chased residents inside.
Ultimately, Dace and his officers encountered several automobiles causing
them to stop, while some 200 yards away Wright met his death. Afterward,
Tandy provided Dace with the license number of the car that dragged Wright,
which he gave to the county prosecutor, along with names of those he recognized in the mob. In subsequent weeks he assisted Blanton's investigation
and testified at the state grand jury.

Dace's and Wallis's lynching reports served their best interests, as did
Donnell's assigning Superintendent Ginn to investigate his own agency's
personnel. Yet Dace was innocent of having abetted the lynchers. No other
lawman responded so swiftly or effectively to the assault on Sturgeon; no
other lawman moved so quickly to protect Wright and then to prevent widespread racial slaughter; no other lawman contributed as much to the effort
to bring the lynchers to justice.

In truth, the charge against Dace revealed the limits of eyewitness accounts and the impact of historical memory. Certainly blacks in Sunset observed among oncoming vehicles a state patrol car bearing the number 84 whose occupants, they said, warned Pastor Crump off the street. Seeing behind it "the truck dragging Cleo's body," and given the commotion, fear of the moment, and nightrider memories in black life and folklore, they realistically judged the troopers to be part of the mob.[95]

Still, either black spectators or Reverend Ross confused decisive points. Specifically, only two patrol cars beat the mob to Sunset Addition: number 31 was driven by Dace and carried Blanton, Fisher, Keller, Bumbarger, and Wilcox; number 84 was operated by Trooper John N. Greim, who had just arrived from Dexter and had Tandy with him.[96] Thus Dace neither drove the automobile that blacks said led the mob nor chased Crump off the street; small wonder that he sought out Ross upon hearing these false accusations. Greim was the driver who told "a negro preacher to help get the people inside" (though he may well have used the term "nigger") but did not take the time to explain "the whole affair" to Crump. Later the cleric verified their conversation, without mentioning the mob.[97]

Perhaps, then, Greim *appeared* to lead the mob. He followed Dace into the Addition, turned off after several blocks, and met the "procession coming from the south." He stopped and waited for it to approach, turn right, and proceed ahead of the patrol car; he remained parked about fifty yards away.[98] It is likely that his and Dace's vehicles came through the neighborhood so close in time to those of the lynchers, all with horns blaring and occupants yelling, that the order and relationship of one vehicle to another were too confusing to determine accurately. In this calamitous atmosphere, patrol car numbers, drivers, and anecdotes became interchangeable.

Moreover, a Ford sedan, not a truck (as indicated by one witness) pulled Wright. And no evidence exists to support the charge that two hours before the lynching "a city policeman and a state patrolman" drove through the community, ordering blacks inside because "we're going to have a little fun."[99] This accusation did not come from Ross and was not among the allegations made by organized protesters, but it indicated the state of black thinking and, like most rumors, contained elements of truth.

From the perspective of Sunset residents, of course, it mattered little who drove what; for them the issue was state-sanctioned trooper involvement in extralegal violence against black people. But Dace and his officers had not given Wright over to the mob; they had fought to protect him. As clearly, certain that his life was lost from the moment lynchers grabbed him, they concentrated thereafter on using "every drastic method" to protect others.

For this reason, Dace ordered his men to alert Sunset residents rather than attempt a bloody rescue of Wright; for this reason, Greim made no effort to interfere with the lynchers (so long as their death parade ignored other blacks). Trooper presence in Sunset before, during, and after Wright's killing limited the bloodshed to a singular act and stemmed the possibility of its becoming a racial pogrom.[100]

Dace and his troopers were well aware of the mob's fury. They decided against drawing their weapons at City Hall out of genuine concern about injuring those trying to help them—though perhaps, too, they hesitated to fire on familiar faces, on persons without "sticks or guns," and in cramped quarters where blood would have been spilled indiscriminately.[101] And, given the lynchers' determination to take Wright, the troopers and others sensed that firing into the crowd would spark "more serious trouble": possibly the loss of their own lives and a full-blown race riot. As Jesse Whittley said, Sikeston men had come to get Wright "one way or the other."[102] In short, bearing only four sidearms (including the police chief's) and facing hundreds of people, the officers lacked sufficient numbers and firepower to protect themselves, much less Wright.

The responsibility for his inadequate protection lay elsewhere, a fact acknowledged by grand jurors and federal attorneys. The state jury members complimented the highway patrolmen, and the federal jury declared that Dace and the other troopers had done "much more than the letter of their duties required."[103] Most significantly, Justice Department lawyers, sifting the facts for evidence of violations by lawmen, determined that state policemen did "everything within reason" to protect Wright and, given the presence of "friendly people," they had "exercised reasonable judgment in not shooting."[104] In the opinion of Judge James C. McDowell, Dace may have been "the best law enforcing officer in southeast Missouri." Now and again his community and racial loyalties surfaced, as when he smugly told a black reporter from St. Louis that he did not have to identify anyone in the mob unless he wanted to.[105] And when ordered by superiors to stay clear of specific events (such as the Caruthersville clashes between unionists and planters), he no doubt obeyed. Still, his integrity and commitment to the law shone through on this occasion.[106] Unlike the inexperienced Perrigan, whose amateurish search of Wright nearly cost him his life, Dace took full measure of the mob, applied standard police procedures, and endeavored to save Wright. He lived up to his oath.

The same could not be said of Sheriff John Hobbs, who was criticized by the NAACP-sponsored delegation for "dereliction of duty."[107] He observed the murder of Wright in Sunset Addition and, charged delegates who sought his suspension, did nothing to prevent it. He took too long to reach Sikeston once he knew the mob was gathering, contended others, including some townspeople. Since he served as an elected official of Scott County, however, he stood beyond gubernatorial jurisdiction.[108]

Little came of these complaints. Hobbs represented the provincialism of his origins. He was born in Cape Girardeau County, son of Joseph V. Hobbs and Frances Brooks, but had spent much of his life in northern Scott County. He served as Chaffee chief of police for fourteen years before becoming deputy sheriff in 1938 and sheriff in 1940. He and his wife, Nona Mae Heeb, making their home in Chaffee, raised two daughters and a foster son. At the time of the lynching, Hobbs was nearing his fifty-third birthday and understood the northern, self-sufficient farming part of the county, with its close-knit, all white, mostly German and Dutch families; like them, he was suspicious of outsiders. He related less well to the southern, plantation economy of the delta region that boasted equally tight though less ethnic families, relied on large numbers of black sharecroppers, and contained the commercial center of Sikeston, which marked the southernmost tip of the county and, in effect, the northernmost point of the delta. In short, Hobbs's loyalties lay above the county seat at Benton. For all practical purposes, he and Sikeston police officials protected separate turf and rarely cooperated with one another.[109]

Against this backdrop, Hobbs received Dace's call for help at 11:00 A.M. on January 25. He arrived at City Hall forty-five minutes later with his deputy sheriff, he said, only to find that "the crowd had just taken the Negro." He and Jim Robert then drove toward Sunset, observed "heavy smoke rising," and found hundreds of people around a burnt body. Hobbs doubted that those in the audience were members of the lynch mob, and he recognized no one.[110] He was not among those who patrolled the black community that evening, but in the weeks that followed he reportedly assisted the county prosecutor's investigation. Most significantly, it was he who selected the jurors to hear Blanton's case and also testified before them.[111]

Hobbs acted deliberately but not urgently. When he took Dace's Mayday call in Benton, he deemed it "impossible to leave" without someone in charge of the county jail, which contained prisoners. Since members of his own family were attending a funeral and were therefore unavailable to spell him as turnkey, he contacted deputies. Lester Miller, living near by, came quickly to secure the lockup, but Jim Robert needed time to dress and drive eight miles from Kelso to Benton, where Hobbs waited. Together, they trav-

eled the eighteen miles over "paved highway" to the Sikeston City Hall, arriving minutes too late to help Dace fend off the mob. Waiting for Robert
cost Hobbs precious time, probably much more than the forty-five minutes
that he estimated between the 11:00 A.M. SOS and his alleged 11:45 A.M. appearance in Sikeston.[112] In fact, if Blanton came to City Hall at 11:35 A.M.
and Trooper Greim pulled up ten minutes or more later, as they each told
federal agents, Hobbs should have showed up just before or right as the mob
apprehended Wright.[113] Trooper Tandy recalled that the patrolmen held the
crowd off "until about 11:45 A.M.," and dragging Wright from his cell to the
street obviously required another five or ten minutes. Assistant Police Chief
Wallace, who checked his watch upon entering the building at 12:07 P.M., said
the "crowd was gone" by then.[114] That Hobbs approached an empty City Hall
and quiet Center Street indicated that he must have arrived at noon or later,
rather than a quarter to the hour.

Hobbs's earlier arrival might have prevented Wright's apprehension
(though that is problematic), but he took his time getting to Sikeston. Within
five minutes of Dace's call he had contacted both deputies and knew them
to be on their way in a matter of minutes; had he departed Benton immediately, at the very latest he would have arrived with Blanton, bolstered the
ranks of lawmen, and created more difficulty for the lynchers—particularly
if he had acted as forcefully as three years earlier when he "seized" a black
man from an Oran crowd endeavoring to run "Negroes out of town."[115]

But this time Hobbs came late and, advancing to the execution site, acted
more as a spectator than a lawman. Nor did he contribute much to either
preparing the state case or testifying against the lynchers. Dace, not Hobbs,
proved "very helpful" to Blanton's investigation, and jurors heard Hobbs say
that "he couldn't identify any of the people . . . around the body."[116] In part,
this signified his racial beliefs: namely, that Wright—unlike the Oran black,
who, he believed, was innocent of wrongdoing—had assaulted the white
woman. Hobbs, who had permitted Wright to play baseball while a county
prisoner, may also have personalized Wright's gross transgression. Consequently, given the sheriff's commitment to the white community, he would
hurt no one in an effort to keep the mob "from getting that nigger." All things
considered, he—like his mountain and southern counterparts—viewed the
mob as having carried out "the spirit of formal law."[117] That Hobbs feuded
with city police, who on this occasion failed to contact him about the previous evening's events, made his delay more predictable.

Whatever the sheriff's intentions, however, policemen more directly responsible for Wright's well-being drew the most attention. NAACP investi-

gators visiting Sikeston shortly after the lynching noted the absence of "a strong protective local police" and the need to probe this issue.[118] More significant, state troopers in defending their own actions had brought into question the behavior of Police Chief Kendall and Assistant Police Chief Wallace. Dace reported that when he arrived at 10:30 A.M. and found would-be lynchers attempting to break into Wright's quarters, no policeman was in the building; that thereafter only Kendall assisted in the unsuccessful effort to fend off the mob; that at no time was the prisoner "in the custody of the Missouri Highway Patrol." In exonerating Dace, Superintendent Ginn emphasized these points, and news stories embellished both their presentations.[119] Mindful of Japan's and Germany's military advances at the time, a local editor joked grimly: "Sikeston officers protected Cleo Wright about as well as our Army and Navy have been protecting American lives and possessions the past few weeks."[120]

Justice Department officials were not laughing. They suspected Sikeston police of having "wilfully denied" Wright the equal protection and due process that might have saved his life. They pressed superiors for a full inquiry by the FBI, and subsequently a grand jury focused solely on Kendall and Wallace. Beyond the seminal issue of protecting a prisoner, they questioned whether the police chief and his assistant had taken seriously the earliest threats against Wright and why they placed him in the insecure women's detention room.[121]

Unlike federal attorneys, Sikeston peace officers sprang from the local region and reflected its personal, pragmatic approach to justice. The police chief was born in 1877 to C.D. and Amanda Kendall and had lived his entire life in town. Educated in its public schools and married to one of its own, Lou LaGrange, he had fathered three daughters and worked at Farmers' Supply Company before becoming a patrolman in 1924. He completed the term of Joe Randol two years later, then was elected police chief in his own right. A very popular lawman for the next sixteen years, he won reelection easily; for example, in 1940 he received 2,800 votes against no opposition.[122] "A fine old gentleman" who often tended his garden on election day, he was "an honorable man" who policed little and treated everyone, regardless of race, respectfully.[123]

Kendall knew most townsfolk and their children and often patrolled afoot and unarmed. Gray-haired, blue-eyed, and kind-looking, yet 6'2" and weighing 225 pounds, he tried to resolve differences through personal diplomacy; he arrested very few transgressors, preferring to look the other way when blacks gambled or to hold them only overnight. Similarly, he toured

downtown white bars, coaxed heavy drinkers to call it an evening, and escorted home those too drunk to make their own way. In 1942 he was nearing his sixty-fifth birthday and lived alone with his wife, their daughters
already having married.[124]

Wallace, younger but somewhat similar in background and build, came
from Fairdealing, southwest of Poplar Bluff. He was born in 1910, one of
several children of James Franklin Wallace and Ida Mae Smith. He moved
into the Bootheel sometime before his twentieth birthday, married Elsie Hale
at Lilbourn, and soon became the parent of four children. Like Kendall, who
probably recommended him for the position in June 1940, Wallace related
well to many residents, including those in the Addition. Yet as an outsider,
and a lawman for less than two years, he lacked the popularity of his mentor. He received mixed evaluations from townspeople, some recalling him
as "much more vigorous" than the police chief and others as less than evenhanded.[125] At thirty-one years old and physically fit, he stood 5'10", weighed
232 pounds, and looked every bit the law enforcer.

For both policemen, January 25, 1942, proved fateful. When Kendall
came on duty that morning, he learned of Wright's attacks while patrolling
the streets, none of his officers having reported them. He went to City Hall
at 9:00 A.M. to find a hundred people outside and a few inside, though "everyone was quiet" and no one approached Wright's chamber. As the crowd
swelled, he claimed to have notified Sheriff Hobbs an hour later and, with
the assistance of Sergeant Dace, cleared the building. Throughout the ordeal that followed he neither called officers Roy Beck and Grover Lewis (because "they had worked all night") nor considered moving Wright from the
detention room to a jail cell. Instead, along with Troopers Dace, Tandy, and
Boisaubin, Kendall held off the ever growing mob, only to lose his prisoner
shortly after Blanton arrived at 11:30 A.M. He then stayed in his office rather
than chase lynchers to Sunset, finally going home for lunch some two hours
later.[126]

By comparison, Wallace began work at 6:00 A.M. and learned of the early
morning bloodshed from Beck and Lewis, whom he met at the bus station.[127]
He drove with them to Wright's house and tried to talk to him. Then he returned downtown, and his fellow officers went off duty. Wallace soon reappeared in Sunset at the request of Wright's in-laws, who asked that he be
taken away. The assistant chief retrieved an ambulance and then, making
his third trip to the black community, brought Wright to City Hall sometime after 9:30 A.M.; he placed him alone in the women's detention room,
believing him close to death. Within half an hour, he, Milem Limbaugh, and

Milburn Arbaugh heard Wright confess to cutting Grace Sturgeon. Thereafter, Wallace continued his "regular police duty," returned to City Hall at
11:15 A.M., spoke with Kendall, Dace, and Boisaubin, "went to the toilet," took
a call "requesting settlement of a trivial dispute among neighbors," and supposedly left the building to resolve it at 11:35 A.M.[128] He considered the three
or four hundred people outside well behaved and unthreatening. When he
returned a little past noon, their absence initially made him think that "the
Negro had died." When he found the building empty and its detention door
broken, he drove to Sunset, observed the crowd from afar, and returned
quickly to town. Later he made his fifth trip to the Addition and helped load
Wright's remains into a truck.

In the aftermath, both policemen claimed not to have recognized anyone at City Hall or, in Wallace's case, Sunset. Wallace also contended that he
had not contacted the highway patrol or the sheriff before Wright's burning
because he had no idea "anything was going to happen." And once federal
intentions to prosecute local lawmen became apparent, Kendall dodged FBI
agents by saying that "he was very busy." By that time, assistant and chief
were the sole targets of the U.S. Justice Department.[129]

From its legal perspective, Kendall deserved prosecution for conduct that
violated his prisoner's civil rights.[130] Though the chief did endeavor to keep
the crowd back after Dace's midmorning arrival, he seemed to have done
nothing before then. Indeed, despite his own recollection, he appeared to
have been elsewhere when the state trooper entered the premises to find
numerous individuals "running in and out" and others attempting to break
into Wright's room; Kendall either left the building open to would-be lynchers between 9:00 and 10:30 A.M. or he was out of Dace's sight.[131] Nor did he
initiate the effort to clear City Hall and call for more help, reacting instead
to the trooper's leadership. In fact, his claim of having called Sheriff Hobbs
at 10:00 A.M. was not confirmed by the phone records. And his contention
of having let Beck and Lewis sleep and left Wallace unsupervised because
their services were unnecessary sounded incredible, for he witnessed Dace's
calls for additional lawmen and watched as the mob grew in size, berated
lawmen, and pushed at the doors in a steady escalation of violence.[132]

Moreover, Kendall provided little help at City Hall. He stood around
rather than engage the lyncher onslaught. And, according to Dace, he denied having keys to lock the front doors of the building and keep out the
crowd, or to open the detention room and jails for the purpose of transfer-
ring Wright from a chamber easily entered to a cell of impenetrable iron bars.
(Kendall subsequently denied that the subject of moving Wright ever came

up, though he did possess keys to the women's detention and the cells.)[133] He neither chased after the lynchers nor alerted Sunset residents; perhaps most disturbing, as a lifelong resident and chief for eighteen years he could identify no one in the very mob that he faced for two hours!

Even more grievously than Kendall, Wallace disregarded Wright's civil rights. He too saw the crowd enlarge and grow ugly between 9:30 A.M., when he placed Wright in the women's room, and two hours later when lynchers dragged him out. Between those events, he, Limbaugh, and Arbaugh heard Wright's confession with at least one lyncher, Mike A., present, and thereafter he walked past those who spoke of killing Wright. Yet when Wallace appeared at City Hall, he observed "nothing unusual," he said—not even minutes before the mob broke through the police line.[134] He entered the building "only once" and left while other officers confronted the crowd that he judged peaceful, recalled Dace; he neither spoke with the chief that morning nor sought his permission to leave on an official call as members of the mob were on the verge of their final charge, remembered Kendall.[135] Nor did Wallace's claim of departing to investigate a dog disturbance jibe with the statements of participants who remembered that as having occurred on another day. Justice Department lawyers believed that he used the incident as an "excuse" to avoid the clash with lynchers and went home to eat lunch.[136] And his afternoon drive to Sunset, only to retreat from the lingering crowd and return to town, hardly seemed fitting for an assistant police chief.

With equal irresponsibility, Kendall failed to treat seriously the possibility of mob violence. Federal agents, as well as one area lawman, theorized that Sikeston police, angered by the attack on Hess Perrigan, took Wright to his own home so that he could be apprehended more easily by lynchers, but Dace and Wright's wife, among others, dismissed such thinking as "ridiculous."[137] Nevertheless, Beck and Lewis, who first delivered Wright to his wife, gave FBI operatives the impression of being "unconcerned" and "indifferent"; despite admonishing troubled blacks to notify them "immediately" if an attempt was made to molest Wright, they went off duty.[138] Kendall, of course, knew nothing of these happenings, but once on duty he must have heard threats among townsfolk abuzz with talk of lynch law. Not a conspirator himself, he did nothing to distract would-be lynchers from their conspiracy.

If Kendall blinked when staring into the eyes of lynchers, Wallace, at the very least, looked the other way.[139] He failed to tell bureau investigators that when he brought Wright to City Hall at 9:00 A.M., blacks had already ex-

pressed concern over talk "about getting him."[140] Later, in fact, probably after having heard Wright's confession, he told Paul Bumbarger about the attacks on Sturgeon and Perrigan, how upset people were, and "what was going
to happen." He seemed to have been informed by the lynchers of their plans
to mob Wright—or so the *Standard* reporter guessed.[141] That would explain
his absence from the battle line of lawmen who clashed with the very individuals who had confided in him. Though not an active member of the mob,
he did its bidding by denying Wright one more protector. Thereafter, he
served as unofficial police spokesman, feeding information to the press that
verified Wright's guilt—his prison record, stalking of Sturgeon, intention to
rape her—and, intentionally or not, giving the impression that he had played
a significant part in the police action.[142]

The assistant chief of police did not, however, place Wright in the
women's room in order to make him more accessible to the mob members
who so easily smashed its wooden panel door. More likely, he believed that
Wright was dying and would be more comfortable alone, on a mattress-cov-
ered cot in the women's room, than on a steel bunk in a jail cell occupied by
other prisoners. In this he was supported by Kendall, who never thought of
moving Wright because he "was in bad shape"; and his stretcher would hardly
fit through a cell door.[143] The police chief's latter point was verified by FBI
agents, who measured the ambulance cot and the entrance.[144]

Perhaps to deflect attention from himself, Wallace told bureau investigators that Wright "was being held for the Sheriff." His remark took on added
intrigue when Hobbs informed the same questioners that Wright should
have been removed to Scott County Jail the moment he had been caught,
implying that his lynching could have been prevented.[145] These comments
lost their potential explosiveness, however, when Mayor George W. Presnell,
himself a physician, opined that moving the badly wounded Wright to
Benton "would have proved instantly fatal." More self-serving for his own
reputation and that of Sikeston police, he added that under the circumstances
Wright received "appropriate protection."[146]

Beyond conspiracy and protection issues, police activity sparked federal inquiry into charges of noncooperation, corruption, and inefficiency.
Neither Kendall nor his officers had contacted Hobbs—or, more surprising,
Blanton—about Wright's violence; that was left for Dace to do long after the
lynchers had gathered. Given the failure of city police to call the sheriff, their
later claim to have been holding Wright for transfer to the county jail proved
disingenuous and substantiated the lack of cooperation between lawmen.

That Kendall did not even speak to Hobbs was a personal manifestation of the "definite friction" that Blanton—himself a county official aligned with Hobbs—noted between city police and county peace officers.[147]

Such friction, involving territorial lines, partly explained Hobbs's dilatory response to the lynching. As significantly, Kendall's and Hobbs's rivalry stemmed from competition over prisoners and spoils. When Sikeston policemen arrested a felon, for example, they would bring him before Justice of the Peace Brown Jewell, who reduced the charge to a misdemeanor and imposed a fine payable to the City of Sikeston instead of the sheriff's office. Essentially, then, Kendall and Brown kept major criminals, normally under county jurisdiction, in their bailiwick and denied the sheriff fees that could total meaningful sums and affect his livelihood. Their act of self-aggrandizement also sharpened the feud and likely affronted Hobbs's self-respect.[148]

It was probably because of this offense that Hobbs charged Sikeston policemen with "receiving money" from black gamblers for permitting crap games in the Addition. He told FBI agents about this (unsubstantiated) corruption within a month of the lynching. However unwittingly, he forced bureau personnel to probe deeper, partly because special prosecutor Jacob M. Lashly sought leverage in the federal case against local lawmen.[149] Investigators found few sources believing, much less corroborating, the rumor of such wrongdoing. Most of those interrogated—including Councilman Matthews and an unnamed informant—considered the allegation specious, as did Dace and Blanton.[150] Hobbs's hearsay about local police receiving bribes found one black resident who named Perrigan and Bartlett but offered no evidence, and years later other Sunset inhabitants disagreed, again without proof either way, as to whether Kendall and Wallace "were on the take."[151]

In truth, Kendall and his officers displayed inefficiency rather than corruption. Few ever questioned the police chief's honesty, but almost everyone considered him and his staff woefully inept: Dace said "untrained." Less objectively, a former department member and present deputy sheriff labeled them "the worst police force in the country."[152] Kendall drew most of the criticism. He winked at gambling in Sunset, never ordering Bartlett to close it down and even informing one operator that he was not violating the law. He heard complaints about white streetwalkers operating out of downtown cafes, and allegedly infecting air cadets with venereal disease, but refused to roust them: "Those prostitutes work as hard for their money as we do for ours."[153] An exasperated Blanton had found it necessary to rely on the sheriff's office to raid Sunset gambling houses. Council members had reduced the police chief's salary to "practically nothing" to dissuade him from seeking reelection in 1940.[154] Yet he ran again without opposition, ever popular with black residents, who purportedly had swung close elections in his favor.[155]

However honest, Kendall's approach to law enforcement boded ill for a major crisis. Having very little crime in Sikeston, he "relaxed in his duties as policeman," spending more time in personal conversation and touring cafes and bars. He made very few arrests, seemingly cared little about enforcing the law, and sometimes ignored calls by simply waiting for another officer to pick up the telephone. He kept no records and lacked a communication system; those needing a patrolman called the town operator, who signaled officers via the red light to contact her.[156]

Thus Kendall's department proved wholly inadequate to handle the lynching; like him, his officers were untrained, lacking in experience, and set in their ways. Collectively, Kendall, Lewis, Beck, Perrigan, and Wallace struck a median age of fifty-two years and boasted little if any knowledge of handling violence-prone criminals or controlling crowds. Hence, Perrigan failed to search Wright adequately, and no officer informed Kendall of the crisis or of black fears that a lynching might occur. Those employed by Kendall, himself neither "an aggressive" officer nor a leader, responded accordingly: Beck and Lewis retired from duty, and Wallace dissembled before the mob.[157] They policed the way they had been taught, as individuals engaged in personal diplomacy rather than a unit authorized to use force; none understood a concept so alien to Kendall's example of law enforcement.

Given these circumstances, little could be expected of Henry Bartlett. He had been hired in May 1940 as the department's sixth man and lone black officer, specifically assigned to police Sunset Addition. He received $30 per month ($70 less than his white counterparts), worked part time as a cook downtown, and served primarily as a liaison between blacks and the larger community.[158] When approached by Lewis early Sunday morning, he directed the officer to Wright's home and then accompanied Wright's in-laws to the hospital. He retired at 6:00 A.M., only to be awakened by someone fearing mob rule and wanting the wounded prisoner moved from his own home. Bartlett, like Beck and Lewis later, dismissed the plaintiff and "went back to sleep." He became very frightened thereafter and, like Wallace, kept out of sight: he never appeared at City Hall to help hold off the mob, never joined the ranks of black homeowners and white lawmen who protected Sunset that night. As the community's duly appointed peace officer, he was ridiculed later for "hiding his ass."[159] In reality, he followed the lead of most white policemen and many black denizens.

Bartlett aside, Kendall and Wallace were the most irresponsible local policemen. Both officers believed Wright guilty and dying, Wallace having heard his midmorning confession and Kendall his weakening groans; their resolve, like Wright's life signs, diminished as lyncher intensity grew.[160] Community loyalty overwhelmed their oath of office, partly because the latter emanated from the very people who now challenged them and partly because the personal approach of policing now made them vulnerable. Kendall and Wallace walked through the crowd and conversed with those who had come to expect lighthanded and, from their perspective, reasonable police behavior. Instead of persuading lynchers to desist, they found themselves lobbied and, in effect, threatened; instead of serving to pacify opposing individuals, they found themselves having to choose sides. They recognized how futile and powerless their position had become in the face of a tyrannical majority, whose emotionalism and numbers made police opposition uncertain—and dangerous.[161]

Clearly, Wallace proved the more vulnerable to communal pressure. Perhaps the assistant chief initially attempted to dissuade the lynchers who approached him; at least he never said that Wright deserved killing, and he did express frustration over his inability to stop the inevitable. Kendall held closer to his sense of duty, refusing to abandon his post, and manifested even clearer signs of exasperation and regret, telling federal agents that he had done all he could—"all a mule can do"— to keep the mob from Wright.[162] Police chief and assistant acted in legally distinct ways, however. Kendall failed to protect the prisoner adequately; Wallace, in making absolutely no effort to shield Wright, committed "wilful 'inaction.'"[163]

Although the grand jury refused to indict either peace officer, Kendall and Wallace surely felt the strain of federal prosecution and—beyond Sikeston—public criticism. They and thirteen other county residents endured grilling that, according to one observer, lacked only "a foot or two of rubber hose" from being the "third degree."[164] Whatever the exaggeration of that quip, the police chief and his assistant received the harshest treatment among witnesses facing federal prosecutors, and they experienced greater anxiety over possible indictment than the lynchers brought before state attorneys. Kendall, in fact, suffered a "very mild" stroke shortly after the inquiry, and within two years he retired.[165] That Wallace succeeded Kendall as police chief indicated their popularity in a community believing itself under siege by outsiders.

In spite of the federal grand jury, which chided local policemen for the lynching (and, ironically, evaluated their department as "no stronger and probably no weaker" than those of similar communities), Sikeston leaders and voters supported Kendall and Wallace from the moment of Wright's killing.[166] Four days later newsman Clint H. Denman publicly commended Kendall and the troopers for having done "their full duty." Shortly thereafter, mayor and council members adopted Ralph E. Bailey's resolution, which expanded appreciation to the chief's subordinates (and the prosecuting attorney) stating that they "did everything in their power to prevent the mob violence." City officials, of course, spoke for several prominent citizens, including Denman, who responded to the "unfortunate publicity" given their city by condemning lynch law, even while protecting the reputations of local lawmen.[167] They also raised the chief's salary from $100 to $125 per month and, two weeks later, that of all white patrolmen by 10 percent.[168]

Wallace, Lewis, Beck, and Perrigan received their increases effective March 1; Kendall waited until the April 7 election for his. The delay reflected municipal ordinance more than displeasure with the police chief; in the national spotlight his stand against the lynchers, however lame, had protected the city's reputation. And yet, a month after he again won reelection without opposition, the council increased his assistant's salary to the level of his own.[169] That Kendall received votes similar in number and distribution to those of all other unopposed citywide candidates indicated his popularity among townspeople. But that he did so in an election characterized by the smallest turnout in recent years reflected not only the absence of servicemen away but public lack of interest and at least some voter disapproval.[170] Whether constituents ignored the polls as an unspoken antilynching protest is difficult to determine, but Kendall's supporters—like those of the mayor, city collector, police judge, treasurer, and assessor—surely revealed public support for the handling of Wright's death. In that sense, Kendall received community payback for having permitted some residents to kill Wright and others to save face for failing to protect him.

Kendall finally lost a three-man race in 1944, outpolled two to one by Wallace, who handled Beck even more easily. His defeat indicated problems of age and health rather than delayed voter opposition to the lynching or a change set in motion by war. Moreover, Kendall, Wallace, and Beck drew as many votes collectively as did all major offices—none of which were contested—and again few constituents turned out, signifying that the immediate postlynching election reflected war-induced trends rather than a divided electorate: one supportive, the other silent.[171] Indeed, in the first election after the war, which Wallace won handily, voter numbers returned to prewar standards.[172]

Not as strange as it appeared, town residents—lynchers and their opponents alike—returned David E. Blanton to office. Despite his opposition to Wright's death and effort to indict the lynchers, he was never snubbed but did find himself at odds with half of Sikeston and their most vociferous spokesman: his own father.[173] In fact, if any two people seemed representative of contesting factions throughout the lynching episode, it was the Blantons.

6   The Blantons

Father and son of one of the locale's most famous families, Charles L. and David E. Blanton found themselves on opposite sides in the matter of Wright's lynching, symbolizing much larger issues of race relations and community development. Their differences revealed the impact of global war on a traditional society whose national government's fight for survival and democracy abroad necessitated social order and racial justice at home. As lynchers, policemen, and the elder Blanton acted in a world that was being lost, the younger Blanton—representative of civic and commercial elites—operated in its modern sequel.[1]

C.L. Blanton publicized the mobbing of Wright as "deserved" and supported those responsible for his death.[2] His position, representing more than that of a racist editor seeking personal notoriety and commercial gain, sprang as much from southern influences and traditional beliefs that mirrored the thinking, if not the lives, of many white townsfolk.

Born September 18, 1863, in Howard County, Missouri, C.L. was one of several children of Mary Harriet Young and Benjamin F. Blanton. Though the origins of his Scottish-Danish parents remain obscure, Benjamin, one of many residents who opposed Missouri unionism during the Civil War, had fought for the Confederate army. He then returned to Missouri's "Little Dixie"—so called because of the area's settlement by migrants from the upper South—and established the *Monroe County Appeal* at Paris, in Monroe County. Given his background, war activity, and publishing venture, he raised C.L. as "a true southerner" in racial attitudes, states' rights beliefs, and Democratic Party politics. He also taught him the newspaper business.[3]

As a young man, C.L. Blanton ventured to Washington, D.C., where—perhaps a result of Benjamin's political contacts—he worked for several years in the Government Printing Office and the Treasury Department before returning home to assist his father. Meantime he courted Mary Agnes Cullen, daughter of a federal employee from Nashville, Tennessee. He married her in 1890 and began a family with the birth of Harry Cullen a year later. Soon he moved them back to the national capital and returned to the Treasury Department, where he remained for sixteen years.

Following residence in Paris, Missouri, from 1909 to 1913, when he entered newspaper publishing anew, C.L. struck out on his own. He borrowed $500, purchased the *Standard* from Fred, George, and Harry Naeter of Cape Girardeau, and brought his wife and their eight children into Sikeston. He published the first issue on March 1, 1913, a four-page weekly that superseded the five-year-old *Hornet*. Thereafter, with the assistance of Mary Agnes and their third child, Charles Lee Jr., he slowly built the area's most profitable and influential newspaper. Increasingly he relied on the advertising skill of Charles Jr., who had learned printing from grandfather Benjamin, attended the University of Illinois, and served in World War I; similar in temperament, father and son complemented one another and, in 1927, made the *Standard* a semiweekly. By 1942 C.L. boasted 2,069 subscribers, numerous advertisers, and a reputation for irreverent, fearless, and entertaining viewpoints that sprang from his father's direct though more tactful style.[4]

C.L.'s fame came as the "Pole Cat" editor, a sobriquet that grew out of his rivalry with Clinton H. Denman of the Republican *Herald*. He disagreed with his somewhat younger, better educated, more deeply religious counterpart on almost everything. He associated with people and things southern; Denman, who was born approximately fifty miles northeast of Sikeston to a Yankee preacher, served in the Spanish American War, earned a college degree, and appeared more cosmopolitan (though no less committed locally). C.L. wrote, said Paul Bumbarger, "to tilt windmills and create sensations" lest townsfolk forget his iconoclasm, while Denman composed serious editorials reflecting his position as a Sunday School teacher, Boy Scout Council president, and Lions and Kiwanis charter member. C.L. joined few organizations and celebrated heritage; Denman, past president of the Missouri Press Association and prominent member of the First United Methodist Church, played "an important role in the civic, intellectual and moral progress of the city."[5]

When Denman publicly remarked in 1936 that Blanton's writings "smelled to high heaven as a polecat would," C.L. delighted in the mock; he retitled his column "The P.C. Editor Says," featured a skunk on its masthead, and hung the hide of one by his desk. He became "the Pole Cat": sharp-tongued, satirical, inimitable. Musing as he operated the two-cylinder press, he would stop it to scribble ideas with pencil stubs and, with gleaming eyes and chuckling voice, read them aloud. Still, he trained cub reporters such as Art L. Wallhausen to be objective and "leave the funny stuff to me," believ-

C.L. Blanton, the "Pole Cat," in his newspaper office, in 1942.
Courtesy of Michael L. Jensen

ing that publishers, for all their individualism, must serve the community.[6]

C.L., of course, cherished editorializing, and relied on Charles Jr. to pacify advertisers alienated by the Pole Cat. His copy revealed an unreconstructed southerner.[7] He opposed the Scott County Milling Company strike in 1941, accusing "union boys" of deception, and two years later encouraged anyone who caught a tire thief to "shoot him like he was a mad dog."[8] Reacting most explosively to assaults on the racial status quo, he endorsed the "swift and impressive" lynchings of alleged black rapists at Charleston in 1924 and Braggadocio in 1927, and advocated "horsewhipping" the primary black organizer and chief white sympathizer of the roadside demonstration centered at Sikeston in 1939. Employing similar rhetorical violence, he offered to duel those who called him a liar or threatened his honor, reminding them of his office hours and desk drawer pistol.[9]

Yet just as surely Blanton embraced a more complicated, seemingly inconsistent concept of race that turned on paternalism and etiquette. He welcomed blacks into the Bootheel as it shifted to a cotton cultivation in the early 1920s but quickly became alienated by their challenge to the color line in religious revivals and local elections. He donated enough pews to fill the Second Baptist Colored Church, reflecting commitments to white philanthropy and racial segregation.[10] Yet despite his support of preachers such as S.D. Woods, whose efforts supposedly curbed asocial and criminal tendencies among blacks, the Pole Cat ridiculed black ministers: there was the parson who, dining with a deacon and asked if he desired some corn, "inadvertently passed his glass instead of his plate." He predicted that Joe Louis would beat Buddy Baer to retain the heavyweight championship yet regularly belittled blacks. He told of the first-time airline traveler who, upon noticing "what appeared to be the same gasoline truck" refueling the plane at every stop, exclaimed that it was "keeping right up with us!"[11] The Pole Cat realized that his column served to control both races, blacks themselves admitting that if you stomped your feet around him "you'd see it in the paper the next day!"[12]

As Sikeston entered the war years, Blanton sounded the trumpet of patriotism and linked it to white supremacy. He referred to "brown bellied Japs," called hero-turned-isolationist Charles Lindbergh a "son-of-a-bitch," and advocated the arrest of anyone calling a strike.[13] Contradictorily, he opposed economic advances for area workers, regardless of race, but endorsed the hiring of 3,000 "competent and willing" blacks by a St. Louis munitions plant.[14] Well into 1942 he played on war exigencies to speak out against union efforts and praise patriotic displays among area blacks, such as the Pinkhook School drum and bugle corps that marched in Charleston to demonstrate "national solidarity." He also expressed concern that the Ethiopian Pacific Movement in that neighboring city was becoming "quite serious" again. Ever the humorist, however, he could not refrain from reporting how he "bit" when asked the location of "no man's land," only to be told that instead of a strategic military position, it was "the opposite side of an old maid's bed"![15]

Seventy-eight years old at the time of Wright's lynching, C.L. Blanton loomed much larger than his nearly 5'9", 170-pound frame. He strolled about town, sporting a gray suit and doffing a gray derby, a smile on his face, a twinkle in his eye, and a firm grip in his handshake. White-haired and mustached, more often than not called "Colonel"—the honorary rank bestowed upon him by Governor Lloyd C. Stark and befitting his self-image—he enjoyed widespread community respect. He lived on Tanner Street in a home purchased nearly thirty years earlier, remodeled according to architectural styles "found in the old south," and kept up by black dayworkers.[16] Once a lady's man, he delighted in escorting "young gals" from his office to a nearby drugstore for a refreshment, collecting "calendar photographs of scantily clad feminine flesh for the 'art gallery' in the press room," and printing jokes that some readers considered vulgar. Once a drinker, though never a smoker, he took pleasure in giving young children nickels and dimes saved from no longer indulging in alcohol. Chivalrous and kind, though hardly religious despite membership in the First Baptist Church, he seemed every bit the southern patriarch.[17]

Above all, C.L. Blanton counted his family first. He boasted of his children's successes, noting that many of them graced public payrolls: Harry a federal attorney, Milton a government economist, J. Benjamin a state public service commissioner, David a county prosecutor, Catherine a former secretary to U.S. Senator Pat Harrison of Mississippi. And Mary's husband worked for the Department of the Interior, leaving only Edna's husband and Charles Jr. in the private sector. An astute party loyalist, the elder Blanton connected his family "from the smallest to the highest level of Democratic politics." Only Charles and David remained in town, but C.L. and Mary Agnes kept abreast of all their children's welfare. During World War II, for example, they visited Charles who spent months in the Mt. Vernon Sanitarium. Those absences were the reason C.L. permitted Paul Bumbarger to ghostwrite an occasional Pole Cat column.[18]

Close-knit and loving, the Blanton children grew up in a surprisingly tolerant home; David in particular developed a very independent personality. Born in Falls Church, Virginia, on October 17, 1908, the fifth son and last Blanton child, he moved with the family to Paris and then, at age four and a half, to Sikeston. He remembered growing up in "a good place." Despite the town's cultural "sparseness" and racial segregation, he experienced "lots of fun" and very little racial friction. He worked as a salesman for Buckner-Ragsdale Company, graduated from Sikeston High School, and put himself through the University of Missouri at Columbia in five years by earning commissions in another clothing store. On his own, in part because of the family's large size and limited income, he managed to save $1,000, obtain a university loan, and borrow from other sources to enter Harvard Law School.[19]

David returned to Sikeston and in 1934 began a successful legal practice. Small-framed, blue-eyed, dark blond, and handsome, he married Mary Anna Hearne of Poplar Bluff in June 1940, and that November he ran successfully for Scott County prosecuting attorney. During his first term of of-

David E. Blanton in 1942. Courtesy of
Michael L. Jensen.

fice he set a record for revenues acquired through fines and fees. He also
enjoyed life on North Park Avenue with Mary and the first of their two children, David Jr.[20]

Several family members influenced David's upbringing, most obviously
his father. From C.L. he learned the value of hard work, self-reliance, and
individualism, especially standing up for one's principles. He also acquired,
as did all Blantons, a commitment to Democratic Party politics and a strong
sense of community. Significantly, though, he did not embrace his father's
feelings toward "colored people." Their differences on this issue loomed large,
blacks recalling that the "ole man had a hard time" and describing his son
as "a nice person."[21] Nor did David display C.L.'s egotism, possibly considering it a countermodel and, in part, a reason to have left Sikeston long
enough to prove himself.

David benefited from the influence of his mother as well. He heard about
the Union side of the family from her, her father having served as a captain
in the Civil War. He learned religious tolerance and the meaning of faith
through her Irish Catholicism and active role in St. Francis Xavier Church,
which offset his father's nominal Baptist membership and irreverence.
(Though baptized a Catholic, as were all the children, he embraced neither

parent's religion; instead, in deference to his bride, he eventually became a deacon in the First Presbyterian Church.) Both parents set the house rules, but David considered his mother more responsible for raising the children and instilling in them "exceptionally fine" values; she was "the family mainstay" who provided stability. Nine years younger and less flamboyant than her husband, Mary Agnes nevertheless ran the home, if not the newspaper, and held her own in the marriage, albeit probably less outspokenly than she did at church.[22]

David also looked to his siblings for life's cues. Raised "in a country town," the youngest of eight brothers and sisters, he learned early to fend for himself—a lesson that reinforced C.L.'s work ethic, combative nature, and independence and Mary Agnes's tolerance and caring. Unlike Charles, who followed the Colonel, he modeled himself after Harry, who seemed more like Mary Agnes and even embraced her Catholicism. David "very much" admired his eldest brother; despite their seventeen years difference, Harry reinforced David's schoolboy desire to become a lawyer and, in uncanny similarity, lived a scenario that the younger brother's would parallel. Harry had stayed behind when the family returned to Paris in 1909, supported himself by selling newspapers in Falls Church, and completed high school in Georgetown; he had worked full time in the Riggs National Bank in Washington, D.C., while earning a law degree from Georgetown University; then, joining the family in Sikeston, he became city attorney and Scott County prosecuting attorney before entering military service in World War I. After the war he returned home, opened a practice, and served the county Democratic Party, which resulted in his appointment as U.S. attorney for the Eastern District after assisting Champ Clark's 1932 election to the U.S. Senate.[23]

So David chose Harry's profession and sought an eastern law degree. Perhaps he also went east thinking that he "needed a change" culturally and to fulfill his own expectations.[24] Then, after he returned to Sikeston and became county prosecutor, a major crisis brought him and Harry together as legal peers and in direct opposition to their father: the face-off of modern and traditional Blantons.

Critics made little distinction between Blantons, ultimately condemning the sons for the viewpoints on lynching espoused by their father. Within hours of Wright's death they questioned David's integrity. Their complaints alleged that he refused to identify mob members after facing them at City Hall and leading them through Sunset Addition. "When a man speaks to a group of men, a number of whom he surely has addressed during his many . . . campaign speeches, and then cannot recognize them," argued one prominent businessman of Kansas City, he must suffer from "very bad memory" or very poor eyesight; in either case, he "put his politics in a safe place." Hence NAACP-sponsored delegates meeting with Governor Donnell, including the letter writer, requested that a special prosecutor replace Blanton.[25]

Blanton's detractors had prejudged him, partly because of his initial press remarks. The Monday after Wright's death the county prosecutor called for a grand jury investigation, yet contended that he and others could not identify the lynchers. That he had encountered unmasked lynchers, including individuals "familiar to him," and ordered no arrests while promising "a vigorous investigation" made little sense to at least one irate St. Louisan, who complained to Donnell.[26] On Tuesday, Blanton next reported "little headway," interpreting the few tips given him as an indication that "the people seem to be well satisfied." Within twenty-four hours he found himself drubbed by liberal editors who misconstrued his words and resented the suggestion that Sikestonians, much less all Missourians, appeared content with letting the inquiry fail.[27]

Whatever Blanton's intentions, his father's column, also published on Tuesday, reinforced the thinking of some critics. The Pole Cat dubbed Wright a knife-wielding ex-convict and his mobbing "unfortunate" but "deserved," the work of dutiful men protecting the wives of "soldier boys" and warning "night prowlers to leave the community"; the elder Blanton's assurances that law-abiding blacks would be given "protection" seemed less noteworthy. Although some editors noted that the son should not be held accountable for his father's views, they seized on the P.C. column as a reason to suggest that the prosecutor demonstrate his own integrity by welcoming "the outside unprejudiced help" offered by the governor.[28]

"Knowing local authorities" in Missouri, however, St. Louis NAACP critics lacked faith that Democrat Blanton—or even Republican Donnell—intended to undertake "a real investigation." Regardless of the younger Blanton's sincerity, which association investigators acknowledged, or his father's typical southern reaction, which David as surely did not share, they believed that only a federal antilynch law would bring justice.[29] Even after an assistant state attorney general joined Blanton in the grand jury investigation, association members—black and white—doubted his ability to prosecute "those friends who elected him to office."[30]

Editors, in turn, flayed away at "the Blanton Clan," so-called by a black Chicagoan who printed a list of family members on the public payroll, indicating that it would "take unusual influence to secure anything like a prosecution in the Sikeston case." He doubted that even the FBI's participation could prove decisive in the face of the Colonel's tribe, itself typical of protagonists in other lynchings. He too deemed federal law "the only remedy to discourage lynching."[31] Following the failure of the state case, one St. Louis journalist wondered anew if—under oath—Blanton had told the truth about mob leaders "with whom he comes into contact almost daily."[32] In short, many critics lacked faith in county and state officials, whatever their names, pedigree, or party affiliation. And their preconceived notions of law enforcement, given the history of racial violence, necessitated reproaching the county prosecutor before, while, and after he played his hand.

David E. Blanton deserved better. Unhesitatingly, he proposed the state grand jury to Donnell on the evening of Wright's death and, once that was endorsed, informed the press that "a vigorous investigation" would serve public interest better than an inquest. In the same conversation he denied knowing any of the mob leaders and made the "little headway" reference that drew withering criticism.[33] Clearly, he could have named some of the lynchers and apparently said otherwise in order to protect his inquiry and himself; rather than try individuals in the newspapers or feel even greater personal pressure, he spoke less than truthfully on the identity of killers and, conversely, too candidly on the lack of cooperation from townspeople. Caught between external and internal forces, which included his father, David found addressing reporters problematic. Nor did he know how much Donnell wanted said or who should say it.

From that moment until Donnell met the black delegation on Thursday, however, Blanton claimed "some progress" and informed the governor of his entire strategy from investigation to grand jury presentment. He anticipated every major obstacle, requesting continual state assistance: troopers for the inquiry and an attorney general for "the trial proper." He explained the latter appeal in legal terms, realizing that he himself would testify and therefore needed someone to question him. Stung by public criticism, he later admitted seeking "outside help" to stem the "whitewashing" accusations. Finally, he reported plans to confer with Judge J.C. McDowell about calling a grand jury.[34] Within two days, Blanton informed Donnell that, unsatisfactory resident cooperation notwithstanding, he and the troopers had identified some of the lynchers and would provide testimony before the jury that McDowell agreed to convene in March. He requested a conference with the governor and State Attorney General Roy A. McKittrick, reiterating his need for someone with "actual practical trial experience in criminal work." This important case, he asserted, sounding very unlike his father or other apologists, should leave no stone unturned in bringing "the guilty parties to the bar of justice."[35]

Thus, between his first encounter with the press and his reports to Donnell, Blanton changed his approach from pessimism to smooth-spoken optimism. He enabled Donnell to tell black protesters on January 29 that progress was under way and on the same day he told newsmen that the "veil of silence" had lifted, that several lynchers were now known, that photographic evidence was available, that a grand jury was forthcoming, that the charge would be murder.[36] In short, the county prosecutor played to his critics, albeit not dishonestly, and wisely declined to comment on the Pole Cat's editorial policy.

The Blanton-Donnell-McKittrick summit occurred on February 9. Afterward, the prosecutor repeated for the press that the probe was "progressing satisfactorily," and the governor revealed that the state attorney general's assistance was under consideration—odd phrasing, since days earlier Donnell had publicized the parley and given assurances that McKittrick would cooperate.[37] In fact, Blanton wanted state assistance and Donnell wanted to give it, but McKittrick balked, no doubt still smarting because the Democrats had both lost the 1940 election to Donnell and failed in their challenge to his victory. Blanton, who offered to let McKittrick lead the prosecution in Benton, thought the attorney general feared that the volatile lynching case would jeopardize his chance for the U.S. Senate nomination and wanted no part in it. Instead, within a week, Blanton received the aid of Assistant Attorney General Harry Kay, the result of a partnership between a Democratic prosecutor and Republican executive.[38]

Political irony aside, Blanton and Donnell understood the need for mutual reliance and came to admire each other. They agreed immediately that lynchers should face prosecution, the governor firmly supporting Blanton in the face of statewide criticism. He assured NAACP officials and black editors that the prosecutor would undertake "a through investigation" and "act vigorously and promptly."[39] He refused to prejudge Blanton, despite mounting pressure and partisan opinion that the prosecutor's father not only supported the lynching but in 1940 had opposed the governor's seating. He awaited Blanton's own reports, appreciative of their quick arrival, decisive strategy, and political sensitivity. Two weeks after the lynching, Donnell again defended Blanton, this time to protesting black ministers, and predicted that the grand jury case would be "adequately presented."[40]

Prosecutor and governor kept in contact, though Blanton received a free hand even as federal agents began their own investigation the day after his meeting with Donnell and McKittrick. Occasionally, Blanton responded to a gubernatorial concern—such as the suggestion of the National Federation for Constitutional Liberties that a reward be offered for information on the lynchers—but for the most part he prepared his own case. He received a copy of the FBI report and permission for a bureau investigator to testify at the grand jury, doubtless through Donnell's intercession and Kay's recommendation.[41] Their very best efforts notwithstanding, grand jurors indicted no one, and only then did Blanton and Donnell part company. They remained friendly, the county prosecutor giving assurances of his continued interest in the case and the governor meeting with McKittrick and Kay to consider his options.[42]

Donnell also agreed to confer with fellow Republican and Sikeston publisher Clint H. Denman, who suggested pressing the case further in criminal court through the testimony of Sergeant Dace (rather than Blanton, whose father would oppose such a maneuver). Donnell considered Denman's desire for justice under state aegis but neither acted on his recommendation nor indicated a willingness to deal Blanton out of future legal proceedings.[43] He found himself preempted by U.S. Attorney General Francis Biddle, who announced one day after the state grand jury decision—and in advance of Blanton's and Denman's letters—that the FBI investigation would continue. Donnell offered state aid but refused, under the advice of McKittrick, Biddle's request for Kay's grand jury notes; and, despite that states' rights-political rendering, he learned of the U.S. attorney general's decision to bring the case before a federal grand jury.[44] Perhaps Donnell delayed meeting with Denman for two months in order to be sure of the federal government's plans; as likely, he realized that the newsman's idea would require placing his governorship, public servants like Sergeant Dace, and the Republican Party under enormous and (in the wake of Biddle's decision) unnecessary pressure.[45]

Though Donnell and Blanton lowered their profile, the prosecutor remained tied to the case. Publicly, he drew criticism for the state grand jury proceeding, one black editor likening him to "Pilate of old" and predicting failure even before the verdict was rendered. Increasingly, he became identified as the brother of U.S. Attorney Harry C. Blanton, who, the same newsman quickly suggested, should withdraw from any federal involvement.[46] Just as his father's sins had dogged David throughout the state prosecution, they now provided critics with reason to deny Harry participation in a national case. David's own efforts to defuse objections to his local ties by requesting state assistance never succeeded among most protesters, who, well in advance of the Scott County defeat, began pushing federal attorneys for a more forceful and independent prosecution.

Most influential were NAACP officials, who defined the federal case that appointed a special prosecutor rather than permit Harry Blanton to perform his duties as ranking attorney of the Eastern District. St. Louis branch president Sidney R. Redmond had raised questions about David E. Blanton with national executive secretary Walter White almost immediately after the lynching occurred.[47] He failed to dislodge Blanton from the state case, but White and staff members regarded local charges against the county prosecutor as gospel. Hence, in releasing their lynching report on February 13, investigators Mary and L. Benoist Tompkins opined that Blanton would "hardly sacrifice both his career and personal friends" for a verdict, and Thurgood Marshall, writing to Biddle's assistant as the county proceeding began on March 9, pressed for "a representative from your office" to present the anticipated federal case. The NAACP special counsel noted that Harry was David's brother, information provided him by St. Louis County branch president E.T. Summytt; he also assumed (wrongly) that David had been involved "in the particular crime being investigated" and (again wrongly) that the FBI inquiry "already revealed" this.[48] Though he did not reiterate Summytt's frantic opinion that "our only chance" to convict members of the mob lay in a federal grand jury—itself "not so good" because of the kinship factor—he believed it.[49]

Marshall and other association insiders must have been surprised when the Justice Department appointed a private citizen as special assistant to the attorney general. The federal officials did so quickly, partly because of NAACP-generated pressure and partly because of their own desire for success. In fact, shortly after receiving Marshall's request and news of the state grand jury's result, Biddle's assistant remarked that the *Chicago Sunday Bee*'s editorial on "Lynching and the Blanton Clan" provided "an interesting background" to the lynching and judged "a prompt presentment" before federal jurors "advisable."[50]

Having decided upon a special prosecutor by March 12, if not earlier, Justice Department higher-ups sought grand jury information from Harry Blanton without revealing their decision to limit his involvement in the federal case. He duly advised them of the grand jury calendar in the Eastern District, which usually convened twice each year, once for the northern division in Hannibal and again for the southeastern division in Cape Girardeau; the latter included Sikeston and would be empaneled in early

May.[51] He soon forwarded a copy of Kay's grand jury notes and a set of summaries about the lynching gleaned from "various reports and hearsay remarks" that required corroboration "by statements in the F.B.I. report." On March 20, Harry also recommended that the federal proceeding be held over for the next regular session so as to delay its decision until October and permit the cooling off of "a good deal of . . . hot blood." Unhesitatingly, he stood ready to press the case if higher-ups deemed the civil rights statutes applicable.[52]

Harry Blanton repeated his willingness "to go along with the Department in whichever direction it wants to travel," requesting further information on the judicial theory and forwarding more data for the case. He asked for a brief and, with a seasoned prosecutor's eye toward a U.S. Supreme Court hearing, recommended that the indictment include only that which could be proved. He suggested anew that the grand jury be empaneled from the entire Eastern District rather than just its southeastern division, thereby drawing jurors from well outside the lynching vicinity. He clarified material regarding the layout of the Sikeston City Hall and reported both the St. Louis woman's allegation that Wright had raped her and Sergeant Dace's charge that Cleo had sought intimacy with another Sikeston white woman.[53] Not until early April did Blanton discover that although superiors had benefited from his suggestions, Jacob Lashly would represent the government. Thenceforth he played an insignificant role in the proceeding, occasionally being called upon to arrange the panel date, comment on new information, and consider extending the session (as jurors labored over their decision).[54]

Before the grand jury reconvened on July 30 to file its official report, however, he defended himself and his office against public criticism and focused attention on Lashly and Biddle's office. Angered by a *Post-Dispatch* editorial on a lynching in Texarkana the previous day, which raised questions about the federal inquiry into Wright's murder, Harry Blanton fired off a letter to the editor. He took umbrage at the contention that his office was letting "dust accumulate on the Sikeston Lynching Case." He informed the editor that even though he had expressed his "willingness to handle this matter," the Justice Department, "for reasons best known to it," had placed the Sikeston lynching in the special prosecutor's hands; thus, no material existed in his office to gather dust.[55] He also informed Biddle's assistant of his complaint and passed along copies of his letter, the editorial "An Unforgettable Crime," and a letter to the editor from Florence A. Mosely, who questioned whether Justice Department personnel were capable of coping with lynch law or were, possibly, the friends of Wright's killers; the St. Louis citizen wondered what the attorney general had to say.[56] As if to underscore his displeasure, Blanton never directly alerted Lashly to the editorial or his response to it, but he did send Biddle's assistant a *Post-Dispatch* cartoon captioned "Unfinished Business": it depicted a lynching tree along a lonely road on which a rope tied with a hangman's noose spelled out "Sikeston."[57] Conscientiously, he also continued to report developments in the federal case, most notably that some jurors were "very insistent" in wanting to explain their action publicly and to provide press comment on their formal verdict, which had failed to remove, in one editor's words, "the shameful blot on this state."[58]

Still, Blanton's resentment continued, from Lashly's appointment on April 11 through the federal jury's final action on July 30. That President Franklin D. Roosevelt renominated him for another four-year term within forty-eight hours of deciding on a special prosecutor appeared more than coincidental, although given his record he surely deserved such consideration, political maneuver or not.[59] Nevertheless, he smarted over his shabby treatment, made even more humiliating by Justice Department deception and Lashly's arrogance. Even before Biddle decided to use an independent attorney, J. Edgar Hoover had instructed FBI agents not to provide copies of their lynching reports to Harry Blanton, whose summaries of Wright's death were thus based on hearsay evidence because no one made bureau findings available to him until late June—fully four months after completion of the first of several probes.[60]

Blanton in fact learned from the local press, rather than Justice Department officials, of Lashly's "discreet" visit to Sikeston, high-powered conference in Washington, and subsequent appointment. He heard from neither Lashly nor his special assistant, Irwin L. Langbein, until nearly two weeks later. Their meeting did not go well, as a proud Blanton indicated his displeasure with the department's tactics and his intention to stay out of the case. He was angered by Lashly's contention that he, the district attorney, should select the jury, perhaps wrongly believing that the special prosecutor expected him to handpick jurors; he must have cringed when Lashly revealed that he "had never been before a Grand Jury" and that therefore the district attorney's participation was imperative. Blanton challenged the assignment—though probably not because he was scheduled to represent the government in a fraud case elsewhere on the date that the grand jury would hear the lynching presentment in St. Louis.[61]

An embittered Blanton soon acted out of character and biased FBI officials against Lashly. To one agent he described the special prosecutor as an overbearing "publicity seeker" capable of doing "anything to pass the buck." He added that the St. Louis lawyer had referred to the bureau's initial report as "rather sloppy" and ordered "further investigation."[62] His comments alarmed agency personnel, who moved to protect themselves should Lashly fail to secure indictments and seek to blame others—"possibly the Bureau" (the latter never occurred). In fact, federal investigators too deemed Lashly's efforts a self-serving "political proposition to satisfy the negroes."[63]

Clearly, Blanton did not like the situation a "damn bit" and assisted Lashly and Langbein in only indirect ways.[64] Despite the Justice Department's original press release announcing Lashly's appointment, which stated that Blanton would "join with" the federal attorney to present the case, he agreed to present only routine matters to the grand jury before turning the proceedings over to Lashly and soon reminded the special prosecutor that the investigation would be "solely in your charge."[65]

Careful consideration should have been given to Blanton, but federal officials bungled the issue. Instead of using the district attorney as one of the best sources to set lynch law precedent, they drove him from the case. They did not even follow up on some of his reports: for example, Justice Department attorneys did not investigate the allegation that Wright had been a rapist before his attempt on Grace Sturgeon until the grand jury proceeding had reached its midpoint.[66] They bowed to political pressure without taking full stock of internal and courtroom realities. In effect, the U.S. attorney general's office created "the Blanton problem."[67]

The Blanton brothers, of course, proved loyal to each other, and if given the chance Harry would have endeavored to punish those responsible for the lynching in their father's town. Before the Lashly appointment they both defied state and local censures. David provided—in spite of McKittrick's legal ruling—the copy of Kay's grand jury notes that found its way into the hands of federal lawyers. Harry prepared himself—in spite of Sikeston's communal mores—to prosecute lawmen he knew personally.[68] Even after learning of the special prosecutor's appointment, neither sibling flinched. David participated with Lashly in an "in-depth discussion" of the state case and testified before the federal grand jury; Harry, however grudgingly, managed the government's grand jury calendar and stayed in touch with jurors.[69]

More than in challenging townspeople and officials, Harry and David showed greatest courage in defying the Pole Cat. Georgetown- and Harvard-trained, they embraced the "duties and obligations" of their profession and viewed the lynching as incompatible with law enforcement.[70] And despite personal prejudices, which very rarely surfaced (as when Harry referred to "darkies" in an official report on black subversive activity),[71] they believed in the letter of the law and its evenhanded, if racially separate, application. Just as racial peace required paternalism, social order necessitated curbing vigilante justice.

Harry and especially David, the more prodigal son, differed with their father on this critical point. Whereas his father stood in the crowd at City Hall, David endeavored to disperse it; whereas his father criticized him by asking why officials neither called out the guard nor used hoses to turn back the mob, David absorbed the curses and blows of its members; whereas his father refused to identify any participants, David named them; whereas his father defended lynchers for protecting white womenfolk, David prosecuted them; whereas his father excused offenders as righteous southerners with "hot blood flowing through . . . [their] veins," David held them deserving of "some penitentiary time"; whereas his father congratulated state grand jurors, David believed that indictments should have been forthcoming; whereas his father preferred that "the incident die, until some other Negro attempts another such brutal crime" prompting "swift action," David cooperated in the federal case; whereas his father felt no humiliation over the mobbing, David considered it "a bad thing."[72]

C.L. Blanton remained the unreconstructed southerner, combining racist threats with kindly gestures: the Pole Cat both warned blacks to stay off downtown streets after dark and sent Grace Sturgeon her first bouquet of flowers.[73] But he also believed, as did David, that punishment for a white man "would have been no less certain or severe."[74] And paramountly, again like David, he opposed outsiders who criticized the town and all its residents for the death of Cleo Wright. For different reasons and in different idioms, then, father and son spoke the same language. As early as his second report to the governor, on January 30, David expressed the "sincere hope" of local law enforcement officials that individuals "far removed from this case" would stop conducting themselves "so as to hamper our work." On the same day, his father predicted that black agitation statewide would create difficulties for Sunset residents who wanted to forget the episode. Hence the Pole Cat invited those organizations looking for trouble into Sikeston, where they would find "plenty of it."[75]

More than on any other event, David's concern for law enforcement and C.L.'s insistence on social control, personal respect, and community reputation focused on the NAACP mass meeting in St. Louis on February 1. They resented most the rally speakers. The Pole Cat advised Mayor William Lee Becker, who condemned the lynching as "class hatred" and urged further protest, to "clean up your own back yard," where "four negro bucks" had recently assaulted a thirteen-year-old white girl and remained untried. The Pole Cat wondered how Fannie Cook, who loved "the colored man," would feel "if some husky black . . . crawl[ed] into her virtuous couch some night." The Pole Cat warned Rev. J.B. Ross, who accused Sergeant Dace of leading the mob into Sunset, that he was inciting "many whites to buy fire arms to protect their homes" and predicted that the cleric would not return. To Frank S. Bledsoe's joy that Wright was resting "where even the 'Pole-Cat Editor' cannot help him," the Pole Cat responded that he did not "give a damn" how much he was ripped "up the back," as everyone knew where he stood.[76]

While his father traded in public diatribe, David expressed his frustration privately and long after the fact. He advised Governor Donnell against offering a reward because the action of such organizations as the National Federation for Constitutional Liberties, metropolitan newspapers, and Mayor Becker produced "a telling effect on an orderly process of law enforcement in Southeast Missouri."[77] In the crossfire of outside criticism and local countercharge, David found securing witnesses for the state impossible; as townspeople adopted a siege mentality—us against them—he "couldn't round up anyone to come in and point the finger." He lamented interference from the black press of St. Louis, especially journalist Willie B. Harmon, who made forceful but unsubstantiated comments.[78] David understood correctly the adverse impact of outside criticism on white witnesses but remained silent on the similar impact of his own father's harangues on residents of both races; he apparently failed to realize that Harmon's claim of ignorance regarding the names of her sources served to protect Sunset residents, which left the legal proceeding to white viewpoints.

Though the Pole Cat railed at outsiders—"half-assed preachers" and "a bunch of niggers" from St. Louis who "might be barbecued as was Wright"— he and David endured the ordeal without exchanging harsh words publicly.[79] Their professional and personality differences dovetailed rather than clashed. The father, an editor with a public ego and tendency to hyperbole, measured success in commercial terms and notoriety: "If you can't compliment us, give us hell, as it is publicity."[80] David, an attorney "low on ego" yet full of self-confidence, embraced diligent research, measured judgments, and total confidentiality as the keys to courtroom victory. Clearly, father and son understood that one "ran the newspaper" and the other "the law office."[81]

So the Pole Cat followed his inclinations in the steady, relentless, and gleeful scribbling of unreconstructed columns. He pridefully announced that *Standard* coverage of the lynching sold eight hundred extra copies and that area weeklies and semiweeklies used its story—written by Paul Bumbarger—rather than one from the metropolitan press. He opened his paper to letter writers who endorsed the lynching. He emerged as the bastion against outside criticism, bragging that the Pole Cat smelled "just as bad to some people as if he was the real article."[82] When he received a request from New York City's *PM* for an "uncommon viewpoint" of the lynching, Bumbarger proceeded to ghostwrite it. He considered it "quite an honor" to be written up in *Collier's* magazine and, if he had known, mocked in a *St. Louis Argus* cartoon several months later.[83] In interviews with Associated Press reporters and mention in news stories nationwide, C.L.'s response to the violence enhanced his public persona.

In advance of his father's new-found notoriety, David entered the crucible as prosecuting attorney. The strategy he devised at City Hall had backfired: he addressed the crowd in hopes of dispersing it; he pleaded with members of the mob to "allow the law to take its course" and threatened them with prosecution, only to hear boos and cries to get Wright.[84] In the rush that followed David sustained a broken rib, and in the aftermath he got criticism from several quarters: Police Chief Kendall, an FBI informant, a lyncher, and a spectator, among others, referred to the prosecuting attorney's gambit as "an error in judgment."[85] Knowing the sources, he later dismissed lambasting that must have stung at the time.[86] Like his father, though in more frightening circumstances, he spoke plainly, gave no quarter, and upheld principles of law.

Although friends and employees never witnessed the family's disagreement over Wright's death, the Blantons discussed it privately. C.L. admitted that within days of the incident his family tried to dissuade him from commenting on the lynching "because of David's position," adding that he would nevertheless print what he thought was right; like his son, he had "a duty to perform."[87] He sometimes chafed when family members failed to approve "what he wrote and what he did"; at other times, he disagreed with the views of his lawyer sons, who marched to "a different drum."[88]

Although his keeping the lynching alive in print made their jobs more difficult, C.L. never tried to control David or Harry. In part this revealed the "space" that existed between father and sons: "whatever he was going to do he did, and that was that." In part it indicated the lessons that he and Mary Agnes had taught their children about self-sufficiency and tolerance (even in selecting one's faith and scattering family members religiously).[89] Surely, C.L. sometimes wished that his sons were more southern, if not Confederate, and more respectful of his racial and vigilante ideas. Yet he understood that David and Harry—much more than Charles, who emulated him—manifested his most important characteristic: individualism.

Given his own indomitable belief in being "a voice not an echo" and a wearer of one's own chain mail, C.L. raised his sons to be themselves, "not a small edition of someone else"—even of himself.[90] He expected them to be duty-bound, well-educated, politically connected, and proud Blantons, but he expected even more that they be individualists. If he "took one hitch" and his sons thought "it wasn't the right hitch," then he taught them to take another hitch. To some a crackpot, to others a sage, C.L. had a reputation that rested, ironically, on the individuality that produced both bombastic columns and independent-thinking sons who loved their father without feeling intimidated by him.[91]

Father's and sons' perspectives went deeper, of course. C.L.'s and David's reactions to the lynching represented much more than generational differences within their family. They acted, respectively, as traditionalist and modernist in a society undergoing change—ultimately, a reshaping of social, economic, and political structures—during an era of great transition. Each represented more than himself, just as Wright's death symbolized more than a singular act of bloodshed. They faced off over an incident that defined the struggle for Sikeston's future, and pitted the Pole Cat against "the Best Elements."

That phrase, which the Pole Cat upgraded from "better element" and tinged with sarcasm, came from the press statement David made when he reevaluated his initial opinion that Sikestonians appeared "well satisfied" with the lynching; in order to parry criticism, he readily corrected himself to report that after "sober reflection . . . the better element came forward" with "names of mob leaders."[92] That elite class then presented its resolution to the city council, expressing "horror" for Wright's crime but "willingness" to bring the lynchers to justice. On the same day, February 5, that Ralph E. Bailey Sr. delivered the resolution to Governor Donnell with the message that local official, civic, and commercial groups disapproved of vigilante law, Clint H. Denman published "We Stand to Defend." He too distinguished "good people" from "misguided men" who "brought shame and disgrace upon us all" and made law-abiding Sikestonians bow "their heads in humiliation."[93]

The Pole Cat counterattacked instantly. A Sikeston citizen "going along with his head bowed," he editorialized on February 10, did so "not for shame about the lynching" but because he was wondering how to pay his income taxes. In fact, he knew of no one in town who expressed humiliation (as

opposed to regret), and the notion of "a blot on the city" was just "rubbish."
Moreover, by agitating for the punishment of those who had protected their
homes, he opined that the "best" element led "bad negroes" to believe themselves as good as whites and, however unwittingly, encouraged them to "run
amuck." The Pole Cat claimed membership in the element that believed in
"protecting our women from either white or black brutes" and wondered
what the best element would do if one of its women were attacked: "sit back
and let the law take its course, or . . . call on the worse element."[94] Nor could
he later resist identifying those who had recommended Cleo Wright's parole as "the real parties responsible for the lynching," suggesting that the FBI
talk to them. Knowing as his readers knew that mayor, councilman, city attorney, and other prominent Sikestonians were among the references, he
again tweaked the best element.[95]

The Pole Cat struck again the day after Denman's March 12 editorial,
"The Grand Jury Report," which began, "Friends of law and order will be
disappointed" with the lack of indictments. Against the Herald publisher's
criticism of the judge's instructions, the witnesses' memory lapse, and the
jurors' failure, the Pole Cat praised the grand jury. He believed the verdict a
shock to Denman and other "best elements," who along with St. Louis blacks
should keep "their mouths shut if they don't want to start a real race war."[96]
Perhaps having gotten wind of Denman's confidential suggestion that Governor Donnell press the case further lest the guilty "go unpunished," the Pole
Cat scorched those "best elements" that were "still bellyaching" because the
jurors—themselves "best element" members—"failed to force indictment
even if there was little or no evidence."[97]

More than anyone else in the Bootheel, the Pole Cat defended its southern, plantation heritage, and he did so as a neo-Radical. Like turn-of-the-
century white supremacists, he feared black freedom in a regional order that
deemed people of color incapable of improvement and therefore requiring
white supervision.[98] He presented himself as a vigilant Confederate, alert to
criminality, particularly sexual assault, and mindful of distinctions between
and within the races. In spite of promising retribution to rapists black or
white, neither of whom was fit "for the dogs to use as a post," he advanced
long-held psychosexual concerns about "black brutes"; he differentiated the
"mean negro" and St. Louis blacks from the "influential men" in Sunset (who
supposedly wanted the incident forgotten), just as he distinguished between
right-thinking white townspeople and the "best element."[99] He believed, too,
the Radical claim that following legal procedures in assaults on "our women

folks"—as advocated by the best element—was "too slow"; such heinous acts required "swift justice."[100]

In addition, the Pole Cat embraced the localism of his southern forebears. He considered it "the highest form of liberty," one that dovetailed with controlling black society and shaping white destiny.[101] Consequently, like antebellum planters and early twentieth-century Radicals, he viewed outside interference, particularly from neoabolitionists and federal representatives such as Fannie Cook and Jacob Lashly, as threats akin to the centralism that the South had cast aside in the wake of Reconstruction.[102] He embraced nineteenth-century traditionalism complete with its provincial outlook, economic unity, and sociopolitical hierarchy wherein "family ties and face-to-face relationships provide[d] structure and cohesion" in a continuous, little-changing, circular passage of time.[103] In his tradition-bound world the Pole Cat served as a living representative of the past, "armed with ancient precedents and cloaked in the authority of ancestral ways." In his southern world he expressed, one critic said, "spicy, irresponsible, and ungrammatical, . . . often vulgar or slanderous" comments that represented the attitude of most readers.[104] Portraying his world in an H.L. Mencken style (minus its elitism), the Pole Cat proved formidable as well as entertaining.[105]

His son possessed a more modern outlook, albeit one that retained southern remnants. For example, David considered *St. Louis Argus*'s Harmon "vicious in her attitude" yet never used racial epithets to describe her or any other black person.[106] He preferred local investigators and state assistance, in keeping with localism and states' rights, and questioned what could be gained by bringing in outsiders; still, he drew from the reports and testimony of FBI agents in the state grand jury proceeding.[107] He judged Wright's death wrong, and even Denman believed him "disappointed that some indictments" never came forward.[108] Moreover, he cooperated in the federal case against local lawmen. Neither hot-blooded nor compulsive like his father, who needed to speak out or "blow up," David never identified himself as a southerner, much less a rabble rouser.[109] His stance, like Denman's, fell between the Pole Cat's "traditional personality" and that of a national "character."[110]

David seemed a neo-Progressive who sought order and assumed that achieving it required acceptance of the region's racial orthodoxy, itself defined by Radicals and kept in place by neo-Radicals like his father.[111] But unlike turn-of-the-century Progressives, much less the Pole Cat, who so precisely and so publicly defined themselves, David engaged in no such self-identity. Rather, he embraced some basic principles, which his father spurned, that characterized modernization: cosmopolitan outlook, diversified economy, and sociopolitical egalitarianism. Over time, these concepts would break personal ties and foster instability in a future-minded "race against death for achievement."[112]

Interestingly, both David and his father accepted certain aspects of modernization. Both, of course, realized and welcomed its economic potential. The elder Blanton had started the *Standard* as a four-page weekly in 1913 and upgraded it to a several-page semiweekly in 1927 as advertisements and subscriptions increased with prosperity, and World War II provided the commercial impetus for the paper to become a daily in 1947.[113] But the Pole Cat never grappled with the sociopolitical aspects of modernization that so threatened his world. Modern life swirled about his desk "but never quite touched him." As one employee later recalled, "The pearl gray derby, the checkered sweater-vest, the items written in long hand, all were part of the old way which until the end he praised as the best way."[114]

While much the same could have been said about the Pole Cat's racial attitudes and endorsement of vigilante law, the opposite was true of his son. David ventured beyond the economics of a modern society and pressed into the southern culture that Progressives found unyielding. In the narrow construct of legal procedure, he stepped beyond Progressives but not as far as the New Deal judicial activists who challenged all provincialism; he concerned himself more with Cleo Wright's life—keeping the mob at bay—than with his civil rights, the subject of the federal attorneys who sought to indict Kendall and Wallace for violating Reconstruction Era statutes damned by the Pole Cat.[115] In short, father and son both sought order, but only David demanded justice. By doing so in court he challenged C.L.'s, his own, and Sikeston's racial orthodoxy.

Notably, if indirectly, David set in legal motion Max Weber's concept of cultural modernity. His father believed in the unified values of knowledge, justice, and beauty; David understood the division of those principles into spheres of science, law, and art. C.L. regarded traditional values as bulwarks for white supremacy; his son realized their modern separation and revaluation as potentially beneficial to the establishment of democratic institutions that would challenge, or even right, past injustices—as would have been the case had he succeeded in convicting the lynchers.[116]

Basically, each Blanton responded to the revolutionary change brought by war, which Wright's attack and death punctuated. David projected an accommodationist position, endeavoring to blend past, present, and future imagery; he looked inward to "self-realization and personal autonomy," made easy by his youthful independence and educational sojourns, more than outward to an equally important sense of "group commitment." Perhaps he sought to rescue himself from aspects of his upbringing, most notably his father's unreconstructed lessons. In efforts to protect Wright and punish his killers, David found "a sense of moral and psychological integrity" and thus a way to the future without turning his back completely on his own or his father's past and present.[117]

The Pole Cat, for his part, responded to the movement of history by finding refuge in his heritage. He emerged a restorationist, embodying "a sense of organic connection with the past" and ascribing "contemporary impurities" to outsiders: FBI agents and black journalists who wanted to prosecute townsmen for protecting their women. Given the enormity of the evil threatening his world, the Pole Cat found it necessary to impugn and chide those "best elements," as well. Predictably, he revealed the paradox inherent in the views of individuals facing historical dislocation; he played on his Confederate blood and martial spirit as symbols to rally American patriotism to the very war that unleashed forces jeopardizing the southern past he so wanted preserved.[118]

In spite of important variations, the elder Blanton and his youngest son represented others of their age groups, sociopolitical bearing, and racial heritage. David spoke for Denman, Bailey, and the civic-commercial elites generally, who felt dishonored by the lynching and censured—in actuality, overwhelmed—by outside forces; they, too, sought integrity by purifying themselves without discarding completely the town's collective past.[119] Denman lamented the presence of reporters in Sikeston for the third time in five years; as with the 1937 flood and 1939 roadside demonstration, they wrote "highly-colored stories" that sometimes "amounted to caricatures of the real facts." He castigated the lynchers for misrepresenting the town and placing "a blot upon us which will take years to erase." And despite the Pole Cat's ridicule of his accommodationism, Denman continued to voice his shame, label mob members "disgraceful," and defend the town's "law-abiding people."[120] His efforts and those of the councilmen and businessmen who through Bailey trumpeted their opposition to the lynching from the state capitol revealed among most elites signs of cultural and psychological accommodation.[121]

Others, by contrast, expressed C.L.'s restoration. The Pole Cat marched before a band that included his former cub reporter and present editor of the *Charleston Enterprise-Courier*. Art Wallhausen seemed even more "belligerently fanatical" in wanting to shore up the area's traditional society.[122] The day after Wright's lynching he suggested that Donnell keep his "gubernatorial nose in the affairs of State" and leave "us to handle our Negro problem." Sounding like the Pole Cat himself, he concluded, "Let your wife or daughter be . . . attack[ed] by some sex maniac, and then take official action." Like overzealous restorationists elsewhere, he actually promoted historical change, for the governor fired back that Missouri operated under law and that he intended to enforce it via a "thorough investigation," grand jury proceeding, and—if that was successful—"prompt trial" of those responsible for "the disgraceful happening."[123]

Scarcely deterred, Wallhausen flailed away at outsiders throughout the state grand jury proceeding. He chided the "Great Uplift Movement" of Mayor Becker, Congressman Dyer, Fannie Cook, and Rabbi Ferdinand M. Isserman for ignoring "the fact that Cleo Wright first perpetrated a most heinous crime," noting that had he done so in their city, he would have incited a race riot on the scale of that in East St. Louis in 1917. He announced a personal boycott of firms associated with their efforts, as well as St. Louis editors, and anticipated future dealings only "with folks of our social, economic, and moral equal." Individuals who placed themselves on the "level of the Negro" and condoned "the rape of white women and the mutilation of peace officers" should be left to themselves. Facetiously, he hoped that they agreed with the state grand jury decision: after nearly half the town had faced criticism and after nearly everybody had entered the case—though someone "overlooked the Boy Scouts and the Lone Ranger"—the county's finest residents had found no one guilty; "Justice had been done."[124]

Even more than his renowned mentor, the Charleston editor attacked Fannie Cook as the region's perennial nemesis. In 1941, for example, Wallhausen ran what she called "vituperative articles" ridiculing her *Post-Dispatch* stories on Bootheel sharecroppers: she had "even found a woman working in an FSA settlement house near Morehouse barefoot!" He wondered what the St. Louis author and Washington University English instructor would say now that the so-called downtrodden were purchasing new automobiles and gambling away "folding money" in the wartime boom.[125] In the wake of the YMCA antilynching meeting a year later, he knew that "Dear Old Fannie" relished the "atmosphere" and reveled in the Great Uplift Movement. He hoped her lot would not be that of Grace Sturgeon, for that might change the viewpoint of "our Fannie," which "would never, never do." And following the state grand jury verdict, he hoped, with equal sarcasm, that "our Friend" was satisfied with its outcome.[126]

In fact, Wallhausen and others, including Grace Sturgeon, exaggerated the tiny role that Fannie Cook played in the protest. She never visited Sikeston to investigate the lynching; though asked to by the St. Louis NAACP, she declined because of illness, leaving the task to the Tompkinses. She never visited the General Hospital, spoke with Sturgeon's mother, or wrote *Post-Dispatch* stories questioning Sturgeon's character (as Grace contended years later). She did appear at the YMCA meeting and, for all of three minutes, delivered "a mild babble of civil-liberties banalities!"[127] Ironically, Fannie Cook benefited from the Sikeston tragedy, which revived the popularity of her novel, *Bootheel Doctor*; her inadvertent celebrity required her presence at autograph parties.[128] She also retained her membership in the Committee for the Rehabilitation of the Sharecropper, which doubtless placed her among Wallhausen's postlynching list of "misdirected nitwits" seeking "to bring about immediate settlement of deeply rooted racial differences."[129] Essentially, though, she served as a phantom enemy reinforcing the siege mentality of Wallhausen, C.L. Blanton, and others who envisioned the North—including St. Louis—as "an emotional idea" rather than a geographic entity.[130]

Even most of the townspeople who opposed the lynching found themselves united in fending off outside censure. No one publicly promoted a complete transformation of society. Restorationists and accommodationists debated the ethics of lynching, sometimes heatedly and always with conviction, but no transformationist entered their dialogue. Those looking to the past stood firm, while accommodationists, like those in periods of historical movement elsewhere, found sustaining their position difficult. Like their counterparts in the post–Civil War South, they lacked "a complete, clear ideology" of order and decision-making: that "ultimate" past of the restorationist or future of the transformationist so necessary for personal and public harmony.[131] Thus, neither David E. Blanton nor Clint H. Denman considered the southern heritage completely evil or Sikeston in need of fundamental remaking; consequently, they agreed with the Pole Cat and Wallhausen on bolstering the color line.

Predictably, the elder Blanton and Denman publicized the issue from diverse and occasionally contentious perspectives. Soon after the lynching the Pole Cat published the letter of an anonymous correspondent who would protect white women by forcing all blacks to carry police-issued passes after dark and, except for domestics, live in a designated area. In short order the Pole Cat proposed a setting curfew for "negro men" and cleaning out "negro roosts in the alleys," sending all their inhabitants to Sunset Addition or "out of town."[132] Thereafter, he periodically took potshots at gambling "dives around town" and reprinted Wallhausen's complaints about white men seeking favors from "dusky" women and white high school students frequenting a "Negro dance hall" in nearby Charleston.[133]

Nonetheless, the Pole Cat left to Denman the organization of drives to enforce segregated housing and curb crime among both races. One of the *Herald* editor's initial comments admitted partial guilt for the lynching: most significantly, beyond failing to protect Wright, Sikestonians had blurred "the line which must always separate the white and black races from each other." A major problem, he said, was that "a few paltry rent dollars" bought blacks— other than servants—living space in white backyard cabins, resulting in lax enforcement of housing laws that relegated blacks to "their own part of town."[134]

As he had in organizing civic-commercial opposition to the lynching, Denman used his newspaper and political contacts to support drives against gambling joints and prostitution haunts soon after the state grand jury proceeding. He criticized local police for ignoring vice and joined forces with Maj. R.C. Rockwood of the Missouri Institute of Aeronautics, who complained of venereal disease among cadets.[135] As a result of their efforts and threatened action by the U.S. Army, the city council created a four-man board—including David E. Blanton—to combat the problem.[136] The county prosecutor and local lawmen ran white streetwalkers out of town and raided several black and white bootlegging and gambling operations. The Pole Cat, for his part, could not resist needling Denman; if a "best element" like himself personally knew where young girls met for immoral purposes, he should file a complaint and give the police "something to act on."[137] Blanton then fell silent, no doubt because he in fact supported the drives.

In association with the lynching furor, and again with the *Herald* editor in their midst, council members also moved on the alley rentals. Picking up the issue in June and questioning the economic and political feasibility of enforcing a segregation ordinance, they focused on sanitation—outdoor toilets, overcrowding, garbage—as a way to rid the cabins of blacks. They condemned some buildings in southeast Sikeston, perhaps coincidentally the quadrant in which Grace Sturgeon lived, but refrained from evacuating all blacks from the alleys.[138]

Nor did race relations show signs of change in the foreseeable future, despite David E. Blanton's effort to impose judicial modernity on lynchers and townsfolk. As no other incident arose during the remainder of World War II to accentuate the divisions between accommodationists and restorationists, Blanton retreated to the provincialism of his father. He ran for reelection; even though he had enlisted for military service and knew he would not serve out the term, he wanted to know whether voters approved of his administration. In August he won the Democratic nomination for a third term as county prosecutor, overcoming Eugene Munger of Benton and John S. Skensenkothen of Kelso. Three months later he defeated Republican Roger A. Bailey, a fellow accommodationist who also had sought punishment for lynchers (though largely on behalf of commercial-civic elite concerns). David won handily over the son of Ralph E. Bailey, receiving 3,686 of 5,624 ballots cast.[139] Significantly, no restorationist sought his office, and during the campaign, no one, publicly or by rumor, mentioned his role in the lynching case. His record was impressive—614 convictions in 1941, double that of the previous year—and his popularity was genuine.[140]

Blanton's reelection forced supporters to consider their own view of the lynching, yet hardly represented an endorsement of his role in pressing the state grand jury. Those who opposed the lynching backed him, but so did many in the mob who, nine months after their act of murder, enjoyed freedom and rationalized that as a public official David had had to do his job. Others probably supported him out of deference to their favorite town crier, the Pole Cat.[141]

In December 1942 David Blanton entered the U.S. Navy and served as a stateside legal officer for three years, mostly at Camp Bradford in Norfolk, Virginia. After the war he returned home to its victorious aftermath. Then on January 8, 1948, he and brother Harry stood over the deathbed of their father, holding his hands and hearing his goodbye. As loving sons, and far removed from the lynching controversy of yesteryear, they experienced a deep personal loss that also marked the end of an era in Blanton and Sikeston history.[142]

Born during the Civil War, C.L. Blanton had carried the Confederate flag throughout his life and waved it most vigorously over the body of Cleo Wright, accentuating the traditional southern heritage that surely explained the dynamics of that killing. David, instead, experienced a wider vision of society and strayed far enough from his father's South to serve as a link with the modernity that the war heightened. In sum, the lynching joined father and son, southern past and national context, in a wrenching personal and— for townspeople—collective experience that simultaneously reached deep into the past and brushed against the future. Like Wright and his lynchers, the Blanton Clan played roles in a well-known ritualistic act of violence which, in this instance, came uniquely from Missouri.

7 From Missouri

Cleo Wright's "spirit in smoke ascended to high heaven" and, in some ways, replicated the previous 3,842 deaths by lynching that had occurred nationwide between 1889 and 1941.[1] His killing followed well-established patterns of racial violence that reached back to southern and mountain heritages. Yet like those bloodlettings his murder, though not "mysterious," was "unique," wrought by social factors and "distinctive conditions" particular to Sikeston. Rather than exemplifying an unchanging "holistic cultural and historical perspective" peculiar to the South or the border states, his slaying verified the evolutionary nature of lynch law.[2] It also revealed the impact of outsiders, modernization (if not modernity), and war on lynchers and their community.

On January 25, 1942, racial violence laid bare the clash between traditional beliefs and modern tendencies in Sikeston. Whites, including David E. Blanton, considered Wright one of those "bad negroes" who periodically terrified the Bootheel.[3] So did the white newsmen who, like their counterparts elsewhere, distorted his life to fit "conventional portraits of black criminals."[4] In fact, unlike most mob victims, Wright possessed both atypical and stereotypical characteristics: neither complete stranger nor lone fugitive, neither vagrant nor feebleminded, he was regarded before the lynching as a quiet, baseball-playing, married oil mill worker; only in the wake of his assaults did he emerge publicly—and for the first time—as "an incorrigible criminal" recognized solely for previous thefts.[5] Hess Perrigan's calling Wright by his first name as he walked toward Sunset indicated that he recognized the man immediately as a member of the community rather than an outlaw in its midst; indeed, before joining the police force, the night marshal had been Wright's supervisor at the Sikeston Cotton Oil Mill.[6]

On the night he entered Grace Sturgeon's home, Wright certainly appeared one-dimensional, but his life to that moment hardly seemed fatalistic. Raised as Ricelor C. Watson in a stable, loving home by parents who encouraged him to achieve yet cautioned him about society's racism, he had sought to integrate their beliefs on his own terms. His experiences away from home, especially in the navy, exposed him to unforgiving whites who dashed his aspirations. Back in Pine Bluff, Ricelor lost his job; coming under brother Wylie's influence, he stole; on the run, he faced anew the "concrete reality" of being black in a white world. However overbearing Alonzo's parenting or conditional Albert's love, he fared worse beyond the home: he and his dreams died in one violent rage—ultimate manifestation of several months, perhaps years, of "surrendered identity."[7]

Ricelor did not yield easily. Unlike many black victims purported to have been unaware of the dangers inherent in racial, particularly sexual encounters, he well understood the risks.[8] In fact, he learned of sexual taboos early and apparently never defied them before coming to Sikeston. As Cleo Wright, he struggled to deliver on his parents' legacy but collapsed under the weight of negative self-images in a town atmosphere, even though it provided more chance in some areas than the countryside from which he had sought freedom originally.[9] From 1937 to 1942 he drifted further from, while trying to hold on to, his origins, his family members and their values. Surreptitiously, he engaged in a love affair with a married white woman. Later, despite his marriage to Ardella, he stole again and, despite her pregnancy, snapped near the end of his parole. Unfulfilled as husband or father-to-be, Wright experienced an identity crisis—"an inescapable turning point"—and evolved from dreamer to rapist. Finally, becoming his enemies' worst nightmare, he slashed at Grace's whiteness more than her gender, manifesting a "sexual expression of power and anger."[10]

Ironically, Wright's attack revealed emotional liberation, sexual preoccupation, and personal protest similar to those of his lynchers.[11] In short, Wright beckoned his own destroyers, and they complied, mirror images of his emotional weakness and insecurity.[12] Unlike black male contemporaries, including Wylie, he could neither wear the mark of oppression nor displace it cathartically.[13] Like all rapists and would-be rapists, his psychological transformation originated in a conflicting upbringing; like black rapists and would-be rapists, it stemmed in larger measure from specific socioeconomic, racist pressures.

Also stereotypically, but in contrast to Wright, Sturgeon seemed an "idealization of women" in a traditional society, the southern beauty to his black beast.[14] Pleasant-looking, polite, and proper, she fought back, defending her honor and, symbolically, white supremacy and patriarchy. These actions endeared her to the lynchers, who sympathized without reinventing her as "a member of one of the very best families in the community"—the way their hill country forebears depicted every white victim of an alleged black rapist.[15] And Sturgeon, unlike numerous southern women who had cried rape falsely—lovers, publicity seekers, or neurotics—did not appear to be anything other than the random target of a stranger. Also unlike bona fide victims of racial assaults in the modern South, she kept her marriage intact; she never lost respect for herself or for Sarge, nor he for her.[16] Still, Grace's ordeal fostered white female fears and white male efforts at protection, which in turn reinforced traditional gender roles.[17]

Significantly, the lynchers reflected both links and breaks with past offenders. Those in Sikeston included riffraff or troublemakers, like southern mob members elsewhere. They were led from above, albeit by entrepreneur Nigel J., salesman Ted C., and flight instructor Preston H. rather than by landed gentry or rich businessmen.[18] Men on the make imposing communal values, the shock troopers and rear guardsmen also resembled frontier vigilantes.[19] Though apparently older and more economically and socially established than the young working- and lower-class turn-of-the-century lynchers, those in Sikeston also included "growing lads" and vengeance seekers—such as, respectively, Steve N. and Ted C.—who equated reputation and heroics with killing blacks.[20] They also numbered an occasional inebriate (for example, Kirk V.), whose drunkenness fulfilled cultural expectations in the southern tradition, and one or two individuals recognized as immoral (such as Lou O.), who resembled their counterparts in earlier "swampeast" mobs.[21] But misfits aside, the mob represented a cross section of townspeople equivalent to the plain folk—landholding farmers and herders—of previous eras, rather than rabble rousers or the poor white southerners normally accused of rope-and-faggot justice. Like culprits of yesteryear, lynchers in Sikeston were identified wrongly by both face-saving elites and dismayed outsiders.[22]

Despite the class differences, Sikeston spectators also resembled earlier lynching witnesses. Neither Grace's relatives nor others tortured Wright according to southern ritual—possibly because of his decimated condition and the influence of urban civilization—yet they provided familial sanction and community approval by witnessing his execution, especially since many onlookers knew the Sturgeon clan.[23] A female friend of Grace felt no "twinge of sympathy" for Wright, seeing beyond his corpse to the bloodshed on Kathleen Avenue. Nor did anyone else feel "the least bit humane," she emphasized, because "there was nothing humane about a woman standing in a pool of blood" clutching her exposed entrails. Typical of both sexes, she deemed Wright's death "swift justice." And some parents wanted to teach their children this lesson of lynch law by exposing them to unforgettable carnage.[24]

Sikeston lynchers and spectators alike "understood perfectly" the logic of their actions, as had southern white mobs dating back to Reconstruction.[25] Faceless before the law yet visible communitywide, their unity bore a collective morality that reached beyond Wright's corpse: their public killing before a mass audience and in full view of Sunset residents was a "schooling" for all who dared challenge racial hierarchy.[26] It drew surprising opposition from local white elites, whose counterparts in another place and time had said little and rarely sought prosecution.

The responses of black residents sprang from their southern, largely delta background yet were shaped in part by individual instinct and town setting.[27] Those who fled did not affect the future demography of blacks in Sikeston (a population replenished by subsequent birthrates and inmigration).[28] Those who guarded their homes and community lacked experience in collective self-defense.[29] Those who complained about the mob played on their gender and status before white elites. Those who addressed the governor or formed a local chapter of the NAACP exhibited municipal influences, but Rev. J.B. Ross's flight and the NAACP chapter's inactivity acknowledged the racial limitations of living in Sikeston.[30] In effect, blacks feared for their lives, yet protected themselves and their honor in ways that both broke with and bore remnants of the past. They knew that whites varied: lynchers such as Richard D. were just "nasty," and peaceful whites of Dr. T.C. McClure's reputation were "good as gold."[31] Courageously, some Sunset residents stood firm, but they lacked the long-term consciousness, know-how, and infrastructure necessary to sustain their protest or turn it into "mass political action."[32]

Whatever the object lessons for blacks, lynchers killed Wright for precise reasons. In the sweeping terms that marked most lynchings, they erupted because he evoked their fears and assaulted Sikeston's color line; in the specific terms that characterized this bloodletting, they destroyed him for having attacked Sturgeon and Perrigan. They cast Wright as rapist and rogue in the late-nineteenth-century image of "Negro as beast."[33] They believed Wright "lust mad" and invoked, as had self-styled executioners of other eras, an "elastic concept" of the most hideous of sexual transgressions.[34] Lynchers, in short, embraced "the rape complex": linking race, sex, and civilization, they associated Wright's attack on Sturgeon—an unprotected, married, white mother—with an attack on all white women and on white Sikeston itself.[35] Perhaps, as is suspected of lynchers generally, some projected their own passions and transgressions onto Wright and, through ritual, dramatized their white, male power over black men and white women—themselves acknowledging the hierarchy and calling for destruction of the beast.[36]

Still, they did not castrate Wright, a ritual symbolizing the permanent eradication of evil. They lived, like southern executioners, in a state that forbade miscegenation, indicating longstanding fears of black sexuality and providing rationalization for lynch law.[37] And sexual phobia affected mob members, for rape was their cry, a black man their target, and "the idea of castration" immanent in their actions.[38] That they did not emasculate Wright evinced his beaten condition, the pressure of approaching lawmen, and the influence of place and time. Perhaps, too, the absence of younger, draft-age participants and individuals suffering from "sexual perversion" limited the level of "primitive brutality."[39]

Those Sikestonians who claimed that a white man would have been punished no less severely than Wright disregarded a fact of mob killings.[40] Eight of the last nine lynchings in Missouri since the Great War had involved black youths accused of assaulting white females, but white mobs killed no alleged white rapists.[41] Indeed, shortly after Wright's death at least two white males in the area received court-determined sentences rather than rope-and-faggot-justice: Otis Morris, a thirty-five-year-old ex-convict extended his case for nearly a year—from April 1941 to February 1942—and won a change of venue before receiving four years in prison for the statutory rape of a fourteen-year-old girl in Oran; a second offender was permitted to change his plea from not guilty of attempting to rape a twelve-year-old girl in Vanduser to guilty of felonious assault. When compared with Wright's fate, even given the vicious brutality of his crime, their treatment by Judge J.C. McDowell and prosecutor David E. Blanton revealed white society's prejudices.[42]

Obviously, "race hatred" magnified interracial crimes involving black offenders and white victims, especially when the infractions were major and sexual. Conversely, local whites never addressed the issue of white men attacking black females, historically unprotected from sexual assault (by either race).[43] Black St. Louis area residents noted that nothing was done to white men who committed crimes against "our women"; on the rare occasion that a white rapist faced prosecution, they contended, his conviction proved most difficult, if not elusive.[44]

But Wright stirred more than Sikeston's psychosexual fears. Coming on the heels of the Sturgeon assault, his equally savage attack on Night Marshal Perrigan unleashed—in the words of the city attorney—"the viciousness" of everyone in the area. Wright, in other words, committed two gross violations of race rule, triggering a southern "ceremony of exorcism."[45] In the face of fallen sexual and legal boundaries, most whites hardly seemed to (distinguish between social control and repressive justice in their act of retribution.[46])

Wright also challenged "white masculine values." Growing up in a traditional, hierarchical, and economically unvaried community, Sikeston men lived in an "honor-bound" society that produced, as it had in the Old South, extremes of behavior: noblesse oblige and violence. They were taught to preserve personal status and protect family integrity in "absolute and indivisible" terms, meshing individual and community mores where necessary. For them, honor dovetailed with masculinity, often necessitated violence, and, in defense against black incursions, elicited "heroic activity."[47] Although the need for order in a town the size of Sikeston had softened the honor code over the previous century, wartime patriotism and, especially, Wright's brutality reassociated it with killing.[48] Lynchers spoke openly of their duty to take the life of a would-be rapist for having attacked the wife of a soldier "off defending the United States."[49] Many knew Sergeant Sturgeon personally; World War I veterans understood his sacrifice; and townsfolk generally identified him as the heart of Company K, whose history evoked pride in them. "Join the Guard and go with the boys you know," boasted truthful recruiters.[50]

Small wonder lynchers combined individual "psychic compensation" and "community honor." Like late nineteenth-century mob members incapable of supporting their families in the midst of economic depression, Sikeston men unable, unwilling, or not yet called to serve abroad discovered their self-worth in the protection of womenfolk.[51] Possibly some of them—such as Yancey T., who soon joined the air school as an instructor—experienced guilt or frustration at neither being in uniform nor protecting the homefront adequately.[52] That lynchers struck under the watchful eyes of uniformed cadets seemed more than symbolic. Unlike those of the 1890s, then, these executioners emerged as "patriots" in national rather than merely regional or provincial terms.[53] Local and statewide apologists equated Wright's violence with Japan's attack on Pearl Harbor and, by inference, lynchers with men in the armed forces. Both crimes made "American blood boil for revenge," and the executioners—troopers in combat—took steps to make it difficult for "negroes, or Japs to molest them or their families" further.[54]

These steps required entering into *communitas*: a bond "over and above any formal social bonds."[55] Many whites had adopted southern paternalism and rigid race relations, which generated intimacy and, in the face of seri-

ous transgressions, intensely hostile reprisal; they believed with the Pole Cat
that insults required an "old fashioned duel." Therefore, when word spread
of Sturgeon's and Perrigan's cutting, townsmen, emulating hundreds of prior
lynchers, deliberately expressed "community will" by ritualistically extermi-
nating Wright and cleansing themselves of his perfidy.[56]

Clearly, as one man wrote the governor, lynchers believed themselves "a
group of men who said, 'I am my brother's keeper.'" They considered their
actions right and honorable, even righteous, and "ethically compatible" with
the common law of their ancestors.[57] This was why lynchers wore no masks,
spectators refused to identify them, and the Sturgeons left Wright's fate in
their hands.[58] Even citizens who opposed vigilantism deemed the arrest of
mob members "a great shame"; ministers seeking reconciliation for the town
condemned none of them, partly in deference to the community will; and
cadets verified the impact of *communitas* on outsiders by offering their blood
for Grace's transfusions.[59]

Townsfolk who struck down Wright were also lashing out, knowingly
or not, at change wrought by modernization. It had been in their midst since
the 1920s, unleashed by the regional shift to cotton cultivation and accelerated by the economic depression that brought federal relief but challenged
social cohesion, political autonomy, and community stability. Though it is
difficult to measure the cumulative effect of volatile race-related events during the late 1930s and early 1940s—including pro-Japanese rallies, labor
strikes, and government-sponsored black farm worker settlements—
Sikestonians struggled with modern intrusions.[60] More recently, they had
complained of cocky blacks and their petty thefts, transgressions that Wright
escalated to a frightening level.[61] Facing that ultimate defiance in an increasingly egalitarian society, lynchers needed both beast and scapegoat.[62] They
drew on the repetition of thought and deed over time to kill Wright in public ceremony: a contradictory event in the long transition from traditional
to modern.[63] Accordingly, Nigel J. countered the county prosecutor's admonition at City Hall—"Why in hell don't you go home where you belong?"[64]—
by expressing ancestral concepts of *communitas* and duty, just as apologists
and opponents closed ranks in the aftermath of violence to display "a siege
mentality" toward outside critics.[65]

Those who killed Wright or condoned his death did so because of their
inability to preserve the old racial order while benefiting economically and
technologically from the new one; they wanted only what they considered
the best of each world. Thus mob members and their supporters sought a
return to normal social relations yet looked forward to economic modern-

ization. They soon shopped in a new Walgreen's, an enlarged J.C. Penney's, and a remodeled Ward's Grocery Store. They laid plans for a regional health facility to replace the small hospital where Sturgeon and Perrigan had recovered; indeed, lynchers and apologists joined their opponents in donations for the modern edifice.[66] Even more portentous was the purchase of the Missouri Institute of Aeronautics by the federal government, thereby increasing its military presence in the area. Surely the townspeople realized that prosperity and centralization would also bring the very race changes they considered so threatening.

Yet Sikestonians probably never thought of their violence as unique or compared it with lynchings nationwide. Like the others, it occurred because a black man had crossed—or appeared to cross—"the invisible but real" socioeconomic and political boundaries established by whites; for this he was labeled an alien to be exterminated during changing times. Like the others, it symbolized the most vicious form of control over all black residents and mirrored in several sociopsychological and physical ways an archetypal southern lynching.[67]

Sikeston lynchers formed a mass mob, since 1880 the "most spectacular" and "most common" type of southern mob in several states. They used technology—telephones and automobiles—to transform traditional bloodshed into "a peculiarly modern ritual," as had lynchers since the last decade of the nineteenth century. They drew sizable numbers, obtained widespread support, and swiftly killed someone charged with dastardly crimes. Well organized, they overpowered lawmen, ritualized Wright's degradation (symbolically that of all blacks), and displayed his corpse for both races to contemplate. Their ranks, though dominated by men, attracted women and children, and their apologists boasted of protecting white womanhood.[68]

In exhibiting these mass mob characteristics, Sikeston lynchers differed from other types of mobs. Unlike secret terrorists, who operated widely in border states, imposed secrecy, and rarely murdered, they held little in common with the planter backlash to Southern Tenant Farmers Union activities in Caruthersville. Unlike vengeful private mobs seeking retribution for crimes against themselves that failed to spark community action, they advanced and gave legitimacy to community punishment. Unlike quasi-legal posses who hunted and often killed alleged lawbreakers, they bore no official sanction.

Yet Sikeston lynchers also displayed specific aspects of private mobs and posses, indicating the limits of specific rope-and-faggot typology. They identified closely with the injury of Grace Sturgeon because of relationships with her husband, and they received the assistance of at least one policeman, as did private mob members elsewhere. They also benefited from the effort of townspeople to forget the entire affair quickly, again paralleling the aftermath of bloodshed involving a private mob. And they struck with the swiftness of the posses that tended to focus on heinous crimes of rape and murder, involved huge numbers of people, and promoted a sense of honor as self-appointed if not deputized protectors of the community.

Sikestonians also broke with important aspects of other mass mobs. They neither killed an innocent suspect nor fabricated his crime in order to justify his death for lesser racial challenges. Representing a minority of lynchings that turned on charges of real or imagined rape, Wright's death reinforced among whites the legitimacy of their action and the belief in black beasts. That lynchers were identified and brought before the law also made them different from past mass mobs, yet as friends, neighbors, and citizens recognizing the status of Grace Sturgeon, they verified contemporary and historical perceptions. Her family members were less than prominent among the lynchers, however, while a handful of malcontents, Kirk V. for one, played major roles in the execution. Still, despite threats to raze Sunset, their violence began and ended with Wright.

Sikestonians differed from members of mass mobs in additional ways because of region, epoch, Wright's condition, and the urban context. They did not torture, shoot, or hang him but limited their ritualized murder to dragging and burning. Knowing of his earlier admission of guilt, they sought no confession, and they wasted no time on prayer or collecting souvenirs from the pyre—activities corresponding to those of legal executions. Photos were taken of the corpse, some even for profit, but no one placed a warning sign on Wright's charred body.

The Sikeston event provided insights into lynchings throughout the state, which totaled eighty-five for the period 1889-1942 and eventually mirrored the South's emphasis on black victims (Table 1 in the Appendix). Whereas southern mobs killed disproportionate numbers of blacks as early as 1889 and reached their peak in the 1890s "like some giant volcanic eruption,"[69] Missourians executed transgressors from both races in near equal numbers in that period: twenty blacks (47.6 percent) versus twenty-two whites (52.4 percent). Over the next forty-three years, however, they lynched thirty-eight blacks and only five whites, most of both races having been shot, hanged, or burned during the first decade (Table 2A). They charged 28.6 percent of their black victims with rape-murder, rape, or attempted rape and 40.0 percent with murder during the twentieth century, when southern counterparts destroyed slightly smaller percentages for those offenses (see Table 3).

That Missourians lagged behind the course of southern violence revealed an overlap of timelines and environments: their frontier society extended into the 1890s to mete out justice across racial boundaries, while their obsession with blacks grew out of that decade and increased with town development and staple crop cultivation. In some cases they killed for what began as a sex offense and escalated to assault or murder. Had Wright's transgression been recorded as an attempted rape of Sturgeon rather than assault, the proportion of rape-related lynchings in the state would have been greater—suggesting that the percentage of alleged sex crimes may have been higher in all states and that the rape complex, however conjured up, was more real in the minds of many lynchers than estimated by lynching critics.

This was the case in Sikeston. And, while the state followed the overall southern pattern of more rape-related lynchings in the nineteenth century and more murder-related killing in the twentieth, its rape-related rate of 45 percent loomed above the 40.7 percent recorded in the South before 1900.[70] Surprisingly, Missouri's rate was even more disproportionate between 1920 and 1942: of nine black deaths in those twenty-three years, six (66.7 percent, the highest percentage for any era) were for rape. Real or imagined sexual transgressions held the attention of Missourians more than of southern lynchers, perhaps reflecting the impact of tradition on urban life (Table 2B-C).

Moreover, Missouri mobs in some instances paralleled and in others broke with trends in other border states and the southern socioeconomic anomaly of Virginia. Like them, they struck in an "ebb and flow" pattern of bloodshed that most affected certain counties (see map of Missouri Lynchings by County).[71] They committed at least one lynching in 40 of 114 counties, 17 above and 23 below the Missouri River, which flows across the upper third of the state. Lynchings clustered along the northern side of the river in the west and, especially, in a diagonal swath from the center of the state to the Mississippi River above St. Louis; they also concentrated in the southwest Ozark Mountains and in the southeast lowlands, especially in the Bootheel counties fronting the Mississippi. Although executions occurred in all three areas during the nineteenth and twentieth centuries, lynchers in the north claimed more lives before 1900, southwesterners during the next decade, and southeasterners after that. Wright's life, then, was taken in a place and at a time consistent with the larger pattern of extralegal killings in the state (Table 4).

Missouri Lynchings
by County, 1889 - 1942

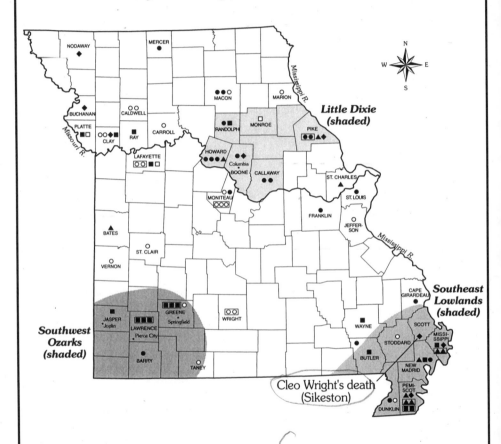

Cleo Wright's death
(Sikeston)

1889 - 1899 • black   ○ white
1900 - 1909 ■ black   □ white*
1910 - 1919 ▲ black*   white*
1920 - 1942 ◆ black*   no white
⟨ 🔲 multiple lynching ⟩

* Four deaths occurred at unknown
   locations and are not indicated:
   ⟨2⟩black (1919, 1920) and
   ⟨2⟩white (1901, 1919).

There were 85 total lynchings
between 1889 and 1942:
58 black and 27 white.

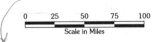

0   25   50   75   100
Scale in Miles

Map recreated by Donna Gilbreath from a map compiled by Jason M. Davis
Source: Missouri Spatial Data Information Service

Mobs appeared more often in some counties than others. They struck more than once in nine northern and nine southern counties; only in Pike above the Missouri River, compared with seven counties below it, did they kill more than one victim in the same incident. Those who claimed the most black as opposed to white lives surfaced in the Missouri and Mississippi valley counties of Howard and Pike, the Ozark counties of Lawrence and Greene, and the Bootheel counties of Mississippi, New Madrid, and Pemiscot. Again like border state and Virginia lynchings, those in Missouri represented the convergence of tradition with labor relations and shifting or (particularly in towns) rapid socioeconomic developments that fostered racial violence.[72]

Missouri lynch mobs emanated from three areas boasting core populations of southern and mountain people; in fact, one such area, comprising six central and two eastern counties above the Missouri River, was known collectively as "Little Dixie."[73] "It's the heart of Missouri, blooded of three, Virginia, Kentucky, and Tennessee," remarked a poet who also described the region that begot C.L. Blanton as "old Jeff Davis a-blowin' on his horn."[74] Each county featured Democratic politics, in part because of pro-slavery sentiment during the Civil War. Howard and Pike also claimed the area's largest number of black lynchings—four each.[75] Mob members of Lawrence and Greene Counties in the southwest took the most lives in a single lynching, three apiece. They drew from similar heritages, though more of the original settlers brought Republican Party politics from eastern Tennessee and, by the turn of the century, resided in mining areas and farmlands adjoining commercial centers such as Pierce City and Springfield. Southeast Missouri, however, recorded the most black deaths in a single county, six in Pemiscot, and the most multiple lynchings in the state. The culture and politics of the lowlands people were akin to those of Little Dixie, their southernness, labor competition, and racial violence having been reinvigorated by the presence of white planters and black sharecroppers.[76] And three of the last eight known lynchings in the state—all after World War I—occurred in the Bootheel, culminating with the death of Cleo Wright (Table 4A).[77]

Those who killed Wright revealed the influence of urban life on their violence. Different from their counterparts in southern and border states, Missourians lynched in a surprisingly large number of small towns and various sized cities.[78] Of fifty-eight black lynchings, twenty-three, or nearly 40 percent, occurred in locales that ranged from 2,500 persons (in minor civil entities, according to census bureau definition) to 80,935 residents (St. Joseph). In contrast, they executed only eight whites in cities (almost 30 percent of the white total), though none in a city larger than Hannibal (12,857) (Table 5A). That they murdered most whites in the 1890s and in countryside settings indicates that white lynching tended to be a more rural phenomenon.

It is also revealing that they killed a greater percentage of blacks in urban settings in each successive lynching period, advancing from 20 percent in the 1890s to nearly 67 percent between 1920 and 1942 (Table 5B).[79] Their violence, after spilling into small towns of under 5,000 residents, threatened to become full-blown pogroms or communal riots in larger, more impersonal communities where traditional beliefs were grafted to modern settings; there, lawmen and judges handled most white and black transgressors yet proved ineffective in the face of large-scale white fear of black assertiveness and socioeconomic competition. Lynchers could turn into rioters as they did in Joplin (1906) and threatened to do in Sikeston (1942), revealing a direct line of rural to urban violence that has been previously overlooked.

In Missouri and elsewhere, white inhabitants of cities threatened by growing numbers and loss of personalism, increasingly viewed blacks as indistinguishable one from another, and thus targeted them as a homogeneous group rather than individual rogues. For example, in Atlanta (1906) crowds excited over press accounts of alleged violations of white women by black men lashed out indiscriminately and tormented, mutilated, and strung up some black victims; and a Springfield, Illinois, mob (1908), frustrated by its failure to lynch an alleged murderer and an accused rapist who were surreptitiously escorted to safety by police, ignited a race riot that included the beating, cutting, and hanging of two black men, again in archetypal lynching fashion. Significantly, countryside and town lynchings evolved into urban riots South and North, in which preserving racial lines required acts of communal bloodshed: white on black combat in the streets.[80]

Wright's killers burst forth in this evolving urban pattern, though his death occurred in a larger city than had most black lynchings. They joined other Bootheel vigilantes who had intimidated and murdered black workers since their labor feuds with proprietors during turn-of-the-century logging days; they joined other postwar mobs who struck in towns, shockingly so in southwest Missouri during the early 1900s. Sikestonians, then, evinced the "culturally inherited blueprint for summary justice" that was present in most other lynchings statewide and bore mass mob characteristics: rumor, crowd formation, dragging, burning, ritual, and site selection. And they manifested the reaction of whites in other lynching towns statewide who questioned their ability to control blacks, particularly during periods of disruptive change. But unlike city dwellers in Virginia, who were outmaneuvered by authorities, they succeeded.[81]

In some specific ways, mob members in Sikeston replicated the bloodshed in southwest Missouri towns. Those in Pierce City (1901), Joplin (1903), and Springfield (1906) experienced unpredictable though not identical provocation: population changes in Pierce City and Joplin; political competition in Joplin and Springfield; and in all these municipalities, criminal activity or racial intimacy that was blamed on black degeneracy (Table 6).[82] Lynchers killed swiftly and ritualistically but did not mutilate blacks alleged to have raped white women or, in Joplin, murdered a police officer; they meant to intimidate black residents—though not as directly as Pierce City and Joplin mobs that entered the black community, attacked its residents, and burned their homes. And, except in Pierce City, they faced prosecution—which, despite the efforts of official counterparts to Forrest C. Donnell and David E. Blanton, proved a mockery.[83]

Sikestonians also shared most of these traits with lynchers in the north central town of Columbia, in Little Dixie's Boone County. There a mob killed James T. Scott in 1923, when perceived black prosperity, population changes, and sexual offenses involving both races triggered the bloodshed one week after his arrest for the attempted rape of a white teenager.[84]

In additional important ways, Sikeston lynchers paralleled the mobs in these towns. They wore no masks; they included no women or youngsters, though both were part of the crowd that gave them anonymity, encouragement, and legitimacy; the groups contained some younger, lower-class, and dissident individuals, even outsiders from nearby locales, yet the leaders and most active participants constituted a cross section of townspeople. Likewise, those few officially accused of involvement in other towns (where sketchy data is suggestive), proved to be residents of longstanding in their thirties and forties, whose occupations ranged from working-class laborers to skilled bricklayers to businessmen, ward heelers, and former officials; sons of prominent citizens also appeared among the activists in Springfield and Columbia. Particulars influenced each mob: for instance, the presence of ex-policemen, their relatives, and friends in Springfield, where a patrolman's wife had given birth to a child fathered by her black lover in 1904. Sikestonians and their peers in Pierce City, Joplin, Springfield, and Columbia, nonetheless, belied the contention that riffraff alone imposed lynch law. And although no arrests occurred and hence no question of bail arose in Sikeston, lynchers had their bail bonds paid by "solid citizens" in Springfield and by the "elite" in Columbia.[85]

However self-serving their actions or predictable their decisions, townspeople more than country residents moved to prosecute mob members. In all these communities except Pierce City, small numbers of citizens pressed for courtroom justice. Some in Joplin risked their lives in a losing tug-of-war with lynchers for control of the rope around Thomas Gilyard's neck; others in Springfield prevented the mob from spilling into the black neighborhoods. Motivated by indignation and apparently, in Springfield, by party politics, prosecutors went after lynchers. And in the Columbia case a grand jury hearing resulted because of outside public pressures, gubernatorial politics, and institutional reputations—especially those of the National Guard, which failed to prevent the murder, and of the University of Missouri, upon whose grounds it occurred. Nonetheless, only laborer Sam Mitchell of Joplin was convicted of a crime, and that verdict was overturned in a second trial. All executioners were freed by respectable citizens serving on grand or trial juries.

As in Sikeston, whites in towns wrecked by mob violence exhibited some disagreement over the lynching. They represented diverse views of white supremacy and race rule, further evidence linking lynchings and riots in an urban context, yet they overwhelmingly shied from convicting anyone for the murder of an alleged black rapist or cop killer. Opposing lynch law differed from protecting neighbors, acquaintances, and themselves in racist and—in the case of Pierce City and portions of Columbia—close-knit societies.[86] Even in Springfield all lynchers went free, despite a sizable population characterized by economic, political, and social diversification. Ironically, in both that city and Columbia seventeen years later, the grand jurors were farmers, representatives of society's traditional past; had they been drawn from more modern segments of the population, the outcome might have been different. Their clash of values with progressive attorneys notwithstanding, those seeking justice were small in number and silenced by the majority and their own commitment to a segregated society—which gave outsiders the mistaken impression that every white resident condoned bloodshed.

Sikeston lynchers killed more than a suspicious young male fairly new to the area. They stressed his prison record, of course, the only characteristic that fit the supposed criminal-prone profile of lynch victims throughout the South. In truth, however, they murdered, as had other mobs in

Missouri towns, a familiar individual—one who, after five years of residency, was regarded by many whites as part of the community.[87] Nor was their victim a cotton worker needing discipline, which explains why his death—occurring in the winter—did not fit the May–September seasonal pattern of most southern lynchings. Only one of the victims in these five towns, Scott of Columbia, was killed in the summer, and none were agricultural laborers.[88]

In fact, only Gilyard, a twenty-three-year-old transient from Mississippi who arrived in Joplin forty-eight hours before his April death, appeared to be a complete stranger. Also in April, Pierce City residents lynched William Godley, thirty-two, married, and employed as a laborer. They knew that he had come from Kentucky several years earlier and had lived in the area with his parents and other kin for some time; they knew, too, that he had a prison record but, after serving seven and a half years for an alleged rape, had been paroled for "orderly and peaceable" conduct. Like the Sikestonians who vouched for Cleo Wright's early release, they never feared him until the failed rape-murder of a landowner's twenty-four-year-old daughter triggered his execution. In contrast, Springfieldians lynched upright, productive citizens, none of whom lived on the edge of society. Horace Duncan, twenty, and Fred Coker, twenty-one, had grown up in Springfield, lived with family members, were steadily employed laborers, and had no criminal records. Nevertheless, in reverse stereotype, white townsfolk took the lives of these "clean cut, hard-working and responsible" youths for the alleged rape of a recently arrived white woman of dubious character who had left her farmer husband in nearby Fair Play.[89] This too occurred in April. Columbians killed an equally respectable resident in August: James T. Scott, thirty-five, a decorated World War I veteran and widower who had left three children with Chicago relatives several years earlier. Despite his identity as a janitor for the University of Missouri who had married a local schoolteacher, owned a car, attended church, lived in a middle-class neighborhood, and had apparently never committed a crime before, they hanged him for allegedly attempting to rape a professor's teenage daughter.

Invariably, one black man served as well as another. Among these victims only Cleo Wright confessed to his crime (and appears to have been guilty); the others professed their innocence and were accused without supporting evidence. Godley was arrested in Pierce City because of his past; Gilyard was found wounded at the crime scene in Joplin where a police officer died from gun shots; Duncan and Coker were at work at the time the estranged wife—who failed to identify them—claimed to have been raped in Springfield; Scott died because the Columbia teenager, and she alone, identified him as her assailant. That black victims stood accused no matter how skimpy the evidence was all that mattered to white townspeople who, like their southern cousins rural and urban, sought immediate racial backlash and example setting rather than justice.

Transgressors, whether Godley in 1901 or Wright forty-one years later, exposed the racial and sexual tension within a city, which necessitated their public execution by white residents attempting to uphold society in spite of its "conflicts and contradictions." "Black beasts" enabled everyday residents to project and channel their fears easily and singularly, much as New Englanders had done with female witches when colonial life was fraught with anxiety.[90] Single women then, like southern blacks later, were social and economic dependents in a society of interpersonal obligations that bred resentment; race and gender marked inherent strains, and public executions brought temporary relief without permanent resolution (which required revamping entire social orders).[91]

Sensing this, blacks in every municipality responded to the cruel object lesson in near-identical acts of survival: they deserted Pierce City, Joplin, and Springfield in sizable numbers. But their lives had been threatened even before the mob violence, as whites—particularly in Springfield—struggled with challenges to segregation and race etiquette; their experience replicated on a much smaller scale that of southern cities such as Atlanta, where the lynching-pogrom connection occurred in 1906.[92] Hence, those who remained lost socioeconomic and political leverage, which in Springfield had been meaningful. Blacks in Columbia and Sikeston also fled, albeit more temporarily. They enjoyed a greater stake in their communities and, in Sikeston, the protection of white paternalism and personalism, which was greatly reduced if not lacking altogether in the more modern context of larger southwestern cities such as Joplin and Springfield.

In several instances blacks also prepared for race war. Pierce City blacks exchanged shots with white lynchers-turned-rioters who entered their neighborhood, killed two inhabitants, and torched several homes. Those in Sikeston and Springfield armed themselves; in the latter city dynamite was provided by a white employer. Few blacks anywhere spoke out in the aftermath, but leaders who did, most notably the ministers J. Lyle Caston of Columbia and J.B. Ross of Sikeston, were warned or run out of town. A handful of ordinary citizens and even three prisoners demonstrated courage by bearing witness against lynchers in Pierce City and Springfield. As in Sikeston, however, protest came largely from outside—the NAACP pressured the governor to prosecute lynchers in Columbia as well as Sikeston—and without much success. NOTE WELL

Many lawmen should have faced prosecution for failing to protect lynching victims. Police in Pierce City made no effort to resist the mob, and some in Springfield joined it; sheriffs in Columbia and Springfield failed to prepare adequately for the lynchers, considered themselves helpless, and abandoned their prisoners easily. Only in Joplin did officers force mob members to push them aside. Missouri guardsmen proved no more effective in Pierce City: when the mayor decided against using them, lynchers broke into the armory to obtain rifles and ammunition. In Columbia, militiamen ignored Governor Arthur Hyde's mobilization call—which the NAACP requested—and, as agitated citizens, augmented the very crowd that he had ordered broken up. Some mayors and lesser officials in Pierce City, Joplin, and Columbia sought to dissuade the mob themselves or, after the lynching, requested the militia to restore peace. None acted with the heroism and determination of County Prosecutor Blanton and Trooper Dace, who nonetheless could not save Wright without firing into the crowd and igniting a full-fledged riot.

Sikeston lawmen, more than those in other urban settings, might have prevented Wright's lynching by a more expressive use of controlled and constrained force, following the example of Blanton, Dace, John Tandy, and Vincent Boisaubin.[93] If Police Chief Kendall had called in Roy Beck, Grover Lewis, and Walter Hughes and if Assistant Police Chief Harold Wallace had remained in City Hall, their numbers—including teenager Jack Johnson—would have totaled ten instead of six and made their chance of turning back the mob certainly possible. Had they held the lynchers at bay for five more minutes, Trooper Jim Greim, Trooper John Morris, and Constable Bob Reed would have brought the number of protectors to thirteen and turned the possibility of success into a probability. Had Sheriff Hobbs and deputy Jim Robert come immediately when summoned, they would have raised the force to fifteen and the prospects of Wright's safety to very probable. By noon, other reinforcements such as Trooper Morley G. Swingle and FBI Agent A.E. Jones would have dashed all opportunity for a lynching.[94]

Numbers alone, of course, would not have saved Wright, for lacking the outlook of Blanton and the troopers, local and county lawmen were unable to suppress racial attitudes, personal rivalries, and provincial loyalties. Otherwise, they could have shielded Wright, if necessary brandishing their weapons; thirteen determined protectors, eleven of them experienced law officers, might have dissuaded the mob until reinforcements arrived to quell the lynching threat. In fact, using firm action, Hobbs had twice prevented mob violence elsewhere in the county, and Dace, Tandy, and Boisaubin would do so four months later in Wyatt.[95] That Blanton and Dace sought to prevent violence while Kendall, Wallace, and Hobbs beckoned it revealed that in lynchings, as in riots, law enforcers participate in and influence the outcome of collective behavior.[96] Whereas Kendall and Wallace permitted Wright's death, state troopers, auxiliary police, and FBI agents prevented a subsequent racial pogrom in Sunset. Prosecutor and troopers represented the promise of justice in a modern context; policemen and sheriff verified the meaning of law and order for a traditional society.[97]

Their actions notwithstanding, Cleo Wright's guilt set him apart from the other victims and gave legitimacy to all previous state lynchings. In other ways too his death differed from those in other towns. Sikeston lynchers acted in an unsettling socioeconomic period that affected the larger area; their striking back at the savagery of Wright's attacks on a white woman and a police officer was somewhat similar to but more single-minded than the actions of Columbia whites fearful of sex offenses crossing racial lines. In contrast, mob members in Pierce City, Joplin, and Springfield, with previous assaults and sexual transgressions heavy on their minds, turned on perpetrators of past crimes whom they considered secondary offenders: Pete Hampton in Pierce City and Will Allen in Springfield, suspected of having murdered, respectively, a marshal and a Confederate veteran. They also targeted the black communities of Pierce City and Joplin. Sikestonians neither sought out yesterday's offenders nor attacked black residents en masse, in part because of the lack of a real or perceived crime wave, the stronger presence of lawmen at the execution, and the fear of black retaliation afterward. The heritage of racial personalism and paternalism, which Columbia shared to a lesser extent but Ozark cities not at all, also proved important in protecting Sunset residents. Cleo Wright stood alone rather than for all black townsmen—a point made by the Pole Cat himself.

Nor did Sikeston's mob seem influenced by a recent lynching nearby, as white residents in both Joplin and Springfield appeared to be. Pierce City's violence pushed racial fears and black refugees into Joplin, which repeated the experience and passed it along to Springfield. Coming so close in time and setting, the three bloodlettings—unique in themselves—seemed a chain reaction, much like the clustering and contagious effect of later race riots; they evinced another weld between lynchings and other forms of collective violence in municipal settings, which modernizing influences—especially "hot," quick television messages of racial confrontation—would accentuate.[98]

And unlike the lynchers in the Ozarks and Little Dixie, those in Sikeston needed no coaxing from sensational editors. Once having acted, however, they faced the greatest barrage of outside pressure and the most sincere legal challenge of all urban lynchers. In this context, Donnell, Blanton, and Dace emerged heroic and historical.

Although municipal mobs killed for reasons of alleged black degeneracy rather than labor conflicts emanating from an agrarian economy beyond city limits, only Sikeston residents lynched in an era of wartime change. Clearly, lynchers experienced different levels of urbanization and, accordingly, different reasons for their rampage. Pierce City residents entered the twentieth century having lost considerable population—black and white— and census bureau status as a civil entity. They also faced a rise in crime, supposedly committed by transients, and a downturn in economics due to area crop failures during the summer of 1901. In contrast to these retrogressive developments, Joplin citizens benefited from enormous growth (161.7 percent) over the 1890s but reeled under the imagined competition of blacks, who, though their numbers had more than doubled by 1900, constituted less than 3 percent of the population. Springfieldians that year and Columbians twenty years later, in turn, enjoyed modest population increases yet manifested sexual fears despite the fact that their black populations, remained constant and lost significant numbers, respectively. In truth, lynchers in each of the expanding municipalities made scapegoats of blacks for socioeconomic disruptions wrought by urbanization. Unsettled by the shift from a traditional to a modern society, whites lashed out at historical aliens (Table 6).

Neither Sikeston nor these other cities matched the pattern of the most lynch-prone areas of the South, where low population density (number of people per square mile) combined with high rates of black population growth. None except Columbia were located in counties characterized by low population densities, and only Joplin and Sikeston experienced high rates of black population growth. In general, they recorded the reverse of state or southern lynchings—rural or urban—before 1930 (Table 6).[99] Sikeston, moreover, combined traditional and modern lynching patterns, high population density with high black population growth, revealing the makings of both the communal and—with the formation of ghettos and heightened black awareness—the commodity riots that converged on Detroit the year after Wright's lynching.

Sikestonians, of course, inhabited one of the medium-sized Missouri municipalities that experienced a twentieth-century lynching, much larger

than Pierce City (2,151) and much smaller than Joplin (26,023) or Springfield (23,267). They numbered 7,944, comparable to Columbians (10,392)
though with a smaller black population at the time of the lynching (Table
6). In the following decade, however, they and the residents of Joplin and
Columbia experienced actual increases in the number of blacks, while those
of Pierce City and Springfield lost population—though attributing the permanent decline of their black populations solely to the bloodshed disregards
the racial emigration that began in the 1890s. As significantly, Sikeston led
all these municipalities in the number (599) and percentage (59.7 percent)
of new black residents, and Scott County alone posted similar gains. These
figures indicate that Wright's killing did not dissuade blacks from living permanently in either the city or the county, as had been the trend in southwest Missouri. In fact, Sikeston's black population grew faster than its
county's, thereby continuing the trend of black urbanization begun before
Wright's death.[100]

Confronting a racial order uniquely accentuated by outside forces,
Sikeston occupied a space between agrarian towns the size of Pierce City—
on the "fringes of urban life"—where race relations were blurred, and much
bigger commercial entities such as Joplin or Springfield, where the potential for racial competition and possible challenge to Jim Crow loomed
large.[101] Its citizens encountered Cleo Wright in this uncertain middle ground
and reckoned, simultaneously, with his rage and global conflict. Moreover,
the war produced in Sikeston circumstances very different from those in all
other Missouri towns or cities where lynchings occurred, regardless of chronology, demography, social order, or economic characteristics. It profoundly
accentuated Wright's personal anxiety, Sturgeon's vulnerability, and the mob's
sense of honor and community, while glorifying traditional violence in a
modern context. Most notable in that respect, it forced the federal government to act.

8 Postmortem

Unforeseen by the tradition-bound killers of Cleo Wright was the long-range significance of their act for constitutional law, one of the most far-reaching sources of modernization. Their ancient blood rite amid global war provoked an unprecedented contemporary, legal response that advanced intermittently into the postwar era toward federal intervention in racially motivated violence. More than reviving earlier concepts of honor and bloodshed, they dragged forward a judicial activism that had begun in the wake of an earlier world war to challenge abuse of black citizens and by the late 1960s reached far beyond Sikeston to envelop the deep South and the entire nation.[1]

Legal efforts growing out of Wright's lynching revealed the shift in race-related cases begun by the NAACP, liberal lawyers, and federal judges during the Progressive Era. Their counterattack rested upon the Civil War constitutional amendments and came before the Supreme Court of Chief Justice Edward Douglass White (1919-21). Most notably, they succeeded in using the Thirteenth and Fifteenth Amendments to strike down peonage and "grandfather clauses," respectively, and the Fourteenth Amendment to point up the rights of black citizens affected by residential segregation and separate-but-equal accommodations. Though hardly dismantling "the legal structure of racism," they held out hope and set precedent for the more fundamental changes of the Great Depression. An improved and increasingly black-dominated NAACP legal staff, a law profession reconsidering its values, and a tolerant Supreme Court brought about a constitutional revolution in civil rights during an era of great change. Their endeavors—which took root in 1937 as Hugo L. Black's appointment created an activist majority on the bench—challenged discrimination in jury selection, voting rights, and state-supported higher education.[2]

On the eve of World War II, however, the NAACP and liberal attorneys had yet to seek legal footing for the equal protection clause of the Fourteenth Amendment in lynching cases. Since the association's inception in 1909, its leaders had sought federal legislation rather than judicial redress to stem mob violence. They knew that Supreme Court decisions had held that lynchings were not in themselves a federal offense (*United States v. Harris,* 1882) and that individuals were exempt from violation of the Fourteenth Amendment (*Hodges v. United States,* 1906). They knew, too, that neither previous presidents nor the Justice Department had supported the earlier legal battles for racial equality.[3] Surprisingly, then, as the NAACP carried on its crusade for congressional action, Wright's murder raised the possibility of broadening the executive branch's commitment to civil rights and, consequently, the Supreme Court's interpretation of the equal protection clause.

Sikeston scarcely seemed the place for a constitutional revolution, particularly one that would expand federal authority and protect black citizens. In fact, after the U.S. Justice Department failed to secure indictments against local lawmen for their role in Wright's death, Attorney General Francis Biddle closed the case. By year's end, however, he had heard of much public dissatisfaction with the proceedings and "several intimations" for another grand jury; of Jacob M. Lashly's hesitance—from the beginning—to accept the theory developed by Civil Rights Section (CRS) attorneys; of "United States v. Walter Kendall, et al." as still "the best case for Federal jurisdiction in the lynching field": should it not be reopened through the office of United States Attorney Harry C. Blanton? Biddle said no.[4] Perhaps he considered the politics of reopening Wright's murder case too risky, or prejudice in the region too overwhelming. Having tested federal power and lost, he seemed disinclined to appear unreasonable by challenging states' rights further. Moreover, the case load facing his department was mounting as national security investigations alone doubled during the 1942-43 fiscal year.[5] Perhaps, too, President Roosevelt, never intending to go beyond the semblance of protecting black civil rights, instructed him to avoid alienating the white majority needed to fight the war abroad.

More likely, Biddle sought a new, stronger case from among subsequent lynchings in Texas and Mississippi; and Roosevelt, who backed away from firm government action in the face of riots the following year, probably preferred dealing with racial violence through CRS initiatives rather than United States Army patrols. In this way the president endeavored to protect democratic rights, thereby stemming Axis propaganda, placating blacks and liberals, but alienating politically powerful unreconstructed racists as little as possible.[6] Indeed, the lynching of Willie Vinson in Texarkana on July 13—two weeks before the federal grand jury issued its report on Wright's murder—doubtless prompted Roosevelt's order that the Justice Department inquire into all black deaths suspected to be the result of lynching. Small wonder that NAACP executive secretary Walter White, who probably learned of the directive from conversations with top officials in the Justice Department, privately confided that "some real results" came from the Sikeston affair.[7]

And they did, largely through the efforts of Biddle, CRS lawyers, and their postwar successors. The "dreaded certainty" of Justice Department officials that other lynchings would occur and further blot the nation's war effort probably influenced Roosevelt's order and proved prophetic, for three black Mississippians were hanged within a span of seven days in October. Given the talk of pressing those cases, one of which involved a jailer and contained strong evidence for prosecution, Biddle decided against reopening the Wright case. He promised "relentless prosecution" and tested CRS theory anew, failing in one grand jury and succeeding in another when jurors—for the first time in forty years—indicted the lawman involved and four others. In federal court, however, the jury acquitted the defendants, despite the confession of one.[8]

Undaunted, Biddle continued the investigation and, where feasible, the prosecution of lynching cases. Of five lynchings that occurred during the remaining two and a half years of his attorney generalship, he advanced beyond grand juries twice. CRS attorneys obtained no convictions, but in *Screws v. United States* (1945) they opened the door to "the potentialities" of Section 52 as "an anti-lynching measure." Slightly more than one year after Wright's death, they had investigated the brutal killing of Robert Hall by three Georgia police officers who handcuffed him and beat him senseless with a blackjack. Following the conviction of Sheriff M. Claude Screws and his henchmen by the United States District Court for violation of Section 52, a divided Supreme Court ordered new trials for the defendants.[9] According to the Court's majority opinion, the district judge had failed to instruct the jury properly on the question of the lawmen's willful intent to deprive Hall of his constitutional rights to life and trial "by a court rather than by ordeal"; hence, the Court limited Section 52's application to state officials acting "under color of law" to divest a citizen of a specific federal right and turned its constitutionality on "the requirement of 'willfulness.'" Nevertheless, CRS lawyers demonstrated the legitimacy of Section 52 despite its vagueness, prosecuted—for the first time before the Supreme Court—a state official for violating personal constitutional rights, and reinforced the concept of "government by injunction" in lynching cases. More significantly for future policy, Justice Department attorneys positioned themselves for ultimate victory.[10]

Although U.S. Attorney General Tom C. Clark, Biddle's successor, ad-

vanced CRS efforts to revitalize the Fourteenth Amendment and Reconstruction statutes, the overwhelming precedent sought in the Wright case still lay
in the future. More lynchings, some involving the gruesome murders of black
veterans, marked the immediate postwar period and triggered enormous
protest from blacks and liberals. Confronted by political problems reminis-
cent of those that had determined Roosevelt's response to Wright's lynching, Harry S Truman created the President's Committee on Civil Rights,
which ultimately evaluated CRS efforts.[11] Publicly, it considered the CRS
record "remarkable" though characterized by serious problems, such as the
difficulty of prosecuting cases under the Reconstruction statutes and relying on the FBI for its investigation; privately, it sharply criticized both
Justice Department agencies, accusing the bureau of "superficial and unin-
telligent work."[12] However fair that appraisal may have been for the CRS's
eight-year history, it hardly did justice to the largely competent handling of
the Sikeston case by CRS attorneys and FBI agents endeavoring to set precedent in a racist, wartime society.

   Internal conflicts, changing priorities, and strict constructionism slowed
Justice Department endeavors for another generation. Seeking positive relations with local lawmen and a favorable image with the public, J. Edgar
Hoover resisted FBI investigations in civil rights cases; facing a conservative
Congress and a Communist threat, President Truman became increasingly
occupied with the Cold War; continuing to advance liberal tenets but not
projecting overwhelming endorsement of full civil rights, the Supreme Court
moved cautiously against only the most obvious forms of discrimination
and, in *Williams v. United States* (1951), held to the limited interpretations
of Sections 51 and 52. Into the 1950s and early 1960s, the Supreme Court
of Chief Justice Earl Warren delivered the crushing legal blow to segregation, Congress enacted relatively tame yet symbolically significant civil rights
laws, and Presidents Dwight D. Eisenhower and John F. Kennedy engaged
in gradualistic, voluntary, and, if necessary, executive action.[13] Yet from 1947
to 1964, no branch of government gave priority to Biddle's and his attorneys' efforts to provide blacks—and, later, white civil rights workers—protection under Sections 51 and 52. Even the Justice Department, which
elevated the CRS unit to division status in 1957, concentrated its resources
on race discrimination and, ironically, reversed its wartime emphasis.[14]

   The resurrection and final success of Biddle's and his staff's strategy in
the Wright lynching came in a rush in 1964, when four civil rights workers
were murdered in the South. Presidential and Justice Department thinking
changed dramatically as the deaths of James Chaney, Andrew Goodman, and

Michael Schwerner in Mississippi and of Lemuel Penn in Georgia triggered public reaction. FBI agents investigated the killings, Civil Rights Division attorneys prosecuted the defendants, and the Supreme Court gave "new vitality" to Sections 51 and 52. In *United States v. Price* (1966), liberal justices reversed the decision of a lower court and ordered new trials for three Mississippi lawmen accused of willfully depriving Chaney, Goodman, and Schwerner of due process as guaranteed them by the Fourteenth Amendment; in *United States v. Guest* (1966), the high court's judicial activists declared Klansmen guilty of conspiring to deny Penn his constitutional rights as assured by both the due process and the equal protection clauses of the Fourteenth Amendment. In essence, the Warren Court upheld and expanded the CRS's original legal theory, placing "prosecutorial discretion" of both sections in the hands of federal attorneys where crimes entailed state involvement or, conversely, state indifference.[15] Going further, it declared in *Guest* that Congress could enact laws "punishing all conspiracies—with or without state action—that interfere with Fourteenth Amendment rights." Although the Biddle and CRS strategy in Wright's and subsequent cases demonstrated the constitutional difficulties involved in applying Sections 51 and 52, black protest, judicial activism, and changing times proved the strategy's worth twenty years later.[16]

In sum, Biddle and CRS attorneys were a small part of the larger constitutional revolution that challenged local legal tradition and, by inference, concepts of white supremacy.[17] Their commitment acquired urgency as the war for democracy abroad brought into question "perversions of democracy at home." Their concerns—and Roosevelt's—were limited to specific minorities and specific rights: the violation of African American civil rights jeopardized the nation's image, but the abrogation of Japanese American civil liberties—for largely political considerations—supposedly bolstered the nation's security. Democratic Party politics and war exigencies limited Justice Department action further, largely to the most flagrant violence. Perhaps Biddle and his staff realized, as had the Supreme Court under Chief Justice White, that lynching, like peonage, was "a hidden, shameful part" of southern racism with few public supporters even among southerners.[18] They played a much less active and cooperative role in the NAACP's successful challenge of white primaries in *Smith v. Allwright* (1944), for they feared alienating southern Democrats—particularly members of the Senate Judiciary Committee, with whom the department "had to get along." Nonetheless, Biddle's and his lawyers' efforts in the Wright case were genuine, and although they fell short during the war and gave the impression that "the system hung on," they laid down judicial arguments that would help "undermine the entire structure."[19]

Nowhere nearly as momentous or immediate as the "judicial shock waves" set in motion by *Smith* and later cases, Biddle's investigation of Wright's death signified the transition of the Justice Department's role in civil rights: instead of sitting on their law books, Justice Department lawyers interpreted them.[20] To be sure, in 1942 Biddle's and his ranking assistants' perspectives were limited to countering enemy propaganda and to deterring racial violence. In the process, however, they brought the federal government more directly into the protection of blacks and the struggle for racial equality than at any time since Reconstruction. Black and liberal contemporaries applauded their efforts, no doubt unaware that Roosevelt's order for future investigations was made informally or that James E. Person's lynching in Illinois in late 1942—legally a weaker case than that of Wright— was pressed relentlessly because Biddle and CRS officials wanted to demonstrate their regional evenhandedness.[21] In that strategy of commitment and expediency lay both the New Deal foundations and the future protection of black constitutional rights.

Like untold numbers of black citizens, Cleo Wright was denied due process, mutilated, and murdered. The taking of his life and the political dimensions of his case symbolized the expendability of black society in the eyes of white lynchers and their government. Unlike his brethren, however, Wright did not die in vain; his death helped set in motion the federal power needed to secure for African Americans the most basic of unalienable rights. Perhaps it was the realization that it would take many more black lives and several more decades to deliver on the promise of personal safety that triggered in Wright the phrase he uttered while mortally wounded in the basement of a segregated hospital: "Oh, God!"

Or it might have been, as Grace Sturgeon wished to believe, confessional remorse for a diabolical act that unleashed violence and tragedy all along the color line of a city in socioeconomic transition. Wright's savage attack combined racial grievance with an explosive ambivalence toward people and things white, a living-out of the cruelest of trickster tales that sought to invert black-white power relationships; it emanated from a traditional society that demanded his own destruction yet occurred in a place and at a time when modernists were struggling to rid themselves of the most blatant forms of backwardness.[22] The lynchers and their supporters, including the Pole Cat, rallied to control their "home ground" and level the social earthquake triggered by Wright. Unlike other southerners who struck at specific conflicts,

they uttered a death cry as far-reaching as his own.[23] Perhaps not even David E. Blanton, who genuinely challenged the mob's right to stand its ground, understood that Wright's lynching signaled the beginning of the end of one kind of racial repression.[24] Though it seemed much like any of the eighty-five executions of black men in Missouri, it alone bore lasting historical significance. Postmortem indeed!

page for incarcerating —

Appendix

Table 1. Lynching Victims in Missouri, 1889-1942

Region:		Setting:		Crime:	Category (Alleged):
LD	Little Dixie	Y	Rural	M	Murder
SE	Lowlands	X	Urban	R	Rape/Rape Murder
SW	Ozarks	U	Unknown	O	Other
O	Other			U	Unknown
U	Unknown				

Date	Race	Name	County	Region/ Setting	Crime
01/21/89	B	Henry Thomas	Mercer	O/Y	M
05/07/89	W	Corber bros.	Moniteau	O/Y	M
	W	Corber bros.	Moniteau	O/Y	M
	W	Corber bros.	Moniteau	O/Y	M
06/21/89	B	Alfred Grizzard	Moniteau	O/Y	O gambling
08/03/89	B	Benjamin Smith	Macon	O/Y	R
09/12/89	W	John Davis	Greene	SW/Y	M
09/17/89	B	George Burke	Boone	LD/X	R
11/17/89	W	Joseph Gebhart	Dunklin	SE/Y	O safecracking
09/03/90	B	Thomas Smith	Butler	O/Y	M
01/20/91	B	Olli Truxton	Howard	LD/Y	R
01/22/92	W	Robt. Helper	Vernon	O/X	M
02/12/92	W	Lewis Gordon	Carroll	O/X	R
02/14/92	W	John F. Bright	Taney	SW/Y	M
04/27/92	B	David Sims	Dunklin	SE/Y	U
02/18/93	B	John Hughes	Randolph	LD/X	O insulting white
09/16/93	W	Redmond Burke	Caldwell	O/Y	O wife beating
01/17/94	B	John Buckner	St. Louis	O/Y	R
06/29/94	B	Ulysses Haydon	Barry	SW/Y	M
07/02/94	B	Joseph Johnson	Callaway	LD/Y	R
11/05/94	W	(unknown man)	St. Clair	O/Y	U

(Continued on next page)

Table 1—continued

Date	Race	Name	County	Region/Setting	Crime
02/17/95	W	George Tracy	Caldwell	O/Y	M
08/15/95	B	Emmett Divens	Callaway	LD/X	M
10/11/95	B	Wm. Henderson	C. Girardeau	O/Y	R
06/27/96	W	James Cocking	Macon	O/Y	M
06/30/96	W	Ceil Wayland	Marion	O/X	R
07/27/96	W	M. Crawford	Moniteau	O/Y	R
09/04/96	W	Thomas Larkin	Jefferson	O/Y	R
12/06/96	W	Jessie Winner	Lafayette	O/X	M
	W	James Nelson	Lafayette	O/X	M
05/22/97	W	John Mitchell	Wright	O/Y	O larceny
	W	Jack Coffman	Wright	O/Y	O larceny
07/10/97	B	Erastus Brown	Franklin	O/Y	R
11/18/97	W	Silas P. Fargo	Clay	O/X	O arson
06/06/98	B	Curtin Young	Pike	LD/Y	M
	B	Sam Young	Pike	LD/Y	M
06/30/98	B	Henry Williams	Macon	O/X	R
08/11/98	W	Benjamin Jones	Clay	O/X	M
11/29/98	B	(unknown man)	New Madrid	SE/Y	M
07/23/99	B	Frank Embree	Howard	LD/Y	R
01/01/99	B	Thomas Hayden	Howard	LD/Y	M
11/16/99	W	Wm. Huff	Stoddard	SE/Y	M
04/28/00	B	Mundee			
		Chowagee	Platte	O/Y	M
05/04/00	B	Henry Darley	Clay	O/Y	R
01/03/01	B	Nelson Simpson	Butler	SE/Y	O prejudice
03/02/01	B	Arthur McNeal	Ray	O/X	M
07/26/01	W	John Mack	Unknown	U/U	U
08/19/01	B	Wm. Godley	Lawrence	SW/Y	M
	B	French Goldley	Lawrence	SW/Y	O prejudice
	B	Peter Hampton	Lawrence	SW/Y	M
02/17/02	B	Louis Wright	New Madrid	SE/Y	O assault
03/26/02	B	Oliver Wright	Randolph	LD/Y	U
05/25/02	W	Abraham			
		Witherups	Monroe	LD/Y	M
07/17/02	W	Joshua Anderson	Lafayette	O/X	M
08/12/02	B	Henry Gates	Lafayette	O/X	M
01/21/03	B	Andy Clark	Wayne	O/Y	M
04/15/03	B	Thomas Gilyard	Jasper	SW/X	M
05/03/03	B	D. Malone	Pemiscot	SE/Y	O prejudice

(Continued on next page)

Table 1—continued

Date	Race	Name	County	Region/Setting	Crime
	B	W.J. Mooneyhon	Pemiscot	SE/Y	O prejudice
05/12/05	B	Robt. Pettigrew	Mississippi	SE/Y	O kidnapping
04/14/06	B	Harry Duncan	Greene	SW/X	R
	B	Fred Coker	Greene	SW/X	R
	B	Wm. Allen	Greene	SW/X	M
08/01/09	W	George Johnson	Platte	O/Y	M
05/30/10	B	(unknown man)	New Madrid	SE/Y	O assault
07/03/10	B	Robert Coleman	Mississippi	SE/X	M
	B	Sam Field	Mississippi	SE/X	M
10/11/11	B	A.B. Richardson	Pemiscot	SE/X	O robbery
	B	Benjamin Woods	Pemiscot	SE/X	R
03/19/14	B	Dallas Shields	Howard	LD/X	M
02/21/15	B	W.F. Williams	Bates	O/U	M
09/01/15	B	Rudd Lane	Pike	LD/X	O theft
01/03/16	B	Samuel Sykes	Pemiscot	SE/Y	O assault
04/03/16	B	Fayette Chandler	St. Charles	O/X	M
00/00/19	B	(unknown man)	Unknown	U/U	U
00/00/19	W	(unknown man)	Unknown	U/U	U
00/00/20	B	(unknown man)	Unknown	U/U	U
08/00/21	B	Roy Hammons	Pike	LD/Y	R
04/29/23	B	James T. Scott	Boone	LD/X	R
12/18/24	B	Roosevelt Grigsby	Mississippi	SE/X	R
08/07/25	B	Walter Mitchell	Clay	O/X	R
10/00/27	B	Will Sherrod	Pemiscot	SE/Y	R
01/12/31	B	Raymond Gunn	Nodaway	O/X	M
11/29/33	B	Lloyd Warner	Buchanan	O/X	R
01/25/42	B	Cleo Wright	Scott	SE/X	O assault

Sources: Comparison and correction of NAACP, *Thirty Years of Lynching in the United States, 1889-1918* (rpt.; New York: Negro Universities Press, 1969), 80-82; Monroe N. Work, ed., *Negro Year Book: An Annual Encyclopedia of the Negro, 1925-1926* (Tuskegee, Ala.: Tuskegee Institute, 1928), 400-402; Walter White, *Rope and Faggot: A Biography of Judge Lynch* (rpt.; New York: Arno, 1969), 256; Jessie Daniel Ames, *The Changing Character of Lynching: Review of Lynching, 1932-1941* (rpt.; New York: AMS Press, 1973), 45-46; *Sikeston Standard,* 30 Jan. 1942, 8; Burton L. Purrington and Judith A Brooks, "Adaptation, Repression, Resistance, and Flight: African Americans in Southwest Missouri, 1865-1920" (meeting of American Society for Ethnohistory, Chicago, 4 Nov. 1989), 6 and table 2; Michael J. Pfeifer, "The Ritual of Lynching: Extralegal Justice in Missouri, 1890-1942," *Gateway Heritage* 13 (Winter 1993): 22-33. See also, for all tables, U.S. Census Reports, *Population,* 1880-1950.

Table 2. Lynching Victims by Race and Alleged Crime, Missouri, 1889-1942

	A. Race									
	1889-1899		1900-1909		1910-1919		1920-1942		Total	
	N	%	N	%	N	%	N	%	N	%
Black	20	47.6	18	81.8	11	91.7	9	100	58	68.2
White	22	52.4	4	18.2	1	8.3	0	0	27	31.8
Total	42		22		12		9		85	

 1889

	B. Crime											
	1889-1899						1900-1909					
	Blk	%	Wh	%	Total	%	Blk	%	Wh	%	Total	%
Murder	8	40.0	12	54.5	20	47.6	8	44.4	3	75	11	50.0
Rape	9	45.0	4	18.2	13	30.9	3	16.7	0		3	13.6
Other	2	10.0	5	22.7	7	16.2	6	33.3	0		6	27.3
Unknown	1	5.0	1	4.5	2	4.8	1	5.6	1	25	2	9.1
Total	20		22		42		18		4		22	

	1910-1919						1920-1942				
	Blk	%	Wh		Total	%	Blk	%	Wh	Total	%
Murder	5	45.4	0		5	41.7	1	11.1	0	1	11.1
Rape	1	9.1	0		1	8.3	6	66.7	0	6	66.7
Other	4	36.4	0		4	33.3	1	11.1	0	1	11.1
Unknown	1	9.1	1		2	16.7	1	11.1	0	1	11.1
Total	11		1		12		9		0	9	

	C. Race and Crime					
	1889-1942					
	Blk	%	Wh	%	Blk/Wh	%
Murder	22	37.9	15	55.6	37	43.5
Rape	19	32.8	4	14.8	23	27.1
Other	13	22.4	5	18.5	18	21.2
Unknown	4	6.9	3	11.1	7	8.2
Total	58		27		85	

Sources: See Table 1.

Table 3. Comparative Lynching Statistics, Missouri and the South, 1900-1942

	Missouri		South[a]	
Alleged Crime	N	%	N	%
Murder	14	40.0	498	37.8
Rape/Rape Murder	10	28.6	337	25.6
Other	11	31.4	481	36.6
Total[b]	35[c]		1,316[d]	

Sources: Calculated from Jessie Daniel Ames, *The Changing Character of Lynching;* Jessie P. Guzman, ed., *The Negro Year Book;* and Stewart E. Tolnay and E.M. Beck, *A Festival of Violence.*

[a]Alabama, Arkansas, Florida, Georgia, Kentucky, Louisiana, Mississippi, North and South Carolina, and Tennessee.

[b]Excludes "Unknown."

[c]All male victims.

[d]Includes 73 females and 24 victims whose gender is not known.

Table 4. Lynching Locations, Missouri, 1889-1942

	A. All Areas									
	1889-1899		1900-1909		1910-1919		1920-1942		Total	
	N	%	N	%	N	%	N	%	N	%
Little Dixie	9	21.4	2	9.1	2	16.7	2	22.2	15	17.6
SW Ozarks	3	7.1	7	31.8	0		0		10	11.8
SE Low-lands	4	9.5	5	22.7	6	50.0	3	33.3	18	21.2
Other	26	62.0	7	31.8	2	16.7	3	33.3	38	44.7
Unknown	0		1	4.5	2	16.7	1	11.1	4	4.7
Total	42		22		12		9		85	

	B. Little Dixie									
	1889-1899		1900-1909		1910-1919		1920-1942		Total	
	N	%	N	%	N	%	N	%	N	%
Black	9	100.0	1	50.0	2	100.0	2	100.0	14	93.3
White	0		1	50.0	0		0		1	6.7
Total	9		2		2		2		15	

(Continued on next page)

Table 4—cont.

	C. SW Ozarks								
	1889-1899		1900-1909		1910-1919		1920-1942		Total	
	N	%	N	%	N	%	N	%	N	%
Black	1	33.3	7	100.0	0		0		8	80.0
White	2	66.7	0		0		0		2	20.0
Total	3		7		0		0		10	

	D. SE Lowlands								
Black	2	50.0	5	100.0	6	100.0	3	100.0	16	88.9
White	2	50.0	0		0		0		2	11.1
Total	4		5		6		3		18	

	E. Other								
Black	8	30.8	5	71.4	2	100.0	3	100.0	18	47.4
White	18	69.2	2	28.6	0		0		20	52.6
Total	26		7		2		3		38	

	F. In Relation to Missouri River				
	1889-1899 (N = 42)	1900-1909 (N = 22)	1910-1919 (N = 12)	1920-1942 (N = 9)	Total (N = 85)
Above					
Black	12	4	3	5	24
White	7	2	0	0	9
Total	19 (45.2%)	6 (27.3%)	3 (25.0%)	5 (55.6%)	33 (38.8%)
Below					
Black	8	14	7	3	32
White	15	1	0	0	16
Total	23 (54.8%)	15 (68.2%)	7 (58.3%)	3 (33.3%)	48 (56.5%)
Unknown					
Black	0	0	1	1	2
White	0	1	1	0	2
Total	0	1 (4.5%)	2 (16.7%)	1 (11.1%)	4 (4.7%)

Sources: See Table 1.

Table 5. Urbanization of Lynching, Missouri, 1889-1942

A. Urban Lynchings, 1889-1942

Pop. Range	BLACK N = 23	%	WHITE N = 8	%	TOTAL N = 31	%
2,500-	13	56.5	6	75.0	19	61.3
5,001-	4	17.4	1	12.5	5	16.1
10,001-	1	4.3	1	12.5	2	6.5
20,001-	3	13.0	0		3	9.7
25,001-	1	4.3	0		1	3.2
50,001-	0		0		0	
80,001-	1	4.3	0		1	3.2

B. Rural v. Urban

	1889-1899						1900-1909					
	BLACK N = 20	%	WHITE N = 22	%	TOTAL N = 42	%	BLACK N = 18	%	WHITE N = 4	%	TOTAL N = 22	%
Rural	16	80.0	15	68.2	31	73.8	12	66.7	2	50.0	14	63.6
Urban	4	20.0	7	31.8	11	26.2	6	33.3	1	25.0	7	31.9
Unknown	0		0		0		0		1	25.0	1	4.5

	1910-1919						1920-1942					
	BLACK N = 11	%	WHITE N = 1	%	TOTAL N = 12	%	BLACK N = 9	%	WHITE N = 0	%	TOTAL N = 9	%
Rural	2	18.2	0		3	25.0	2	22.2	0		2	22.2
Urban	7	63.6	0		7	58.3	6	66.7	0		6	66.7
Unknw	2	18.2	1	100.0	2	16.7	1	11.1	0		1	11.1

	1889-1942					
	BLACK N = 58	%	WHITE N = 27	%	TOTAL N = 85	%
Rural	32	55.2	17	63.0	49	57.6
Urban	23	39.7	8	29.6	31	36.5
Unknown	3	5.1	2	7.4	5	5.9

Sources: Federal Census, 1890-1950; see also Table 1.

Table 6. Lynchings in Selected Towns and Counties, Missouri, 1890-1950

Location	Pop.[a]	% Change Before	After	Blk Pop./%	Blk % Change Before	After	Density County	State
Sikeston (1942)	7,944	+40.0	+46.5	1,003/ 12.6	+123.9	+59.7		
Scott	30,377	+21.8	+8.1	2,261/ 7.4	+43.7	+21.7	72.5	54.6
Pierce City (1901)	2,151	-14.3	-16.0	175/ 8.1	-14.6	NA		
Lawrence	31,662	+20.7	-16.0	283/ .9	-22.3	-67.8	51.7	45.2
Joplin (1903)	26,023	+161.7	+20.1	733/ 2.8	+113.7	+9.3		
Jasper	84,018	+66.4	+6.7	1,428/ 1.7	+56.4	-4.2	132.9	45.2
Sprgfld (1906)	23,267	+6.5	+51.3	2,268/ 9.7	+.4	-12.0		
Greene	52,713	+8.4	+21.1	3,298/ 6.3	+1.7	-20.4	78.9	45.2
Columbia (1923)	10,392	+7.6	+44.0	1,919/ 18.5	-14.6	+19.9		
Boone	29,672	-2.8	+4.5	3,471/ 11.7	-7.1	-5.1	43.1	49.5

Source: Federal Census, 1890-1950.

[a]Population is the last census figure prior to the lynching.

[b]Percent change from one census to the next (i.e., Sikeston "before" from 1930 to 1940; "after" from 1940 to 1950).

[c]Density is the average number of people per square mile.

Notes

In this — when we were will seen in 2063 ...

Abbreviations and Short Forms

ARCHIVES AND FILES

FBIF	Federal Bureau of Investigation Files, Washington, D.C.
FBI Report	Federal Bureau of Investigation, "Report," 23 Feb., 13 March, 27 April, 16 May, 4 and 16 June 1942, FBIF
FBI Survey	Federal Bureau of Investigation, "Survey of Racial Conditions in the United States" (1944), Box 21, OF 10B, Franklin D. Roosevelt Library, Hyde Park, New York
FCDP	Forrest C. Donnell Papers, UMSH
JCC	Jefferson County Courthouse, Pine Bluff, Arkansas
MHSL	Missouri Historical Society Library, St. Louis, Missouri
MSHP	Missouri State Highway Patrol Files, Jefferson City, Missouri
NAACP	National Association for the Advancement of Colored People Papers, Library of Congress, Washington, D.C.
NARS	National Archives and Records Service, Washington, D.C.
RHUA	Regional History and University Archives, Kent Library, Cape Girardeau, Missouri
SCCH	Scott County Courthouse, Benton, Missouri
SCH	Sikeston City Hall, Sikeston, Missouri
SCJ	Scott County Jail, Benton, Missouri
STFU	Southern Tenant Farmers Union Papers, microfilm edition, Kent Library, Cape Girardeau, Missouri
TLF	Tuskegee Lynching Files, Hollis Burke Frissell Library, Tuskegee, Alabama
UMSH	Joint Collection, University of Missouri Western Historical Manuscript Collection and State Historical Society of Missouri Manuscripts, Elllis Library, Columbia, Missouri
USED	Office of United States Attorney for the Eastern District of Missouri Files, Justice Department, Washington, D.C.
USIP	Office of Information and Privacy Files, Justice Department, Washington, D.C.
USJD	Criminal Division Files, Justice Department, Washington, D.C.
USJD	United States Justice Department, "Summary and Excerpts from Summary Statements of Persons Interviewed by Agents of the Fed-

eral Bureau of Investigation in re Lynching of Cleo Wright," 20 (received) and 22 (filed) April 1942, Box 460, Record Group 60, NARS

WNRC   Washington National Records Center, Suitland, Maryland

NEWSPAPERS

Argus	*St. Louis Argus*
Call	*Kansas City Call*
Herald	*Sikeston Herald*
NYT	*New York Times*
Post-Dispatch	*St. Louis Post-Dispatch*
Standard	*Sikeston Standard*

CENSUS REPORTS
(see Bibliography for publication information)

Eleventh Census (1890)
Twelfth Census (1900)
Thirteenth Census (1910)
Fourteenth Census (1920)
Fifteenth Census (1930)
Sixteenth Census (1940), *Housing*
Sixteenth Census (1940), *Population*
Seventeenth Census (1950)

Preface

1. James R. McGovern, *Anatomy of a Lynching: The Killing of Claude Neal* (Baton Rouge: Louisiana State Univ. Press, 1982); Stewart E. Tolnay and E.M. Beck, *A Festival of Violence: An Analysis of Southern Lynchings, 1882-1930* (Urbana: Univ. of Illinois Press, 1995). See Bibliography for additional works on lynchings written during this period.   **2.** Michael J. Pfeifer, "The Ritual of Lynching: Extralegal Justice in Missouri, 1890-1942," *Gateway Heritage* 13 (Winter 1993): 22-33; W. Fitzhugh Brundage, *Lynching in The New South: Georgia and Virginia, 1880-1930* (Urbana: Univ. of Illinois Press, 1993); Tolnay and Beck, *Festival of Violence.*   **3.** Perhaps as many as twenty-seven lynchings occurred between 1882 and 1888, though verification and analysis are beyond the scope of this book. See sources in Chapter 7, n. 70; and Monroe N. Work, ed., *Negro Year Book: An Annual Encyclopedia of the Negro, 1925-1926* (Tuskegee, Ala.: Tuskegee Institute, 1925), 402.

Chapter 1   Sikeston

1. The following account is based on Dominic J. Capeci Jr., "The Lynching of Cleo Wright: Federal Protection of Constitutional Rights during World War II," *Jour-*

nal of American History 77 (March 1986): 862-63, and "Violence in Three Acts: A Lynching in Wartime Sikeston, 1942" (National Council for Geographic Educators Conference, Springfield, Mo. 21 Oct. 1987), 17-25.   **2.** This chapter draws heavily on Thad Snow, *From Missouri* (Boston: Houghton Mifflin, 1954), and "History of Swampeast, Missouri" (n.d.), 1-14, folder 20, Snow Papers, RHUA; Leon Parker Ogilvie, "The Development of the Southeast Missouri Lowlands" (Ph.D. diss., Univ. of Missouri, 1967); Charles E. Hudson, "A Geographic Study Examining the Major Elements Involved in the Rise of Cotton Production in Southeast Missouri, 1922-1925" (M.A. thesis, Western Michigan Univ., 1967); A. James Meigs, "The Delta Area of Southeast Missouri: A Case Study in Economic Change," *Monthly Review* 38 (July 1956): 81-86; Max R. White et al., *Rich Land, Poor People* (Indianapolis: Farm Security Administration, 1937); Louis Cantor, *A Prologue to the Protest Movement: The Missouri Sharecropper Roadside Demonstration of 1939* (Durham, N.C.: Duke Univ. Press, 1969); William E. Foley, *A History of Missouri*, vol. 1, *1673-1820* (Columbia: Univ. of Missouri Press, 1971), 162-65, 170-71, 173; Russel L. Gerlach, *Settlement Patterns in Missouri: A Study of Population Origins, with a Wall Map* (Columbia: Univ. of Missouri Press, 1986), 30, 36-37, 54, 59, 66-69, 73-74; William E. Parrish, *A History of Missouri*, vol. 3, *1860-1875* (Columbia: Univ. of Missouri Press, 1973), 59-86; Michael Fellman, *Inside War: The Guerrilla Conflict in Missouri during the American Civil War* (New York: Oxford Univ. Press, 1989), 161, 163-64; David P. Thelen, *Paths of Resistance: Tradition and Dignity in Industrializing Missouri* (New York: Oxford Univ. Press, 1986), 92-93. Most Missourians supported the Union, but Confederate sympathizers were ever present, especially in the Bootheel and the Missouri River Valley, where large proportions of southerners resided. In southeastern Missouri those who favored the South were more nearly equal to the pro-Unionists than elsewhere in the state.   **3.** Snow, "History of Swampeast," 2, 5.   **4.** *Fifteenth Census* (1930). vol. 3, pt. 1, table 13, pp. 1339, 1341, 1343-46, compares the data for 1920 and 1930. In 1920, whites constituted 93.8 percent of the state population (Hudson, "A Geographic Study," 67-68).   **5.** Snow, *From Missouri*, 159; Hudson, "A Geographic Survey," 21 and table 2.

   6. *Fifteenth Census* (1930), vol. 3, pt. 1, table 13, pp. 1339, 1341, 1343-46. In 1920 the black population in the seven counties was 9,104 persons, or 5.2 percent of the total; by 1930 it exceeded that percentage in every county except Dunklin, though the number of its black residents jumped from 147 to 461 for a 213.6 percent increase over the previous census. More revealing, only Butler, which registered an increase of 6.2 percent (90 blacks), failed to record at least 160 percent growth during the decade: Mississippi, +2,686 blacks (204.8 percent increase); New Madrid, +3,667 (188.1 percent); Pemiscot, +6,175 (159.8 percent); Scott, +1,166 (319.5 percent), Stoddard, +1,675 (9,852.9 percent). In actual numbers and percentages of black populations in 1930, the riverfront counties—Mississippi (3,997, 25.4 percent), New Madrid (5,617, 18.6 percent), Pemiscot (10,040, 26.9 percent)—led the way. See Snow, *From Missouri*, 160; Mary Taussig Tompkins and L. Benoist Tompkins, "An Informal Report on Attitudes in Southeast Missouri Relative to the Lynching of Cleo Wright, Negro, Jan. 25, 1942" (n.d.), 8, Box A381, General Office Files, NAACP (all NAACP Papers references cite these files unless otherwise indicated). **7.** White, *Rich Land, Poor People,* 6-8: Dunklin, Pemiscot, and New Madrid indicate similar conditions in the other lowland counties. **8.** Snow, "History of Swampeast," 7; Fannie Cook, *Boot-Heel Doctor* (New York: Dodd, Mead, 1941), 111. **9.** Irvin G. Wyllie, "Race and Class Conflict on Missouri's Cotton Frontier," *Journal of Southern History* 20 (May 1954): 185. **10.** Snow, *From Missouri,* 169, 172.

11. For the wider background, context, and significance of the Pacific Movement of the Eastern World and its splinter-group rival, the Original Independent Benevolent Afro-Pacific Movement of the World, Inc. (OIBAPMW), see FBI Survey (Box 21), 532, 541-42, 571-73, 578, 585; and Ernest Allen Jr., "When Japan Was 'Champion of the Darker Races': Satokata Takahashi and the Flowering of Black Messianic Nationalism," *Black Scholar* 24 (Winter 1994): 23-46. For their activities in southeast Missouri, see *Post-Dispatch,* 5 March 1942, 1A, 7A; U.S. Department of War, Military Intelligence Department (MID), "Racial Disturbances in Southeastern Missouri" (23 Oct. 1942), 2, Box 3542, RG 165, WNRC; and Ernest Allen Jr., "Waiting for Tojo: The Pro-Japan Vigil of Black Missourians, 1932-1943," *Gateway Heritage* 15 (Fall 1994): 16-33. **12.** On support for these organizations in southeast Missouri, see FBI Survey, 544; and Allen, "Waiting for Tojo," 29-30. Supposedly including the Pacific Movement among the pro-Japan organizations he had formed, Naka Nakane boasted 20,000 members in St. Louis, 6,000 in Kansas City, and "smaller numbers in other towns," which FBI agents considered "greatly exaggerated"; neither gave specific figures for Missouri. Allen contends that the Pacific Movement alone attracted "tens of thousands of black Missourians" whose "pro-Japanese sentiment persisted" long after their Pacific Movement and OIBAPMW chapters declined. No specific membership lists were found; the number of actual members—as opposed to sympathizers—most likely fell between the equally self-serving high of Nakane and low of federal agents, and doubtless were greater in urban centers with viable nationalist heritages and organizational structures than in rural areas. No evidence indicates substantial pro-Japanese feelings among black lowlanders afterward, though Allen demonstrates that Pacific Movement and OIBAPMW activities in the mid-1930s revealed deep-seated bitterness against white supremacy and desire for black self-determination, if not clearly defined instances of nationalism and millennialism. **13.** Allen, "Waiting for Tojo," 24 (interpretation is mine). **14.** Louis Cantor, "A Prologue to the Protest Movement: The Missouri Sharecropper Roadside Demonstration of 1939," *Journal of American History* 55 (March 1969): 804-22, and *Prologue to the Protest Movement,* 64-65, 161-63; Donald H. Grubbs, *Cry from the Cotton: The STFU and the New Deal* (Chapel Hill: Univ. of North Carolina Press, 1971), 181, for quotation; Thad Snow, "Labor Policy in Cotton Control" (n.d.), 1-10, and "Planters and Farm Legislation" (n.d.), 1-3, folders 27 and 30, Snow Papers, RHUA, for problems of agricultural legislation. **15.** Nicholas Natanson, *The Black*

Image in the New Deal: The Politics of FSA Photography (Knoxville: Univ. of Tennessee Press, 1992), 126, 113-41; Thad Snow, "Farm Control After Five Years" (n.d.), 1, folder 30, Snow Papers, RHUA.

16. *Sixteenth Census* (1940), *Population*, vol. 2, pt. 4, table 22, p. 363, and table 30, p. 436. Scott County recorded 30,377 inhabitants, including 2,261 blacks.
17. Robert S. Douglass, *A History of Southeast Missouri* (Chicago: Lewis, 1912), 291-92, 524-25; Audrey Chaney, "Excerpts of Early Times: History of Sikeston" (n.d.), 1-14, Sikeston Public Library, and *A History of Sikeston* (Cape Girardeau, Mo.: Ramfire, 1960); Edison Shrum, *The History of Scott County, Missouri: Up to the Year 1880* (Sikeston, Mo.: Scott County Historical Society, 1984), 106-7, 113, 118-19, 218-29.
18. *Fourteenth Census* (1920), vol. 3, table 11, p. 564; and *Fifteenth Census* (1930), vol. 3, pt. 1, table 16, pp. 1356-57. Between 1920 and 1940, blacks increased from 90 to 1,003 for a growth rate of 1,014.4 percent.   **19.** Interviews with Griffen (6 and 7 June 1988; see Bibliography for full list of author's interviews with dates), who estimated that Sunset residents owned 20 to 25 homes by 1940; however, of 715 owner-occupied units in Sikeston, blacks owned 58 (8.1%) higher than Griffen estimated, and some owned more than one property (though probably all within Sunset). Black tenants occupied 308 (19.6%) of 1,569 rental homes, whose ownership is not identified by race (but according to Griffen was mostly white) and whose location is not given but included more than the Addition. Making up 12.6% of the city population, black proprietors and renters accounted for 16% of all occupied residences. See *Sixteenth Census* (1940), *Housing*, vol. 2, pt. 3, table 22, p. 910, and table 24, p. 956.
20. Bea Harmon, "My Trip to Sikeston," *Argus*, 6 Feb. 1942, 1; interview with Griffen, 5 Nov. 1987. Black households seemed to parallel but, according to oral history, fall behind those of whites: 64.3% occupied one-family units, 75.2% heated by stove, 93.1% read by electric light, and 54.2% enjoyed flush toilets—yet, for example, they used most of the outdoor privies. See *Sixteenth Census* (1940), *Housing*, vol. 2, pt. 3, table 22, p. 910, and table 23, p. 937.
21. Interviews with Lee, Gardner, and Ingram (5 Nov. 1987); editorial, "All Can Help," *Herald*, 11 June 1942, 4.   **22.** Phone conversations with Everett Nixon (28 June 1990, St. Louis) and subject B (7 June 1988; phone conversations originated in Sikeston unless cited otherwise); interviews with Gardner, Ingram, Lee, Frank Ferrell, Dotson (18 May 1987), Griffen (18 May 1987), Crews, and subject C; interviews with James H. (Pete) Schwabb (24 June and 7 Aug. 1987, Cape Girardeau), RHUA.
23. Census employment figures by race exist only for the county, but comparison with racially descriptive city data and oral history suggests that most black males worked as common laborers or in domestic service; fewer black than white females worked outside the home, but those who did toiled as domestics in much greater numbers; and regardless of race or gender, only very tiny groups of less than seventy people worked for public emergency agencies like the Works Progress Administration, or were seeking employment as the depressed economy gave way to wartime boom. Whites, of course, shared these employment opportunities, while also

monopolizing many others closed to black professionals, managers, craftsmen, operatives, salespersons, and clerks, or open in only a very limited way to black proprietors of rentals and personal services. See *Sixteenth Census* (1940), *Population*, vol. 2, pt. 2, introduction, p. 9, table 23, p. 378, and table 30, p. 436; *Standard*, 16 Sept. 1941, 1 (202 white workers at milling company); interviews with Grace Sturgeon (7 Nov. 1987: 600 white workers at shoe factory, nearly equal numbers of men and women, in 1942); Lee, Schwabb (24 June and 7 Aug. 1987), and Law. **24.** Interviews with Griffen (5 Nov. 1987, 6 June 1988). **25.** Walter Griffen, Minnie B. Sprowls, Eula Burns, and William Hobson, "History of the West End Missionary Baptist Church, Sikeston, Missouri" (1975), in author's possession, courtesy of Walter Griffen; Chaney, *History of Sikeston*, 126-29; interviews with Brown and Griffen (5 Nov. 1987), for information on the First (West End Missionary) Baptist Church, Second (St. John's Missionary) Baptist Church, Smith (Methodist) Chapel, Bethel (African Methodist Episcopal) Church, Central Methodist Episcopal Church, God in Christ Church, and others that had failed by 1940.

26. Ogilvie, "Southeast Missouri Lowlands," 253; interviews with Griffen (5 Nov. 1987, 6 June 1988, 11 June 1990), Lee, and Gardner; phone conversation with Nixon; *Standard*, 5 Sept. 1941, 1, and 14 Nov. 1941, 2; *Herald*, 23 April 1942, 1. **27.** Cantor, *Prologue to the Protest Movement*, 10; interviews with Julia Renfro (13 June 1990) and Gardner; *Standard*, 6 Feb. 1943, 2. **28.** Snow, *From Missouri*, 280-81; Cantor, "Prologue to the Protest Movement," 813; Sam B. Armstrong, "Sharecroppers, Ordered Evicted, To Camp On Road," *Post-Dispatch*, 8 Jan. 1939, 1A; Cantor, *Prologue to the Protest Movement*, 64; interview with Fred Smith (18 May 1987). Data for the city are based on the 97.1% of all employed people reporting their occupations; they lack reference to race, but record gender (one female farm worker). The minuscule number of farm workers—27 out of a total of 2,816 individuals—suggests that few if any of the 1939 demonstrators came from Sikeston, much less Sunset, and corroborates eyewitness and oral history accounts. See *Sixteenth Census* (1940) *Population*, vol. 2, pt. 4, table 23, p. 378. **29.** P. George Hummasti, "From Immigrant Settlement to Ethnic Community: The Maturing of American Finntown," *Locus: Regional and Local History of the Americas* 7 (Spring 1995): 93-110; interviews with Brown, Gardner, and Griffen (5 Nov. 1987). **30.** *Sixteenth Census* (1940), *Population*, vol. 2, pt. 4, p. 436; interviews with Griffen (18 May 1987), subject C, Lee, Ingram, Sturgeon (7 Nov. 1987, 8 June 1988), and subject E.

31. See Chaney, "Excerpts of Early Times," 7-9, and *History of Sikeston*, 77-111, 121-24; "History of the First United Methodist Church, 1867-1992" (1992), in author's possession, courtesy of Rev. Charles E. Buck; Jane B. Gillespie, "First Presbyterian Church of Sikeston, Missouri," 19 Oct. 1959, in author's possession, courtesy of Sybil Wathen; "The Church Register of the Sikeston Methodist Church, 1932-1948," First United Methodist Church, Sikeston, Mo. (1,412 congregants as of 31 Dec. 1939); "Records of the First Baptist Church of Sikeston, 1937-1946" (902 congregants as of 31 Dec. 1941); "History of Sikeston [Hunter Memorial First] Presbyterian

Church for 1940," (13 new congregants; total membership not given). Several churches began between the world wars—such as the First Christian Church (1918), Church of Christ (1924), Church of God of Prophecy (c. 1930)—but their numbers were small, and none responded to my research inquiry.   32. Chaney, "Excerpts of Early Times," 7-8; "Our History" (n.d.), author's possession, courtesy of Monsignor William Stanton; interviews with Mitchell (9 June 1988) and P.J. Schlosser (22 Nov. 1991).   **33.** Interviews with subject B and Lee.   **34.** Interview with Lee.   **35.** Interviews with Mitchell (9 June 1988), Geraldine Schlosser, and subject G; "Centennial, St. Francis Xavier Church, Sikeston, Missouri, 1892-1992" (1992), 12; Catholic Center, Springfield, Mo.: 57% interfaith marriages in 1929, revealing both the practical limits of endogamy in a small population and some genuine religious tolerance.

36. Interviews with Lee and Mitchell.   **37.** Interview with Mitchell; George M. Fredrickson, *White Supremacy: A Comparative Study in American and South African History* (New York: Oxford Univ. Press, 1981), 86-87.   **38.** Interview with subject B; Mark Zborowski and Elizabeth Herzog, *Life Is with People: The Jewish Little-Town of Eastern Europe* (New York: International Univ. Press, 1952); Leonard Dinnerstein, *Antisemitism in America* (New York: Oxford Univ. Press, 1994), 184-85; and Milton M. Gordon, *Assimilation in American Life: The Role of Race, Religion, and National Origins* (New York: Oxford Univ. Press, 1964), 67-83, 190-95.   **39.** Interviews with subject F and Mitchell; Will Herberg, *Protestant-Catholic-Jew: An Essay in American Religious Sociology*, rev. ed. (Garden City, N.Y.: Anchor, 1960), 36.   **40.** Interviews with Geraldine Schlosser, and P.J. Schlosser; Anonymous, "Preface: Sikeston, Missouri" [1957], State Historical Society of Missouri, Reference Library, Columbia; *Herald*, 25 Dec. 1941, 24, and Editorial, "The Three Bulwarks," 1 Jan. 1942, 4.

41. Herberg, *Protestant-Catholic-Jew*, 38; George M. Fredrickson, *The Black Image in the White Mind: The Debate on Afro-American Character and Destiny, 1817-1914* (New York: Harper & Row, 1971), 61, 267, 322, for *Herrenvolk* theory of Pierre L. van den Berghe.   **42.** George C. Wright, *Life Behind a Veil: Blacks in Louisville, Kentucky, 1865-1930* (Baton Rouge: Louisiana State Univ. Press, 1985), 5.   **43.** Michael P. Johnson and James L. Roark, eds., *No Chariot Let Down: Charleston's Free People of Color on the Eve of the Civil War* (New York: Norton, 1984), 10; David Potter, *The South and the Sectional Conflict* (Baton Rouge: Louisiana State Univ. Press, 1968), 16.   **44.** Interviews with Ingram, Gardner, Jesse Whittley, and Bartley. Northerners, by contrast, were said to "love the race and hate the individual Negro." **45.** Ira Berlin, *Slaves without Masters: The Free Negro in the Antebellum South* (New York: Random House, 1974); Eugene D. Genovese, *Roll, Jordan, Roll: The World the Slaves Made* (New York: Pantheon, 1974), 4-5, 6-7; James Oakes, *The Ruling Race: A History of American Slaveholders* (New York: Random House, 1982), 197, for geographic boundaries of paternalism. James L. Roark, *Masters without Slaves: Southern Planters in the Civil War and Reconstruction* (New York: Norton, 1977), 198-203, apparently overstates postbellum abandonment of paternalism, given the quasi-feudal system of race relations introduced in southeast Missouri by early twentieth-century Mississippi and Arkansas planters.

46. Interviews with Schwabb (14 July 1987, 7 Aug. 1987) and Whittley.   **47.** Genovese, *Roll, Jordan, Roll*, 5-6, 91-92, 148-49, 597-98.   **48.** Interview with Ingram. **49.** Interviews with Griffen (11 June 1990, 6 June 1988).   **50.** Interview with Griffen (11 June 1990); Ogilvie, "Southwest Missouri Lowlands," 374-84; Sikeston City Council, Minutes, 6 April 1938, 2 April 1940, 8 April 1942, SCH; *Fifteenth Census* (1930), vol. 3, pt. 1, table 16, p. 1357. Griffen estimated the number of black voters at 400, but it must have been lower: election returns from Ward 2 in 1938, 1940, and 1942 dropped from 755 to 525 for all voters—black and white. In 1930, 305 blacks (68%) were of voting age; by ten years later their numbers had expanded to 682, assuming a constant percentage of black adults (the census no longer recorded race by age for cities under 10,000).

51. Interviews with Brown and Griffen (11 June 1990); Charles S. Johnson, *Backgrounds to Patterns of Negro Segregation* (rpt.; New York: Apollo, 1970), 258. **52.** *Standard*, 30 Jan. 1942, 8; J. William Harris, "Etiquette, Lynching, and Racial Boundaries in Southern History: A Mississippi Example," *American Historical Review* 100 (April 1995): 391-93; Wright, *Life behind a Veil*, 5.   **53.** "The P.C. Editor Says," *Standard*, 24 Oct. 1941, 1; 5 Dec. 1941, 5, 7; 12 Dec. 1941, 6; 16 Dec. 1941, 1, 11; 19 Dec. 1941, 1; *Herald*, 11 Sept. 1941, 1, and 12 Feb. 1942; John Hobbs and Ralph C. Rockwood interviews, FBI Report, 23 Feb. 1942, 34, and 27 April 1942, 8. **54.** *Standard*, 28 Oct. 1941, 1, and 28 Nov. 1941, 10; interview with Bruce (6 Nov. 1987).   **55.** *Standard*, 10 Oct. 1941, 1, 8; 14 Oct. 1941, 3; 28 Oct. 1941, 1; and 21 Nov. 1941, 5. See William Lynwood Montell, *Killings: Folk Justice in the Upper South* (Lexington: Univ. Press of Kentucky, 1986), 162, for theory; interview with Ferrell, for application in Sikeston.

56. *Standard*, 7 Nov. 1941, 5; 5 Dec. 1941, 1, 7; and 20 Jan. 1942, 8; Snow, "History of Swampeast," 4; *Herald*, 4 Dec. 1941, 1. George King, seventeen, and Norman Votaw, twenty, received ninety-nine-year prison terms for the slaying of State Trooper Fred L. Walker.   **57.** *Standard*, 16 Sept. 1941, 1; 30 Sept. 1941, 1; 3 Oct. 1941, 1; 7 Oct. 1941, 1, 2; 10 Oct. 1941, 1, 4; and 2 Jan. 1942, 1.   **58.** Ogilvie, "Southeast Missouri Lowlands," 390-92; interviews with Sturgeon (7 Nov. 1987) and Whittley; "The P.C. Editor Says," *Standard*, 10 Oct. 1941, 1; Leslie Woodcock Tentler, *Wage-Earning Women: Industrial Work and Family Life in the United States, 1900-1930* (New York: Oxford Univ. Press, 1979), 58-80.   **59.** "The P.C. Editor Says," *Standard*, 10 Oct. 1941, 1.   **60.** Fannie Cook to Mr. Walton, 25 Oct. 1941, Box 5, Cook Collection, MHSL; *Standard*, 5 Sept. 1941, 6; 7 Oct. 1941, 2; and 9 Dec. 1941, 1; *Herald*, 11 Sept. 1941, 1; 25 Sept. 1941, 1; and 20 Nov. 1941, 1.

61. *Herald*, 30 Sept. 1941, 1; 14 Oct. 1941, 8; 17 Oct. 1941, 5; and 21 Oct. 1941, 4.   **62.** *Standard*, 17 Oct. 1941, 6.   **63.** Interview with subject C; *Herald*, 25 Sept. 1941, 9; 6 Nov. 1941, 12; and 1 Jan. 1942, 1.   **64.** *Herald*, 6 Nov. 1941, 1; and 8 Jan. 1942, 4. **65.** *Herald*, 11 Sept. 1941, 1, 4.

66. *Standard*, 7 Oct. 1941, 1; *Herald*, 25 Dec. 1941, 6; 8 Jan. 1942, 9; and 22 Jan. 1942, 1; Richard R. Lingeman, *Don't You Know There's a War On? The American Home Front, 1941-1945* (New York: Putnam, 1970), 234-70.   67. Richard D. Brown, *Modernization: The Transformation of American Life, 1600-1865* (New York: Hill & Wang, 1976), 8, 10, 11, 13-14.

Chapter 2   Bloodshed

1. *Standard*, 9 Dec. 1941, 1.   2. *Herald*, 11 Dec. 1941, 1, 4; *Standard*, 9 Dec. 1941, 1, 2d quotation.   3. *Standard*, 12 Dec. 1941, 1, 6; "The P.C. Editor Says," *Standard*, 9 Dec. 1941, 1; "War to the End," *Herald*, 11 Dec. 1941, 4.   4. Interview with Law. 5. Company K information is taken from *Missouri National Guard Yearbook*, 1939, Office of the Adjutant General of Missouri, Jefferson City; and James E. McGhee, "Historical Sketch, HHC 135th Engr. Gp., HHC and Co. A 140th Engr. Bn., Missouri Army National Guard, Cape Girardeau County, Missouri" (n.d.), 6-10, Sikeston Armory.   6. *Standard*, 2 Jan. 1942, 1.   7. *Herald*, 4 Sept. 1941, 12; 16 Oct. 1941, 1; and 20 Nov. 1941, 14.   8. *Herald*, 18 Dec. 1941, 1; *Standard*, 23 Dec. 1941, 7.   9. *Standard*, 6 Jan. 1942, 1; *Herald*, 8 Jan. 1942, 4, 9; 22 Jan. 1942, 1, 7; editorial, "Our Program for 1942," *Herald*, 1 Jan. 1942, 4.   10. *Herald*, 22 Jan. 1942, 7; Claude F. Cooper to H.L. Mitchell, 12 Feb. 1942, and Claude F. Cooper to Forrest C. Donnell (n.d.), reel 20, STFU.   11. *Herald*, 29 Jan. 1942, 1; *Standard*, 23 Jan. 1942, 9.   12. Interview with Sturgeon (19 May 1987).   13. Quoted in Paul R. Bumbarger, "Jail-Storming Mob Burns Negro Knifer," *Memphis Commercial Appeal*, 26 Jan. 1942, TLF.   14. Interview with Sturgeon (19 May 1987); *Herald*, 29 Jan. 1942, 1.   15. Interviews with Sturgeon (19 May 1987, 7 Nov. 1987, 19 July 1990).   16. *Standard*, 27 Jan. 1942, 8.   17. Interview with Whittley, 6 June 1988; Maxine Croder interview, FBI Report, 13 March 1942, 5. Residents needing police assistance after dark called the operator, who activated a red light visible from almost anywhere in the city; officers then contacted the operator.   18. Hess Perrigan and Roy Beck interviews, FBI Report, 23 Feb. 1942, 4, 6.   19. *Standard*, 27 Jan. 1942, 8; Beck interview, FBI Report, 6.   20. Phone conversation with James Sturgeon, 16 Dec. 1990, Chino, Calif.   21. Beck interview, FBI Report, 6; *Standard*, 27 Jan. 1942, 1.   22. Perrigan interview, FBI Report, 4; interview with Sturgeon (19 July 1990).   23. Perrigan interview, FBI Report, 4; interview with Whittley; *Standard*, 27 Jan. 1942, 8; interview with Arthur Bruce (6 Nov. 1987).   24. Perrigan interview, FBI Report, 4; interview with Whittley; Melvin Dace interview, FBI Report, 23 Feb. 1942, 13-14; Hess Perrigan statement, USJD Summary; *Standard*, 27 Jan. 1942, 8 (this and the next paragraph).   25. Quoted in Beck interview, FBI Report, 6.   26. Interview with Sturgeon (7 Nov. 1987); Dr. M.G. Anderson interview, FBI

Report, 23 Feb. 1942, 8; Perrigan interview, FBI Report, 4; Bumbarger, "Jail-Storming Mob Burns Negro Knifer"; *Standard*, 8 May 1942, 1. Perrigan never recalled how he got to the hospital. **27.** Beck interview, FBI Report, 6; interview with Whittley. **28.** Dr. E.J. Nienstedt interview, FBI Report, 23 Feb. 1942, 8; Dace interview, FBI Report, 14. **29.** Minnie Gates (Gay), Ardella Wright, and Henry Bartlett interviews, FBI Report, 23 Feb. 1942, 12, 10, 11-12; Beck interview, FBI Report, 6. **30.** Grover H. Lewis interview, FBI Report, 23 Feb. 1942, 9.

31. Gates (Gay) and Wright interviews, FBI Report, 11-12; Richard Gay interview, FBI Report, 27 April 1942, 11; *Argus*, 30 Jan. 1942, 7. Ardella Wright and her parents later told FBI agents that they had not feared a lynching, but immediately after his death Minnie Gay informed a black reporter: "I was afraid for Cleo from the beginning." **32.** Harold Wallace interview, FBI Report, 23 Feb. 1942, 23; J.D. Grisham interview, FBI Report, 23 Feb. 1942, 40. **33.** Croder interview, FBI Report, 5, 6; interview with Sturgeon (19 May 1987). **34.** Interviews with Mitchell (9 June 1988), subject E, and Sturgeon (19 May 1987). **35.** *Call*, 30 Jan. 1942, 24; "Identifying Ten Members of Missouri Lynching Mob," *Chicago Defender*, 7 Feb. 1942, TLF; Bartlett interview, FBI Report, 10-11; *Argus*, 30 Jan. 1942, 7.

36. Billy Walker interview, FBI Report, 13 March 1942, 4. **37.** Richard Gay interview, FBI Report, 11; Toni Morrison, *Beloved* (New York: Knopf, 1987), 157. **38.** Interviews with Clinton, subject C, and Ingram (5 Nov. 1987); Tompkins and Tompkins, "An Informal Report," 2. **39.** *Standard*, 27 Jan. 1942, 1, 8; interview with Clinton. **40.** Beck interview, FBI Report, 6; *Post-Dispatch*, 27 Jan. 1942, 4C.

41. Milburn Arbaugh interview, FBI Report, 23 Feb. 1942, 26. **42.** Harry Malcolm statement, USJD Summary, 68; Milburn Arbaugh and Milem Limbaugh interviews, FBI Report, 27 April 1942, 10. **43.** Quoted in *Herald*, 29 Jan. 1942, 4. For discrepancies in the time and the mood of the mob as Wallace, Arbaugh, and Limbaugh left Wright, cf. their interviews, FBI Report, 23 Feb. 1942, 23-24, 26-27, 28. **44.** Dace interview, FBI Report, 14, 15; Melvin Dace, "Lynching of Cleo Wright, Sikeston, Missouri" (official report, 31 Jan. 1942), 2-3, MSHP. **45.** *Standard*, 27 Jan. 1942, 1.

46. *Post-Dispatch*, 26 Jan. 1942, 3; David E. Blanton interview, FBI Report, 23 Feb. 1942, 29; Walter Kendall statement, USJD Summary, 33. **47.** Blanton interview, FBI Report, 30-31; Dace interview, FBI Report, 16; *Post-Dispatch*, 30 Jan. 1942, 3A. **48.** *Post-Dispatch*, 30 Jan. 1942, 3A. **49.** H.C. Henry interview, FBI Report, 23 Feb. 1942, 47; interview with subject E. **50.** Bumbarger, "Jail-Storming Mob Burns Negro Knifer"; Arbaugh interview, FBI Report, 27.

51. *Post-Dispatch*, 26 Jan. 1942, 3; *Herald*, 29 Jan. 1942, 4; interview with Dempster. **52.** Charles E. Latham interview, FBI Report, 23 Feb. 1942, 37; "Eye Witness Tells of Burning Horror," *Amsterdam News* (New York), n.d., TLF. **53.** Interview with Griffen (18 May 1987). **54.** Blanton interview, FBI Report, 31; John N. Greim, "Mob Violence at Sikeston, Jan. 25, 1942" (n.d.), 1, MSHP. Planter Leo Fisher and cleaner Tip Keller rode with Blanton and Dace.   **55.** Blanton interview, FBI Report, 31; John Tandy, "Lynching of Cleo Wright at Sikeston" (n.d.), 1, MSHP; Dace interview, FBI Report, 16.

56. Tompkins and Tompkins, "An Informal Report," 2; interviews with subjects D and F.   **57.** Interview with Brown.   **58.** *Argus*, 30 Jan. 1942, 1, 7. Contrary to reports, Ardella Wright did not see her husband's body.   **59.** Interview with Arthur Renfro; conversation with Griffen (13 June 1990).   **60.** Interview with Gardner.

61. Interview with Griffen (18 May 1987).   **62.** Blanton interview, FBI Report, 31, 32; *Post-Dispatch*, 30 Jan. 1942, 3A; interview with subject D; "Negro Is Lynched by Missouri Crowd," *NYT*, 26 Jan. 1942, TLF (300 persons); Hobbs interview, FBI Report, 34 (300-400 persons); John Morris, "Mob Violence at Sikeston" (1 Feb. 1942), 1 (1,000 persons), MSHP.   **63.** [J.B. Ross], "Sikeston Lynching, Jan. 25, 1942" (27 Jan. 1942), 1, Box A381, NAACP.   **64.** *Argus*, 30 Jan. 1942, 7, quoting Mattie D. Smith; Mattie D. Smith interview, FBI Report, 23 Feb. 1942, 44-45.   **65.** Interview with Clinton.

66. Bumbarger, "Jail-Storming Mob Burns Negro Knifer"; interviews with subject D, Mitchell, and Bumbarger (6 Nov. 1987).   **67.** *Argus*, 27 Feb. 1942, TLF; phone conversation with subject I (20 May 1987); *Post-Dispatch*, 30 Jan. 1942, 3A.   **68.** Interview with subject D; phone conversation with subject I; interviews with Ingram, subject F, and Smith.   **69.** Ross, "Sikeston Lynching," 3; *Call*, 30 Jan. 1942, 1, and *Post-Dispatch*, 27 Jan. 1942, 4C.   **70.** *Call*, 30 Jan. 1942, 1; Ross, "Sikeston Lynching," 3; interview with Dotson (18 May 1987). See Mary Louise Ellis, "'Rain Down Fire': The Lynching of Sam Hose" (Ph.D. diss., Florida State Univ., 1992), 121-25, and Charles Crowe, "Racial Massacre in Atlanta, September 22, 1906," *Journal of Negro History* 54 (April 1969): 164-65, for white employer efforts to shield blacks.

71. Interviews with Brown and Gardner; Ida B. Wells-Barnett, "Lynch Law in All Its Phases," in Mildred I. Thompson, ed., *Ida B. Wells-Barnett: An Exploratory Study of An American Black Woman, 1893-1930* (Brooklyn, N.Y.: Carlson, 1990), 176-77, for religious associations in the 1892 Memphis lynching; John Dittmer, *Black Georgia in the Progressive Era, 1900-1920* (Urbana: Univ. of Illinois Press, 1977), 126-27, for family bonds and personal courage in the 1906 Atlanta riot.   **72.** Interview with Gardner; Joe William Trotter Jr., "Race, Class, and Industrial Change: Black Migration to Southern West Virginia, 1915-1932," and Peter Gottlieb, "Rethinking the Great Migration: A Perspective from Pittsburgh," both in *The Great Migration in Historical Perspective: New Dimensions of Race, Class, and Gender*, ed. Joe William Trotter Jr. (Bloomington: Indiana Univ. Press, 1991), 55, 73.   **73.** Interview with Julia Renfro (13 June 1990); Deborah Gray White, *Ar'n't I a Woman? Female Slaves in the Plantation South* (New York: Norton, 1985), 72-74, 119-21.   **74.** Jacqueline Jones, *Labor of Love, Labor of Sorrow: Black Women, Work, and the Family, from Slavery to the Present* (New York: Basic Books, 1985), 279-80.   **75.** *Argus*, 30 Jan. 1942, 1, 7; Smith interview, FBI Report, 44 (Mattie also attempted to call the sheriff).

76. *Argus*, 30 Jan. 1942, 1; Morris, "Mob Violence at Sikeston," 1; Henry Bartlett interview, FBI Report, 27 April 1942, 6; interviews with Gardner and Griffen (5 May 1987). **77.** Interview with Smith. **78.** Ross, "Sikeston Lynching," 1; interviews with Griffen (6 June 1988, 18 May 1987). **79.** Earl Lewis, "Expectations, Economic Opportunities, and Life in the Industrial Age," in Trotter, *The Great Migration in Historical Perspective*, 34; interview with Gardner. **80.** Forrest C. Donnell, "Sikeston Notes" (n.d. [25-26 Jan. 1942]), 1-5, folder 3623, FCDP; City Council, Minutes, 25 Jan. 1942, 246, SCH; *Standard*, 27 Jan. 1942, 5; George Presnell interview, FBI Report, 23 Feb. 1942, 33.

81. Interview with Jesse Whittley; *Herald*, 29 Jan. 1942, 4 (naming the five deputies G.W. Kiser, Oscar Cooper, A. Miller, A.Z. Holt, and Joe Deal); *NYT*, 26 Jan. 1942, 17. **82.** C.E. Wallis, "Mob Violence at Sikeston, January 25, 1942," 3, MSHP; Dace interview, FBI Report, 17; Morris, "Mob Violence at Sikeston," 2; *NYT*, 26 Jan. 1942, 17. **83.** Wallis, "Mob Violence at Sikeston," 3; interview with Griffen (18 May 1987); Morris, "Mob Violence at Sikeston," 2. **84.** Ross, "Sikeston Lynching," 2; interview with Griffen (6 June 1988). **85.** Donnell, "Sikeston Notes," 8.

86. Wallis, "Mob Violence at Sikeston," 3; Ross, "Sikeston Lynching," 3, quoting Presnell. George Scott and probably Revs. Kater E. Crump and S.D. Woods were the other agitators. **87.** Donnell, "Sikeston Notes," 8; Paul Bumbarger, "More Mob Violence Hinted at Sikeston," *Memphis Commercial Appeal*, Jan. 1942, TLF. **88.** *Post-Dispatch*, 27 Jan. 1942, 4C; *Herald*, 29 Jan. 1942, 4; Wallis, "Mob Violence at Sikeston," 3; Morris, "Mob Violence at Sikeston," 1; Morley G. Swingle, "Sikeston Lynching, Jan. 25, 1942," 1, MSHP. **89.** Donnell, "Sikeston Notes," 6, 8. **90.** Phone conversation with subject I.

91. Interviews with Griffen (11 and 13 June 1990, 18 May 1987). **92.** *Standard*, 27 Jan. 1942, 8. **93.** Interview with Ingram; *Herald*, 29 Jan. 1942, 4; Richard Gay interview, FBI Report, 11; *Argus*, 30 Jan. 1942, 1; *Standard*, 27 Jan. 1942, 8. **94.** "Sikeston Negro Who Slashed White Woman Is Burned," *Charleston Democrat*, 12 Feb. 1942, FBIF. **95.** Phone conversation with Nixon.

96. Interviews with Griffen (6 June 1988) and Gardner; Albert J. Raboteau, *Slave Religion: The "Invisible Institution" in the Antebellum South* (New York: Oxford Univ. Press, 1978), 217-19. **97.** Interviews with Griffen (5 Nov. 1987) and Gardner; Florette Henri, *Black Migration: Movement North, 1900-1920* (Garden City, N.Y.: Anchor, 1976), 58, 63-64, 75; James R. Grossman, *Land of Hope: Chicago, Black Southerners, and the Great Migration* (Chicago: Univ. of Chicago Press, 1989), 16-18, 32. **98.** W.J. Cash, *The Mind of the South* (New York: Knopf, 1941), 312; interview with Clinton. **99.** Interviews with Currin, Crews, and Gardner. **100.** *Kansas City* (Kan.) *Plaindealer*, "Burn Negro to Crisp in Wake of Church Hour; Rape Cry Weak," 30 Jan. 1942, TLF.

101. Ross, "Sikeston Lynching," 2; interview with Griffen (5 Nov. 1987); Charlotte B. Crump to Rev. S.W. Wolfe, 25 Feb. 1942, Box C93, NAACP; interview with Brown. **102.** Louis Galambos, "The Emerging Organizational Synthesis in Modern American History," *Business History Review* 44 (Autumn 1970): 279-90; Gerald

D. Nash, *The Crucial Era: The Great Depression and World War II, 1933-1945*, 2d ed. (New York: St. Martin's, 1992), 173-74.   **103.** *Standard*, 6 Feb. 1942, FBIF; phone conversation with subject B (8 June 1988); interview with Gardner; Minnie Gay interview, FBI Report, 27 April 1942, 11.   **104.** Morris, "Mob Violence at Sikeston," 2; interviews with Frank Ferrell (7 June 1988) and Law.   **105.** "The P.C. Editor Says," *Standard*, 27 Jan. 1942, 1.

   106. Barbara Jeanne Fields, *Slavery and Freedom on the Middle Ground: Maryland during the Nineteenth Century* (New Haven, Conn.: Yale Univ. Press, 1985), 143. **107.** Allen D. Grimshaw, "A Study in Social Violence: Urban Race Riots in the United States" (Ph.D. diss., Univ. of Pennsylvania, 1959), 313-14.   **108.** John A. O'Hara to the Editor, *Standard*, 6 Feb. 1942, 2; anonymous to Forrest C. Donnell, 31 Jan. 1942, folder 3599, FCDP.   **109.** Interviews with Law and Gardner; phone conversation with subject H (18 May 1987).   **110.** Interviews with Crews, subject D, and Lee.

   111. Editorial, "We Stand to Defend," *Herald*, 5 Feb. 1942, 2, 4. Read's sermon was not printed.   **112.** *Herald*, 12 Feb. 1942, 2; interviews with Crews, Lee, subjects C and T; Pete Daniel, *Standing at the Crossroads: Southern Life since 1900* (New York: Hill & Wang, 1986), 56.   **113.** Phone conversation with subject A (7 June 1988). **114.** Interviews with subject F and Law.   **115.** Interview with Sturgeon (8 June 1988).

   116. This and the next paragraph are based on my interview with Elbridge W. Bartley Jr., 27 April 1992.   **117.** E.W. Bartley, *If I Had Wings* (n.d.), 3, pamphlet in author's possession, courtesy of Elbridge W. Bartley Jr. and John Bartley.   **118.** Elbridge W. Bartley Jr., ed., "Memoirs of Reverend Elbridge W. Bartley," 91, in author's possession, courtesy of Elbridge W. Bartley Jr.   **119.** "Minutes," 12 Feb. 1942, First Baptist Church, Sikeston, Mo., for the meeting after Wright's death. Neither local press nor congregants recorded that Owen addressed the issue publicly. **120.** Interviews with P.J. Schlosser, Geraldine Schlosser, and Charles M. Mitchell; "Centennial, St. Francis Xavier Church, Sikeston, Missouri, 1882-1992" (1992) 13, 29, 30, Catholic Center, Springfield, Mo.; Herberg, *Protestant-Catholic-Jew*, 27-45. Mitchell alone recalled that O'Neil condemned the lynching from the pulpit.

   121. Zborowski and Herzog, *Life Is with People*, 224, 415, 424. Sikeston did not appear to have a *proster yid* (common class) of Jews.   **122.** Harry Golden, *Only in America* (Cleveland: World, 1958), 131; Joel Williamson, *The Crucible of Race: Black-White Relations in the American South since Emancipation* (New York: Oxford Univ. Press, 1984), 471, 552 n 14. See above, chapter 1, p. 8, and Leonard Dinnerstein, *The Leo Frank Case* (New York: Columbia Univ. Press, 1968).   **123.** Phone conversation with subject B.   **124.** *Herald*, 29 Jan. 1942, 4; *Post-Dispatch*, 26 Jan. 1942, 3.   **125.** Interviews with Brown, subject F, and Gardner.

   126. Interviews with Griffen (6 June 1988), subject F, and Lee.   **127.** Genovese, *Roll, Jordan, Roll*, 5.   **128.** Interview with Griffen (5 Nov. 1987). The curfew suggestion Griffen attributed to Blanton actually came from anonymous to C.L. Blanton, *Standard*, 30 Jan. 1942, 2. Griffen said the lawman was fired, but no corroborating evidence has been found. **129.** Daniel, *Standing at the Crossroads*, 165; interview with Dotson. **130.** *Standard*, 6 Feb. 1942, 1; Sikeston City Council, Minutes, 2 Feb. 1942, SCH: present—Presnell, Frank S. Miller, S.L. Lawrence, Gust Zacher, T.F. Rafferty, E.H. Smith, and Charles H. Butler; absent—Joseph L. Matthews and Loomis Mayfield. **131.** *Post-Dispatch*, 5 Feb. 1942, 3A. **132.** *Herald*, 5 Feb. 1942, 4. **133.** Editorial, *NYT*, 27 Jan. 1942, 20; E.P. Coleman Jr. to Editor, *NYT*, 7 Feb. 1942, 16. J.F. Cox Sr. had joined Coleman and Denman in approaching Bailey. **134.** *Standard*, 6 Feb. 1942, 5; Resolution of the American Legion, Henry Meldrum Post No. 114, Sikeston, Mo. (n.d.), folder 3605, FCDP; *Herald*, 29 Jan. 1942, FBIF; René Girard, "Generative Scapegoating," in *Violent Origins: Ritual Killing and Cultural Formation*, ed. Walter Burkert, René Girard, and Jonathan Z. Smith (Stanford, Cal.:Stanford Univ. Press, 1987), 101-03. **135.** Sikeston City Council, Minutes, 25 Jan. 1942, SCH; "Negro Is Lynched by Missouri Crowd," *NYT*, 29 Jan. 1942, TLF. **136.** *Herald*, 12 Feb. 1942, 1; interview with Sturgeon (19 July 1990). **137.** City Council, Minutes, 25 Jan. 1942, SCH; *Standard*, 6 Feb. 1942, 4. **138.** *Argus*, 6 Feb. 1942, 1, 11; *Pittsburgh Courier*, "Mob Victim's Widow Gets Real Help," n.d., TLF. **139.** Interview with subject F; phone conversation with subject J (12 June 1990). **140.** See James M. Jones, *Prejudice and Racism* (Reading, Mass.: Addison-Wesley, 1972), 112, for theory in this and next two paragraphs. **141.** Harry Malcolm statement, USJD Summary, 68; Susie King Taylor, *A Black Woman's Civil War Memoirs*, ed. Patricia W. Romero (New York: Markus Wiener, 1988), 144 n 6. **142.** Interview with Frank Ferrell. **143.** Interviews with Ingram and Law. **144.** Interview with subject F. **145.** *Standard*, 20 March 1942, 6. **146.** *Call*, 30 Jan. 1942, 167. **147.** *Argus*, 10 April 1942, 1. **148.** Interviews with Gardner and Julia Renfro; phone conversation with Nixon; White, *Ar'n't I a Woman?* 157-60; John Blassingame, *The Slave Community: Plantation Life in the Antebellum South*, rev. ed. (New York: Oxford Univ. Press, 1979), 151, 187-88, 189-91. **149.** Phone conversation with Julia Renfro (14 June 1990). **150.** Phone conversation with Nixon. **151.** Phone conversation with subject K (12 June 1990). **152.** Interview with Julia Renfro (13 June 1990); Gladys-Marie Fry, *Night Riders in Black Folk History* (Knoxville: Univ. of Tennessee Press, 1975), 3, 73, 75, 113, 160, 162-69. **153.** Interview with Griffen (18 May 1987); "Eye Witness Tells of Burning Horror," *Amsterdam News*, n.d., TLF. **154.** FBI Survey (Box 21), 204; interview with Currin. **155.** W.M. Tucker to Donnell, 27 Jan. 1942, folder 3607, FCDP.

Chapter 3   Law and Order

1. Interview with Bumbarger (6 Nov. 1987). **2.** Lee Finkle, *Forum for Protest: The Black Press during World War II* (Rutherford, N.J.: Fairleigh Dickinson Univ. Press, 1975), 61, 89, 108, 112. **3.** Arthur Euing to Donnell, n.d., folder 3146, and Lorenzo

J. Greene, 26 Jan. 1942, folder 3620, FCDP.   **4.** Ralph Shaw, *New York Daily Worker*, 29 Jan. 1942, TLF; John T. Clark to the Editor, *Post-Dispatch*, 28 Jan. 1942, 2C; *Argus*, 30 Jan. 1942, 8.   **5.** Walter White to Carl R. Johnson, 12 Jan. 1942, Box C90, Missouri Branch Files, NAACP; E.T. Summytt and William Mickens to Walter White, 29 Jan. 1942, Box A381, General Office Files, NAACP. In 1942 there were fourteen NAACP chapters in Missouri.

    6. [Sidney R. Redmond], "Sikeston Lynching," 27 Jan. 1942, Box A381, NAACP. Redmond's statement was based on information provided by Rev. J.B. Ross. Redmond had lived in St. Louis since 1929 and, as local NAACP counsel, had played a major role in *Missouri rel. Gaines v. Canada* (1938). See Mark V. Tushnet, *The NAACP's Legal Strategy against Segregated Education, 1925-1950* (Chapel Hill: Univ. of North Carolina Press, 1987), 70-77.   **7.** This and the next three paragraphs draw chiefly on *Argus*, 30 Jan. 1942, 1; and *Call*, 6 Feb. 1942, 1.   **8.** Willard B. Gatewood, *Aristocrats of Color: The Black Elite, 1880-1920* (Bloomington: Indiana Univ. Press, 1990), 300-322; U.S. Falls to Donnell, 26 Jan. 1942, folder 3627, and Carl R. Johnson telegram to Donnell, 27 Jan. 1942, folder 3626, FCDP.   **9.** See, e.g., Dorothy [Davis] to Roy [Wilkins], 29 Jan. 1942, Box A381, NAACP.   **10.** N.A. Sweets et al., "Sikeston, Missouri—Mob Violence," [29 Jan. 1942], folder 3622, FCDP; *Call*, 6 Feb. 1942, 5.

    11. *Call*, 6 Feb. 1942, 1; S.R. Redmond to Donnell, 30 Jan. 1942, Box A381, NAACP; C.A. Franklin to Donnell, 29 Jan. 1942, folder 3605, FCDP.   **12.** Dorothy [Davis] to Roy [Wilkins], 29 Jan. 1942, Box A381, NAACP; Bea Harmon, "My Trip to Sikeston," *Argus*, 6 Feb. 1942, 1; *Standard*, 17 March 1942, 2.   **13.** *Call*, 30 Jan. 1942, 1, 2; *Argus*, 30 Jan. 1942, 1, 8. No copies of the *St. Louis American* could be found.   **14.** Virgus C. Cole to Donnell, 30 Jan. 1942, folder 3616, FCDP.   **15.** S.R. Redmond to Walter White, 1 Feb. 1942, Box C91, Missouri Branch Files, NAACP; *Post-Dispatch* clippings, 2 Feb. 1942, NAACP.

    16. Robert L. Zangrando, *The NAACP Crusade against Lynching, 1909-1950* (Philadelphia: Temple Univ. Press, 1980), 170, 210-16; Sweets et al., "Sikeston, Missouri—Mob Violence," 4; *Argus*, 30 Jan. 1942, 1; *Post-Dispatch*, 2 Feb. 1942, 34; S.R. Redmond to Walter White, 1 Feb. 1942, Box C91, Missouri Branch Files, NAACP.   **17.** *Post-Dispatch*, 7 Feb. 1942, 3A, and 9 Feb. 1942, 6A; Lee Etta Summytt to NAACP, 13 Feb. 1942, Box A381, NAACP.   **18.** Carl R. Johnson telegram to Walter White, 27 Jan. 1942; Roy Wilkins to Johnson, 28 Jan. 1942; "Missouri N.A.A.C.P. Branch List," n.d.; and NAACP Press Release, 30 Jan. 1942, all in Box A381, NAACP. White received Redmond's telegram on Jan. 27 and spoke with him that evening.   **19.** C.B. [Johnson] to Donnell, 3 Feb. 1942, folder 3600, FCDP.   **20.** A.L. Reynolds and L.D. Hardiman to Donnell, 11 Feb. 1942, folder 3608, FCDP; *Argus*, 13 Feb. 1942, 8.

    21. E.g., *Negro Labor News* (Houston), 30 Jan. 1943; *Pittsburgh Courier*, 7 Feb. 1942; and *Chicago Defender*, 7 Feb. 1942, all in TLF.   **22.** Franklyn R. Johnson to Roosevelt, 26 Jan. 1942, and Johnson to Walter White, 27 Jan. 1942, Box A381, NAACP. **23.** White telegram to Roosevelt, 26 Jan. 1942, Box A381, NAACP.   **24.** NAACP Press

Release, 26 Jan. 1942, and White to Sidney R. Redmond, 27 Jan. 1942, Box A381, NAACP; *Argus*, 30 Jan. 1942, 1. **25.** White to Redmond, 27 Jan. 1942, Box A381, NAACP; Zangrando, *The NAACP Crusade against Lynching*, 10, 41, 92-94; Walter White, *Rope and Faggot* (rpt.; New York: Arno, 1969); *Call*, 20 Feb. 1942, TLF, for Tompkinses racial identity.

26. Tompkins and Tompkins, "An Informal Report," 1. **27.** [J.B. Ross], "Statement," 27 Jan. 1942, Redmond, "Sikeston Lynching," and Dorothy [Davis] to Roy [Wilkins], 29 Jan. 1942, Box A381, NAACP. **28.** E.T. Summytt and William Mickens to Walter White, 29 Jan. 1942; NAACP Press Release, 26 and 30 Jan. and 2 Feb. 1942, Box A381, NAACP. **29.** Russell S. Brown to Donnell, 28 Jan. 1942, folder 3616, and Truth Truly to Donnell, 2 Feb. 1942, folder 3599, FCDP; James Wilson Jr. to the Editor, *Chicago Defender*, 7 Feb. 1942, TLF, probably written before the press release. **30.** Neil A. Wynn, *The Afro-American and the Second World War* (New York: Holmes & Meier, 1975), 101.

31. Walter White to Sidney R. Redmond, 13 Feb. 1942, Box A381, NAACP; *Daily Worker*, 25 Feb. 1942, TLF; Elliott M. Rudwick, *Race Riot at East St. Louis, July 2, 1917* (Carbondale: Southern Illinois Univ. Press, 1964), 134-35; Zangrando, *The NAACP Crusade against Lynching*, 38. **32.** Roy Wilkins to Lee Etta Summytt, 14 Feb. 1942, Box A381, NAACP. **33.** Quoted in NAACP Press Release, 13 Feb. 1942; examples in *Kansas City Plaindealer*, 20 Feb. 1942, and *Chicago Bee*, 1 March 1942, TLF. **34.** Frank D. Reeves to E.T. Summytt, 19 Feb. 1942, Box A381, NAACP, for suggestions of Sidney E. Sweet, pastor, Church of Christ Cathedral, and Spencer McCulloch, editor-in-chief of the *Post-Dispatch*. **35.** Wendell Berge to Thurgood Marshall, 13 Feb. 1942, and Berge to Walter White, 14 Feb. 1942, Box A381, NAACP.

36. Roy Wilkins with Tom Mathews, *Standing Fast: The Autobiography of Roy Wilkins* (New York: Viking, 1982), 189. **37.** S.R. Redmond to Walter White, 1 Feb. 1942; Daisy Lampkin telegram to Richetta Randolph, 18 Feb. 1942; and NAACP Press Release, 13 March 1942, all in Box C91, Missouri Branch Files, NAACP. **38.** Memorandum to [Roy] Wilkins from Charlotte B. Crump, 24 Feb. 1942, Box A381, NAACP. **39.** Quoted in *Post-Dispatch*, 31 Jan. 1942, 3A; Frank L. Williams to Donnell, 27 Jan. 1942, folder 3609, FCDP. **40.** H.H. Lewis, "Possession," n.d., Box 1, Lewis Papers, RHUA.

41. Lindell F. Bagley to the Editor, *Post-Dispatch*, 16 Feb. 1942, 2C; A Citizen to Donnell, n.d., folder 3599, FCDP. **42.** *Herald*, 5 Feb. 1942, 4; *Post-Dispatch*, 31 Jan. 1942, 3A. **43.** Emily C. Franklin to Donnell, 6 Feb. 1942, folder 3606; Warren Hilsiker telegram to Donnell, 27 Jan. 1942, folder 3605; Julius Hecht to Donnell, 4 Feb. 1942, folder 3608; Harry H. Ball Jr. to Donnell, 8 Feb. 1942, folder 3619 (for St. Louis National Alliance of Postal Workers, a secular example), FCDP. **44.** *Call*, 6 Feb. 1942, 22, quoting *St. Louis Globe-Democrat* and *Kansas City Journal*. **45.** *St. Louis Star-Times* clipping, 27 Jan. 1942, Box C91, Missouri Branch Files, NAACP.

46. C.A. Franklin to Donnell, 4 Feb. 1942, folder 3605, FCDP. **47.** Editor, "Two Crimes at Sikeston," *Post-Dispatch*, 26 Jan. 1942, 2C; Sidney E. Sweet to E.T. Summytt,

12 Feb. 1942, Box A381, NAACP; Marion R. Lynes to Donnell, 3 March 1942, folder 3621, FCDP.   **48.** Interview with Bumbarger (6 Nov. 1987).   **49.** *Herald*, 29 Jan. 1942, 4.   **50.** Mrs. George R. Smith to Donnell, 27 Jan. 1942, folder 3612; J.W. Nadal to Donnell, 9 April 1942, folder 3609; James Baare Turnball to Donnell, 13 Feb. 1942, folder 3611; and Mrs. Brooks to Donnell, 18 Feb. 1942, folder 3599, all in FCDP.

51. Helen Deering to Donnell, n.d., folder 3615, and Mrs. H.L. Slage to Donnell, 18 Feb. 1942, folder 3599, FCDP.   **52.** Mrs. Attwood R. Martin et al., telegram to Donnell, 30 Jan. 1942, folder 3620, and Mrs. R.E. Connell to Donnell, 27 Jan. 1942, folder 3616, FCDP.   **53.** Katherine Gardner to Donnell, 28 Jan. 1942, folder 3604, and Progress Club of Ohio University, "Petition," n.d., folder 3625, FCDP.   **54.** George Marshall and A.J. Isserman to Donnell, 29 Jan. 1942, Box A381, NAACP. **55.** Editor, "Mob Murder," *Washington Post*, 27 Jan. 1942, TLF; *Herald*, 5 Feb. 1942, 4, for Tampa and Chicago newspapers.

56. *Standard*, 27 Jan. 1942, 5; Donnell, "Sikeston Notes," 1-7. Between 12:47 A.M. and 6:30 P.M., Donnell spoke with Mayor Presnell, Prosecutor Blanton, Missouri State Troop Commander Col. Stanley Ginn, and others.   **57.** Quoted in *Post-Dispatch*, 26 Jan. 1942, 3; S.R. Redmond to Donnell, 30 Jan. 1942, Box A381, NAACP; Editor, "Missouri Shame!" *Call*, 30 Jan. 1942, 22.   **58.** Fredrickson, *The Black Image in the White Mind*, 312.   **59.** Edward A. Purcell Jr., *The Crisis of Democratic Theory: Scientific Naturalism and the Problem of Value* (Lexington: Univ. Press of Kentucky, 1973), 138, 269-72.   **60.** *Who's Who in American Politics* (New York: Bowker, 1977), 268; *Who's Who in America* (Chicago: Marquis, 1978), 1:867; phone conversation with Ruth Rogers (Donnell's daughter), 29 July 1985, and interviews with Rogers (22 May 1993) and Bay; Leonidas C. Dyer to Donnell, 26 Jan. 1942, folder 3620, FCDP.

61. Folders 3599, 3600, 3604-21, FCDP (100+ protests).   **62.** C. Ellis to Donnell, 10 Feb. 1942, folder 3614; Alzonia I. Bryant to Donnell, 3 Feb. 1942, folder 3616; and Mrs. George R. Smith to Donnell, 27 Jan. 1942, folder 3612, FCDP.   **63.** Editor, "Don't Be Misled," *Herald*, 5 Feb. 1942, 4.   **64.** Lyman Russell Mitten II to Dominic J. Capeci Jr., 15 July 1985; Donnell, "Sikeston Notes," 8; U.S. Falls to Donnell, 26 Jan. 1942, folder 3627, and Peter F. Keyes to Donnell, 27 Jan. 1942, folder 3607, FCDP. **65.** *Call*, 30 Jan. 1942, 1, 4.

66. Duane G. Meyer, *The Heritage of Missouri*, 3d ed. (St. Louis: River City, 1982), 671-72; David D. March, *The History of Missouri* (New York: Lewis Historical, 1967), 2:1409-20; Lyle W. Dorsett, *The Pendergast Machine* (New York: Oxford Univ. Press, 1968), 118-37.   **67.** State of Missouri, *Official Manual, 1941-1942* (Jefferson City, Mo.: Mid-State, 1943), 241-42; Larry Henry Grothaus, "The Negro in Missouri Politics, 1890-1941" (Ph.D. diss., Univ. of Missouri, 1970), 138-71; *Post-Dispatch*, 6 Nov. 1940, A2, and 7 Nov. 1940, A10; Thomas F. Soapes, "The Governorship 'Steal' and the Republican Revival," *Bulletin of the Missouri Historical Society* 32 (April 1976): 158-72.   **68.** Dorothy W. Twine to Donnell, 1 Feb. 1942, folder 3610, FCDP.   **69.** Interview with Blanton (18 May 1987).   **70.** A Voter to Donnell, 6 Feb. 1942, folder

3600; anonymous postcard to Donnell, 6 Feb. 1942; and newspaper clipping, n.d., all in FCDP.

71. John Edgar Hoover to Special Agent in Charge (St. Louis), 16 Feb. 1942, FBIF. **72.** Victor W. Rotnem memorandum to Wendell Berge, 2 Feb. 1942, USJD; *Amsterdam News*, 7 Feb. 1942, TLF. **73.** Berge to Thurgood Marshall, 13 Feb. 1942, USJD; Marshall to E.T. Summytt, Box A381, NAACP. **74.** Rotnem to Berge, 2 Feb. 1942, USJD; Berge memorandum to Attorney General, 10 Feb. 1942, USIP; and Biddle to Donnell, 10 Feb. 1942. **75.** Walter White telegram to Franklin D. Roosevelt, 26 Jan. 1942, Box A381, NAACP.

76. *Call*, 6 Feb. 1942, 3. **77.** *NYT*, 5 Oct. 1968, 35; *The National Cyclopedia of American Biography* (Clifton, N.J.: James T. White, 1973), 54:382-83; Francis Biddle, *In Brief Authority* (New York: Doubleday, 1962), 155. **78.** Frank Freidel, *FDR and the South* (Baton Rouge: Louisiana State Univ. Press, 1965), 72-73; *Call*, 6 Feb. 1942, 3; Dominic J. Capeci Jr., *The Harlem Riot of 1943* (Philadelphia: Temple Univ. Press, 1977), 94-98, 148-56. **79.** Biddle, *In Brief Authority*, 169, 269; Peter Irons, "Politics and Principles: An Assessment of the Roosevelt Record on Civil Rights and Liberties," *Washington Law Review* 59, no. 4 (1984): 711-20, for defense exigencies, especially the internment of Japanese Americans, that overrode Biddle's liberal instincts. **80.** Edward A. Purcell Jr., "American Jurisprudence between the Wars: Legal Realism and the Crisis of Democratic Theory," *American Historical Review* 75 (Dec. 1969): 424-46; Paul L. Murphy, *The Constitution in Crisis Times, 1918-1969* (New York: Harper & Row, 1972), 172.

81. Irons, "Politics and Principles," 699, 703-4. **82.** Robert M. Cover, "The Origins of Judicial Activism in the Protection of Minorities," *Yale Law Journal* 91 (June 1982): 1291, quoting Supreme Court Justice Harlan Fiske Stone; Louis Lusky, "Footnote Redux: A *Carolene Products* Reminiscence," *Columbia Law Review* 82 (Oct. 1982): 1093-1105. **83.** Zangrando, *NAACP Crusade against Lynching*, 154-55; Richard Kluger, *Simple Justice: The History of Brown v. Board of Education and Black America's Struggle for Equality* (New York: Knopf, 1975), 196-213. **84.** Henry A. Schweinhaut, "The Civil Liberties Section of the Department of Justice," *Bill of Rights Review* 1 (Spring 1941): 206-16; Robert K. Carr, *Federal Protection of Civil Rights: Quest for a Sword* (Ithaca, N.Y.: Cornell Univ. Press, 1947), 24-31; John T. Elliff, "Aspects of Federal Civil Rights Enforcement: The Justice Department and the FBI, 1939-1964," *Perspectives in American History* 5 (1971): 605, 606-7; Sidney Fine, *Frank Murphy: The Washington Years* (Ann Arbor: Univ. of Michigan Press, 1984), 76-82; Harvard Sitkoff, *A New Deal for Blacks: The Emergence of Civil Rights as a National Issue* (New York: Oxford Univ. Press, 1978), 216-43. Several scholars have contended that between 1940 and 1945 (except for Japanese American internment and Hawaiian military government) civil liberties largely survived wartime exigencies. Revisionists have challenged this viewpoint; see Alfred H. Kelly, Winifred A. Harbison, and Herman Belz, *American Constitution: Its Origins and Development*, 6th ed. (New York: Norton, 1983), 571; and Irons, "Politics and Principles," 721-22. **85.** Peter J.

Kellogg, "Civil Rights Consciousness in the 1940s," *Historian* 42 (Nov. 1979): 30; Oliver C. Cox, "Lynching and the Status Quo," *Journal of Negro Education* 14 (Fall 1945): 586.   **86.** Biddle to Forrest Donnell, 10 Feb. 1942, USIP; Biddle telegram to Donnell, 28 Feb. 1942, FBIF.   **87.** *Post-Dispatch*, 13 Feb. 1942, 3A; Edward A. Tamm memorandum for D.M. Ladd, 28 Feb. 1942, FBIF.   **88.** John Edgar Hoover to Special Agent in Charge, 16 Feb. 1942, C.B. Norris to Director, 23 Feb. 1942, and FBI Report, 23 Feb. 1942, 1-48, all in FBIF; *Herald*, 19 Feb. 1942, 1; interview with Mitchell (9 June 1988); [Paul Bumbarger], "The Goat Editor Says," *Standard*, 24 Feb. 1942, 1.   **89.** Interview with subject E.   **90.** FBI Report, 23 Feb. 1942, 47-48; R.P. Kramer memorandum for D.M. Ladd, 28 Feb. 1942, FBIF.

91. Interviews with subject C and subject E.   **92.** J.A. Cimperman memorandum for D.M. Ladd, 17 March 1942, and James Rowe Jr., memorandum for J. Edgar Hoover, 2 March 1942, FBIF.   **93.** Interview with Blanton (13 June 1990).   **94.** *Post-Dispatch*, 30 Jan. 1942, 3A, and 1 March 1942, 2C; Melvin Dace to Commanding Officer, 31 Jan. 1942, 4, MSHP; interview with Blanton (6 Nov. 1987). The press reported that Scott County Sheriff John Hobbs assisted Blanton's investigation (*Herald*, 29 Jan. 1942, 1) but Blanton never mentioned him, and no sheriff reports have been found.   **95.** USJD Summary, 62, 66; interviews with Ingram (5 Nov. 1987) and Law; *Argus*, 27 Feb. 1942, TLF.

96. Vincent P. Boisaubin interview, FBI Report, 23 Feb. 1942, 19; Blanton interview, FBI Report, 27 April 1942, 5, and "Undeveloped Leads," 14, FBIF.   **97.** Interview with Blanton (13 June 1990); *Des Moines Bystander*, 29 Jan. 1942, TLF; *Chicago Bee*, 22 Feb 1942, FBIF.   **98.** Interview with Blanton (18 May 1987). Blanton denied ever seeing photos or using them in the grand jury presentation; FBI records mention Blanton's photographic evidence, but not films; in 1987 an individual assured me that he had film of the lynching but never produced it.   **99.** David E. Blanton to Donnell, 28 Jan. 1942, folder 3623, FCDP.   **100.** *Standard*, 20 Feb. 1942, 1, and 3 March 1942, 1; *Herald*, 5 March 1942, 1.

101. Interview with Blanton (6 Nov. 1987); Lyman Russell Mitten II, "The Lynching of Cleo Wright: A Study" (senior thesis, Southeast Missouri State Univ., 1974), 33.   **102.** Interview with Blanton (18 May 1987); *Herald*, 29 Jan. 1942, 1; *Standard*, 3 Feb. 1942, 1.   **103.** *Standard*, 3 Feb. 1942, 1, 4; 24 Feb. 1942, 1; 10 March 1942, 1.   **104.** *Circuit Court Criminal Record, Scott County*, 11:237, SCCH; *Standard*, 13 March 1942, 4. Matthews withdrew late, and Miller replaced him the day of the proceeding, after Harry C. Watkins Sr. and Alden Pinney excused themselves.   **105.** Shrum, *History of Scott County, Missouri*, 119; Douglass, *History of Southeast Missouri*, 291.

106. *Standard*, 10 March 1942, 4, and 13 March 1942, 4.   **107.** Interview with Blanton (6 Nov. 1987); Harry Kay, "Notes on Testimony before the Grand Jury at Benton, Missouri," 9-10 March 1942, 1-12, folder 3624, FCDP (cited as Kay, State Grand Jury Notes).   **108.** Interview with Bumbarger (6 Nov. 1987); Mitten, "The Lynching of Cleo Wright," p. 33.   **109.** *Standard*, 13 March 1942, 1; *Circuit Court*

Criminal Record, 11:238.   **110.** Editor, "A Lesson for Missouri," *Call*, 27 Feb. 1942, 22; Donald D. Landon, "Clients, Colleagues, and Community: The Shaping of Zealous Advocacy in Country Law Practice," *American Bar Foundation Research Journal* 1985 (Winter): 84-91.

111. Tompkins and Tompkins, "An Informal Report," 9; Edward L. Ayers, *Vengeance and Justice: Crime and Punishment in the 19th-Century American South* (New York: Oxford Univ. Press, 1984), 17; interview with Blanton (6 Nov. 1987).   **112.** Interview with Clinton; phone conversation with subject I.   **113.** *Kansas City Star*, 3 Feb. 1942, Cook Collection, MHSL; Tompkins and Tompkins, "An Informal Report," 6-7.   **114.** Editor, "Missouri's Shame!" *Call*, 30 Jan. 1942, 22; "A Lesson for Missouri," *Call*, 27 Feb. 1942, 22.   **115.** Interview with Bumbarger (6 Nov. 1987).

116. *Standard*, 10 March 1942, 4.   **117.** Editor, "The Sikeston Lynching Inquiry Fiasco," *Post-Dispatch*, 12 March 1942, 2C.   **118.** *Standard*, 10 March 1942, 4; Jack Greenberg, *Race Relations and American Law* (New York: Columbia Univ. Press, 1959), 394-96.   **119.** *Standard*, 3 Feb. 1942, 4; Kay, State Grand Jury Notes, 5.   **120.** Interviews with Blanton (18 May 1987, 13 June 1990).

121. Floyd Calvin Shoemaker, ed., *Missouri and Missourians: Land of Contrasts and People of Achievements* (Chicago: Lewis, 1943), 3:584; *Argus*, 13 March 1942, 7; *Post-Dispatch*, 2 Feb. 1942, 3A.   **122.** Editor, "Another Blot on Missouri," *Argus*, 13 March 1942, 8.   **123.** Editor, "The Grand Jury's Report," *Herald*, 12 March 1942, 4; Fredrickson, *The Black Image in the White Mind*, 293.   **124.** Art L. Wallhausen to Donnell, 26 Jan. 1942, folder 3604, FCDP.   **125.** Editor, "The Sikeston Lynching Inquiry Fiasco," *Post-Dispatch*, 12 March 1942, 26; Helen Musil to the Editor, *Post-Dispatch*, 14 March 1942, 4A; Gamma Omega Chapter (Alpha Kappa Alpha) telegram to Donnell, 12 March 1942, folder 3611, FCDP.

126. Editor, "Another Blot on Missouri," *Argus*, 13 March 1942, 8; "That Sikeston Grand Jury," *Argus*, 6 March 1942, 8.   **127.** Editor, "Another Blot on Missouri," *Argus*, 13 March 1942, 8; William Senter telegram to Donnell, 11 March 1942, folder 3604, FCDP.   **128.** Donnell to Henry D. Espy, 19 March 1942, folder 3626, FCDP; *Post-Dispatch*, 14 March 1942, 3A.   **129.** Donnell to William Senter, 12 March 1942, folder 3604, FCDP.   **130.** S.R. Redmond to Francis Biddle, 13 March 1942, USJD.

131. Tompkins and Tompkins, "An Informal Report," 9.   **132.** E.T. Summytt to Frank D. Reeves, 1 March 1942, Box A381, NAACP.   **133.** James H. Chadbourn, *Lynching and the Law* (Chapel Hill: Univ. of North Carolina Press, 1933), 13.   **134.** *Post-Dispatch*, 9 April 1942, 3A.   **135.** Victor W. Rotnem, "Clarifications of the Civil Rights' Statutes," *Bill of Rights Review* 2 (Summer 1942): 260; Dominic J. Capeci Jr., *Race Relations in Wartime Detroit: The Sojourner Truth Housing Controversy of 1942* (Philadelphia: Temple Univ. Press, 1984).

136. Justice Department Press Release, 11 March 1942, FBIF; *St. Louis American*, April 1942, FBIF; Wendell Berge memorandum for J. Edgar Hoover, 13 March 1942, USJD.   **137.** Schweinhaut, "The Civil Liberties Section," 207; Carr, *Federal Protection of Civil Rights*, 56-77, 163-76; Elliff, "Aspects of Federal Civil Rights Enforcement," 608. Section 51 originated as Section 6 of the Enforement Act (1870), becoming Section 5508 of the *Revised Statutes* (1873), Section 19 of the *Criminal Code* (1909), and Section 51 of Title 18 of the *U.S. Code* (1925); Section 52 originated in Section 2 of the Civil Rights Act (1866) and in Sections 16 and 17 of the Enforcement Act (1871), becoming Section 5510 in the *Revised Statutes* (1873), Section 20 of the *Criminal Code* (1909), and Section 52 of Title 18 of the *U.S. Code* (1925). By 1968, Sections 51 and 52 became Sections 241 and 242, Title 18, *U.S. Code.* See Carr, *Federal Protection of Civil Rights,* 57-58, 70-71. **138.** Victor W. Rotnem, "The Federal Civil Right 'Not to Be Lynched,'" *Washington University Law Quarterly* 28 (Feb. 1943): 60. Supreme Court decisions had held that lynchings were not a federal offense (*United States v. Harris,* 1882) and that individuals were exempt from violation of the Fourteenth Amendment (*Hodges v. United States,* 1906). **139.** Victor W. Rotnem, "Criminal Enforcement of Federal Civil Rights," *Lawyers Guild Review* 2 (May 1942): 18-23, and "Clarifications of the Civil Rights' Statutes," 252-61. Section 51 carried harsher penalties because its violation was a felony; violation of Section 52, a misdemeanor. **140.** Wendell Berge memorandum for J. Edgar Hoover, 10 Feb. 1942, FBIF.

141. Rotnem, "The Federal Civil Right 'Not to Be Lynched'" 70-73; Carr, *Federal Protection of Civil Rights,* 70, 77. **142.** Elliff, "Aspects of Federal Civil Rights Enforcement" 609, 615; Darlene Clark Hine, *Black Victory: The Rise and Fall of the White Primary in Texas* (Millwood, N.Y.: KTO Press, 1979), 202-6. **143.** Berge to Marshall, 13 Feb. 1942, and Marshall to Berge, 16 Feb. 1942, USJD; E.T. Summytt to Frank D. Reeves, 1 March 1942, Marshall to Summytt, 9 March 1942, and Marshall to Berge, 9 March 1942, Box A381, NAACP. Summytt of Webster Groves suggested the need for federal court action and questioned the objectivity of Harry C. Blanton, which paralleled the earlier concern of Sidney R. Redmond and others who protested David E. Blanton's role in the state grand jury. **144.** Rotnem to Berge, 12 March 1942, USJD; Berge memorandum for J. Edgar Hoover, 13 March 1942, and *Chicago Bee,* 22 Feb. 1942, FBIF; Berge to Jacob M. Lashly, 27 March and 3 April 1942, USIP; Rotnem to Lashly, 28 March 1942, and Lashly telegram to Rotnem, 11 April 1942, USIP. **145.** E.g., Walter White to Attorney General, 16 April 1942, USJD.

146. Donnell telegram to Francis Biddle, 27 Feb. 1942, and Donnell to Biddle, 13 March 1942 and 8 April 1942, USIP; Donnell to Roy McKittrick, 24 March 1942, folder 3622, FCDP. For criticism, see, e.g., Editor, "Department of Justice Enters Lynching Case," *Argus,* 17 April 1942, 8. **147.** John Edgar Hoover memorandum for Attorney General, 30 April 1942, FBIF; *Argus,* 3 April 1942, 2; *Call,* 3 April 1942, 1. For examples, see *Norfolk Journal and Guide,* 4 April 1942; *Indianapolis Recorder,* 4 April 1942; *Detroit Tribune,* 4 April 1942; *Amsterdam News,* 4 April 1942; *Chicago Defender,* 4 April 1942; *Philadelphia Independent,* 5 April 1942; (Baltimore) *Afro-American,* 4 April 1942, FBIF. **148.** Harry C. Blanton to Wendell Berge, 6 April 1942, USED. **149.** Lashly to Rotnem, 14 April 1942, and Berge telegram to Lashly, 15 April 1942, USIP. **150.** FBI Report, 27 April 1942, 16 May 1942, and 4 June 1942.

151. Berge to Lashly, 27 March 1942, and Rotnem to Lashly, 28 March 1942, USIP. 152. Sylvester P. Meyers memorandum for Irwin L. Langbein, 2 May 1942, USIP. See Carr, *Federal Protection of Civil Rights*, 74, for Section 550: "Whoever directly commits any act constituting an offense defined in any law of the United States, or aids, abets, counsels, commands, induces, or procures its commission, is a principal." 153. Lashly to Berge, 30 March 1942, USIP. 154. Irwin L. Langbein memorandum for Victor Rotnem, 8 May 1942, USIP. 155. S.P. Meyers memorandum for Victor W. Rotnem, 13 May 1942, USJD.

156. Lashly to Berge, 30 March 1942, USIP. 157. Rotnem memorandum for Berge, 13 May 1942, USJD. 158. Langbein to Lashly, 29 May 1942, USIP. 159. *Standard*, 19 May 1942, 1; *Call*, 29 May 1942, 1; Jacob M. Lashly, "Case of Cleo Wright" (n.d.), USIP; interview with Clinton. 160. Ross, "Statement"; Redmond, "Sikeston Lynching"; Lashly, "Case of Cleo Wright"; David E. Blanton interview (23 Feb. 1942), FBI Report, 31; *Call*, 30 Jan. 1942, 24; Charles E. Latham interview (23 Feb. 1942), FBI Report, 37-38; anonymous white witness interview (13 March 1942), FBI Report, 4; anonymous white witness interview (4 June 1942), FBI Report, 3.

161. Redmond, "Sikeston Lynching," 2; Tompkins and Tompkins, "An Informal Report," 1; Irwin L. Langbein memorandum for Rotnem, 8 May 1942, USIP; Dace interview, FBI Report, 16. 162. Lashly to Berge, 30 March 1942, USIP. 163. Walter Kendall and Harold Wallace interviews, FBI Report, 23 Feb. 1942, 21, 24-25. 164. Floyd A. Buchanan to Irwin L. Langbein, 1 Aug. 1942, USIP; *Argus*, 29 May 1942, 1; *Call*, 5 June 1943, 1; *Standard*, 9 June 1942, 8; *Post-Dispatch*, 2 July 1942, 3A. No files of the federal grand jury could be located in the U.S. District Court (Eastern District of Missouri) or the archives at Kansas City. 165. Jacob M. Lashly to Francis Biddle, 2 July 1942, USIP; J.K. Mumford memorandum for D.M. Ladd, 30 July 1942, FBIF.

166. Justice Department Press Release, 30 July 1942, USJD. 167. *Post-Dispatch*, 31 July 1942, 2C. 168. Frankie Weaver Johnson, untitled declaration, 14 Aug. 1942, FBIF. 169. Rotnem, "The Federal Civil Right 'Not to Be Lynched,'" 57-73. 170. *Call*, 29 May 1942, 1, and 5 June 1942, 22; *Standard*, 9 June 1942, 8; interview with Clinton.

171. Ellis L. Arenson memorandum for Victor Rotnem, 18 June 1942, USJD; Rotnem, "The Federal Civil Right 'Not to Be Lynched,'" 73; Lashly to Berge and Rotnem, 2 July 1942, USIP. 172. Lashly to Berge, 30 March 1942, USIP. 173. R.P Kramer memorandum to D.M. Ladd, 5 May 1942, FBIF; Lashly to Francis Biddle, 2 July 1942, USIP; *Post-Dispatch*, 30 July 1942, 1A, 5A. 174. Lashly to Berge, 11 June 1942, USIP. 175. White to Biddle, 16 April 1942, USJD.

176. Shoemaker, *Missouri and Missourians*, 4:378-79; interview with Rogers (22 May 1993); R.P. Kramer memorandum for D.M. Ladd, 5 May 1942, FBIF. 177. Langbein to Rotnem, 12 May 1942, USIP. 178. Berge to Lashly, 19 June 1942, and Rotnem to Lashly, 19 June 1942, USIP. 179. Rotnem memorandum for Berge, 12 March 1942, USJD. Baldwin also suggested Roscoe Anderson, former U.S. attorney

and president of the Missouri Bar Association.   **180.** *Post-Dispatch*, n.d., FBIF.
181. Lashly to Berge and Rotnem, 2 July 1942, USIP.   **182.** Lashly to Berge, 21
July 1942, Lashly to Rotnem, 24 July 1942, and Lashly telegram to Justice Depart-
ment, 30 July 1942, USIP; *Call*, 10 July 1942, 1.   **183.** Langbein memorandum re
Sikeston case, 23 July 1942, USIP; Justice Department Press Release, 30 July 1942,
USJD.   **184.** M.E. Gilfond memorandum for the Attorney General, 29 July 1942,
USIP.   **185.** Biddle to Lashly, 13 April 1942, and Berge to Lashly, 10 April 1942, USIP;
"Mr. Lashly's Appointment," *Post-Dispatch*, 13 April 1942.

186. Lashly to Berge, 30 March 1942, USIP.   **187.** Lashly to Berge and Rotnem,
2 July 1942, USIP.   **188.** Biddle to Lashly, 21 July 1942, USIP.   **189.** Justice Department Press Release, 30 July 1942, USJD.   **190.** James T. Patterson, *The New Deal
and the States: Federalism in Transition* (Princeton, N.J.: Princeton Univ. Press, 1969),
207.

191. Cantor, *Prologue to the Protest Movement*, 132; Murphy, *Constitution in Crisis
Times*, 174.   **192.** Lashly to Berge, 30 March 1942, USIP. See *Call*, 22 and 29 May
1942, TLF, for profile of jury members. Lee Bowman, the only juror from Sikeston,
was excused, apparently at his own request—another example of the close-knit bonds
of white townsfolk.   **193.** Caucasin to the Editor, *Post-Dispatch*, 15 April 1942, 2C.
194. Lashly to Berge and Rotnem, 2 July 1942, USIP.   **195.** Mitten, "The Lynching
of Cleo Wright," 31.

Chapter 4   Autopsy

1. "Promise Probe in Mo. Lynching," *Atlanta Daily World*, Feb. 1942, TLF; *Standard*, 27 Jan. 1942, 1; Redmond, "Sikeston Lynching," 2; Tompkins and Tompkins,
"An Informal Report," 1-9.   **2.** *Circuit Court Criminal Record*, 10:360; Cleo Wright
entry, 21 Sept. 1942, *County Jail Record*, SCJ; Sheriff Bill Ferrell to author 1 June 1987.
Wright might have been suspected of petty theft before the car tampering convic-
tion: FBI record 1387618, FBIF, for erroneous date, conviction, and sentence of a
1936 violation; Cleo Wright, File 54168, Missouri State Prison Record, 1, Missouri
Department of Corrections and Human Resources, Jefferson City (cited as Wright
Prison Record) for self-reported 1937 "suspicion of larceny."   **3.** Wright Prison
Record, 1; *Circuit Court Criminal Record*, 11:50-51; Cleo Wright entry, 18 May 1940,
County Jail Record, SCJ.   **4.** Wright Prison Record, "Trade or Profession" page; interview with Sturgeon (19 July 1990), quoting Limbaugh; *Call*, 30 Jan. 1942, 4.
5. Ardella Wright interview, FBI Report, 23 Feb. 1942, 12; interviews with Griffen
(11 June 1990) and Dotson (18 May 1987); *Call*, 30 Jan. 1942, 1.

6. Cleo Wright Supervision Report, 29 Dec. 1941, Board of Probation and Parole, Jefferson City, Missouri; *Call*, 30 Jan. 1942, 4; *Standard*, 6 April 1942, 1.
7. Interview with Griffen (5 Nov. 1987). Wright was in the Scott County Jail 21 Sept.
to 9 Dec. 1937 and 18 May to 16 July 1940.   **8.** Interview with Ingram (5 Nov. 1987).
9. Interview with Brown; Ardella Wright interview, FBI Report, 23 Feb. 1942, 12.

10. Interview with Brown; *Argus*, 30 Jan. 1942, 7; interview with Linetta Watson Koonce (23 Aug. 1992), Pine Bluff, Ark.   **11.** *Standard*, 6 April 1942, 1; Richard Wright, *Black Boy: A Record of Childhood and Youth* (New York: Harper, 1945), 175.   **12.** Interview with Schwabb, 7 Aug. 1987, RHUA; *Standard*, 6 April 1942, 1.   **13.** Interview with Blanton (18 May 1987); Perrigan interview, FBI Report, 4.   **14.** Milem Limbaugh interview, FBI Report, 23 Feb. 1942, 28; interview with Dempster (20 May 1987); anonymous to Forrest C. Donnell, 31 Jan. 1942, folder 3599, FCDP.   **15.** Interview with Bumbarger (6 Nov. 1987).

16. Interview with Griffen (5 Nov. 1987).   **17.** Interviews with Dotson (18 May 1987)and Brown.   **18.** Interview with Gardner; George C. Wright, *Racial Violence in Kentucky, 1865-1940: Lynchings, Mob Rule, and "Legal Lynchings"* (Baton Rouge: Louisiana State Univ. Press, 1990), 103.   **19.** *Standard*, 27 Jan. 1942, 9; *Chicago Tribune*, 26 Jan. 1942, TLF.   **20.** Grace Sturgeon interview, FBI Report, 23 Feb. 1942, 3.

21. Perrigan interview, FBI Report, 4; interview with Jesse Whittley.   **22.** See, e.g., Wright, *Black Boy*, 59; interview with Sturgeon (19 May 1987).   **23.** Wallace, Arbaugh, and Limbaugh interviews, FBI Report, 23 Feb. 1942, 24, 26, 27; Bartlett interview, FBI Report, 23 Feb. 1942, 11.   **24.** Interviews with Sturgeon (19 May 1987, 8 June 1988); phone conversation with Laverne Sturgeon (19 Oct. 1992, Somerville, Tex.). Grace never mentioned the sighting to FBI agents in 1942. Perhaps being in shock at the time created some confusion, for using the hospital's rear entrance to the basement did not necessitate passing Grace's room, and the front entrance would have required escorting Wright through a crowd of angry whites, a most risky venture.   **25.** Interviews (19 May 1987, 8 June 1988); and phone conversations (21 Nov. 1991, 21 Aug. 1993) with Grace Sturgeon.

26. Interviews with Sturgeon (19 May 1987, 8 June 1988, 7 Nov. 1987).   **27.** Bartlett interview, FBI Report, 11; interview with Whittley.   **28.** Richard Gay interview, FBI Report, 11; Wallace interview, FBI Report, 23 Feb. 1942, 24.   **29.** FBI Report, 23 Feb. 1942, 36, for Wright's physical description; interview with James Walker (22 Aug. 1992); Beck interview, FBI Report, 6; interviews with Whittley and Griffen (11 June 1990).   **30.** Perrigan interview, FBI Report, 4.

31. *Standard*, 7 Nov. 1941, 1, and 28 Nov. 1941, 1. Ardella Wright said Cleo had no gun; Beck said he was carrying three .38 caliber cartridges when captured (interviews, FBI Report, 23 Feb. 1942, 12, 6).   **32.** Interview with Sturgeon (20 May 1987).   **33.** *Standard*, 3 March 1942, 1.   **34.** Bumbarger, "Jail-Storming Mob Burns Negro Knifer"; interviews with Law and Sturgeon (19 July 1990, 8 June 1988).   **35.** *Charleston Democrat*, 12 Feb. 1942, FBIF; interview with Dotson (18 May 1987); Bartlett interview, FBI Report, 23 Feb. 1942, 11; Redmond, "Sikeston Lynching"; interview with Currin.

36. Interview with Julia Renfro (13 June 1990); Trudier Harris, *Exorcising Blackness: Historical and Literary Lynching and Burning Rituals* (Bloomington: Indiana

Univ. Press, 1984) 26. Such white women were sometimes ostracized and scorned, if rarely physically abused, by community members. **37.** Johnson, *Backgrounds to Patterns of Negro Segregation*, 147; John Dollard, *Caste and Class in a Southern Town*, 3d ed. (Garden City, N.Y.: Doubleday Anchor, 1957), 170; Harris, *Exorcising Blackness*, 27. **38.** Interview with Griffen (11 June 1990); Dollard, *Caste and Class in a Southern Town*, 278. **39.** Bartlett interviews, FBI Report, 23 Feb. 1942, 11, and 27 April 1942, 6; Ardella Wright interviews, FBI Report, 23 Feb. 1942, 12, and 27 April 1942, 12. **40.** Phone conversation with Linetta Watson Koonce (21 June 1993, Albuquerque).

   41. Interview with Brown. **42.** Interview with Koonce (23 Aug. 1992), for discrepancies in Ardella's statements to her and the FBI. **43.** Interview with Sturgeon (19 July 1990). **44.** Howard Smead, *Blood Justice: The Lynching of Mack Charles Parker* (New York: Oxford Univ. Press, 1986), 93; interview with subject L (14 June 1990). **45.** Interviews with Glenda Whittley, David E. Blanton (18 May 1987), and Clinton.

   46. USJD Summary, 16. **47.** Interview with Sturgeon (8 June 1988); Frankie Weaver Johnson, untitled declaration, 14 Aug. 1942, FBIF. **48.** E.g., Melvin Dace to Commanding Officer [Troop E], 21 Aug. 1942, MSHP. **49.** Interview with Sturgeon (19 May 1987). **50.** Interview with Sturgeon (19 July 1990); Laural Myrtle Wiedmann interview, FBI Report, 27 April 1942, 8; interviews with Dotson (18 May 1987) and Clinton.

   51. Blanton and Rockwood interviews, FBI Report, 27 April 1942, 4, 8. **52.** Dace interviews, FBI Report, 23 Feb. 1942, 19, and 13 March 1942, 2. **53.** Harry C. Blanton to Attorney General, 6 April 1942, USED. **54.** Letter to "Dear One," 18 Jan. 1939, FBI Report, 13 March 1942, 2; interview with Koonce (10 Aug. 1993), who said it sounded like something her brother Cleo might have written; its place and date also coincided with Wright's return to Arkansas for his grandmother's funeral in late December. **55.** Dace interview, FBI Report, 13 March 1942, 2; C.L. Wallis to Commanding Officer, 29 Jan. 1942, MSHP.

   56. Wright Prison Record, 1. **57.** Harry C. Blanton to Attorney General, 6 April 1942, USED. Her physical characteristics should have been irrelevant to the veracity of her story, since rape is a "sexual expression of hostility and aggression" that turns on the assailant's need to resolve his own inadequacies, not on his victim's physical attributes; see A. Nicholas Groth with H. Jean Birnbaum, *Men Who Rape: The Psychology of the Offender* (New York: Plenum. 1979), 104-9. **58.** Wright Prison Record, 3; interview with Koonce (10 Aug. 1993). **59.** Ardella Wright interview, FBI Report, 27 April 1942, 12. **60.** Interview with Julia Renfro (13 June 1990); Hortense Powdermaker, *After Freedom: A Cultural Study in the Deep South* (New York: Atheneum, 1968), 164.

   61. Koonce to author, 19 Oct. 1992; interviews with Andrew Walker (22 June 1992) and John Henry Rasberry. **62.** This and the next paragraph are based on interviews with James Walker (22 Aug. 1992) and Andrew Walker (22 June 1992);

Clora quoted in *Pine Bluff Commercial*, 2 April 1972, 13; interview with Rasberry. **63.** Interviews with Koonce (23 Aug. 1992, 10 Aug. 1993); phone conversation with James Woolfolk (12 Sept. 1992, Pine Bluff, Ark.); Temp Humphrey and Alonzo Woolfork [*sic*], Marriage License (15 Aug. 1907) and Certificate of Marriage (18 Aug. 1907), Marriage Records, Book P, 537, JCC; Alonzo Humphrey and Wiley Humphrey vs. Bettie Humphrey Rasberry, Decree, 6 March 1909, Chancery Court Records, Book Q, n.p., JCC. Temp died six months after marrying Alonzo, and Wiley was born six months after his father's death; Alonzo and Bettie—wife of John Rasberry, mother of John Henry and Adam—became neighbors and ultimately friends. **64.** Albert Watson and Alonzo Humphrey, Marriage License (19 Jan. 1910) and Certificate of Marriage (24 Jan. 1910); Albert Watson and Bessie Lusby, Marriage License (7 June 1904) and Certificate of Marriage (8 June 1904), Marriage Records, Book R, 409, and Book O, 33, JCC; interviews with Koonce (23 Aug. 1992, 10 Aug. 1993). No record of the Watson-Lusby divorce was found. **65.** Phone conversation with Koonce; interview with Rasberry.

    66. Interviews with James Simms (20 June 1992) and Andrew Walker (22 June 1992). **67.** Phone conversation and interview with Koonce (22 Aug. 1992). **68.** Interview with Andrew Walker (22 June 1992); phone conversation and interview with Koonce (23 Aug. 1992); interview with Rasberry; phone conversation with Woolfolk. Alonzo began teaching in 1916 and received the Woolfolk land in 1944. **69.** Phone conversation and interview with Koonce (23 Aug. 1992); interview with James Walker (22 Aug. 1992); phone conversation with Woolfolk. **70.** Interviews with Rasberry and Koonce (23 Aug. 1992).

    71. White, *Ar'n't I a Woman?*, 96; interview with James Walker (22 Aug. 1992). **72.** This and next two paragraphs based on interview with Koonce (23 Aug. 1992). **73.** Interview with James Walker (22 Aug. 1992). **74.** Interview with Koonce (23 Aug. 1992). **75.** Phone conversations with Koonce, and Woolfolk; interviews with James Walker (22 Aug. 1992) and Koonce (10 Aug. 1993).

    76. Interviews with James Walker (22 Aug. 1992) and Koonce (23 Aug. 1992). **77.** Interviews with Rasberry, Andrew Walker (22 June 1992), James Walker (22 Aug. 1992), and Koonce (23 Aug. 1992). **78.** Wiley Arnett Humphrey, Prison Record No. 35847, Arkansas Department of Corrections, Pine Bluff, Ark. (cited as Humphrey Prison Record); phone conversation with Woolfolk; interviews with Rasberry and Koonce (23 Aug. 1992). **79.** Wright Prison Record, 3, 4; interview with Koonce (23 Aug. 1992), who denied that Cleo was forced to quit school. **80.** Michigan State Police file and FBIF, Humphrey Prison Record.

    81. Interview with Koonce (23 Aug. 1992). **82.** Ricelor Cleodas Watson (Cleo Wright's given name), Military Record No. 346-60-26, 9, 12, National Personnel Record Center, St. Louis, Mo. (cited as Military Record); *U.S.S. Wyoming* Logbook, entries of 31 Dec. 1935 and 31 Mar. 1936, Military Reference Branch, NARS. Cleo's disaffection with military service was compounded by his inability to attend the funeral of his sister Alice on 29 Jan. 1936: interview with Koonce (10 Aug. 1994).

83. [U.S. Navy], *Bureau of Navigation Manual*, Section 1. Discharges, Article D-911 (Military Reference Branch, NARS), authorizes the discharge of "a man for unsuitability due to immaturity or other cause wherein it is not desired to discharge him for inaptitude." **84.** Rebecca Livingston (Military Reference Branch, NARS) to author, 6 Aug. 1992. **85.** FBI Report, 23 Feb. 1942, 36, for dishonorable discharge belief; Wright Prison Record, 5, for Pine Bluff occupation; interviews with Koonce (23 Aug. 1992), and James Simms (20 June 1992).

86. Wright Prison Record, 5. **87.** Interviews with Andrew Walker (22 June 1992), James Walker (22 Aug. 1992), and Simms; Michigan State Police file and Arkansas State Penitentiary file, Humphrey Prison Record. **88.** Interviews with Andrew Walker (22 June 1992) and Koonce (23 Aug. 1992). **89.** Phone conversation (21 June 1992) and interview (23 Aug. 1992) with Koonce; Koonce to author, 15 Feb. 1993. **90.** Interview with Koonce (23 Aug. 1992); State of Arkansas v. Wiley Arnett Humphrey, Criminal Court Record, Book 13, 127, JCC; Supervisor of Paroles to T.C. Cogbill, 17 June 1937, and Notice of Release, 4 Sept. 1941, Humphrey Prison Record. Wiley served four years.

91. Interview with James Walker (22 Aug. 1992). **92.** Ardella Wright interviews, FBI Report, 23 Feb. 1942, 11, and 27 April 1942, 12. **93.** Wright Supervision Report. **94.** Daniel, *Standing at the Crossroads*, 57. **95.** Interview with Koonce (23 Aug. 1992).

96. See Dollard, *Caste and Class in a Southern Town*, 275. **97.** Erich Fromm, *Escape from Freedom* (New York: Farrar & Rinehart, 1945); Wright Prison Record, 5. **98.** Interview with Koonce (23 Aug. 1992). There is no record that a Ricelor C. Watson or Cleo Wright committed a crime in Jefferson County, which includes Pine Bluff; neither name appears in the Index of Criminal Cases, Appeal and Cost Bonds of Jefferson County Circuit Court, vol. 2 (1919-38), JCC, which registers felonies. Municipal court files of Pine Bluff (containing mostly lesser offenses) do not exist for the period before 1948. **99.** Ian Robertson, *Sociology*, 3d ed. (New York: Worth, 1987), 194-95, for cultural transmission concept; Henry Allen Bullock, "Urbanism and Race Relations," in *The Urban South*, ed. Rupert B. Vance and Nicholas J. Demerath (rpt.; Freeport, N.Y.: Books for Libraries, 1971), 209, for urbanization theory. **100.** Bartlett interview, FBI Report, 23 Feb. 1942, 11; interview with Rasberry.

101. Interviews with Koonce (23 Aug. 1992) and Andrew Walker (22 June 1992). **102.** Phone conversation with Woolfolk; interview with James Walker (21 Aug. 1992). **103.** Paul Bohannan with Lawrence A. Miller, "Cross-Cultural Comparison of Aggression and Violence," in *Violence in America: Crimes of Violence*, vol. 13, ed. Leon Friedman (rpt.; New York: Chelsea House, 1983), 113-20. **104.** Eugene D. Genovese, *In Red and Black: Marxian Explorations in Southern and Afro-American History* (New York: Pantheon, 1968), 149. **105.** James P. Comer, "The Dynamics of Black and White Violence," in *Violence in America: Historical and Comparative Perspectives*, vol. 2, ed. Hugh D. Graham and Ted R. Gurr (Washington, D.C.: Government Printing Office, 1969), 345, 347, 348.

106. Cf. Wright, *Black Boy*, 227.   107. Erik H. Erikson, *Childhood and Society*, 2d ed. (New York: Norton, 1963), 242; Robertson, *Sociology*, 207-8.   108. Bertram Wyatt-Brown, "The Mask of Obedience: Male Slave Psychology in the Old South," *American Historical Review* 93 (Dec. 1988):1233.   109. Interview with Koonce (23 Aug. 1992).   110. Wyatt-Brown, "The Mask of Obedience," 1250; Herbert G. Gutman, *The Black Family in Slavery and Freedom, 1750-1925* (New York: Pantheon, 1976), 219-20; Genovese, *Roll, Jordan, Roll*, 511-12; William H. Grier and Price M. Cobbs, *Black Rage* (New York: Bantam, 1969), 52-53.

111. Wright, *Black Boy*, 87.   112. Interview with Koonce (23 Aug. 1992). 113. Erik H. Erikson, *Insight and Responsibility: Lectures on the Ethical Implications of Psychoanalytic Insight* (New York: Norton, 1964), 233; interviews with Koonce (23 Aug. 1992, 10 Aug. 1993); Alonzo Watson interview, FBI Report, 16 June 1942, 3. 114. Wright Prison Record, 3-4.   115. Interview with Dr. Whipple (14 Jan. 1988); Austin L. Porterfield and Robert H. Talbert, "Crime in Southern Cities," in Vance and Demerath, *The Urban South*, 186-88.

116. Mary Frances Berry and John W. Blassingame, *Long Memory: The Black Experience in America* (New York: Oxford Univ. Press, 1982), 364. Frantz Fanon, *The Wretched of the Earth*, trans. Constance Farrington (New York: Grove , 1968), is the fullest theory of violence as necessary for the psychological freedom of oppressed people.   117. This and next eight paragraphs are based on interviews (19 May 1987, 7 Nov. 1987, 19 July 1990, 14 Sept. 1992) and phone conversation (21 Aug. 1993) with Grace Sturgeon,   118. Ogilvie, "Development of the Southeast Missouri Lowlands," 238-39.   119. Phone conversation with Sturgeon (13 Dec. 1993). A brother, Charles, also died in infancy.   120. Phone conversation with James Sturgeon (16 Dec. 1990, Chino, Calif.). Dillard was born 30 Oct. 1910; his son Jimmy, 22 Oct. 1933.

121. *Herald*, 27 Nov. 1941, 8.   122. Phone conversation with Laverne Sturgeon (19 Oct. 1992); *Herald*, 27 Nov. 1941, 8. Laverne and John were married in Stevens, Ark., on 30 August 1941.   123. Interview with Grace Sturgeon (14 Sept. 1992). 124. Interview with Sturgeon (14 Sept. 1992) for this and next paragraph.   125. Interviews (8 June 1988, 19 July 1990) and phone conversation (21 Aug. 1993) with Sturgeon.

126. Interviews with Sturgeon (7 Nov. 1987, 8 June 1988), for this and next paragraph.   127. Anonymous to Forrest C. Donnell, 31 Jan. 1942, folder 3599, FCDP; interview with Sturgeon (7 Nov. 1987).   128. Ronald M. Holmes, *Sex Crimes* (Newbury Park, Calif.: Sage, 1991), 78-80; Susan Brownmiller, *Against Our Will: Men, Women and Rape* (New York: Simon & Schuster, 1975), 182, 184, 186. Cleo was not yet the father of small children (though he was a father-to-be), nor did he travel on the job as did many modern rapists.   129. *Chicago Tribune*, 26 Jan. 1942, TLF. 130. Interview with Sturgeon (19 May 1987); anonymous to Forrest C. Donnell, 31 Jan. 1942, folder 3599, FCDP; *Standard*, 27 Jan. 1942, 8.

131. Interview with Sturgeon (19 May 1987); and phone conversations with

Grace (21 Aug. 1993) and Laverne Sturgeon; *Standard*, 27 Jan. 1942, 8. Laverne spoke about the gun incident within two days of Wright's assault, but years later Grace claimed that no such weapon was in the house. **132.** Interviews with Sturgeon (19 May 1987, 7 Nov. 1987, and 14 Sept. 1992). **133.** Phone conversation with Laverne Sturgeon. **134.** Interviews with Sturgeon (19 July 1990, 14 Sept. 1992); interview with Glenda Whittley. Laverne did not recall these incidents. **135.** See Brownmiller, *Against Our Will*, 205, for example of Albert DeSalvo. Grace and Cleo both said that he acted alone, despite the testimony of neighbor W.A. Sturgeon that he had three times noticed *two* men loitering near his home the evening before the attack, and of H.D. Davenport that he saw two men running away from the Sturgeon house immediately after the assault (*Standard*, 27 Jan. 1942, 8); neither witness could identify the race of those seen. Possibly Cleo had a lookout who was no part of the attack.

136. Holmes, *Sex Crimes*, 78-79; Brownmiller, *Against Our Will*, 184; interviews with Sturgeon (7 Nov. 1987, 19 July 1990). **137.** Carole-Rae Reed, Ann W. Burgess, and Carol R. Hartman, "Victim Assessment: The Dimensions of Rape Interview Schedule (DORIS)," in *Rape and Sexual Assault III: A Research Handbook*, ed. Ann Wolbert Burgess (New York: Garland, 1991), 18; Grace Sturgeon interview, FBI Report, 2. **138.** Interview with Sturgeon (19 May 1987). **139.** Brownmiller, *Against Our Will*, 184-85, 207-8; Ron Langevin, "The Sex Killer," in *Rape and Sexual Assault*, 259, 262, 268. **140.** Martin Duberman, "A Matter of Difference," *Nation* 257 (5 July 1993): 23; Eugene D. Genovese, *The Political Economy of Slavery: Studies in the Economy and Society of the Slave South* (New York: Random House, 1965), 74.

141. Robert Jay Lifton, *History and Human Survival: Essays on the Young and Old, Survivors and the Dead, Peace and War, and on Contemporary Psychohistory* (New York: Vintage, 1971), 219, on "counterfeit nurturance"; Genovese, *In Red and Black*, 149, for its manifestation in slavery. **142.** Interview with Dr. Whipple (17 Jan. 1988); Comer, "The Dynamics of Black and White Violence," 347; Brownmiller, *Against Our Will*, 185, 206. **143.** Dollard, *Caste and Class in a Southern Town*, 137. **144.** Robert Staples, *Black Masculinity: The Black Male's Role in American Society* (San Francisco: Black Scholar Press, 1982), 118; Grier and Cobbs, *Black Rage*, 76. **145.** Frantz Fanon, *Black Skin, White Masks*, trans. Charles Lam Markmann (New York: Grove, 1968), 63, on self-worth; Malcolm X with Alex Haley, *The Autobiography of Malcolm X* (New York: Grove, 1965), 67, 68, 96, for status factor.

146. Harry C. Blanton to Attorney General, 20 March 1942, USED. **147.** Dollard, *Caste and Class in a Southern Town*, 297-98; Genovese, *In Red and Black*, 211; Brownmiller, *Against Our Will*, 180-81; Eldridge Cleaver, *Soul on Ice* (New York: Dell, 1968), 14. **148.** David O. Sears and John B. McConahay, *The Politics of Violence: The New Urban Blacks and the Watts Riot* (Boston: Houghton Mifflin, 1973), 33.

149. Angela Y. Davis, *Women, Race, and Class* (New York: Vintage, 1983), 197; Jacquelyn Dowd Hall, "'The Mind That Burns in Each Body': Women, Rape, and Racial Violence," in *Powers of Desire: The Politics of Sexuality*, ed. Ann Snitow, Christine Stansell, and Sharon Thompson (New York: Monthly Review Press, 1983), 341, 346.   **150.** Groth, *Men Who Rape*, 12-17, 25-31, 44-49.

151. See Holmes, *Sex Crimes*, 79, for characteristics of rapists' parents.   **152.** Ardella Wright interviews, FBI Report, 27 April 1942, 12, and 23 Feb. 1942, 12; Minnie Gay interview, FBI Report, 27 April 1942, 11.   **153.** Calvin C. Hernton, *Sex and Racism in America* (New York: Grove, 1965), 84; Staples, *Black Masculinity*, 115; interview with Dr. Whipple (23 Sept. 1993).   **154.** Interview with Koonce (23 Aug. 1992); Ardella Wright interview, FBI Report, 23 Feb. 1942, 12.   **155.** This and next paragraph based on FBI Report, 16 June 1942, 1-3.

156. Interview with Koonce (23 Aug. 1992), for this and next paragraph. **157.** Interview with subject M.   **158.** Interviews with Koonce (23 Aug. 1992, 10 Aug. 1994).   **159.** Interviews with Rasberry, Andrew Walker (22 June 1992), James Walker (22 Aug. 1992), and Strong; Koonce to author, 25 Sept. 1993.   **160.** Military Record, 2; Wright Prison Record, 2.

161. Notice of no birth certificate on file for Cleo Wright or Ricelor Cleodas Watson, 13 Nov. 1992, Mississippi State Department of Health and Vital Records (author's possession); phone conversation with Bettye Teague, Arkansas Department of Health (20 Oct. 1992, Pine Bluff, Ark.); Koonce to author, 19 Oct. 1992. **162.** Court records revealed the marriage between Josephine Watson (no relation to Albert) and George Wright (1894), and divorces for Julia Wright and George J. Wright (1908) and Rinda Wright and Henry Wright (1918). No other information (including race) could be found for these Wrights, but the chronology makes the first two men unlikely candidates as Ricelor's father; and the fact that Henry Wright sued Rinda for divorce, instead of vice versa, suggests that neither was he. Marriage Records, Book I, 294; Chancery Court Records, Book P (12 Feb. 1908) and Book X (16 April 1918), JCC.   **163.** Interview with Hilton; phone conversation with James Walker (25 July 1993, Gethsemane, Ark.); *Pine Bluff* (Ark.) *Commercial*, 2 April 1972, 13.   **164.** Interview with subject M.   **165.** Interviews with Koonce (23 Aug. 1992) and James Simms (20 June 1992).

166. Arkansas State Penitentiary file, Humphrey Prison Record; Wright Prison Record, 2, 8.   **167.** Wright Prison Record, 4; Alonzo Watson interview, FBI Report, 3.   **168.** Cf. the letter to "Dear One," with Wright Prison Record, 8, for his limited spelling ability.   **169.** Phone conversation with Woolfolk and interviews with Koonce (23 Aug. 1992, 10 Aug. 1993); the interpretation is mine. Had Ricelor lived, he would have inherited one-fourth of Alozno's share of the Woolfolk property (37 acres) and one-sixth of Alonzo's inheritance of the Humphrey property (45 acres, half of which was allotted to Wylie, Temp Humphrey's son): 16.75 acres in all. **170.** Interview with Koonce (23 Aug. 1992). No record of this contact appears in the NAACP Papers; possibly Alonzo relinquished the idea and never approached the association.

171. Koonce to author, 15 Feb. 1993; my interpretation.   **172.** Interview with Koonce (10 Aug. 1993); my interpretation.   **173.** Brownmiller, *Against Our Will*,

348, 358, 360.   **174.** Hall, "The Mind That Burns," 337; Brownmiller, *Against Our Will*, 366; interviews with Sturgeon (19 May 1987, 8 June 1988, 19 July 1990, 14 Sept. 1992), for this and next paragraph.   **175.** Interview with Sturgeon (7 Nov. 1987); phone conversation with James Sturgeon.

176. Interviews with Sturgeon (7 Nov. 1987, 8 June 1988).   **177.** Interviews with Sturgeon (19 May 1987, 14 Sept. 1992).   **178.** Phone conversation with James Sturgeon.   **179.** Reed, Burgess, and Hartman, "Victim Assessment," 23; interview with Sturgeon (8 June 1988).   **180.** Interviews with Sturgeon (19 May 1987, 7 Nov. 1987, 8 June 1988).

181. Phone conversation with Laverne Sturgeon; interview with Sturgeon (14 Sept. 1992); Reed, Burgess, and Hartman, "Victim Assessment," 22-24.   **182.** Interviews with Sturgeon (19 July 1990, 14 Sept. 1992); phone conversation with James Sturgeon; phone conversation with Laverne Sturgeon.   **183.** American Psychiatric Association (APA), *Diagnostic and Statistical Manual of Mental Disorders*, 3d ed. rev. (Washington, D.C.: APA, 1987), 247-50; Zella Luria, Susan Friedman, and Mitchel D. Rose, *Human Sexuality* (New York: Wiley, 1987), 607-8; A.W. Burgess and L.L. Holmstrom, "Rape Trauma Syndrome," *American Journal of Psychiatry* 131 (1974): 981-86.   **184.** Groth, *Men Who Rape*, 24-25; interview with Dr. Whipple (22 Sept. 1993).   **185.** Phone conversation with James Sturgeon; interview with Koonce (23 Aug. 1992).

186. Dollard, *Caste and Class in a Southern Town*, 185; Wyatt-Brown, "The Mask of Obedience," 1249.   **187.** Interview with Dr. Whipple (22 Sept. 1993); Groth, *Men Who Rape*, 61, 104-9; Rollo May, *Man's Search for Himself* (New York: Norton, 1953), 250.   **188.** James Weldon Johnson, *Along This Way* (rpt.; New York: Da Capo Press, 1973), 170; Janet Saxe, review of *Black Rage* by William H. Grier and Price M. Cobbs, in *Black Scholar* 1 (March 1970): 58-62, and Davis, *Women, Race and Class*, 172-201, for criticism of authors—black males Grier, Cobbs, Hernton, and Cleaver, as well as Brownmiller—who distort the sexual dimension of black society, especially that of rapists.

Chapter 5   Burial

1. E.P. Coleman Jr. to Editor, *NYT*, 7 Feb. 1942, 16; Special Investigator to Forrest C. Donnell, 12 Feb. 1942, folder 3599, FCDP.   **2.** Kay, State Grand Jury Notes, 9-10 March 1942, 9, for testimony of Paul Bumbarger; H.C. Henry interview, FBI Report, 23 Feb. 1942, 47,   **3.** Bumbarger interview, FBI Report, 23 Feb. 1942, 47; Kay, State Grand Jury Notes, 9; interview with Bumbarger (6 Nov. 1987).   **4.** Interview with Clinton; *Atlanta Daily World*, n.d., TLF.   **5.** Phone conversation with subject I (8 June 1988).

6. Landon, "Clients, Colleagues, and Community," 84-91; Editorial, "An Unforgettable Crime," *Post-Dispatch*, 14 July 1942, 2B.   **7.** Tompkins and Tompkins, "An Informal Report," 3.   **8.** FBI Report, 8 June 1942, 1-3; interview with Griffen (18

May 1987).   **9.** George Scott interview, FBI Report, 23 Feb. 1942, 44; Ross, "Statement," 2; Kay, State Grand Jury Notes, 10, 12.   **10.** Kendall and Hobbs interviews, FBI Report, 23 Feb. 1942, 22, 34; *Standard*, 11 Jan. 1977, 8.

11. Interview with Dotson (18 May 1987); Bartlett interview, FBI Report, 23 Feb. 1942, 11.   **12.** *Post-Dispatch*, 30 Jan. 1942, 1.   **13.** Tip Keller and Leo Fisher interviews, FBI Report, 23 Feb. 1942, 43, 44; interview with Griffen (18 May 1987), about McClure.   **14.** Donnell, "Sikeston Notes"; informant TA interview, FBI Report, 23 Feb. 1942, 45.   **15.** The identities of lynchers, determined by examining several documents, have been masked with bogus first names and last initials, since no one was found guilty.

16. Kay, State Grand Jury Notes, 1, 2, 3, 7; Blanton interview, FBI Report, 23 Feb. 1942, 30.   **17.** Dace interview, FBI Report, 23 Feb. 1942, 17; Redmond, "Sikeston Lynching," 1; Ross, "Statement," 2.   **18.** Kay, State Grand Jury Notes, 2, 3; Blanton interview, FBI Report, 23 Feb. 1942, 81; Redmond, "Sikeston Lynching," 1.   **19.** Martin X. interview, FBI Report, 23 Feb. 1942, 37.   **20.** Kay, State Grand Jury Notes, 5, 6-11; informant TA interview, FBI Report, 4 June 1942, 3; Mike A. interview, FBI Report, 23 Feb. 1942, 46.

21. Kay, State Grand Jury Notes, 5, 12; Richard D. and Wade L. interviews, FBI Report, 13 March 1942, 4.   **22.** See Chapter 3; Boisaubin interview, FBI Report, 23 Feb. 1942, 19-20.   **23.** Quoted in Tompkins and Tompkins, "An Informal Report," 3.   **24.** Interviews with Dempster, Dotson (18 May 1987), and Blanton (18 May 1987).   **25.** Bumbarger, "Jail-Storming Mob Burns Negro Knifer"; Blanton interview, FBI Report, 23 Feb. 1942, 31; interviews with Mitchell (9 June 1988) and Blanton (6 Nov. 1987).

26. Barbara Welter, "The Cult of True Womanhood, 1820-1860," *American Quarterly* 18 (Summer 1966): 151-75; Jacquelyn Dowd Hall, *Revolt against Chivalry: Jessie Daniel Ames and the Women's Campaign against Lynching* (New York: Columbia Univ. Press, 1979), 291.   **27.** Anonymous to Forrest C. Donnell, 31 Jan. 1942, folder 3599, FCDP; Arthur F. Raper, *The Tragedy of Lynching* (rpt.; Montclair, N.J.: Peter Smith, 1969), 12-13; Teresa Montseny [Layton], "Hope's Daughters: Women in Collective Violence" (Mid-America Conference on History, Lawrence, Kan., 17 Sept. 1992), 27, quoting Allen D. Grimshaw.   **28.** Of 20, $N = 10$: 30 years (exact ages); $N = 14$: 33.7 years (ten exact ages and four estimated from data indicating one 30, one 42, and two 50). The median age without the estimates is 34. See, e.g., *Standard*, 6 Sept. 1941, 1.   **29.** Comments on age based on known data. Of $N = 20$: 10 unknown marital and parent status; 10 married, 6 with children.   **30.** *Sixteenth Census* (1940), *Population*, vol. 2, pt. 4, table 30, p. 436, shows median education of 8.5 years for all persons 25 years and older. Five of twenty lynchers (25%) had completed high school or its equivalent, a proportion higher than the 15% of the town population generally (636 of 4289).

31. Ibid., p. 9, for occupation categories, and table 30, p. 436, for Sikeston data. The comparison is based on 2,125 working males aged 14 and over with known occupations, including public emergency work. Of $N = 17$ v. city statistics: 7 (47%) proprietors/1 manager v. 283 (13.3%); 3 (17.6%) crafts v. 289 (13.6%); 2 professionals (11.8%) v. 112 (5.3%); 2 (11.8%) operatives v. 529 (24.9%); 1 (5.9%) service v. 116 (5.5%); 1 sales (5.9%) v. 319 (15.0%). The lynchers strikingly included no laborers (10% of all workers) or members of the other categories (such as domestic service workers) that together constituted the remaining 12.4% of all workers.   **32.** Phone conversation with subject B (8 June 1988); Richard D. interview, FBI Report, 13 March 1942, 4.   **33.** "Records of the First Baptist Church of Sikeston, 1937-1946"; interview with subject C.   **34.** "Church Register of the First Presbyterian Church" (Hunter Memorial) for example of Ned B.; (church records were found for only the largest congregations: First Baptist, First United Methodist, and Hunter Memorial Presbyterian); interview with Bartley.   **35.** W.G. Henderson to Forrest C. Donnell, 8 Feb. 1944, folder 310, FCDP.

36. Elbridge W. Bartley Jr. to author, 17 March 1992.   **37.** White, *Rope and Faggot*, 40-53, 246.   **38.** *Post-Dispatch*, 26 Jan. 1942, 3; interview with subject E. Of the eight who came from the area, one each originated in Campbell, Charleston, Morley, Sikeston, and Yount; the other three came from farms in Scott or New Madrid County.   **39.** Kay, State Grand Jury Notes, 1, 2, 6; interview with subject E. Roger Brown, *Social Psychology* (New York: Free Press, 1965), 758, contends that mob leadership "falls to those in whom the norms are weakest," identifying them as "persons of low status." But southerners outside their milieu, like Preston H., would also question Sikeston norms. And the other ringleaders—proprietor Nigel J. and salesman Ted C.—had considerable socioeconomic status; their challenge to the norms may have come from dominant if not authoritarian personalities. See McGovern, *Anatomy of a Lynching*, 9.   **40.** *Standard*, 27 Jan. 1942, 8.

41. Blanton and Kirk V. interviews, FBI Report, 23 Feb. 1943, 31-32, 42; Kay, State Grand Jury Notes, 3; interview with Mitchell (9 June 1988).   **42.** USJD Summary, 65: local press stories of 1941 and 1942, unspecified to protect the identities of Lou O. and Stan E.; Kay, State Grand Jury Notes, 1.   **43.** This and next paragraph based on interview with subject C.   **44.** Kay, State Grand Jury Notes, 1.   **45.** Lance W. interview, FBI Report, 23 Feb. 1942, 43.

46. Ibid.; Kay, State Grand Jury Notes, 7.   **47.** This and next paragraph based on interview with subject E.   **48.** Subject E interview, FBI Report, 13 March 1942, 4.   **49.** Kay, State Grand Jury Notes, 12; Synopsis, FBI Report, 13 March 1942, 1.   **50.** Ayers, *Vengeance and Justice*, 245; Bumbarger, "Jail-Storming Mob Burns Negro Knifer."

51. Interviews with Blanton (18 May 1987), and Frank Ferrell.   **52.** Hobbs interview, FBI Report, 23 Feb. 1942, 34; interviews with subject E and subject F; *Herald*, 29 Jan. 1942, 4.   **53.** Brundage, *Lynching in the New South*, 38; Dace, "Lynching of Cleo Wright," 3-4.   **54.** Brown, *Social Psychology*, 736, 754, 760; interview with Blanton (18 May 1987) for confirmation of Brown's theory.   **55.** Interview with subject F.

56. Kay, Grand Jury Notes, 11; *Post-Dispatch*, 26 Jan. 1942, 3. That the relative was the brother-in-law of Grace Sturgeon is disputed by contemporary sources. 57. Blanton interview, FBI Report, 23 Feb. 1942, 29; Kay, State Grand Jury Notes, 4; Dace, "Lynching of Cleo Wright," 3. 58. Ross, "Statement," 1; Mattie Smith interview, FBI Report, 23 Feb. 1942, 45. 59. Lewis Coser, *The Functions of Social Conflict* (Glencoe, Ill.: Free Press, 1956), 107; see also Roberta Senechal, *The Sociogenesis of a Race Riot: Springfield, Illinois, in 1908* (Urbana: Univ. of Illinois Press, 1990), 126-29. 60. Richard D. interview, FBI Report, 13 March 1942, 4; R. Lance Shotland, "Spontaneous Vigilantism: A Bystander Response to Criminal Behavior," in *Vigilante Politics*, ed. H. Jon Rosenbaum and Peter C. Sederberg (Philadelphia: Univ. of Pennsylvania Press, 1976), 43.

61. Croder interview, FBI Report, 13 March 1942, 5; Hall, "The Mind That Burns in Each Body," 335. 62. Ayers, *Vengeance and Justice*, 240-42; Williamson, *The Crucible of Race*, 309; interview with Bruce (6 Nov. 1987). 63. Grisham interview, FBI Report, 23 Feb. 1942, 40; Kay, State Grand Jury Notes, 2. 64. Morris, "Mob Violence at Sikeston," 2. 65. Interview with Blanton (18 May 1987).

66. Kay, State Grand Jury Notes, 3. 67. Tompkins and Tompkins, "An Informal Report," 2; interview with subject C. 68. Phone conversation with James D. Sturgeon (16 Dec. 1990, Chino, Calif.). 69. Interview with Frank Ferrell; Bertram Wyatt-Brown, *Southern Honor: Ethics and Behavior in the Old South* (New York: Oxford Univ. Press, 1982), 369; Brundage, *Lynching in the New South*, 11, 51-52; McGovern, *Anatomy of a Lynching*, 9. 70. Dace, "Lynching of Cleo Wright," 3; interview with subject F.

71. Brundage, *Lynching in the New South*, 52; Wright, *Racial Violence in Kentucky*, 101. 72. F.E. Mount and Bartley R. Schwegler telegram to Forrest C. Donnell, 7 Feb. 1942, folder 3604, FCDP; interviews with subject C and Dempster. 73. H. Jon Rosenbaum and Peter C. Sederberg, "Vigilantism," in Rosenbaum and Sederberg, *Vigilante Politics*, 7; interviews with Frank Ferrell and Clinton. 74. Interviews with Bartley and Lee. 75. Interviews with Ingram and Geraldine Schlosser.

76. Interviews with Sturgeon (18 May 1987) and subject E. 77. Tompkins and Tompkins, "An Informal Report," 2; *Missouri National Guard Yearbook, 1939*; Dace, "Lynching of Cleo Wright," 3. 78. *Herald*, 29 Jan. 1942, 1; Perrigan interview, FBI Report, 23 Feb. 1942, 4, 7; interviews with Jesse Whittley and subject E. 79. Interviews with Sturgeon (19 May 1987, 8 June 1988, 14 Sept. 1992) and interview with subject U. 80. See David W. Blight, *Frederick Douglass' Civil War: Keeping Faith in Jubilee* (Baton Rouge: Louisiana State Univ. Press, 1989), 44; the description of Douglass's perfect enemy (the slaveholder) approximates the lynchers' view of Wright.

81. Interviews with Clinton and Frank Ferrell; Kay, State Grand Jury Notes, 3. 82. Dace, "Lynching of Cleo Wright," 3; Hall, *Revolt against Chivalry*, 149-57. 83. Dr. Nienstedt and Blanton interviews, FBI Report, 23 Feb. 1942, 8, 30. 84. Phone conversation with Everett Nixon; interviews with Glenda Whittley and Gardner. 85. Carl

R. Johnson telegram to Forrest C. Donnell, 27 Jan. 1942, folder 3626, and Tucker to Donnell, 27 Jan. 1942, folder 3607, FCDP.

86. Sweets et al., "Sikeston, Missouri–Mob Violence," *Argus*, 6 Feb. 1942, 11, and 13 Feb. 1942, 8.   **87.** Donnell, "Sikeston Notes," 8.   **88.** Ross, "Statement," 2; *Call*, 30 Jan. 1942, 1.   **89.** Redmond, "Sikeston Lynching"; *Call*, 6 Feb. 1942, 1.   **90.** *Herald*, 5 Feb. 1942, 4, and 5 Feb. 1942, 3A.

91. *Post-Dispatch*, 1 Feb. 1942, 3A; *Standard*, 3 Feb. 1942, 4; *St. Louis Globe Democrat*, 2 Feb. 1942, FBI File.   **92.** Henry D. Espy to Donnell, 13 March 1942, and Donnell to Espy, 19 March 1942, folder 3626, FCDP.   **93.** *Standard*, 19 Nov. 1985, 5; "Troopers: Former and Present," in *Missouri State Highway Patrol, 1931-1981: 50th Anniversary* (commemorative yearbook), Government Documents, Meyer Library, Southwest Missouri State University; "Records of the Sikeston First Baptist Church"; *Argus*, 13 March 1942, 7.   **94.** Interview with Sturgeon (19 May 1987). This and the next three paragraphs are based on Dace, "Lynching of Cleo Wright," 1, and Dace interview, FBI Report, 23 Feb. 1942, 13-17.   **95.** Redmond, "Sikeston Lynching," 2; *Call*, 30 Jan. 1942, 1; Fry, *Night Riders in Black Folk History*, 154-69.

96. Dace, "Lynching of Cleo Wright," 4; Blanton interview, FBI Report, 23 Feb. 1942, 31.   **97.** Tandy, "Lynching of Cleo Wright at Sikeston," 1; Greim, "Mob Violence at Sikeston," 1; Rev. Kater E. Crump, untitled statement, n.d., MSHP. Crump served the Second Baptist Church (St. John's Missionary), having left the First Baptist Church (West End Missionary) some time after 1939; Rev. C.H. Flowers was pastor at First Baptist in 1942.   **98.** Greim, "Mob Violence at Sikeston," 1.   **99.** *Call*, 30 Jan. 1942, 1.   **100.** Dace, "Lynching of Cleo Wright," 4; Harry C. Blanton to Attorney General, 20 March 1942, USED.

101. Dace, "Lynching of Cleo Wright," 3; interviews with Frank Ferrell and subject D; *Argus*, 13 March 1942, 7, quoting Dace.   **102.** *Post-Dispatch*, 5 Feb. 1942, 3A, quoting Ralph E. Bailey; interview with Jesse Whittley.   **103.** *Circuit Court Criminal Record*, 11:238; *Herald*, 30 July 1942, 1.   **104.** Irwin L. Langbein memorandum for Victor W. Rotnem, 8 May 1942, 2, USIP.   **105.** *Argus*, 13 March 1942, 7.

106. Frank McCallister, "Report on Caruthersville, Missouri, Investigation" (n.d.), 6, reel 20, STFU; interview with Blanton (18 May 1987).   **107.** Sweets et al., "Sikeston, Missouri—Mob Violence," 3.   **108.** *Atlanta Daily World*, 5 Feb. 1942, TLF; Editorial, "The Grand Jury," *Herald*, 5 March 1942, 4; *Post-Dispatch*, 30 Jan. 1942, 3A.   **109.** *Standard*, 11 Jan. 1977, 8; interview with Bill Ferrell.   **110.** Hobbs interview, FBI Report, 23 Feb. 1942, 34.

111. Interview with Griffen (6 June 1988); *Herald*, 29 Jan. 1942, 1, and 5 March 1942, 1; Kay, State Grand Jury Notes, 10.   **112.** John Hobbs, Lester Miller, and Jim Robert interviews, FBI Report, 23 Feb. 1942, 34, 35; Harry C. Blanton to Attorney General, 20 March 1942, USED.   **113.** Blanton interview, FBI Report, 23 Feb. 1942, 29; Greim, "Mob Violence at Sikeston," 1.   **114.** Tandy, "Lynching of Cleo Wright," 1; Wallace interview, FBI Report, 23 Feb. 1942, 24.   **115.** Hobbs interview, FBI Report, 23 Feb. 1942, 35.

116. Interview with Blanton (6 Nov. 1987); Kay, State Grand Jury Notes, 10. 117. Interview with Griffen (5 Nov. 1987); Cleo Wright, No. 287, Prisoner List, 1940, SCJ, for Wright's county jail stay from 18 May to 16 July 1940; interview with Bom; Brundage, *Lynching in the New South*, 180. 118. Tompkins and Tompkins, "An Informal Report," 3. 119. Dace interview, FBI Report, 23 Feb. 1942, 15, 16, 17; *Post-Dispatch*, 11 Feb. 1942, 3A; *Call*, 13 Feb. 1942, 1. 120. *Herald*, 19 Feb. 1942, 4.

121. Wendell Berge memorandum for J. Edgar Hoover, 10 Feb. 1942, 1, FBIF; USJD Summary, 4; *Roanoke World News*, 16 April 1942, TLF. 122. *Standard*, 14 Sept. 1953, 1; FBI Report, 27 April 1942, 2. Kendall had a half-brother and a half-sister. 123. Interviews with Blanton (13 June 1990), Dempster, and Griffen (18 May 1987). 124. FBI Report, 23 Feb. 1942, 22, and 27 April 1942, 13; interviews with Dempster, Dotson (18 May 1987), and Ingram. 125. *Standard*, 28 Nov. 1982, 16; Wallace and informant TA interviews, FBI Report, 23 Feb. 1942, 23, 25, 46; FBI Report, 27 April 1942, 2. (FBI agents wrongly recorded his birth date as 1912); interviews with Dempster and Bumbarger (6 Nov. 1987).

126. Kendall interview, FBI Report, 23 Feb. 1942, 20-22; *Post-Dispatch*, 27 Jan. 1942, 4C. 127. This paragraph is based on Wallace interview, FBI Report, 23 Feb. 1942, 23-25. 128. Langbein memorandum for Rotnem, 8 May 1942, 1, USIP. 129. Wallace interview, FBI Report, 23 Feb. 1942, 24; Kendall interview, FBI Report, 27 April 1942, 12; U.S. Attorney, 22 April 1942, Index File (March-June, 1942), USJD. 130. Jacob M. Lashly to Wendell Berge, 30 March 1942, USIP.

131. Dace, "Lynching of Cleo Wright," 2. 132. Hobbs interview, FBI Report, 23 Feb. 1942, 34; FBI Report, 27 April 1942, 5. 133. Blanton interview, FBI Report, 23 Feb. 1942, 29; Dace, "Lynching of Cleo Wright," 4; Kendall interview, FBI Report, 23 Feb. 1942, 21. 134. Mike A. and Wallace interviews, FBI Report, 23 Feb. 1942, 46, 24. 135. Dace and Kendall interviews, FBI Report, 23 Feb. 1942, 17, 22.

136. Langbein memorandum to Rotnem, 8 May 1942, 1, USIP. 137. Thomas Scott (former Scott County sheriff and warden of the State Penitentiary), Dace and Ardella Wright interviews, FBI Report, 27 April 1942, 8-9, 4, 12. 138. USJD Summary, 4. 139. Raper, *The Tragedy of Lynching*, 14. 140. Grisham and Wallace interviews, FBI Report, 23 Feb. 1942, 40, 23.

141. Interview with Bumbarger (6 Nov. 1987). 142. *Standard*, 27 Jan. 1942, 8; *Afro-American*, n.d., and *Macon Telegraph*, n.d., TLF. 143. Wallace and Kendall interviews, FBI Report, 23 Feb. 1942, 23, 21. 144. FBI Report, 27 April 1942, 10, 12-13. Agents also verified that "a number of 'sleepers'" occupied the regular cells when Wright was placed in the women's room. 145. Wallace and Hobbs interviews, FBI Report, 23 Feb. 1942, 24, 34.

146. Presnell interview, FBI Report, 23 Feb. 1942, 34. 147. Hobbs and Blanton interviews, FBI Report, 23 Feb. 1942, 34, 33. 148. Dace interview, FBI Report, 27 April 1942, 4. 149. Hobbs interview, FBI Report, 23 Feb. 1942, 34, and 27 April 1942, 5; Special Agent, confidential memorandum, 29 April 1942, 2, FBIF. 150. Jo-

seph L. Matthews, informant TA, Dace, and Blanton interviews, FBI Report, 27 Apr. 1942, 3, 9, 5.

151. FBI Report, 16 May 1942, 4-5, for black resident (name expunged); interviews with Griffen (18 May 1987) and Dotson (18 May 1987).   **152.** Dace and Claude McManus interviews, FBI Report, 27 April 1942, 3, 6;   **153.** Bartlett and Rockwood (quoting Kendall) interviews, FBI Report, 27 April 1942, 6, 8; see also 7; **154.** Blanton interview, FBI Report, 23 Feb. 1942, 33; Matthews interview, FBI Report, 27 April 1942, 3. In January 1942, Kendall received $100 per month as did his patrolmen Beck, Lewis, and Perrigan, and $10 less than Assistant Chief Wallace: Sikeston City Council, Minutes, 2 Feb. 1942, SCH.   **155.** Informant TA interview, FBI Report, 27 April 1942, 9; City Council, Minutes, 6 April 1938, SCH. Ward 2, in which most black voters resided, voted heavily for Kendall in 1938, his last contested election, but so did Wards 1, 3, and 4; black and white voters together reelected him over George L. Dye 1,993 to 1,133, Ward 2 contributing 487 or 65% of its ballots for 24.4% of his total.

156. Interview with Blanton (13 June 1990); Bartlett interview, FBI Report, 27 April 1942, 6, and 7 for the white source (name expunged).   **157.** Sikeston City Attorney W.P. Wilkerson interview, FBI Report, 27 April 1942, 11. Officers' ages: Kendall, 64; Lewis, 56; Beck, 52; Perrigan, 37, Wallace, 31.   **158.** FBI Report, 27 April 1942, 2; City Council, Minutes, 2 Feb. 1942, SCH; interview with Griffen (18 May 1987). Bartlett was discharged in August 1941 and reappointed two months later after council members investigated the need for "police protection" in Sunset and the "character" of applicants for the position: City Council, Minutes, 4 Aug. 1941, 2 Sept. 1942, and 3 Nov. 1941, SCH.   **159.** Bartlett interview, FBI Report, 23 Feb. 1942, 11; interviews with Gardner and with Dotson (18 May 1987).   **160.** Wallace and Kendall interviews, FBI Report, 23 Feb. 1942, 24, 21.

161. Interview with subject F.   **162.** Interviews with Bumbarger (6 Nov. 1987) and subject O; Kendall interview, FBI Report, 23 Feb. 1942, 21.   **163.** Rotnem to Lashly, 28 March 1942, USIP.   **164.** *Call*, 22 May 1942, TLF; *Standard*, 26 May 1942, 4.   **165.** *Standard*, 22 May 1942, 1, quoting Dr. H.E. Reuber; Chaney, *History of Sikeston*, 57.

166. Justice Department Press Release, 30 July 1942, USJD.   **167.** *Herald*, 29 Jan. 1942, 1, and 5 Feb. 1942, 5; *Standard*, 6 Feb. 1942, 1.   **168.** City Council, Minutes, 2 Feb. 1942 and 16 Feb. 1942, SCH; *Herald*, 5 Feb. 1942, 4. Council also reappointed Wallace, Beck, Lewis, and Perrigan (without mention of Bartlett) when their terms expired in April and added William Carson to the force: City Council, Minutes, 9 April 1942, SCH.   **169.** City Council, Minutes, 2 Feb. 1942 and 4 May 1942, SCH.   **170.** City Council, Minutes, 2 April 1940 and 8 April 1942, SCH; *Herald*, 9 April 1942, 1. Total votes cast in the three elections declined from 3,278 in 1938 to 2,096 in 1940 to 1,698 in 1942. Kendall received slightly over 1,600 in 1942, as did all unopposed candidates; only Mayor Presnell faced an opponent, Charles H. Butler, whom he defeated with 65 percent of the vote: 1,104 to 594.

171. City Council, Minutes, 4 April 1944, SCH. Of 1,348 votes cast, Wallace received 760, Beck 209, and Kendall 379. That Wallace received his highest number (253) and percentage (66.6) of votes from Ward 2, which included Sunset Addition, indicated further how little the lynching influenced the election. **172.** City Council, Minutes, 2 April 1946, SCH. Of 3,505 votes cast, Wallace received 2,492, Henry Cooper 738, George Seufert 160, and Tice Martin 115. Again Wallace's highest number (952) and percentage (80) came from voters in Ward 2. **173.** Interview with Blanton (6 Nov. 1987).

Chapter 6. The Blantons

1. Brundage, *Lynching in the New South*, 221; Blaine A. Brownell, *The Urban Ethos in the South, 1920-1930* (Baton Rouge: Louisiana State Univ. Press, 1975), xv-xxi, 217-20. **2.** "Sentiment in Sikeston," *St. Louis Star-Times*, 29 Jan. 1942, Box A381, NAACP. **3.** This and next two paragraphs are based on interviews with David E. Blanton (18 May 1987, 13 Dec. 1993). Blanton is unsure of his grandmother's maiden name. See also *Herald*, 15 Jan. 1948, 4; *Standard*, 20 Jan. 1962, 1, 6; and Robert M. Crisler, "Missouri's Little Dixie," *Missouri Historical Review* 42 (Jan. 1948): 130-39. **4.** *Standard*, 1 March 1973, 1, 16. **5.** Interview with Bumbarger (6 Nov 1987); Shoemaker, *Missouri and Missourians*, 3:292, 293; *Standard*, 17 Feb. 1962, 1. Denman was born near Marquand (Madison County) 10 July 1879, son of Jabez H. Denman and Sarah King; he married Minnie Watts in 1901, and they raised six children before her death twenty years later; he married Ella Sackman in 1923. The *Herald* began publication in 1903.

6. *Standard*, 13 March 1942, 2, and 9 Jan. 1948, 1. **7.** *Standard*, 12 Aug. 1991, 1; interview with Bumbarger (6 Nov. 1987). **8.** "The P.C. Editor Says," *Standard*, 3 Oct. 1941, 1, and 9 Jan. 1942, 1. **9.** Ogilvie, "Development of the Southeast Missouri Lowlands," 261; Snow, *From Missouri*. 273; interview with Crews. **10.** Ogilvie, "Development of the Southeast Missouri Lowlands," 258-59, 378-79; Chaney, *History of Sikeston*, 126.

11. "The P.C. Editor Says," *Standard*, 2 Sept. 1941, 1; 9 Jan. 1942, 1; and 9 Sept. 1941, 1. **12.** Interview with Dotson (18 May 1987). **13.** "The P.C. Editor Says," *Standard*, 9 Dec. 1941, 1, and editorial, 4; "The P.C. Editor Says," *Standard*, 12 Dec. 1941, 1. **14.** Editorial, *Standard*, 23 Jan. 1942, 4. **15.** "The P.C. Editor Says," *Standard*, 29 May 1942, 1; 12 May 1942, 1; 17 March 1942, 1; and 9 Dec. 1941, 1. **16.** *Standard*, 9 Jan. 1948, 1; interview with Blanton (13 Dec. 1993). **17.** Interviews with Crews, Bumbarger (6 Nov. 1987), and Blanton (13 June 1990); *Standard*, 13 March 1942, 2, and 12 Jan. 1948, 1; "Records of the Sikeston First Baptist Church." Although a church member, C.L. was a only a nominal Baptist until near his death. **18.** *Des Moines Bystander*, 29 Jan. 1942, TLF; interviews with Blanton (13 June 1990) and Bumbarger (6 Nov. 1987); *Standard*, 27 Nov. 1978, 1; "The P.C. Editor Says," *Standard*, 9 Dec. 1941, 1; phone conversation with Bumbarger (19 Jan.

1995, Memphis).   **19.** Interviews with Blanton (13 June 1990, 18 May 1987).
20. *Standard*, 26 May 1942, 1; Blanton interview, FBI Report, 23 Feb. 1942, 28; interview with Blanton (13 Dec. 1993). David married Mary Anna on 15 June 1940; David Jr. was born in 1941 and Kate (Dempsey) in 1947.

21. Interviews with Blanton (18 May 1987), Dotson (18 May 1987), and Griffen (18 May 1987).   **22.** Interviews with Blanton (18 May 1987, 13 June 1990, 13 Dec. 1993); *Standard*, 20 Jan. 1962, 1, 6; interview with Geraldine Schlosser. Mary Agnes was born 21 Jan. 1872.   **23.** Interview with Blanton (13 June 1990); *Standard*, 20 March 1973, 1; *Who's Who in America*, ed. Albert N. Marquis (Chicago: Marquis, 1942), 337.   **24.** Interview with Blanton (13 June 1990).   **25.** U.S. Falls to Forrest C. Donnell, 26 Jan. 1942, folder 3627, FCDP; *Call*, 6 Feb. 1942, 1; Sweets et al., "Sikeston, Missouri—Mob Violence."

26. *Post-Dispatch*, 26 Jan. 1942, 3; Peter F. Keyes to Donnell, 27 Jan. 1942, folder 3607, FCDP.   **27.** *Post-Dispatch*, 27 Jan. 1942, 4C, and "Missouri Is Not 'Satisfied,'" 28 Jan. 1942, 2C.   **28.** "Sentiment in Sikeston," *St. Louis Star-Times*, 29 Jan. 1942, Box A381, NAACP; *Pittsburgh Courier*, 7 Feb. 1942, 5, for *Star-Times* reprint.   **29.** E.T. Summytt and William Mickens to Walter White, 29 Jan. 1942, Box A381, NAACP; Tompkins and Tompkins, "An Informal Report," 1.   **30.** NAACP Press Release, 13 Feb. 1942, 2, and [Charlotte B. Crump], "Sikeston, USA," n.d. [24 Feb. 1942], 2, Box A381, NAACP.

31. "Lynching and the Blanton Clan," *Chicago Sunday Bee*, 22 Feb. 1942, FBIF. **32.** "Another Blot on Missouri," *Argus*, 13 March 1942, 8.   **33.** Donnell, "Sikeston Notes," 7; *NYT*, 26 Jan. 1942, 17; "Grand Jury Lynch Probe Is Indicated," *Standard* clipping, n.d., FBIF; *Philadelphia Tribune*, n.d., and *Dayton Newsweek*, n.d., TLF. **34.** Blanton to Donnell, 28 Jan. 1942, folder 3623, FCDP; interview with Blanton (6 Nov. 1987).   **35.** Blanton to Donnell, 30 Jan. 1942, folder 3622, FCDP.

36. *Post-Dispatch*, 30 Jan. 1942, 3A.   **37.** *Herald*, 12 Feb. 1942, 1; *Standard*, 13 Feb. 1942, 5; *Post-Dispatch*, 6 Feb. 1942, 2C.   **38.** Thomas F. Soapes, "Barak Mattingly and the Failure of the Missouri Republicans," *Missouri Historical Review* 87 (Jan. 1993): 168-87; interviews with Blanton (6 Nov. 1987, 13 Dec. 1993); Blanton to Roy McKittrick, 13 and 16 Feb. 1942, folder 3624, FCDP.   **39.** Donnell to Carl R. Johnson, 27 Jan. 1942, and Donnell telegram to J.E. Mitchell, 28 Jan. 1942, folder 3623, FCDP. **40.** A Citizen to Donnell, n.d., folder 3599, and Donnell to Blanton, 3 Feb. 1942, folder 3622, FCDP; *Post-Dispatch*, 7 Feb. 1942, 3A.

41. Donnell to Blanton, 7 March 1942, folder 3627, FCDP; James Rowe Jr. memorandum for J. Edgar Hoover, 2 March 1942, FBIF.   **42.** Blanton to Donnell, 12 March 1942, and Donnell to Blanton, 14 March 1942, folder 3624, FCDP.   **43.** Denman to Donnell, 18 March 1942, folder 3606, FCDP.   **44.** Justice Department Press Release, 11 March 1942, FBIF; Donnell to Biddle, 13 March and 8 April 1942, USIP. **45.** Donnell to Denman, 31 March and 1 May 1942, folder 3606, FCDP.

46. "That Sikeston Grand Jury," *Argus*, 6 March 1942, 8; "Department of Justice

Enters Lynching Case," *Argus*, 17 April 1942, 8. **47.** Redmond, "Sikeston Lynching," 2. Redmond's information came from Rev. J.B. Ross. **48.** NAACP Press Release, 13 Feb. 1942, 2, Box A381, NAACP; Marshall to Berge, 9 March 1942, USJD. **49.** Summytt to Reeves, 1 March 1942, and Marshall to Summytt, 9 March 1942, Box A381, NAACP. **50.** Rotnem to Berge, 12 March 1942, and Berge memorandum for J. Edgar Hoover, 13 March 1942, USJD.

51. Harry C. Blanton to Wendell Berge, 11 March 1942, USED. **52.** Blanton to Berge, 11 March and 20 March 1942, USED. **53.** Blanton to Berge, 25 March, 6 and 7 April 1942, USED. **54.** Blanton to Berge, 8 May and 29 June 1942, USED; Berge memorandum for FBI Director, 20 June 1942, FBIF. **55.** Harry C. Blanton to the Editor, *Post-Dispatch*, 17 July 1942, 2C.

56. Blanton to Berge, 24 July 1942, USED; "An Unforgettable Crime," *Post-Dispatch*, 14 July 1942, 2B; Florence A. Moseley, "Where Stands the Sikeston Case?" *Post-Dispatch*, 23 July 1942, 2C. **57.** Lashly to Berge and Rotnem, 17 July 1942, USIP; Blanton to Berge, 27 July 1942, and "Unfinished Business," *Post-Dispatch*, 25 July 1942, USED. **58.** Blanton to Berge, 24 July 1942, USED; Blanton to Rotnem, 31 July 1942, and "Lessons of the Sikeston Lynching," *St. Louis Globe-Democrat*, 31 July 1942, USED. **59.** *Standard*, 17 April 1942, 1. **60.** John Edgar Hoover to Special Agent in Charge, 16 Feb. 1942, FBIF; Harry C. Blanton to Rotnem, 20 March 1942, USED; Blanton to Berge, 9 June 1942, and Berge memorandum for FBI Director, 20 June 1942, FBIF.

61. R.P. Kramer memorandum for D.M. Ladd, 5 May 1942, FBIF. **62.** Special Agent (Cape Girardeau), confidential memorandum, 29 April 1942, FBIF. **63.** Kramer memorandum for Ladd, 5 May 1942, FBIF. **64.** Special Agent (Cape Girardeau), confidential memorandum, 29 April 1942, FBIF. **65.** Harry C. Blanton to Jacob M. Lashly, 29 April 1942, USED; *Standard*, 14 April 1942, 1; *Post-Dispatch*, 11 May 1942, 3A.

66. Berge memorandum for FBI Director, 17 July 1942, FBIF. **67.** Langbein to Rotnem, 12 May 1942, USIP. **68.** Harry C. Blanton to Rotnem, 20 March 1942, USED. **69.** Interview with David E. Blanton (13 June 1990); Harry C. Blanton to Berge, 29 June and 24 July 1942, USED. **70.** Interview with Blanton (13 June 1990).

71. Harry C. Blanton to Berge, 9 June 1942, FBIF. **72.** "The P.C. Editor Says," *Standard*, 30 Jan., 6 and 10 Feb., and 31 March 1942 (p. 1 in all cases); interviews with Blanton (13 June 1990, 18 May 1987); A Citizen to Forrest C. Donnell, n.d., folder 3599, FCDP; Kay, State Grand Jury Notes, 7-8; Editorial, *Standard*, 3 Feb. 1942, 4. **73.** "The P.C. Editor Says," *Standard*, 3 Feb. 1942, 1; interviews with Griffen (18 May 1987) and Sturgeon (19 May 1987). **74.** "Lynch Law," *Standard*, 10 Feb. 1942, 2; *Call*, 30 Jan. 1942, 1. **75.** Blanton to Donnell, 30 Jan. 1942, folder 3622, FCDP; Editorial, *Standard*, 30 Jan. 1942, 4.

76. "The P.C. Editor Says," *Standard*, 3 Feb. 1942, 1; Bledsoe in *St. Louis Globe-Democrat*, 2 Feb. 1942, 4A. **77.** Blanton to Donnell, 12 March 1942, folder 3624, FCDP. **78.** Interview with Blanton (6 Nov. 1987); Kay, State Grand Jury Notes, 9.

79. "The P.C. Editor Says," *Standard*, 6 Feb. 1942, 1; Editorial, *Standard*, 24 Feb. 1942, 4.   **80.** "The P.C. Editor Says," *Standard*, 3 Feb. 1942, 1.

81. Interviews with Blanton (18 May 1987, 13 June 1990).   **82.** *Standard*, 30 Jan. and 6 Feb. 1942, 2, 4; "The P.C. Editor Says," *Standard*, 3 and 6 Feb. 1942, 1. **83.** Interview with Bumbarger (6 Nov. 1987); "The P.C. Editor Says," *Standard*, 24 March 1942, 1; *Argus*, 15 May 1942.   **84.** Blanton interview, FBI Report, 23 Feb. 1942, 29-30; Wallis, "Mob Violence at Sikeston," 3; USJD Summary, 3; Dace interview, FBI Report, 23 Feb. 1942, 15.   **85.** Harry C. Blanton to Rotnem, 20 March 1942, USED; Kendall and informant TA interviews, FBI Report, 23 Feb. 1942, 21, 45, Art U. interview, FBI Report, 13 March 1942, 5; interview with Clinton.

86. Interview with Blanton (13 June 1990).   **87.** *Post-Dispatch*, 30 Jan. 1942, 3A; interview with Blanton (13 Dec. 1993).   **88.** Interview with Bumbarger (6 Nov. 1987).   **89.** Interviews with Blanton (18 May 1987, 13 Dec. 1942).   **90.** *Standard*, 12 Jan. 1948, 1, quoting Rev. E.D. Owen.

91. Interview with Blanton (13 Dec. 1993); "The P.C. Editor Says," *Standard*, 27 and 30 Jan. 1942, n.p., NAACP.   **92.** *Post-Dispatch*, 27 Jan. 1942, 4C, and 30 Jan. 1942, 3A.   **93.** *Herald*, 5 Feb. 1942, 1, 4; *Post-Dispatch*, 5 Feb. 1942, 3A.   **94.** "The P.C. Editor Says," *Standard*, 10 Feb. 1942, 1.   **95.** Editor, *Standard*, 24 Feb. 1942, 4, and 6 Feb. 1942, 1.

96. *Herald*, 12 March 1942, 4; "The P.C. Editor Says," *Standard*, 13 March 1942, 1.   **97.** Denman to Donnell, 18 March 1942, folder 3606, FCDP; "The P.C. Editor Says," *Standard*, 20 March 1942, 1.   **98.** Willamson, *The Crucible of Race*, 111-19. **99.** "The P.C. Editor Says," *Standard*, 30 Jan. 1942, 1, and 10 Feb. 1942, 1. **100.** Fredrickson, *The Black Image in the White Mind*, 275; "The P.C. Editor Says," *Standard*, 10 Jan. 1942, 1, and 9 June 1942, 1.

101. Genovese, *The Political Economy of Slavery*, 31.   **102.** Clement Eaton, "Mob Violence in the Old South," *Mississippi Valley Historical Review* 29(Dec. 1942): 356; Fredrickson, *The Black Image in the White Mind*, 293.   **103.** Brown, *Modernization*, 7, 9-11.   **104.** David H. Fischer, *Growing Old in America* (New York: Oxford Univ. Press, 1977), 221; Snow, *From Missouri*, 258.   **105.** Interview with Bumbarger (6 Nov. 1987).

106. Interview with Blanton (18 May 1987).   **107.** Blanton to Donnell, 30 Jan. 1942, folder 3622, FCDP; Kay, State Grand Jury Notes, 7-8.   **108.** Denman to Donnell, 18 May 1942, folder 3606, FCDP.   **109.** "The P.C. Editor Says," *Standard*, 30 Jan. 1942, 1; Editorial, *Standard*, 3 Feb. 1942, 4.   **110.** Brown, *Modernization*, 11.

111. Jack Temple Kirby, *Darkness at the Dawning: Race and Reform in the Progressive South* (New York: Lippincott, 1972), 4, 25.   **112.** Brown, *Modernization*, 13, 14-22.   **113.** *Standard*, 1 March 1973, 1, 16. The *Standard* incorporated in 1948 (the year of C.L. Blanton's death), purchased and combined with Denman's *Herald* in 1954, and adopted offset printing in 1964.   **114.** *Standard*, 9 Jan. 1948, 1. **115.** Dewey W. Grantham, *Southern Progressivism: The Reconciliation of Progress and*

Tradition (Knoxville: Univ. of Tennessee Press, 1983), 421; interview with Blanton (13 June 1990). **116.** See Matthew Mancini, *Alexis de Tocqueville* (New York: Twayne, 1994), 23-24, for a brilliant application of Weber's theory to a historical figure. **117.** Lifton, *History and Human Survival*, 58-59, 71, 73, 74-75. **118.** Ibid., 58-59, 66, 67, 70-71, 75-76; Editorial, *Standard*, 9 Dec. 1941, 4. **119.** Brownell, *The Urban Ethos in the South*, 217-20; Lifton, *History and Human Survival*, 71, 73. **120.** *Herald*, 29 Jan. 1942, 4, and 5 Feb. 1942, 4.

121. *Standard*, 6 Feb. 1942, 1. Denman, E.P. Coleman Jr., and J.F. Cox Sr. joined to mobilize civic-commercial elites. **122.** Lifton, *History and Human Survival*, 71. **123.** Wallhausen to Donnell, and Donnell to Wallhausen, 26 Jan. 1942, folder 3604, FCDP. **124.** *Standard*, 10 Feb. 1942, 2; 17 Feb. 1942, 2; and 17 March 1942, 4. **125.** Cook to Mr. Walton, 25 Oct. 1941, Box 5, Cook Collection, MHSL; *Standard*, 14 Oct. 1941, 8, and 21 Oct. 1941, 4.

126. Quoted in *Standard*, 10 Feb. 1942, 2. **127.** Cook to Mr. Lewis, 5 and 17 Feb. 1942, Box 13, Cook Collection, MHSL; interview with Sturgeon (18 May 1987). Sturgeon's confusion of fact with fancy was perhaps caused by her need to reinvent portions of the past so as to cope with it: therapy for rape trauma syndrome. **128.** Cook to Mr. Lewis, 19 March 1942, Box 13, Cook Collection, MHSL. **129.** *Charleston Enterprise-Courier*, 29 Jan. 1942, FBIF. Cook also served on the St. Louis Race Relations Commission from its inception in Sept. 1943 to Sept. 1946, when she resigned. See Patricia L. Adams, "Fighting for Democracy in St. Louis: Civil Rights during World War II," *Missouri Historical Review* 80 (Oct. 1985): 67, 73-74; Cook to Edwin B. Meissner, 26 Sept. 1946, Box 9, Cook Collection, MHSL. **130.** Sheldon Hackney, "Southern Violence," *American Historical Review* 74 (Feb. 1969): 924-25; William Faulkner, *Intruder in the Dust* (New York: Random House, 1948), 149.

131. Roark, *Masters without Slaves*, 207; Lifton, *History and Human Survival*, 61-65, 75, 77. **132.** *Standard*, 30 Jan. 1942, 2; "The P.C. Editor Says," *Standard*, 3 Feb. 1942, 1. **133.** "The P.C. Editor Says," *Standard*, 6 Feb. 1942, 1; reprints in *Standard*, 3 and 10 Feb. 1942. **134.** *Herald*, 29 Jan. 1942, 4. **135.** *Herald*, 2 April 1942, 4.

136. City Council, Minutes, 6 April 1942, SCH; *Herald*, 9 April 1942, 1; *Standard*, 10 April 1942, 1. **137.** Blanton and Rockwood interviews, FBI Report, 27 April 1942, 4, 8; *Standard*, 28 April 1942, 1; "The P.C. Editor Says," *Standard*, 31 March 1942, 1. **138.** City Council, Minutes, 16 March 1942, 1, 5, 22, and 29 June 1942, SCH; *Herald*, 11 June 1942, 1; 25 June 1942, 4; and 2 July 1942, 1. **139.** *Herald*, 11 June 1942, 1; 6 Aug. 1942, 1; and 5 Nov. 1942, 1. **140.** Interview with Blanton (18 May 1987); *Herald*, 30 July 1942, 4.

141. Interview with subject C. **142.** Interview with Blanton (13 Dec. 1993).

Chapter 7. From Missouri

1. Claude McKay, "The Lynching," in *Black American Literature: 1760-Present*, ed. Ruth Miller (Beverly Hills: Glencoe, 1971), 336; Raper, *The Tragedy of Lynching*, 1; Jessie Daniel Ames, *The Changing Character of Lynching. Review of Lynching, 1931-1941* (rpt.; New York: AMS Press, 1973), 33. **2.** Ayers, *Vengeance and Justice*, 255; Brundage, *Lynching in the New South*, 13; Montell, *Killings*, 165. **3.** *Call*, 31 Jan. 1942, 1; Wyllie, "Race and Class Conflict on Missouri's Cotton Frontier," 186. **4.** E.g., see *Standard*, 27 Jan. 1941, 1; Brundage, *Lynching in the New South*, 80. **5.** Ayers, *Vengeance and Justice*, 244; Neil R. McMillen, *Dark Journey: Black Mississippians in the Age of Jim Crow* (Urbana: Univ. of Illinois Press, 1990), 226; Williamson, *The Crucible of Race*, 189.

6. Perrigan interview, FBI Report, 23 Feb. 1942, 4; interview with Jesse Whittley. **7.** Erikson, *Childhood and Society*, 231, 236-37, 241-45; Robert Coles, "It's the Same, but It's Different," 272, and Erik H. Erikson, "The Concept of Identity in Race Relations: Notes and Queries," 231 (quoting C. Van Woodward), both in *The Negro American*, ed. Talcott Parsons and Kenneth B. Clark (Boston: Beacon Press, 1967). **8.** Brundage, *Lynching in the New South*, 81. **9.** Allison Davis and John Dollard, *Children of Bondage: The Personality Development of Negro Youth in the Urban South* (rpt.; New York: Harper & Row, 1964), 247. **10.** Erikson, "The Concept of Identity in Race Relations," 242; Harris, *Exorcising Blackness*, 25; Groth and Birnbaum, *Men Who Rape*, 2.

11. Fanon, *Black Skin, White Masks*, 72; Richard M. Brown, *Strain of Violence: Historical Studies of American Violence and Vigilantism* (New York: Oxford Univ. Press, 1975), 216. **12.** Allison Davis, *Leadership, Love, and Aggression* (New York: Harper & Row, 1983), 12; Groth and Birnbaum, *Men Who Rape*, 5. **13.** Abram Kardiner and Lionel Ovesey, *The Mark of Oppression: Explorations in the Personality of the American Negro* (Cleveland; World, 1962), 368-87; John Dollard et al., *Frustration and Aggression* (New Haven, Conn.: Yale Univ. Press, 1939), 89. **14.** Hall, "The Mind That Burns in Each Body," 337; Harris, *Exorcising Blackness*, 20. **15.** Wright, *Racial Violence in Kentucky*, 81.

16. Smead, *Blood Justice*, 93-94. **17.** Peter Loewenberg, "The Psychology of Racism," in *The Great Fear: Race in the Mind of America*, ed. Gary B. Nash and Richard Weiss (New York: Holt, Rinehart & Winston, 1970), 195; interviews with Deal and Lee. **18.** Brundage, *Lynching in the New South*, 38; Ayers, *Vengeance and Justice*, 245; Ross, "Statement," 1. **19.** Rosenbaum and Sederberg, "Vigilantism," 10; Richard M. Brown, "The American Vigilante Tradition," in Friedman, *Violence in America*, 2:138. **20.** Francis B. Simkins and Charles P. Roland, *A History of the Old South*, 4th ed. (New York: Knopf, 1972), 497; Cash, *The Mind of the South*, 123; Kay, State Grand Jury Notes, 1, 8.

21. Kay, State Grand Jury Notes, 7; David E. Blanton interview, FBI Report, 23 Feb. 1942, 31; Ayers, *Vengeance and Justice*, 14; Wyllie, "Race and Class on Missouri's

Cotton Frontier," 187-91; interview with Griffen (18 May 1987). **22.** Williamson, *The Crucible of Race*, 188, 301-2; Frank L. Owsley, *Plain Folk of the Old South* (Baton Rouge: Louisiana State Univ. Press, 1949), v; interview with Blanton (18 May 1987). **23.** H.C. Brearley, "The Pattern of Violence," in *Culture in the South*, ed. W.T. Couch (Chapel Hill: Univ. of North Carolina Press, 1953), 680; Blanton interview, FBI Report, 23 Feb. 1942, 29; interview with Sturgeon (19 May 1987). **24.** Anonymous to Forrest C. Donnell, 31 Jan. 1942, folder 3599, FCDP. **25.** Fields, *Slavery and Freedom on the Middle Ground*, 143.

26. Brown, *Social Psychology*, 733, 760; Wright, *Racial Violence in Kentucky*, 14; Brundage, *Lynching in the New South*, 41, 48; Cox, "Lynching and the Status Quo," 585. **27.** McMillen, *Dark Journey*, 227; Brundage, *Lynching in the New South*, 46, 81, 183. **28.** Neil Fligstein, *Going North: Migration of Blacks and Whites from the South, 1900-1950* (New York: Academic Press, 1981), 133; *Sixteenth Census* (1940), *Population*, vol. 2, pt. 4, table 30, p. 436; and *Seventeenth Census* (1950), vol. 2, pt. 25, table 34, p. 70. In 1950, blacks numbered 1,602 persons or 13.8% of Sikeston's population, up from 1,003 persons or 12.6% ten years earlier. **29.** Interview with Griffen (6 June 1988). **30.** Brundage, *Lynching in the New South*, 81, 184; Coser, *The Functions of Social Conflict*, 84.

31. Interview with Griffen (18 May 1987). **32.** Doug McAdam and Kelly Moore, "The Politics of Black Insurgency, 1930-1975," in *Violence in America: Protest, Rebellion, Reform*, ed. Ted Robert Gurr (Newbury Park, Calif.: Sage, 1989), 2:258. **33.** Grimshaw, "A Study in Social Violence," 41; Allen D. Grimshaw, ed., *Racial Violence in the United States* (Chicago: Aldine, 1969), 6-8; Fredrickson, *The Black Image in the White Mind*, 256-82. **34.** *Charleston Democrat*, 12 Feb. 1942, FBIF; Brundage, *Lynching in the New South*, 61. **35.** Cash, *The Mind of the South*, 117.

36. Hall, *Revolt against Chivalry*, 156; anonymous to Forrest C. Donnell, 31 Jan. 1942, folder 3599, and anonymous to Donnell, 1 Feb. 1942, folder 3600, FCDP. **37.** William Cohen, *At Freedom's Edge: Black Mobility and the Southern White Quest for Racial Control, 1861-1915* (Baton Rouge: Louisiana State Univ. Press, 1991), 213; Franklin Johnson, *The Development of State Legislation concerning the Free Negro* (rpt.; Westport, Conn.: Greenwood, 1979), 136-37. **38.** Joel Kovel, *White Racism: A Psychohistory* (New York: Pantheon, 1970), 67. **39.** NAACP, "Why a Congressional Investigation of Lynching in the United States?" (1919), 2, quoting Dr. A.A. Brill, in NAACP (microfilm) pt. 7, reel 28, ser. B. See also Wyllie, "Race and Class on Missouri's Cotton Frontier," 193, and *Atlanta Constitution*, 10 Dec. 1924, TLF, for southeast Missouri; and Brundage, *Lynching in the New South*, 66, for evidence that southeast Missourians—like lynchers elsewhere—did not always mutilate alleged rapists. **40.** Interview with subject C.

41. *Standard*, 30 Jan. 1942, 8; Work, *Negro Year Book*, 401, lists an unidentified victim in 1920; Pfeifer, "The Ritual of Lynching," 33 n 27. **42.** *Standard*, 25 Nov. 1941, 1, and 17 Feb. 1942, 1. **43.** Brearley, "The Pattern of Violence," 680; White, *Ar'n't I a Woman?* 164-65; Darlene Clark Hine, "Rape and the Inner Lives of

Black Women in the Middle West: Preliminary Thoughts on the Culture of Dissemblance," *Signs: Journal of Women and Culture in Society* 14 (Summer 1989): 912-20. **44.** Virgus C. Cole to Forrest C. Donnell, 30 Jan. 1942, folder 3616, and Peter F. Keyes to Donnell, 27 Jan. 1942, folder 3607, FCDP.   **45.** Interview with Dempster; Ayers, *Vengeance and Justice*, 252. See Richard Slotkin, "Narratives of Negro Crime in New England, 1675-1800," *American Quarterly* 25 (March 1973): 28, for "exorcism," also applicable to later lynchings.

46. Grimshaw, "A Study in Social Violence," 31-32; James M. Inveriarity, "Populism and Lynching in Louisiana, 1889-1896: A Test of Erikson's Theory of the Relationship between Boundary Crises and Repressive Justice," *American Sociological Review* 41 (April 1976): 262-80 (see also criticism in 42 [April 1977]); Dennis B. Downey and Raymond M. Hyser, *No Crooked Death: Coatesville, Pennsylvania, and the Lynching of Zachariah Walker* (Urbana: Univ. of Illinois Press, 1991).   **47.** Ayers, *Vengeance and Justice*, 14, 19, 26; Wyatt-Brown, *Southern Honor*, 371, 364; Cash, *The Mind of the South*,125.   **48.** Brundage, *Lynching in the New South*, 52, 70, 71; Herbert Kelman, "Violence without Moral Restraint," in *Varieties of Psychohistory*, ed. George M. Kren and Leon H. Rappoport (New York: Springer, 1976), 305.   **49.** Dace interview, FBI Report, 23 Feb. 1942, 15.   **50.** Interview with Sturgeon (7 Nov. 1987); McGhee, "Historical Sketch, HHC 135th Engr. Gp., HHC and Co. A 140th Engr. Bn.," 8.

51. Williamson, *The Crucible of Race*, 115; Brundage, *Lynching in the New South*, 52.   **52.** Phone conversation with James Sturgeon (16 Dec. 1990, Chino, Calif.), for frustration of those "left behind"; Snow, "History of Swampeast Missouri," for guilt of even the most law-abiding residents too old for military service.   **53.** Tompkins and Tompkins, "An Informal Report," 2.   **54.** Mrs. W.M. Gill to Forrest C. Donnell, 28 Jan. 1942, folder 3613, and Anonymous to Donnell, 31 Jan. 1942, folder 3599, FCDP.   **55.** Wyatt-Brown, *Southern Honor*, 369-71; Victor Turner, *The Ritual Process: Structure and Anti-Structure* (Ithaca, N.Y.: Cornell Univ. Press, 1977), 131-65, and *Dramas, Fields, and Metaphors: Symbolic Action in Human Society* (Ithaca, N.Y.: Cornell Univ. Press, 1974), 45, 47, 169.

56. Coser, *The Functions of Social Conflict*, 60-65; "The P.C. Editor Says," *Standard*, 30 Jan. 1942, 1; Wyatt-Brown, *Southern Honor*, 402.   **57.** Howard L. Yeager to Forrest C. Donnell, 27 Jan. 1943, folder 3607, FCDP; James E. Cutler, *Lynch-Law: An Investigation into the History of Lynching in the United States* (rpt.; Montclair, N.J.: Patterson Smith, 1969), 267-79; interview with subject C; Wyatt-Brown, *Southern Honor*, 401.   **58.** Anonymous interviews, FBI Report, 23 Feb. 1942, 43, and 13 March 1942, 4; interview with Sturgeon (19 May 1942).   **59.** Anonymous to Forrest C. Donnell, 31 Jan. 1942, folder 3599, FCDP; interviews with Bartley and Sturgeon (13 Dec. 1993).   **60.** None of those interviewed forty-five years later associated these events with the lynching, yet government reports and press accounts indicate their unsettling effect on residents of wartime Sikeston.

61. Tompkins and Tompkins, "An Informal Report," 4-6.   **62.** Cash, *The Mind* *of the South*, 119; Lawrence J. Friedman, *The White Savage: Racial Fantasies in the Postbellum South* (Englewood Cliffs, N.J.: Prentice-Hall, 1970), 11; Fredrickson, *The Black Image in the White Mind*, 256-82, 311-12; Williamson, *The Crucible of Race*, 318.   **63.** Brown, *Modernization*, 8, 10-13.   **64.** Blanton interview, FBI Report, 23 Feb. 1942, 30; Richard M. Brown, "Southern Violence—Regional Problem or National Nemesis? Legal Attitudes Toward Southern Homicide in Historical Perspective," *Vanderbilt Law Review* 32 (Jan. 1979): 233-34 (and 251-59 for criticism by Dennis R. Nolan), and *No Duty to Retreat* (New York: Oxford Univ. Press, 1991), 3-37, for homicide theory as applied to the lynching.   **65.** Hackney, "Southern Violence," 924.

66. Gail Williams O'Brien, "Return to 'Normalcy': Organized Racial Violence in the Post–World War II South," in Gurr, *Violence in America*, 2:238; *Herald*, 5 March, 18 and 25 June 1942, and 23 July 1942, all p. 1.   **67.** Brown, *Strain of Violence*, 214, 215-18.   **68.** This and next four paragraphs based on Brundage, *Lynching in the New South*, 36, 37-44, 18-35; Grace Elizabeth Hale, "Deadly Amusement: Spectacle Lynchings and Southern Whiteness, 1890-1940," in *Varieties of Southern History: New Essays on a Region and Its People*, ed. Bruce Clayton and John Salmond (Westport, Conn.: Greenwood, 1996), 65. See also John R. Ross, "At the Bar of Judge Lynch: Lynching and Lynch Mobs in America" (Ph.D. diss., Texas Tech Univ., 1983). **69.** Williamson, *The Crucible of Race*, 117.   **70.** The rape statistic for the South, 1889-1899, is derived from Tolnay and Beck, *Festival of Violence*, 49, 271; the rape statistic they establish for the South for 1882-1899 is 38.1 percent.

71. Brundage, *Lynching in the New South*, 141.   **72.** Pfeifer, "The Ritual of Lynching," 24; Brundage, *Lynching in the New South*, 137-38, 145. Moniteau recorded the most white lynching victims: four between 1889 and 1899.   **73.** Boone, Howard, Randolph, Monroe, Ralls, Pike, Audrain, and Callaway Counties; small portions of neighboring counties shared some of their characteristics, such as voting patterns. See Howard Wight Marshall, "The Concept of Folk Region in Missouri: The Case of Little Dixie" (Ph.D. diss., Indiana Univ., 1976), 1:9, 239-44; Milton D. Rafferty, *Historical Atlas of Missouri* (Norman: Univ. of Oklahoma Press, 1982), map 33. **74.** "Little Dixie" by Albert Edmund Trombly, quoted in Lawrence O. Christensen, "Missouri: The Heart of the Nation," in *HeartLand*, ed. James H. Madison (Bloomington: Indiana Univ. Press, 1988), 90.   **75.** Crisler, "Missouri's 'Little Dixie,'" 130-39.

76. See Chapter 1 and Gerlach, *Settlement Patterns in Missouri*,   **77.** See *Columbia Daily Tribune*, 26 April 1989, 1, for hanging of Andre Roland. Lacking contrary evidence, authorities ruled his death a suicide, but the black fourteen-year-old's mother, Norma, suspected that it was a racially motivated lynching.   **78.** Since scholars have rarely analyzed the urban dimension of lynchings, scant data exist for comparison. Mary Elizabeth Hines, "Death at the Hands of Persons Unknown: The Geography of Lynching in the Deep South, 1882 to 1910" (Ph.D. diss., Louisiana State Univ. and A&M College, 1992), 168-77, 197, shows low rates—under 10%—in "urbanized counties" of Alabama, Georgia, Mississippi, and Louisiana; Terence R. Finnegan, "'At the Hands of Parties Unknown': Lynching in Mississippi and South Carolina, 1882-1940" (Ph.D. diss., Univ. of Illinois, 1993), 320, gives examples of 22.2% and 15.2% over a longer time span. **79.** *Seventeenth Census* (1950), vol. 2, pt. 25, table 4, p. 10. **80.** Crowe, "Racial Massacre in Atlanta," 150-69; Senechal, *The Sociogenesis of a Race Riot*, 25-46, for evidence on this typology.

81. Pfeifer, "The Ritual of Lynching," 29; Brundage, *Lynching in the New South*, 156. **82.** These municipalities (and Columbia in Table 6) were selected because of their locations (in the areas of greatest lynching), population sizes, and available histories. Only Pierce City fluctuated from a census-recognized minor civil entity of 2,511 in 1890 to an unrecognized one of 2,151 in 1900: *Eleventh Census* (1890), pt. 1, table 19, pp. 466-67; *Twelfth Census* (1900), pt. 1, table 8, pp. 459-61. **83.** This and the next several paragraphs are based on Murray Stringer-Bishoff, "The Lynching That Changed Southwest Missouri," *Monett Times*, 14, 15, and 16 Aug. 1991 (all starting on p. 1); Burton L. Purrington and Penny L. Harter, "The Easter and Tug-of-War Lynching and the Early Twentieth-Century Black Exodus from Southwest Missouri," in *Visions and Revisions: Ethnohistoric Perspectives on Southern Cultures*, ed. George Sabo III and William M. Schneider (Athens: Univ. Of Georgia Press, 1987), 59-82; Mary N. Clary, "The Easter Offering: A Missouri Lynching, 1906" (M.A. thesis, Southwest Missouri State Univ., 1972); Katherine Lederer, "And Then They Sang a Sabbath Song," *Springfield!* 2 (April; May; June 1981): 26-28, 33-36, 24-26. **84.** Information on this lynching from Patrick J. Huber, "The Lynching of James T. Scott: The Underside of a College Town," *Gateway Heritage* 12 (Summer 1991): 19-21, 18-37, table 5 for population changes; Proctor Neal Carter, "Lynch-Law and the Press of Missouri" (M.A. thesis, Univ. of Missouri, 1933), 19, for sex crimes. **85.** Clary, "The Easter Offering," 9; Huber, "The Lynching of James T. Scott," 32.

86. Dominic J. Capeci Jr., Comments on "'Violators of the Law in Boone County': Columbia Elites, the University of Missouri and the James Scott Lynching" by Patrick J. Huber (Missouri Conference on History, Cape Girardeau, 6 April 1991). **87.** Brundage, *Lynching in the New South*, 81. **88.** Tolnay and Beck, *A Festival of Violence*, 32-34, 141, 255, correlates lynching with seasonal cotton cultivation; Finnegan, "Who Were the Lynching Victims?" 80, shows that most victims in Mississippi and South Carolina were familiar agricultural workers. **89.** Stringer-Bishoff, "The Lynching That Changed Southwest Missouri," 14 Aug. 1991, 5; Clary, "The Easter Offering," 5. **90.** S.F. Nadel, "Witchcraft in Four African Societies: An Essay in Comparison," in *Cultures and Societies of Africa*, ed. Simon and Phoebe Ottenberg (New York: Random House, 1960), 407-19; Bill Rogers, "Witchcraft and Women: A Study of Sexist Attitudes in Western Europe and New England during the Fifteenth, Sixteenth, and Seventeenth Centuries" (seminar paper, Southwest Missouri State Univ., 1986), 1-23; and conversations with Teresa Montsney [Layton], Springfield, Mo., 1993.

91. Some witches were older and married, yet, as with lynch victims, the unattached among them were overrepresented; lacking male protectors (husbands and prominent whites) put them at greater risk when accused of "deviant" behavior. In reality, both groups threatened society's normal functioning by refusing to stay in their ascribed places: women no longer capable of childbearing yet economically reliant on others or, if heirs, preventing "the orderly transmission of property from one generation of males to another"; blacks seeking greater economic and social opportunities, sometimes across the color line. In some way, these white females and black men expressed dissatisfaction with society's "power arrangements" and, more specifically, challenged the favored position of white males who believed their own gender and race superior to those they destroyed in rituals fraught with sexual fantasies and white masculine reaffirmations. See Carol F. Karlsen, *The Devil in the Shape of a Woman: Witchcraft in Colonial New England* (New York: Norton, 1987), 46-76, 116, 152. Hence, witches and lynch victims seemed lower-class and repeat offenders, abrasive women and uppity men deserving of their fate. That they, like Wright, possessed other characteristics as well meant little to their killers, witch-hunters manifesting "tremors of uncertainty" and projecting uncomfortable personal feelings onto their prey (John Putnam Demos, *Entertaining Satan: Witchcraft and the Culture of Early New England* [New York: Oxford Univ. Press, 1982], 93-94, 202-8, 210). See also Mary Daly, *Gyn/Ecology: The Metaethics of Radical Feminism*, 2d ed. (Boston: Beacon, 1990), 178-222.   **92.** Crowe, "Racial Massacre in Atlanta," 150-69; John Dittmer, *Black Georgia in the Progressive Era, 1900-1920* (Champaign: Univ. Of Illinois Press, 1977), 123-31. *Afro-American*, 29 Sept. 1906, 5, recounts a lynching within the riot. **93.** Allen D. Grimshaw, "Actions of Police and the Military American Race Riots," in Grimshaw, *Racial Violence in the United States*, 269-87.   **94.** Dace, "Lynching of Cleo Wright"; Greim, "Mob Violence at Sikeston"; Morris, "Mob Violence at Sikeston"; Kay, State Grand Jury Notes, 11; chapter 5.   **95.** Hobbs interview, FBI Report, 23 Feb. 1942, 35; *Herald*, 4 June 1942, 4.

   96. Grimshaw, "A Study in Social Violence," 262.   **97.** See Kenneth A. Lockridge, "The American Revolution, Modernization, and Man: A Critique," in *Tradition, Conflict, and Modernization: Perspectives on the American Revolution*, ed. Richard M. Brown and Don E. Fehrenbacher (New York: Academic Press, 1976), 110-19. **98.** Morris Janowitz, "Patterns of Collective Racial Violence," in Friedman, *Violence in America*, 3:33-34.   **99.** Edward L. Ayers, *The Promise of the New South: Life after Reconstruction* (New York: Oxford Univ. Press, 1992), 156, 497 n 71. County densities are defined as low or high in relation to the state density, which serves as the norm.   **100.** No official statistics exist for Pierce City, but Lawrence County's black population loss of 67.8 percent (192 persons) over the postlynching decade represented municipal and area tendencies of the previous thirty years. Joplin (9.3 percent) and Columbia (19.9 percent) experienced increased black urbanization after the respective lynchings, but all counties save Scott recorded negative black population growth.

   101. Brundage, *Lynching in the New South*, 123. See Robert P. Ingalls, *Urban Vigi-*

lantes in the New South: Tampa, 1882-1936 (Knoxville: Univ. of Tennessee Press, 1988), 204-14, and Walter T. Howard, *Lynchings: Extralegal Violence in Florida during the 1930s* (Selinsgrove, Pa.: Susquehanna Univ. Press, 1995), 133-42, for diverse patterns of urban lynchings in southern municipalities over time and in seven communities during one decade. See also McGovern, *Anatomy of a Lynching,* for one of the last, most significant rural lynchings.

Chapter 8. Postmortem

1. Capeci, "The Lynching of Cleo Wright," 859-60, 882-87 (original version of this chapter); Michal R. Belknap, *Federal Law and Southern Order: Racial Violence and Constitutional Conflict in the Post-Brown South,* 2d ed. (Athens: Univ. of Georgia Press, 1995).   2. Alexander M. Bickel and Benno C. Schmidt Jr., *The Judiciary and Responsible Government, 1910-1921* (New York: Macmillan, 1984), 725-27; August Meier and Elliott Rudwick, "Attorneys Black and White: A Case Study of Race Relations within the NAACP," *Journal of American History* 62 (March 1976): 913-46; Sitkoff, *A New Deal for Blacks,* 216-43; Jerold S. Auerbach, *Unequal Justice: Lawyers and Social Change in Modern America* (New York: Oxford Univ. Press, 1976), 3-230; Cover, "Origins of Judicial Activism in the Protection of Minorities," 1287-1316. 3. Zangrando, *The NAACP Crusade against Lynching,* 3-21; Hine, *Black Victory,* 12-13, 18-19.   4. Wendell Berge memorandum for Attorney General, 2 Nov. 1942, USIP, and Biddle's response, handwritten on the memo by an aide: "The AG is of the view it should not be reopened (11-5-42)."   5. *NYT,* 10 Oct. 1943, 9.

6. Capeci, *The Harlem Riot of 1943,* 90-96, 148-56.   7. *NYT,* 13 July 1942, 17; Carr, *Federal Protection of Civil Rights,* 163-64; Walter White to Mary Taussig Tompkins, 5 Aug. 1942, Box A381, NAACP.   8. Frank Coleman, "Freedom from Fear on the Home Front," *Iowa Law Review* 29 (March 1944): 426-27; Carr, *Federal Protection of Civil Rights,* 163-76; *NYT,* 21 Oct. 1942, 11. Federal attorneys released two defendants; the jury found the remaining three not guilty. See also James A. Burran III, "Racial Violence in the South during World War II" (Ph.D. diss., Univ. of Tennessee, 1977).   9. Guzman, *The Negro Year Book,* 305; Carr, *Federal Protection of Civil Rights,* 169-76; Julius Cohen, "The Screws Case: Federal Protection of Negro Rights," *Columbia Law Review* 46 (Jan. 1946), 106.   10. *NYT,* 8 May 1945, 34; Eugene Gressman, "The Unhappy History of Civil Rights Legislation," *Michigan Law Review* 50 (June 1952): 1351 and 1352; Robert J. Harris, *The Quest for Equality: The Constitution, Congress, and the Supreme Court* (Baton Rouge: Louisiana State Univ. Press, 1960), 128; Cover, "The Origins of Judicial Activism in the Protection of Minorities," 1314. See Fine, *Frank Murphy,* 396-402, for opinions of individual judges.

11. William C. Berman, *The Politics of Civil Rights in the Truman Administration* (Columbus: Ohio State Univ. Press, 1970), 41-78; Donald R. McCoy and Richard T. Ruetten, *Quest and Response: Minority Rights and the Truman Administration* (Lawrence: Univ. of Kansas Press, 1973), 44-54; Barton J. Bernstein, "The Ambigu-

ous Legacy: The Truman Administration and Civil Rights," in *Politics and Policies of the Truman Administration*, ed. Barton J. Bernstein (Chicago: Quadrangle, 1970), 269-314. **12.** President's Committee on Civil Rights, *To Secure These Rights: The Report of the President's Committee on Civil Rights* (Washington, D.C.: Government Printing Office, 1947), 114; William E. Juhnke, "President Truman's Committee on Civil Rights: The Interaction of Politics, Protest, and Personality" (manuscript, 1984), 23-24, in author's possession, courtesy of Juhnke. **13.** Elliff, "Aspects of Federal Civil Rights Enforcement," 630, 640, 652; Kenneth O'Reilly, *"Racial Matters": The FBI's Secret File on Black America, 1960-1972* (New York: Free Press, 1989), 23-27; Murphy, *The Constitution in Crisis Times* 211-12, 275-77, 354; Kluger, *Simple Justice*, x, 700-747; Robert Fredrick Burk, *The Eisenhower Administration and Black Civil Rights* (Knoxville: Univ. of Tennessee Press, 1984), 226, 253-66; Carl M. Brauer, *John F. Kennedy and the Second Reconstruction* (New York: Columbia Univ. Press, 1977), 11, 94-97, 152-79, 309-20. **14.** The Justice Department's deemphasizing the protection of blacks from lynch mobs and police brutality occurred in part because departmental lawyers looked to the President's Committee on Civil Rights to correct the deficiencies in Sections 51 and 52; legal scholars questioned the merits of the statutes, given the limitations placed on them in *Screws* and *Williams*; and politicians stressed moderation in civil rights. See Tom C. Clark, "A Federal Prosecutor Looks at the Civil Rights Statutes," *Columbia Law Review* 47 (March 1947): 184-85; Zechariah Chaffee Jr., "Safeguarding Fundamental Human Rights: The Tasks of States and Nation," and Robert G. Dixon Jr., "Civil Rights: Recent Variations on a Theme of Moderation," *George Washington Law Review* 27 (April 1959): 527-28, 540-46. **15.** Elliff, "Aspects of Federal Civil Rights Enforcement," 668-69; Mary Frances Berry, *Black Resistance, White Law: A History of Constitutional Racism in America* (New York: Appleton-Century-Crofts, 1971), 201; Philip B. Kurland, *Politics, the Constitution, and the Warren Court* (Chicago: Univ. Of Chicago Press, 1970), 145, 149; Belknap, *Federal Law and Southern Order*, 157-82, and "The Legal Legacy of Lemuel Penn," *Harvard Law Journal* 25 (1982): 457-524.

   16. Kelly, Harbison, and Belz, *The Constitution*, 619, 623. **17.** Lawrence M. Friedman and Harry N. Scheiber, eds., *American Law and the Constitutional Order: Historical Perspectives* (Cambridge, Mass.: Harvard Univ. Press, 1978), viii; William Cohen, "Negro Involuntary Servitude in the South, 1865-1940: A Preliminary Analysis," *Journal of Southern History* 42 (Feb. 1976): 59; Cover, "The Origins of Judicial Activism in the Protection of Minorities," 1294. **18.** See sources in chapter 3, note 84, and Irons, "Politics and Principles," 716-20; Bickel and Schmidt, *Judiciary and Responsible Government*, 906. **19.** Kluger, *Simple Justice*, 234-35; Lawrence M. Friedman, *American Law* (New York: Norton, 1984), 264; Hine, *Black Victory*, 237. **20.** Hine, *Black Victory*, 337; Kluger, *Simple Justice*, 64.

   21. Carr, *Federal Protection of Civil Rights*, 164 n 22, 172; Berry, *Black Resistance, White Law*, 170, 185, 187-204. **22.** Phyllis Greenacre, "Youth, Growth, and Violence," in *The Psychoanalytic Study of the Child* (New York: International Universities Press,

1970), 25:358; Charles Joyner, *Down By the Riverside: A South Carolina Slave Community* (Urbana: Univ. of Illinois Press, 1984), 180, 194.   **23.** Richard E. Rubenstein, *Rebels in Eden: Mass Political Violence in the United States* (Boston: Little, Brown, 1970); Charles David Phillips, "Exploring Relations among Forms of Social Control: The Lynching and Execution of Blacks in North Carolina, 1889-1918," *Law and Society Review* 21 (1987): 372-73.   **24.** Brown, *No Duty to Retreat,* 156-57.

Selected Bibliography

Manuscript Collections

Ellis Library, University of Missouri, Columbia, Joint Collection, University of Missouri Western Historical Manuscript Collection and State Historical Society of Missouri Manuscripts.
> Forrest C. Donnell Papers.

Kent Library, Southeast Missouri State University, Cape Girardeau Regional History and University Archives.
> John Buxton Oral History Interview, 18 July 1979.
> H.H. Lewis Papers.
> James H. (Pete) Schwabb Oral History Interviews, 24 June 1987 and 7 Aug. 1987.
> Thad Snow Papers.
> Southern Tenant Farmers Union Papers (microfilm).

Library of Congress, Washington, D.C.
> National Association for the Advancement of Colored People Papers.

Missouri Historical Society Library, St. Louis.
> Fannie Cook Papers.

National Archives and Records Service, Washington, D.C., Record Group 60.
> U.S. Department of Justice Index File, 1942.

Hollis Burke Frissell Library, Tuskegee University, Tuskegee, Alabama.
> Lynching Files.

Records of Government Agencies

Arkansas Department of Correction, Pine Bluff.
> Wiley Arnett Humphrey, File No. 35847.

Federal Bureau of Investigation, Washington, D.C.
> Cleo Wright, File No. 44-532.

Jefferson County Courthouse, Pine Bluff, Arkansas.
> Chancery Court Records.
> Criminal Court Records.
> Marriage Records.

Missouri Department of Corrections and Human Resources, Jefferson City.
> Cleo Wright, File No. 54168.
> Cleo Wright, Supervision Report.

Missouri Department of Public Safety, Jefferson City, State Highway Patrol Reports.
> Cleo Wright Lynching.
> Rev. J.B. Ross Incident.

National Personnel Records Center, St. Louis, Missouri.
  Ricelor C. Watson, File No. 346-60-26.
Scott County Courthouse, Benton, Missouri.
  Circuit Court Criminal Records, 1937, 1940, 1942.
Scott County Jail, Benton, Missouri.
  Jail Records, 1937, 1940.
Sikeston City Hall, Sikeston, Missouri.
  City Council Minutes, 1936-1945.
U.S. Department of Justice, Washington, D.C.
  Criminal Division Files.
  Office of United States Attorney for the Eastern District of Missouri Files.
  Office of Information and Privacy Files.

Census Reports

U.S. Census Office, Department of the Interior. Eleventh Census: 1890. *Population*.
  Pt. 1. Washington, D.C., 1895.
———. *Twelfth Census: 1900. Population.* Pt. 1. Washington, D.C., 1901.
U.S. Bureau of the Census, Department of Commerce. *Thirteenth Census of the United
  States: 1910. Population.* Vol. 2. Washington, D.C., 1913.
———*Fourteenth Census of the United States: 1920. Population.* Vol. 3. Washington,
  D.C., 1921.
———*Fifteenth Census of the United States: 1930. Population.* Vol. 3, pt. 1. Washing-
  ton, D.C., 1932.
———*Sixteenth Census of the United States: 1940. Population.* Vol. 2, pts. 3-4. Wash-
  ington, D.C., 1943.
———*Sixteenth Census of the United States: 1940. Housing.* Vol. 2, pt. 3. Washing-
  ton, D.C., 1943.
———*Seventeenth Census of the United States: 1950. Population.* Vol. 2, pt. 25. Wash-
  ington, D.C., 1952.

Author's Interviews

All interviews not otherwise located were conducted in Sikeston, Mo.

Elbridge W. Bartley Jr., 27 April 1992.
C. Arch Bay, 9 Feb. 1989, Springfield, Mo.
David E. Blanton, 18 May 1987, 6 Nov. 1987, 13 June 1990, and 13 Dec. 1993.
Jess Bogy, 22 Aug. 1992, Wabbaseka, Ark.
Mitchell Bogy, 22 Aug. 1992, Altheimer, Ark.
Lecher Bom, 20 May 1987, Benton, Mo.
Milton Brown, 13 June 1990.
Arthur Bruce, 6 Nov. 1987 and 12 June 1990.

Paul Bumbarger, 6 Nov. 1987, Sikeston; 19 Jan. 1995, Memphis.

Gilbert Clinton, 16 June 1990, Cape Girardeau, Mo.

Raymond Crews, 9 June 1988.

Helen Currin, 19 May 1988, Charleston, Mo.

Herschel Deal, 8 June 1988.

Robert A. Dempster, 20 May 1987.

Alvin Dotson, 18 May 1987 and 7 Nov. 1987.

Bill Ferrell, 13 June 1990.

Frank Ferrell, 7 June 1988.

Alberta Gardner, 7 June 1988.

Rev. Tom Geers, 13 June 1990.

Walter Griffen, 18 May 1987, 5 Nov. 1987, 6 June 1988, 7 June 1988, 11 June 1990, and 13 June 1990.

Barbara Hilton, 23 Aug. 1992, Altheimer, Ark.

Lynn Ingram, 5 Nov. 1987.

Michael L. Jensen, 7 June 1988 and 21 Nov. 1991.

Linetta Watson Koonce, 21 June 1992 and 10 Aug. 1993, Albuquerque, N.M.; 23 Aug. 1992, Pine Bluff, Ark.

J.M. Law, 14 June 1990.

Margaret Lee, 8 June 1988.

Charles M. Mitchell, 9 June 1988 and 12 Nov. 1991.

Everett Nixon, 13 June 1990, St. Louis.

John Henry Rasberry, 20 June 1992, Altheimer, Ark.

Arthur Renfro, 13 June 1990.

Julia Renfro, 13 June 1990 and 14 June 1990.

Ruth Donnell Rogers, 29 July 1985 and 22 May 1993, Webster Groves, Mo.

Geraldine Schlosser, 22 Nov. 1991.

P.J. Schlosser, 22 Nov. 1991.

James Simms, 20 June 1992 and 6 July 1992, Wabbaseka, Ark.

Johnnie Simms, 20 June 1992, Wabbaseka, Ark.

Fred Smith, 18 May 1987.

Minnie Strong, 20 June 1992, Altheimer, Ark.

Grace Sturgeon, 19 May 1987, 20 May 1987, 7 Nov. 1987, 8 June 1988, 19 July 1990, 21 Nov. 1991, 14 Sept. 1992, 21 Aug. 1993, and 13 Dec. 1993.

James Sturgeon, 16 Dec. 1990, Chino, Calif.

Laverne Sturgeon, 19 Oct. 1992, Somerville, Tex.

Andrew Walker, 22 June 1992 and 27 June 1992, Gethsemane, Ark.

James Walker, 22 Aug. 1992 and 25 July 1993, Gethsemane, Ark.

Dr. Clifford I. Whipple, 14 Jan. 1988 and 22 Sept. 1993, Springfield, Mo.

Glenda Whittley, 6 June 1988.

Jesse Whittley, 6 June 1988.

James Woolfolk, 12 July 1992, Pine Bluff, Ark.

Anonymous Subjects: A, 7 June 1988; B, 8 June 1988; C, 8 June 1988; D, 8 June 1988;

E, 8 June 1988; F, 21 Nov. 1991; G, 21 Nov. 1991; H, 18 May 1987; I, 20 May 1988; J, 12 June 1990; K, 12 June 1990; L, 14 June 1990; M, 22 Aug. 1992, Altheimer, Ark.; N, 13 June 1990; O, 14 June 1990; P, 5 Nov. 1987; Q, 23 Nov. 23 1991; R, 23 Nov. 1991; S, 22 Nov. 1991; T, 9 June 1988; U, 7 June 1988.

Secondary Works

Adams, Patricia L. "Fighting for Democracy in St. Louis: Civil Rights during World War II." *Missouri Historical Review* 80 (Oct. 1985): 58-75.

Allen, Ernest, Jr. "Waiting for Tojo: The Pro-Japan Vigil of Black Missourians, 1932-1943." *Gateway Heritage* 15 (Fall 1994): 16-33.

Ames, Jessie Daniel. *The Changing Character of Lynching: Review of Lynching, 1932-1941.* Reprint. New York: AMS Press, 1973.

Ayers, Edward L. *The Promise of the New South: Life after Reconstruction.* New York: Oxford Univ. Press, 1992.

———. *Vengeance and Justice: Crime and Punishment in the 19th-Century American South.* New York: Oxford Univ. Press, 1984.

Belknap, Michal R. *Federal Law and Southern Order: Racial Violence and Constitutional Conflict in the Post-Brown South.* 2d ed. Athens: Univ. of Georgia Press, 1995.

———. "The Legal Legacy of Lemuel Penn." *Howard Law Journal* 25 (1982): 457-524.

Berry, Mary Frances. *Black Resistance, White Law: A History of Constitutional Racism in America.* New York: Appleton-Century-Crofts, 1971.

Biddle, Francis. *In Brief Authority.* New York: Doubleday, 1962.

Blassingame, John W. *The Slave Community: Plantation Life in the Antebellum South.* Rev. ed. New York: Oxford Univ. Press, 1979.

Brearley, H.C. "The Pattern of Violence." In *Culture in the South,* ed. W.T. Couch. Chapel Hill: Univ. of North Carolina Press, 1953.

Brown, Richard D. *Modernization: The Transformation of American Life, 1600-1865.* New York: Hill & Wang, 1976.

Brown, Richard M. *No Duty to Retreat.* New York: Oxford Univ. Press, 1991.

———. "Southern Violence—Regional Problem or National Nemesis? Legal Attitudes toward Southern Homicide in Historical Perspective." *Vanderbilt Law Review* 32 (Jan. 1979): 225-50.

———. *Stain of Violence: Historical Studies of American Violence and Vigilantism.* New York: Oxford Univ. Press, 1975.

Brown, Roger. *Social Psychology.* New York: Free Press, 1965.

Brownell, Blaine A. *The Urban Ethos in the South, 1920-1930.* Baton Rouge: Louisiana State Univ. Press, 1975.

Brownmiller, Susan. *Against Our Will: Men, Women, and Rape.* New York: Simon & Schuster, 1975.

Brundage, W. Fitzhugh. *Lynching in the New South: Georgia and Virginia, 1880-1930.* Urbana: Univ. of Illinois Press, 1993.

Burgess, A.W., and L.L. Holmstrom. "Rape Trauma Syndrome." *American Journal of Psychiatry* 131 (1974): 981-86.

Burran, James A., III. "Racial Violence in the South during World War II." Ph.D. diss., Univ. of Tennessee, 1977.

Cantor, Louis. "A Prologue to the Protest Movement: The Missouri Sharecropper Roadside Demonstration of 1939." *Journal of American History* 55 (March 1969): 804-22.

————. *A Prologue to the Protest Movement: The Missouri Sharecropper Roadside Demonstration of 1939.* Durham, N.C.: Duke Univ. Press, 1969.

Capeci, Dominic J., Jr. "The Lynching of Cleo Wright: Federal Protection of Constitutional Rights during World War II." *Journal of American History* 77 (March 1986): 859-87.

————. "Violence in Three Acts: A Lynching in Wartime Sikeston, 1942." Paper presented to National Council for Geographic Educators Conference, Springfield, Mo., 21 Oct. 1987.

Carr, Robert K. *Federal Protection of Civil Rights: Quest for a Sword.* Ithaca, N.Y.: Cornell Univ. Press, 1947.

Carter, Proctor Neal. "Lynch-Law and the Press of Missouri." M.A. thesis, Univ. of Missouri, 1933.

Cash, W.J. *The Mind of the South.* New York: Knopf, 1941.

Chadbourn, James H. *Lynching and the Law.* Chapel Hill: Univ. of North Carolina Press, 1933.

Chaney, Audrey. *A History of Sikeston.* Cape Girardeau, Mo.: Ramfire Press, 1960.

Christensen, Lawrence O. "Missouri: The Heart of the Nation." In *Heart Land,* ed. James H. Madison. Bloomington: Indiana Univ. Press, 1988.

Clark, Tom C. "A Federal Prosecutor Looks at the Civil Rights Statutes." *Columbia Law Review* 47 (March 1947): 175-85.

Clary, Mary N. "The Easter Offering: A Missouri Lynching, 1906." M.A. thesis, Southwest Missouri State Univ., 1972.

Coleman, Frank. "Freedom from Fear on the Home Front." *Iowa Law Review* 29 (March 1944): 415-29

Cook, Fannie. *Boot-Heel Doctor.* New York: Dodd, Mead, 1941.

Coser, Lewis. *The Functions of Social Conflict.* Glencoe, Ill.: Free Press, 1956.

Cover, Robert M. "The Origins of Judicial Activism in the Protection of Minorities." *Yale Law Journal* 91 (June 1982): 1287-1316.

Cox, Oliver C. "Lynching and the Status Quo." *Journal of Negro Education* 14 (Fall 1945): 576-88.

Crisler, Robert M. "Missouri's Little Dixie." *Missouri Historical Review* 42 (Jan. 1948): 130-39.

Crowe, Charles. "Racial Massacre in Atlanta, September 22, 1906." *Journal of Negro History* 54 (April 1969): 150-73.

Cutler, James E. *Lynch-Law: An Investigation into the History of Lynching in the United States.* Reprint. Montclair, N.J.: Patterson Smith, 1969.

Daniel, Pete. *Standing at the Crossroads: Southern Life since 1900.* New York: Hill & Wang, 1986.

Davis, Allison, and John Dollard. *Children of Bondage: The Personality Development of Negro Youth in the Urban South.* Reprint. New York: Harper & Row, 1964.

Davis, Angela Y. *Women, Race, and Class.* New York: Vintage Books, 1983.

Dinnerstein, Leonard. *The Leo Frank Case.* New York: Columbia Univ. Press, 1968.

Dollard, John. *Caste and Class in a Southern Town.* 3d ed. Garden City, N.Y.: Doubleday Anchor Books, 1957.

Douglass, Robert S. *A History of Southeast Missouri.* Chicago: Lewis, 1912.

Downey, Dennis B., and Raymond M. Hyser. *No Crooked Death: Coatesville, Pennsylvania, and the Lynching of Zachariah Walker.* Urbana: Univ. of Illinois Press, 1991.

Elliff, John T. "Aspects of Federal Civil Rights Enforcement: The Justice Department and the FBI, 1939-1964." *Perspectives in American History* 5 (1971): 605-73.

Ellis, Mary Louise. "'Rain Down Fire': The Lynching of Sam Hose." Ph.D. diss., Florida State Univ., 1992.

Erikson, Erik H. *Childhood and Society.* 2d ed. New York: Norton, 1963.

Fellman, Michael. *Inside War: The Guerrilla Conflict in Missouri during the American Civil War.* New York: Oxford Univ. Press, 1989.

Finnegan, Terence R. "'At The Hands of Parties Unknown'": Lynching in Mississippi and South Carolina, 1881-1940." Ph.D. diss., Univ. of Illinois, 1993.

———. "Who Were the Victims of Lynchings? Evidence from Mississippi and South Carolina, 1881-1940." In *Varieties of Southern History: New Essays on a Region and Its People,* ed. Bruce Clayton and John Salmond. Westport, Conn.: Greenwood Press, 1996.

Fligstein, Neil. *Going North: Migration of Blacks and Whites from the South, 1900-1950.* New York: Academic Press, 1981.

Foley, William E. *A History of Missouri,* vol. 1, *1673-1820.* Columbia: Univ. of Missouri Press, 1971.

Fredrickson, George M. *The Black Image in the White Mind: The Debate on Afro-American Character and Destiny, 1817-1914.* New York: Harper & Row, 1971.

Friedman, Leon, ed. *Violence in America.* 16 vols. Reprint. New York: Chelsea House, 1983.

Fromm, Erich. *Escape from Freedom.* New York: Farrar & Rinehart, 1945.

Genovese, Eugene D. *Roll, Jordan, Roll: The World the Slaves Made.* New York: Pantheon Books, 1974.

Gerlach, Russel L. *Settlement Patterns in Missouri: A Study of Population Origins, with a Wall Map.* Columbia: Univ. of Missouri Press, 1986.

Girard, René. "Generative Scapegoating." In *Violent Origins: Ritual Killing and Cultural Formation,* ed. Walter Burkert, René Girard, and Jonathan Z. Smith. Stanford, Calif.: Stanford Univ. Press, 1987.

Graham, Hugh D., and Ted R. Gurr, eds. *Violence in America: Historical and Comparative Perspectives.* 2 vols. Washington, D.C.: Government Printing Office, 1969.

Grier, William H., and Price M. Cobbs. *Black Rage.* New York: Bantam Books, 1969.

Grimshaw, Allen D. "A Study in Social Violence: Urban Race Riots in the United States." Ph.D. diss., Univ. of Pennsylvania, 1959.

————, ed. *Racial Violence in the United States.* Chicago: Aldine, 1969.

Groth, Nicholas, with H. Jean Birnbaum. *Men Who Rape: The Psychology of the Offender.* New York: Plenum Press, 1979.

Grothaus, Larry H. "The Negro in Missouri Politics, 1890-1941." Ph.D. diss., Univ. of Missouri, 1970.

Gurr, Ted R. *Violence in America,* vol. 2, *Protest, Rebellion, Reform.* Newbury Park, Calif.: Sage, 1989.

Guzman, Jessie P., ed. *Negro Year Book: A Review of Events Affecting Negro Life, 1941-1946.* Atlanta: Foote & Davies, 1947.

Hackney, Sheldon. "Southern Violence." *American Historical Review* 74 (Feb. 1969): 906-25.

Hale, Grace Elizabeth. "Deadly Amusements: Spectacle Lynchings and Southern Whiteness, 1890-1940." In *Varieties of Southern History: New Essays on a Region and Its People,* ed. Bruce Clayton and John Salmond. Westport, Conn.: Greenwood Press, 1996.

Hall, Jacquelyn Dowd. "'The Mind That Burns in Each Body': Women, Rape, and Racial Violence." In *Powers of Desire: The Politics of Sexuality,* ed. Ann Snitow, Christine Stansell, and Sharon Thompson. New York: Monthly Review Press, 1983.

————. *Revolt against Chivalry: Jessie Daniel Ames and the Women's Campaign against Lynching.* New York: Columbia Univ. Press, 1979.

Harris, J. William. "Etiquette, Lynching, and Racial Boundaries in Southern History: A Mississippi Example." *American Historical Review* 100 (April 1995): 387-410.

Harris, Trudier. *Exorcising Blackness: Historical and Literary Lynching and Burning Rituals.* Bloomington: Indiana Univ. Press, 1984.

Hernton, Calvin C. *Sex and Racism in America.* New York: Grove Press, 1965.

Hine, Darlene Clark. "Rape and the Inner Lives of Black Women in the Middle West: Preliminary Thoughts on the Culture of Dissemblance." *Signs: Journal of Women and Culture in Society* 14 (Summer 1989): 912-20.

Hines, Mary Elizabeth. "Death at the Hands of Persons Unknown: The Geography of Lynching in the Deep South, 1882 to 1910." Ph.D. diss., Louisiana State Univ. and A&M College, 1992.

Holmes, Ronald M. *Sex Crimes.* Newbury Park, Calif.: Sage, 1991.

Howard, Walter T. *Lynchings: Extralegal Violence in Florida during the 1930s.* Selinsgrove, Pa.: Susquehanna Univ. Press, 1995.

Huber, Patrick J. "The Lynching of James T. Scott: The Underside of a College Town." *Gateway Heritage* 12 (Summer 1991): 18-37.

————. "Town versus Gown: The James T. Scott Lynching and the Social Fracture between the University of Missouri and the Larger Columbia Community." Senior thesis, Univ. of Missouri, 1990.

————. "'Violators of the Law in Boone County': Columbia Elites, the University of Missouri and the James T. Scott Lynching." Paper presented to Missouri Conference on History, Cape Girardeau, Missouri, 6 April 1991.

Hudson, Charles E. "A Geographic Study Examining the Major Elements Involved in the Rise of Cotton Production in Southeast Missouri, 1922-1925." M.A. thesis, Western Michigan Univ., 1967.

Hummasti, P. George. "From Immigrant Settlement to Ethnic Community: The Maturing of American Finntown." *Locus: Regional and Local History of the Americas* 7 (Spring 1995): 93-110.

Ingalls, Robert P. "Lynching and Established Violence in Tampa, 1858-1935." *Journal of Southern History* 53 (Nov. 1987): 613-44.

———. *Urban Vigilantes in the New South: Tampa, 1882-1936.* Knoxville: Univ. of Tennessee Press, 1988.

Irons, Peter. "Politics and Principles: An Assessment of the Roosevelt Record on Civil Rights and Liberties." *Washington Law Review* 59, no. 4 (1984): 693-722.

Johnson, Charles S. *Backgrounds to Patterns of Negro Segregation.* Reprint. New York: Apollo Editions, 1970.

Kirkendall, Richard S. *A History of Missouri,* vol. 5, *1919-1953.* Columbia: Univ. of Missouri Press, 1986.

Landon, Donald D. "Clients, Colleagues, and Community: The Shaping of Zealous Advocacy in Country Law Practice." *American Bar Foundation Research Journal,* 1985 (Winter): 81-111.

Layton, Teresa L. "Hope's Daughters: Women in Collective Violence." Paper presented to Mid-America Conference on History, Lawrence, Kansas, 17 Sept. 1992.

Lederer, Katherine. "And Then They Sang a Sabbath Song." *Springfield!* 2 April 1981, 2 May 1981, and 2 June 1981.

Lifton, Robert Jay. *History and Human Survival: Essays on the Young and Old, Survivors and the Dead, Peace and War, and on Contemporary Psychohistory.* New York: Vintage Books, 1971.

Lockridge, Kenneth A. "The American Revolution, Modernization, and Man: A Critique." In *Tradition, Conflict, and Modernization: Perspectives on the American Revolution,* ed. Richard M. Brown and Don E. Fehrenbacher. New York: Academic Press, 1976.

Mancini, Matthew. *Alexis de Tocqueville.* New York: Twayne, 1994.

March, David D. *The History of Missouri.* Vol. 2. New York: Lewis Historical, 1967.

Marshall, Howard Wright. "The Concept of Folk Region in Missouri: The Case of Little Dixie." Ph.D. diss., Indiana Univ., 1976.

May, Rollo. *Man's Search for Himself.* New York: Norton, 1953.

McGovern, James R. *Anatomy of a Lynching: The Killing of Claude Neal.* Baton Rouge: Louisiana State Univ. Press, 1982.

McMillen, Neil R. *Dark Journey: Black Mississippians in the Age of Jim Crow.* Urbana: Univ. of Illinois Press, 1990.

McPherson, James M. "From Limited to Total War: Missouri and the Nation, 1861-1865." *Gateway Heritage* 12 (Spring 1992): 4-19.

Meigs, A. James. "The Delta Area of Southeast Missouri: A Case Study in Economic Change." *Monthly Review* 38 (July 1956): 82-86.

Meyer, Duane G. *The Heritage of Missouri.* 3d ed. St. Louis. Mo.: River City, 1982.

Mitten, Lyman Russell, II. "The Lynching of Cleo Wright: A Study." Senior thesis, Southeast Missouri State Univ., 1974.

Montell, William Lynwood. *Killings: Folk Justice in the Upper South*. Lexington: Univ. Press of Kentucky, 1986.

Nash, Gerald D. *The Great Depression and World War II: Organizing America, 1933-1945*. New York: St. Martin's Press, 1979.

Natanson, Nicholas. *The Black Image in the New Deal: The Politics of FSA Photography*. Knoxville: Univ. of Tennessee Press, 1992.

National Association for the Advancement of Colored People. *Thirty Years of Lynching in the United States, 1889-1918*. Reprint. New York: Negro Universities Press, 1969.

Noland, Dennis R. "Comment: Southern Violence—Regional Problem or National Nemesis?" *Vanderbilt Law Review* 32 (Jan. 1979): 251-59.

Ogilvie, Leon Parker. "The Development of the Southeast Missouri Lowlands." Ph.D. diss., Univ. of Missouri, 1967.

Parrish, William E. *A History of Missouri*, vol. 3, *1860-1875*. Columbia: Univ. of Missouri Press, 1973.

Parsons, Talcott, and Kenneth B. Clark, eds. *The Negro American*. Boston: Beacon Press, 1967.

Pfeifer, Michael J. "The Ritual of Lynching: Extralegal Justice in Missouri, 1890-1942." *Gateway Heritage* 13 (Winter 1993): 22-33.

Phillips, Charles D. "Exploring Relations among Forms of Social Control: The Lynching and Execution of Blacks in North Carolina, 1889-1918." *Law and Society Review* 21 (1987): 361-74.

Potter, David. *The South and the Sectional Conflict*. Baton Rouge: Louisiana State Univ. Press, 1968.

Powdermaker, Hortense. *After Freedom: A Cultural Study in the Deep South*. Reprint. New York: Atheneum, 1968.

Purcell, Edward A., Jr. "American Jurisprudence between the Wars: Legal Realism and the Crisis of Democratic Theory." *American Historical Review* 75 (Dec. 1969): 424-46.

Purrington, Burton L., and Judith A. Brooks. "Adaptation, Repression, Resistance, and Flight: African Americans in Southwest Missouri, 1865-1920." Paper presented to American Society for Ethnohistory Meeting, Chicago, 4 Nov. 1989.

Purrington, Burton L., and Penny Harter. "The Easter and Tug-of-War Lynching and the Early Twentieth-Century Black Exodus from Southwest Missouri." In *Visions and Revisions: Ethnohistoric Perspectives on Southern Cultures*, ed. George Sabo III and William M. Schneider. Athens: Univ. of Georgia Press, 1987.

Rafferty, Milton D. *Historical Atlas of Missouri*. Norman: Univ. of Oklahoma Press, 1982.

Raper, Arthur F. *The Tragedy of Lynching*. Reprint. Montclair, N.J.: Patterson Smith, 1969.

Rosenbaum, H. Jon, and Peter C. Sederberg, eds. *Vigilante Politics*. Philadelphia: Univ. of Pennsylvania Press, 1976.

Ross, John R. "At the Bar of Judge Lynch: Lynching and Lynch Mobs in America." Ph.D. diss., Texas Tech Univ., 1983.

Rotnem, Victor W. "Clarifications of the Civil Rights Statutes." *Bill of Rights Review* 2 (Summer 1942): 252-61.

———. "Criminal Enforcement of Federal Civil Rights." *Lawyers Guild Review* 2 (May 1942): 18-23.

———. "The Federal Civil Right 'Not to Be Lynched.'" *Washington University Law Quarterly* 28 (Feb. 1943): 57-73.

Schweinhaut, Henry A. "The Civil Liberties Section of the Department of Justice." *Bill of Rights Review* 1 (Spring 1941): 206-16.

Senechal, Roberta. *The Sociogenesis of a Race Riot: Springfield, Illinois, in 1908.* Urbana: Univ. of Illinois Press, 1990.

Shoemaker, Floyd, ed. *Missouri and Missourians: Land of Contrasts and People of Achievements.* 5 vols. Chicago: Lewis, 1943.

Shrum, Edison. *The History of Scott County, Missouri: Up to the Year 1880.* Sikeston, Mo.: Scott County Historical Society, 1984.

Sitkoff, Harvard. *A New Deal for Blacks: The Emergence of Civil Rights as a National Issue.* New York: Oxford Univ. Press, 1978.

Smead, Howard. *Blood Justice: The Lynching of Mack Charles Parker.* New York: Oxford Univ. Press, 1986.

Snow, Thad. *From Missouri.* Boston: Houghton Mifflin, 1954.

Soapes, Thomas F. "Barak Mattingly and the Failure of the Missouri Republicans." *Missouri Historical Review* 87 (Jan. 1993): 168-87.

———. "The Governorship 'Steal' and the Republican Revival." *Bulletin of the Missouri Historical Society* 32 (April 1976): 158-72.

Staples, Robert. *Black Masculinity: The Black Male's Role in American Society.* San Francisco: Black Scholar Press, 1982.

Stringer-Bishoff, Murray. "The Lynching That Changed Southwest Missouri." *Monett Times,* 14-16 Aug. 1991.

Thelen, David P. *Paths of Resistance: Tradition and Dignity in Industrializing Missouri.* New York: Oxford Univ. Press, 1986.

Tolnay, Stewart E., and E.M. Beck. *A Festival of Violence: An Analysis of Southern Lynchings, 1882-1930.* Urbana: Univ. of Illinois Press, 1995.

Trotter, Joseph W., Jr., ed. *The Great Migration in Historical Perspective: New Dimensions of Race, Class, and Gender.* Bloomington: Indiana Univ. Press, 1991.

Vance, Rupert B., and Nicholas J. Demerath, eds. Reprint. *The Urban South.* Freeport, N.Y.: Books for Libraries, 1971.

White, Deborah Gray. *Ar'n't I a Woman? Female Slaves in the Plantation South.* New York: Norton, 1985.

White, Max R., Douglas Ensminger, and Cecil L. Gregory. *Rich Land, Poor People.* Indianapolis: Farm Security Administration, 1937.

White, Walter. *Rope and Faggot: A Biography of Judge Lynch.* Reprint. New York: Arno, 1969.

Williamson, Joel. *The Crucible of Race: Black-White Relations in the American South since Emancipation.* New York: Oxford Univ. Press, 1984.

Wright, George C. *Racial Violence in Kentucky, 1865-1940: Lynchings, Mob Rule, and "Legal Lynchings."* Baton Rouge: Louisiana State Univ. Press, 1990.

Wright, Richard. *Black Boy: A Record of Childhood and Youth.* New York: Harper, 1945.

Wyatt-Brown, Bertram. "The Mask of Obedience: Male Slave Psychology in the Old South." *American Historical Review* 93 (Dec. 1988): 1228-52.

————. *Southern Honor: Ethics and Behavior in the Old South.* New York: Oxford Univ. Press, 1982.

Wyllie, Irvin G. "Race and Class Conflict on Missouri's Cotton Frontier." *Journal of Southern History* 20 (May 1954): 183-96.

Wynn, Neil A. *The Afro-American and the Second World War.* New York: Holmes & Meier, 1976.

Zangrando, Robert L. *The NAACP Crusade against Lynching, 1909- 1950.* Philadelphia: Temple Univ. Press, 1980.

Index

1,000